IRISH, CATHOLIC AND SCOUSE

CW00923935

Irish, Catholic and Scouse

The History of the Liverpool-Irish,
1800–1939

JOHN BELCHEM

Liverpool University Press

First published 2007 by
Liverpool University Press
4 Cambridge Street
Liverpool L69 7ZU

Copyright © 2007 John Belchem

The right of John Belchem to be identified as the author of this work
has been asserted by him in accordance with the Copyright, Designs and
Patents Act 1988.

All rights reserved. No part of this book may be reproduced, stored
in a retrieval system, or transmitted, in any form or by any means,
electronic, mechanical, photocopying, recording, or otherwise, without
the prior written permission of the publisher.

British Library Cataloguing-in-Publication data

A British Library CIP record is available

ISBN 978–1–84631–107–9   cased
      978–1–84631–108–6   limp

Typeset by Carnegie Book Production, Lancaster
Printed and bound in the European Union by Bell and Bain Ltd, Glasgow

Contents

List of Tables

List of Abbreviations

BT	Board of Trade Papers, National Archives, Kew
CBS Précis	Home Office Crime Department: Special Branch. Précis of information relative to secret societies, National Archives, Dublin and National Archives, Kew
CO	Colonial Office Papers, National Archives, Kew
CT	*Catholic Times*
DP	*Daily Post*
HO	Home Office Papers, National Archives, Kew
LAB	Ministry of Labour Papers, National Archives, Kew
LCH	*Liverpool Catholic Herald*
LFP	*Lancashire Free Press*
LM	*Liverpool Mercury*
LVRO	Liverpool Record Office
MH	Ministry of Health Papers, National Archives, Kew
NAD	National Archives, Dublin
NLI	National Library of Ireland
NP	*Northern Press*
PP	Parliamentary Papers
PRO	Domestic Records of the Public Record Office, National Archives, Kew
PRONI	Public Record Office of Northern Ireland
RCFBS	Report of the Commissioners appointed to inquire into Friendly and Benefit Societies
RCLv	Archdiocese of Liverpool Papers, Lancashire Record Office
RRO	Home Office Directorate of Intelligence (Special Branch): Report on Revolutionary Organisations in Cabinet Office Papers, CAB24, National Archives, Kew
T	Treasury Papers, National Archives, Kew
TCD	Trinity College Dublin
THSLC	*Transactions of the Historic Society of Lancashire and Cheshire*
UI	*United Irishman*
UL	University of Liverpool Library Special Collections

Acknowledgements

THIS BOOK has been long in the making, put on hold while I undertook a succession of administrative and managerial roles, necessary tasks that tend to befall academics of a certain age – in my case, Head of the new School of History, then Dean of the Faculty of Arts at the University of Liverpool. Its final completion owes much to the generosity of external funding bodies. I would like to record my thanks to the British Academy for a Larger Research Grant (LRG33569) for extensive archival visits in Britain and Ireland; and to the Leverhulme Trust for the award of a Major Research Fellowship, allowing me time and scope to place the Irish within the wider context and broad sweep of Liverpool history.

Throughout this unduly lengthy period, I have received invaluable help from colleagues who have shared their knowledge and expertise, commented on drafts, corrected my blunders and encouraged me to persevere. Particular thanks to Don Akenson, Joan Allen, Frank Boyce, Sean Connolly, Enda Delaney, Marianne Elliott, Jim Epstein, David Fitzpatrick, Roy Foster, Peter Hart, Michael Huggins, Kevin Kenny, Jack McGinley, Don MacRaild, Frank Neal, Paddy O'Sullivan, Colin Pooley, Richard Price, Roger Swift and John Walton.

Over the years, I have relied on the in-house knowledge and efficient service of librarians and archivists throughout the United Kingdom and the Republic of Ireland. The list includes: the British Library, St Pancras; the Newspaper Library, Colindale; the National Archives, Kew; Liverpool Record Office; the Athenaeum, Liverpool; Lancashire Record Office; the Public Record Office of Northern Ireland; Trinity College, Dublin; University College, Dublin; National Library of Ireland; National Archives, Dublin; Dublin Diocesan Archives; and Diocese of Clogher Archives, Monaghan. Special thanks to Maureen Watry and her staff in Special Collections and Archives, Sydney Jones Library, University of Liverpool, my bolthole in intervals between committee meetings.

Liverpool University Press has offered invaluable support and advice from the outset – my thanks to Robin Bloxsidge, Anthony Cond, Andrew Kirk and other members of the hard-working LUP team. I am also deeply indebted to David Stoker, manager of the Liverpool Record Office, who has helped in so many ways, not least in aiding my access to sources and illustrations.

Finally, my thanks to my partner, Mary, who has had to live with this book for too long. After all this time and effort, errors and omissions are, of course, entirely my responsibility.

John Belchem
Liverpool
January 2007

Preface

As studies of diasporas, migration and identities proliferate, the need for a full-length historical survey of the Irish in Liverpool, the 'floodgate of the old world', becomes more urgent. The most significant 'ethnic' group in nineteenth- and early twentieth-century pre-multi-cultural Britain, the Irish in Liverpool were also one of the most sizeable and pivotal Irish formations within the Irish diaspora. Based on extensive archival research, this book highlights the complex interplay of cultural and structural factors experienced by migrants who remained in the port of entry, 'the nearest place that wasn't Ireland', as they acquired a distinctive hybrid hyphenated identity as Liverpool-Irish.

At the hub of the Irish diaspora, the Liverpool-Irish cannot be studied in isolation from their migrant compatriots who continued on their travels. Remaining in the 'last seaport of the Old World', the Irish in Liverpool jostled in cosmopolitan (if not always harmonious) inter-cultural action alongside a range of other 'moving Europeans' as well as innumerable seafaring and trading groups from across the 'black Atlantic' and the oceans beyond. Hence, in line with the best practice commended by historians responding to the challenge of globalisation theory and transnational sociology, this study of Irish migrants offers some 'divergent' and 'convergent' comparative reflections: it recognises the need for migration (or mobility) history that 'combines the diasporic or transnational with the comparative or cross-national'.[1] Liverpool itself, proverbially a city apart in British historiography, needs to be considered in

---

1   For useful introductions to the latest theoretical and methodological developments, see the papers by Nancy L. Green, 'The comparative method and poststructural structuralism: New perspectives for migration studies', in J. Lucassen and L. Lucassen, eds, *Migration, Migration History, History: Old Paradigms and New Perspectives*, Berne, 1997, pp.57–72, and 'Time and the study of assimilation', *Rethinking History*, 10, 2006, pp.239–58. See also, Donna R. Gabaccia, 'Do we still need immigration history?', *Polish American Studies*, 15, 1998, pp.45–68; and Kevin Kenny, 'Diaspora and comparison: The global Irish as a case study', *Journal of American History*, 90, 2003, pp.134–62.

international comparative perspective.[2] Famously described as 'a sort of sunless Marseille',[3] it is perhaps best understood within the kind of socio-economic and demographic analysis applied to other world port cities characterised by dependent labour markets, long-distance in-migration and exposure to infectious disease – in this case, 'Irish fever'.[4]

Such comparative cross-reference notwithstanding, there is perforce an exclusionary aspect to the history of the Liverpool-Irish. This book charts the contingent historical process by which Irish and Catholic became synonymous in Liverpool, an ethno-sectarian formulation which served to exclude the considerable number of Protestant migrants, some 25 per cent or so of the total who arrived from across the Irish Sea. Recent studies of the 'Orange diaspora' have drawn long-overdue attention to the considerable contribution of Protestants, in particular those Irish migrants who sailed on from Liverpool, the gateway of empire, out to the colonies.[5] However, those who remained in Liverpool, the point of entry to mainland Britain, are less readily identified as ethno-culturally distinctive. When their Catholic compatriots were stigmatised on arrival as the 'internal other', Protestant migrants in Liverpool chose not to articulate an alternative non-Catholic representation of Irishness but to adopt forms of associational and political culture conforming to wider British norms, affiliation and membership. Encrypted within broader British formulations, the residual Irishness of Protestant migrants is difficult to decode, although it is to be hoped this crucial and challenging task will soon be undertaken: it will require a book in itself. The purpose of the present study is to show how, when and why Catholic migrants and their descendants in Liverpool made Irishness their own.

---

2   John Belchem, 'A city apart: Liverpool, Merseyside and the North West region', in D. Newton and N. Vall, eds, *An Agenda for Regional History*, forthcoming, 2007.

3   Paul Du Noyer, *Liverpool: Wondrous Place. Music from the Cavern to the Coral*, London, 2002, p.5

4   W.R. Lee, 'The socio-economic and demographic characteristics of port cities: a typology for comparative analysis?', *Urban History*, 25, 1998, pp.147–72.

5   For a useful discussion of the growing literature on the 'Orange diaspora', see Donald M. MacRaild, *Faith, Fraternity and Fighting: The Orange Order and Irish Migrants in Northern England, c. 1850–1920*, Liverpool, 2005, ch. 8. David Fitzpatrick's article, 'Exporting brotherhood: Orangeism in South Australia', *Immigrants and Minorities*, 23, 2005, pp.277–310, concludes with some interesting comparative reflections on Liverpool, Glasgow and New York.

Introduction: 'A Piece Cut Off from the Old Sod Itself'

F OR ALL ITS COSMOPOLITAN and imperial pretensions, the great Victorian seaport of Liverpool was often depicted and perceived as 'Irish'. The self-proclaimed second city of empire, Liverpool was also known as the capital of Ireland in England, in A.M. Sullivan's words, 'a piece cut off from the old sod itself'.[1] By the early years of the twentieth century, Liverpool's climacteric, the numbers of Irish and Catholics, regarded as synonymous terms at the time, was calculated at up to 200,000: roughly one-third of the population.[2] This sizeable presence notwithstanding, there is as yet no full-scale history of the Liverpool-Irish and their distinctive hyphenated identity. Studies abound of the sufferings and tensions of the Famine influx from Ireland in the late 1840s, offering a short-term 'crisis' perspective on such issues as health, housing, welfare, crime and sectarian violence in this main port of entry.[3] There is an urgent need for a longer-term assessment of crisis, continuity and change as the Liverpool-Irish, the most significant 'minority' community in pre-multi-cultural Britain, adjusted to what T.P. O'Connor described as their 'curious middle place'.[4]

---

[1]   *Nationalist* 6 Dec. 1884.

[2]   In the Liverpool section of his study of *The Irish in Britain*, London, 1892, p.252, John Denvir produced a range of figures to confirm that 'we are almost, if not quite, one-third'.

[3]   See in particular the exemplary works by Frank Neal with their enviable mastery of statistical detail and technique: for example, 'Liverpool, the Irish steamship companies and the Famine Irish', *Immigrants and Minorities*, 5, 1986, pp.28–61; 'Lancashire, the Famine Irish and the Poor Laws: a study in crisis management', *Irish Economic and Social History*, XXII, 1995, pp.26–48; 'A criminal profile of the Liverpool Irish', *THSLC*, 140, 1991, pp.161–99; and a longer-term but episodic study, *Sectarian Violence: The Liverpool Experience 1819–1914*, Manchester, 1988.

[4]   T.P. O'Connor, 'The Irish in Great Britain', in F. Lavery, ed., *Irish Heroes in the War*,

The chronological boundaries adopted here are political: from the Act of
Union to the supposed 'final settlement' between Britain and Eire in the late
1930s, a time-span which highlights the constitutional complexities, confusion
and controversy over the status of Irish migrants first within the United Kingdom
and then as a 'free state' dominion with the British Empire. Attitudes towards
the Irish tended to harden at times of political crisis and tension, a variable not
entirely independent, however, of fluctuations in the trade cycle and labour
market. The economic consequences of the Act of Union became apparent
once free trade, implemented in phases, took full (and devastating) effect
in the 1820s: domestic industries went into rapid decline; Ireland became a
country exporting food and cheap labour.[5] A fortuitous conjuncture, transport
developments facilitated the mass migration outflow, a major advance in global
communications ignored by sociologists who date and attribute transnationalism
to the late-twentieth-century advent of cheap air travel. With the introduction
of steam navigation in the 1820s, fares fell sharply for the passage across the Irish
Sea and, if desired, for subsequent trans-shipment on the new 'Atlantic ferry'.
Passenger traffic contributed much to Liverpool's growth and prosperity in the
nineteenth century as it sought new markets and a re-branded 'cosmopolitan'
image following abolition of the infamous slave trade in 1807. North American
shippers, having concentrated their cotton, flaxseed and Canadian timber
imports through Liverpool, filled out the low-volume return cargoes with
increasing numbers of passengers. Liverpool, indeed, quickly established itself as
the premier European emigration port, the human entrepôt through which some
9 million 'moving Europeans' passed, not always without adverse incident.[6]
Thus, the increasing numbers of Irish who arrived in Liverpool entered what
historical geographers call a 'diaspora space', a contact zone between different
ethnic groups with differing needs and intentions as transients, sojourners or
settlers. By no means mutually exclusive, these categories were often blurred,
particularly when hard luck, accident, poverty or other factors precluded
intended onward movement – the majority of patients in the Northern Hospital
in 1849 and 1850 were classified as Irish and 'foreigners'. A critical question

London, 1917, p.32. The Irish in nineteenth-century Britain form the opening case-study
of Leo Lucassen's analysis of *The Immigrant Threat: The Integration of Old and New Migrants in
Western Europe since 1850*, Chicago, 2005, pp.27–49.
5   John Saville, *1848: The British State and the Chartist Movement*, Cambridge, 1987, p.30.
6   G. Read. 'The flood-gate of the Old World: A study in ethnic attitudes', *Journal of
American Ethnic History*, 13, 1993, pp.31–47. Eric Richards, *Britannia's Children: Emigration
from England, Scotland, Wales and Ireland since 1600*, London, 2004, p.292.

Table 0.1 *Origin and occupation of patients in the
Liverpool Northern Hospital 1849 and 1850*

Occupation	1849	1850
Labourers	1086	1204
Sailors	719	830
Mechanics	292	270
Women	415	475
Children	297	359
Total	**2809**	**3138**

Origin	1849	1850
Liverpool	564	591
Different parts of England	457	561
Ireland	916	1149
Scotland	124	114
Wales	112	89
Foreigners	636	634
Total	**2809**	**3138**

Source: *Report, List of Subscribers, and Statement of Account of the Liverpool
Northern Hospital, for 1849* and *for 1850*, Liverpool, n.d.

addressed in this book is why did so many Irish remain in Liverpool, the 'black
spot on the Mersey'?

Some were trapped, having fallen victim to Liverpool's notorious 'sharpers',
a generic term for the unscrupulous band of lodging-house keepers, ticket
brokers, 'runners', currency converters and other heartless fraudsters who
fleeced those awaiting trans-shipment, often leaving them penniless and hence
immobile. To the dismay of Vere Foster, the Irish emigration philanthropist,
waterfront Liverpool lacked any reception and induction facilities to match the
services provided on arrival at journey's end by the Irish Emigrant Society of
New York.[7] As it was, new arrivals from Ireland were greeted on arrival at
Clarence Dock by the sight of Liverpool's most famous 'Irish' pub run by Jack

7   See the correspondence between Vere Foster and A.M. Sullivan and the addresses
of the Irish Emigrant Society of New York in the Irish Emigration Database available at
PRONI.

Langan, a former champion boxer, immediately recognisable by the effigy of St Patrick, shamrock in hand, high on its walls. Thereafter, as they awaited trans-shipment, they had to be on their guard against all kinds of tricksters and hustlers in sailortown Liverpool.

Such was Liverpool's infamous reputation in this regard that some migrant groups, such as the Mormons from Scandinavia en route to Utah, kept themselves insulated and apart in their own self-contained mission and accommodation houses in the port.[8] For their own safety, migrants bound for Australia were kept in a form of quarantine in an emigrant depot across the Mersey in Birkenhead.[9] The local Jewish community, in fear of being overwhelmed by new arrivals requiring relief, provided a comprehensive 'in transit' service to ensure the safe onward journey of European and Russian Jews fleeing pogroms. A special Liverpool Commission of the Mansion House Relief Fund provided local board, lodging and medical inspection for refugees arriving from Hamburg via Grimsby and West Hartlepool, and bulk-purchase steamship tickets to America together with suitable clothing and kosher food for the voyage, an initiative that assisted 6274 poor Jews across the Atlantic in 1881–82 at a cost of just over £30,000.[10] The efforts of Vere Foster and others notwithstanding, the Irish awaiting trans-shipment across the Atlantic were less well shielded.

Fleecing the emigrant, the *Liverpool Catholic Herald* rued, had been 'elevated to the dignity of a fine art in the days when Irish emigration was at its height'.[11] The Irish press protested vigorously against the horrors and cruelties of what the *Irishman* described in 1859 as 'the organized system of plunder directed in Liverpool against Irish emigrants'.[12] Despite the promotion of alternative routes, Liverpool dominated the market: in 1845, as the Great Famine exodus began, well over 90 per cent of Irish emigrants to the United States travelled via the great seaport on the Mersey.[13] Having learnt through bitter experience, those who reached America offered helpful survival tips, written on the back

---

[8]   See the pages on Mormon emigration on the Norway Heritage website at www. norwayheritage.com, last accessed 9 May 2007.

[9]   D. Hollett, *Merseyside and the Nineteenth-Century Emigrant Trade to Australia*, Birkenhead, 1988.

[10]   *Persecution of the Jews in Russia. Mansion House Relief Fund. Liverpool Commission*, Liverpool, 1882.

[11]   *LCH* 25 Jan. 1913.

[12]   *Irishman* 1 Jan. 1859.

[13]   David N. Doyle, 'The Irish in North America, 1776–1845', in W.E. Vaughan, ed., *A New History of Ireland*, vol. 5: *Ireland under the Union*, Oxford, 1989, pp.682–725, here pp.700–701.

of tickets posted back across the Atlantic to friends and relatives, next in line on the migration chain. 'Liverpool is full of Imposters [sic] if they can trick any person they can lay hold of', Howard Berne was warned: 'you will require to be very cautious & clever & no way shy without getting your rights'. Alice Cleland was directed to a small court 'opposit the cloureness dock liverpool ... you would be safer there thane aney other plase when you lave the steem boat'.[14] As it happened, some Liverpool-Irish of a street-wise disposition were to be found in the ranks of the 'infamous land pirates'. The Liverpool 'man-catchers', the *Morning Chronicle* reported, were 'principally Irishman themselves, and knew both the strength and weakness of the Irish character – many of whom, poor and miserable as they look, have sovereigns stitched amid the patches of their tattered garments – and persuade them into the purchase of various articles, both useful and useless'.[15]

Beyond the 'sharpers' were the perils, by no means merely physical, of the Atlantic crossing itself. Vere Foster suffered several months of ill health after travelling incognito on an emigrant packet in 1850, enduring unduly cramped conditions, inadequate and irregular food and the mindless brutality of the crew.[16] Having been encouraged 'in the Confessional' to leave 'unfortunate' Liverpool, Francis Dyer reported back to Father Hickey, parish priest of St Michael's, expressing outrage at the misconduct on board the SS *Commonwealth* en route to 'Catholic' Montreal and the seduction of 'some of the poor Irish girls'.[17]

Besides those fleeced by sharpers or deterred by the prospect of the voyage on the 'Atlantic ferry', the great mass of those who perforce remained in Liverpool were characterised by contemporaries in most unflattering terms as 'the scum left by the tide of migration between Europe and the continent of

---

14   Quoted in J. Matthew Gallman, *Receiving Erin's Children: Philadelphia, Liverpool and the Irish Famine Migration, 1845–1855*, Chapel Hill, NC, and London, 2000, pp.2–3. Another migrant, wise by experience, averred that 'if a man had 7 senses, it would take 500 senses largely developed to counteract the sharpers of Liverpool', Thomas Reilly to Kelly, 19 June 1848, NLI MS 10,511 (2).

15   'Emigration – Emigrants and Man-Catchers', *Morning Chronicle* 15 July 1850. Locals, it seems, were not to the fore in this infamous and long-continued trade: 'It is a curious fact, one perhaps of some credit to this country, that in nearly all cases the people who have cheated the strangers within our gates have themselves been aliens', *Watch Committee: Report on the Police Establishment 1908*, Liverpool, 1909, p.46.

16   M.A. Busteed, 'A Liverpool shipping agent and Irish emigration in the 1850s: Some newly discovered documents', *THSLC*, 129, 1980, pp.145–61.

17   Dyer, July 1903, Father Hickey Papers, NLI MS 8479.

America'.[18] Those from Ireland were condemned as 'the residuum of the Irish – that is, those cases who had not "wing" enough, when they came from Ireland to carry them across the Atlantic'.[19] 'Only fitted for the ruder form of labour', they were labelled as 'the dregs' by Father Nugent, an Irish-Liverpudlian himself, a kind of underclass, unable, unwilling or unsuited to take advantage of opportunities elsewhere in Britain or the New World.[20] It was 'Irishness' of this order – immobile, inadequate and irresponsible – that purportedly set Liverpool and its notorious social problems part. The Liverpool-Irish (of whom Heathcliff, the great other/outsider of Victorian literature, brought starving and houseless from the streets of Liverpool, may well have been one) suffered the prejudice and negative reputation that came to blight the city itself.[21] 'Do you want to hear my theory about Scousers', the Lake District hotel owner asks the job-seeking Liverpudlian Danny Kavanagh in Jimmy McGovern's television drama series *The Lakes* (1997–99): 'Bone idle. It's not your fault you understand, it's in your genes. You're all descended from the feckless Irish. Half starved, you get on a boat, you get as far as Liverpool and say, "Sod that, I'm not going any further, this'll do."' [22]

While providing an invaluable statistical portrayal of the city's demographic mosaic, census-based studies, a specialist feature of Liverpudlian historiography, have done little to reassess or rehabilitate the Liverpool-Irish, seemingly immovably located at the bottom of the local occupational and social hierarchy.[23] Factor analysis of the (pre-Famine influx) 1841 census,

---

18   *Watch Committee Report*, 1908, p.46.

19   *LCH* 27 Jan. 1905.

20   PP 1870 (259) VIII, Select Committee on Prisons and Prison Ministers Acts 1870, q. 4148.

21   Terry Eagleton, *Heathcliff and the Great Hunger*, London, 1995, pp.1–26.

22   Quoted in Philip Smith, '"I've got a theory about Scousers": Jimmy McGovern and Linda la Plante', in Michael Murphy and Deryn Rees-Jones, eds, *Writing Liverpool: Essays and Interviews*, Liverpool, 2007.

23   R. Lawton and C.G. Pooley, 'The social geography of Merseyside in the nineteenth century', final report to the SSRC, July 1976, Dept of Geography, University of Liverpool; R. Lawton, 'The population of Liverpool in the mid nineteenth century', *THSLC*, 107, 1955, pp.89–120; and Colin G. Pooley, 'The residential segregation of migrant communities in mid-Victorian Liverpool, *Transactions of the Institute of British Geographers*,

by which time there were already 49,639 Irish-born in Liverpool, some 17.3 per cent of the population, has highlighted three main clusters of interrelated variables, a three-class model with an Irish/unskilled/lodging/ industrial service/court house cluster at the base.[24] Comparative analysis confirmed the picture, presenting the Irish as what Caradog Jones termed in his pioneer *Social Survey* a 'blot' in the otherwise positive impact of migration on Merseyside: all migrant groups were under-represented in the unskilled stratum, except the Irish; all migrant groups, except the Irish, were of a higher socio-economic status than the locally born. By their very weight, such census statistics tend to obscure the minority of Liverpool-Irish above the adverse variables and lowly occupations.[25]

Table 0.2 *Estimated number of Irish Catholics in Liverpool*

Year	Estimated no. of Irish Catholics
1800	4950
1810	8244
1820	11,016
1830	18,900
1833	24,156

Source: PP1836(40)XXXIV: Royal Commission on the Condition of the Poorer Classes in Ireland: Appendix G, The State of the Irish Poor in Great Britain, p.9.

II, 1977, pp.364–82; 'Migration, mobility and residential areas in nineteenth-century Liverpool', unpublished PhD thesis, University of Liverpool, 1978; and 'The Irish in Liverpool *circa* 1850–1940', in M. Engman, F.W. Carter, A.C. Hepburn and C.G. Pooley, eds, *Ethnic Identity in Urban Europe*, Aldershot, 1992, pp.71–97. See also J.D. Papworth, 'The Irish in Liverpool 1835–71: segregation and dispersal', unpublished PhD thesis, University of Liverpool, 1982.

24 Iain Taylor, 'Black spot on the Mersey: A study of environment and society in eighteenth- and nineteenth-century Liverpool', unpublished PhD thesis, University of Liverpool, 1976, pp.114–15, and 213–20.

25 D. Caradog Jones, *A Study of Migration to Merseyside, with Special Reference to Irish Immigration*, Liverpool, 1931; and *Social Survey of Merseyside*, 3 vols, vol. 2, Liverpool, 1934.

Table 0.3 *Irish-born residents of Liverpool, 1841–1951*

Year	Total population	No of Irish-born	Irish-born as %
1841	286,656	49,639	17.3
1851	375,955	83,813	22.3
1861	443,938	83,949	18.9
1871	493,405	76,761	15.5
1891	517,980	66,071	12.6
1901	684,958	45,673	6.7
1911	746,421	34,632	4.6
1921	802,940	31,287	3.9
1931	855,688	26,836	3.3
1951	788,659	17,929	2.3

Source: Census of Population

The essential starting point for analysis, census statistics enumerate only the first generation Irish-born migrants and give no indication of religious affiliation. Despite various computer-aided attempts to produce more meaningful figures, the most useful (and neatly symmetrical) formulation for calculating numbers remains that applied by Abraham Hume in 1858: 'the number of Irish is just equal to the number of Roman Catholics, the protestants of Irish birth being exactly balanced by the Roman Catholics of English birth'.[26] This is not just a handy statistical formula, however: as noted already, Irish and Catholic came to carry synonymic force in nineteenth-century Liverpool. As understood and defined in Liverpool, Irishness excluded the considerable number of Protestant migrants, perhaps some 25 per cent of the total who arrived from Ireland.

Although Leinster was to the fore, the migrant inflow into Liverpool included substantial numbers, both Catholic and Protestant, from sectarian Ulster and the adjoining counties, 'these silly people retaining here', Head Constable Whitty reported in 1836, 'the absurd enmities which disgraced and

---

[26]   Abraham Hume, *Condition of Liverpool, Religious and Social*, Liverpool, 1858, pp.14–15. For examples of recent statistical techniques, see the application of the 'Widnes factor' in W.J. Lowe, *The Irish in Mid-Victorian Lancashire: The Shaping of a Working-Class Community*, New York, 1989, and the cross-matching of burial data with census material in Lynda Letford, 'Irish and non-Irish women living in their households in nineteenth-century Liverpool: Issues of class, gender and birthplace', unpublished PhD thesis, University of Lancaster, 1996.

degraded them at home'.[27] Catholic Ribbonmen from the north were to rally their fellow countrymen and co-religionists in Liverpool, otherwise divided by intense regional and factional divisions, into united hostility to the Protestant Orangemen. At the same time, the sizeable presence of Ulster Protestants, a catalyst absent in most other English towns, served to activate latent British anti-Catholicism. Implanted by these migrants and the 'Irish brigade' of ultra-Protestant Anglican pastors in Liverpool (the Rev. Hugh McNeile's 'thirty-nine articles'), Orangeism was soon incorporated into the local Tory narrative of providential Protestant religious and constitutional freedom, attesting to *British* allegiance, an inclusive national identity for all Protestants. Anglo-Irish migrants were enthusiastic (often demagogic) advocates of Britishness, the populist Protestant identity which secured Tory hegemony in Liverpool until the Second World War and beyond.[28]

While Ulster-Anglican migrants readily affirmed their Britishness in this way, Ulster-Scots migrants (and their distinct Irish Presbyteries) disappeared quietly from view, denied any equivalent to the 'Scotch-Irish' identity of their compatriots in America. The Irish Islington Church in Liverpool, formed in 1843 by Irish Presbyterian migrants, connected itself with the Presbytery of Belfast. A bitter dispute ensued with the Presbytery of Lancaster which was not resolved until the name Irish was deleted, and the General Assembly of the Presbyterian Church in Ireland had disclaimed 'any intention of invading the jurisdiction or territory of the English Synod'.[29] Members of the Reformed Presbyterian Congregation in Liverpool, part of the Eastern Synod of the Reformed Presbyterian Church in Ireland, tried to retain ministerial (and other) links with Belfast, but were finally compelled to transfer allegiance to the Reformed Presbytery of Glasgow in 1857 (under whose auspices a church was built in Shaw Street).[30] On an informal level, however, they continued to

---

[27]   PP 1836 (40) XXXIV, Royal Commission on the Condition of the Poorer Classes in Ireland, Appendix G: The State of the Irish Poor in Great Britain, p.21.

[28]   For McNeile as the 'real creator' of Liverpool Conservatism, see P.J. Waller, *Democracy and Sectarianism: A Political and Social History of Liverpool 1868–1939*, Liverpool, 1981, p.11.

[29]   'The rise and progress of Presbyterianism in Liverpool', in *Jubilee Memorial of Canning Street Presbyterian Church*, n.p., n.d., pp.119–20. *Minutes of the General Assembly of the Presbyterian Church in Ireland*, Belfast, 1850, pp.315 and 381.

[30]   PRONI: CR5/3, Reformed Presbyterian Church Records: Shaw Street, Liverpool; Presbyterian Historical Society of Ireland, *Minutes of the Annual Meeting of the Eastern Reformed Synod in Ireland at its Meeting in Belfast 1857*, p.20.

provide a reception service at Liverpool for emigrant Ulster Presbyterians en route to America.[31]

Vacated by Protestant migrants, Anglican and Presbyterian, Irishness became the derogatory label applied to the 'contagion' of Catholic migrants from famine-ridden Ireland. In the absence of any phenotypic or linguistic difference (the overwhelming majority of the migrants being English-speakers), this pejorative host ascription served to differentiate Irish Catholics, technically internal migrants in a single market and united kingdom, as the local underclass, stigmatised by crude prejudice as the 'internal other'. The migrants, however, were by no means passive victims of such crude prejudice and denigratory stereotyping. They were soon to formulate their own versions of Irishness, an ethno-confessional affiliation which served at first protective and defensive functions against disadvantage, disability and discrimination, but then became increasingly assertive, leading to a form of home rule in pre-First World War Irish Liverpool. Ethnic agency was a positive force, aided and empowered by the sheer scale of the 'enclave'. However lowly the conditions, here was a milieu (or 'habitus') of solidarity and security – mobilised around the court and core street, the pub and the parish – which tended to preclude further movement, the uncertain quest for 'success' elsewhere.[32]

The symbiosis which 'made Irish, Catholic, and Catholic, Irish' developed out of a dynamic and contingent historical process, drawing upon factors of cultural continuity, adjustment and invention. The necessary components of ethnic agency, or ethno-confessional affiliation, were not all in place, ready for instant activation. As the leading scholars of American ethnic history have shown, migrant 'ethnicisation' required 'constant invention, innovation, negotiation and renegotiation on the part of those seeking to organize identities, patterns of daily life, or the competitive struggle for social resources around ethnic symbols'.[33] Ethnic entrepreneurs and culture brokers played a critical role in projecting and promoting Irishness, in superimposing a wider ethnic affiliation upon traditional and instinctive sub-national loyalties, the clan,

---

31   Letter from Liverpool to James Staveley, 1 Dec. 1860, Irish Emigration Database.

32   See my essays on 'Ribbonism, nationalism and the Irish pub' and 'Charity, ethnicity and the Catholic parish' in John Belchem, *Merseypride: Essays in Liverpool Exceptionalism*, Liverpool, 2000, 2nd edn, 2006.

33   K.N. Conzen, D.A. Gerber, E. Morawska, G.E. Pozzetta and R.J. Vecoli, 'The invention of ethnicity: A perspective from the USA', *Journal of American Ethnic History*, 12, 1992, pp.3–41. For a useful introduction to the sociology of ethnicity, see J. Hutchinson and A.D. Smith, *Ethnicity*, Oxford, 1996.

regional and faction networks of chain migration. Here was a 'middle-class' contribution to Irish Liverpool unduly ignored in historical demography.

For middle-class migrants, Liverpool was generally perceived as stepwise entrepôt, not as place of destination. As the 'second metropolis', Victorian Liverpool was an important staging-post in career development for the Irish middle class (forerunners of today's brain-drain 'Eirepreneurs'), a convenient testing-ground for their journalistic, legal, medical, clerical, entrepreneurial and other talents.[34] When Justin McCarthy came to Liverpool as a 'stepping-stone on my way to London', he found that the majority of the staff on the *Northern Daily Times* was also Irish.[35] Not all were to move on, and of those who remained several came forward as culture brokers and political leaders of the Liverpool-Irish, able to span the enclave and the city. A survey of the local medical profession in the early 1870s identified a number of long-established Irish practices (replenished by professional chain migration) located both in fashionable areas and in the north end Irish 'ghetto', including such practitioners as the Bligh brothers, close friends of Parnell, and prominent figures in local nationalist politics and Irish cultural affairs.[36]

The 'western emporium of Albion', Liverpool attracted a considerable number of Irish merchants from across the Irish Sea. Generous and gregarious, Phelin O'Flighty was accorded a major supporting role in *The True and Wonderful History of Dick Liver*.[37] The Irish presence was noted by Samuel Derrick, master of the ceremonies at Bath, on a visit to Liverpool in 1760, as the port pulled ahead of Bristol and other west coast rivals. 'This great increase of commerce', he reported to the Earl of Corke,

> is owing to the spirit and indefatigable industry of the inhabitants, the majority of whom are either native Irish, or of Irish descent: a fresh proof,

34   Mary P. Corcoran, 'Emigrants, *Eirepreneurs* and opportunists: A social profile of recent Irish immigration in New York City', in Ronald H. Bayor and Timothy J. Meagher, eds, *The New York Irish*, Baltimore, MD, and London, 1997, pp.461–80. For the Irish middle-class presence in London, see Craig Bailey, 'The Irish network: A study of ethnic patronage in London, 1760–1840', unpublished PhD thesis, University of London, 2004. See also my essay, 'Micks on the make on the Mersey', in *Merseypride*.

35   J. McCarthy, *Story of an Irishman*, London, 1904, p.102.

36   J.F. McArdle, *A Patient in Search of a Doctor*, Liverpool, 1872.

37   *The True and Wonderful History of Dick Liver: shewing how from small beginnings he became a man of substance; and how he was robbed while he was asleep; and relating his ineffectual attempts to get into his own house and recover his property. By Timothy Touchstone, Historiographer*, Liverpool, 1824.

my lord, that the Hibernians thrive best when transplanted. They engage in trade as battle, with little or no spirit at home, but with unparalleled gallantry abroad.[38]

Economic historians have focused on the exotic (and financially less secure) trans-oceanic trade, but Liverpool's prosperity as global seaport was underwritten by its near-hegemony in the movement of goods and people within and around the 'inland' Irish Sea, Liverpool's 'private Celtic empire', trade accompanied by a significant Irish mercantile presence.[39] Reporting to the Irish Confederation in 1848 on the state of 'Irish trade, with or through, Liverpool, import and export', George Smyth calculated its value as 'between eleven or twelve millions a year ... greater than that of any other country of the world, the United States of America alone excepted'.[40] Liverpool was Ireland's most convenient point of access to distribution networks in Britain and overseas: Ireland supplied over 75 per cent of the cattle, pigs, oats, oatmeal, butter, eggs, lard and preserved meats imported coastwise at Liverpool.[41] *The Picturesque Hand-book to Liverpool* directed visitors to the Clarence Dock to observe the arrival of the Irish packets: 'At the stern will be seen, as usual, a freight of bipeds, old and young, holding converse in a jargon that it would be difficult to interpret; while the rest of the deck will be crowded with a medley of sheep, pigs and oxen.' [42] The Anglo-Irish cattle trade was dominated by the Liverpool firm of Cullen and Verdon, comprising Michael and James Cullen, brothers of Cardinal Paul Cullen of Dublin, and their brother-in-law, Peter Verdon. Noted for their wealth and contribution to Catholic orphanages and other charities, they set up temporary hospital facilities on their premises for destitute Irish migrants during the Famine influx.[43] In nationalist circles, however, they were depicted as 'ruthless exterminators'. 'They are said to have swept large tracts of land in Meath clear of peasants, whom they have replaced with bullocks to be fattened for the English market',

[38]   Samuel Derrick, *Letters Written from Leverpoole, Chester, Corke, the Lake of Killarney, Dublin, Tunbridge Wells, Bath*, 2 vols, London, 1767, pp.23–24.

[39]   See the interesting portrayal of 'Liverpool and the Celtic Sea', in Robert Scally, *The End of Hidden Ireland: Rebellion, Famine and Emigration*, New York, 1995, ch. 9.

[40]   *Nation* 15 Jan. 1848.

[41]   Valerie Burton, 'Liverpool's mid-nineteenth century coasting trade', in Valerie Burton, ed., *Liverpool Shipping, Trade and Industry*, Liverpool, 1989, pp.26–66.

[42]   *The Picturesque Hand-book to Liverpool; a manual for the resident and visitor, being a new and greatly improved edition of the Stranger's Pocket Guide*, Liverpool, 1842, p.40.

[43]   Peadar Mac Suibhne, *Paul Cullen and His Contemporaries*, 5 vols, Nass, 1967–77, vol. 4, p.28.

T.P. O'Connor noted in his pocket-book: 'Father Lavelle calls this process the Cullenization of Ireland'.[44]

Differing considerably in background, Irish merchants displayed a bewildering gamut of political, cultural and 'ethnic' attitudes towards Ireland and Irishness. The most successful of all, William Brown, a merchant prince in the Atlantic trade, forsook his Ulster heritage to secure his position (and a baronetcy) within the Liverpool mercantile elite and the Lancashire establishment. Presbyterianism was abandoned in favour of Anglicanism, and his benefaction was expended, much to the annoyance of Irish nationalists, not on his native Ballymena but on funding the magnificent Liverpool museum, an immortalising symbol of the culture of commerce in the would-be 'Florence of the north'.[45] Among Irish Catholic merchants, it is possible to detect a rough division between the charitable and cultural Irish projects sponsored by those at the apex (those members of the middle class whose business interests and commercial practices extended above and beyond Ireland and the Irish-Liverpool enclave) and the ardent 'revolutionary' nationalist politics (examined in Chapter 6) pursued by lesser Catholic merchants in the Irish trade (whose business interests took them regularly across to famine-stricken Ireland) in association with members of professions, notably doctors, in daily contact with poor Irish migrants. Then there were those who kept a low profile, such as Edward Smith (c. 1808–80), a penniless migrant from Co. Down, who made a fortune through colliery ownership, acquired a desirable residence in Abercromby Square, the most fashionable part of town, but appears not to have donated to charitable or political causes, his staunch Catholicism notwithstanding.[46]

At the time of the Famine influx, the most prominent Irish Catholic merchant in the Atlantic trade, with extensive business interests in the Caribbean, was Richard Sheil (commemorated in the name of a local park), cousin of the Irish Liberal MP and orator of the same name. The principal Catholic layman in Liverpool and for long the only Catholic member of the council, Sheil quickly adjusted to the Tridentine norms and Liberal politics of the small and socially exclusive indigenous Catholic community.[47] However, he never lost his 'rich,

---

[44] 'Cardinal Cullen', NLI MS 27,991, Notebook in the hand of T.P. O'Connor.

[45] See the biographical article on Brown by Francis Bigger in *Belfast News-Letter* 7 June 1926.

[46] Personal information kindly provided by Cornelius Smith, Blackrock, Co. Dublin, who is writing a family history.

[47] Sheil is listed in fifteenth place in the capitalisation of Liverpool trading firms, 1855–70 in Graeme Milne, *Trade and Traders in Mid-Victorian Liverpool: Mercantile Business and the Making of a World Port*, Liverpool, 2000, p.127.

mellifluous brogue' nor his love for Ireland. His assimilationist profile notwithstanding, what mattered to Sheil was not making the Irish British but keeping
the Irish Catholic in the corrupting environment of Liverpool. In guarding
against leakage from the faith and Protestant proselytisation, his never-ending
fund-raising activities enabled the church to 'hibernicise' its mission to reach
out to 'the destitute Irish in our workhouses, the branded Irish in the gaols,
the homeless and unsheltered Irish in the streets'.[48]

While helping to sponsor the Catholic framework of charitable and
institutional provision (analysed in Chapter 3) to safeguard the 'low Irish' in
their holy sanctity of poverty, the rich merchants otherwise remained aloof from
the Liverpool-Irish enclave. As founder of the Catholic Club, Sheil embedded
a form of socially exclusive Liberal politics (examined in Chapter 5) which
ultimately failed to adapt and accept the emergence of a new middle class or
petite bourgeoisie, an upwardly mobile group who made their living catering to
the needs of the Irish in Liverpool. Like their compatriots elsewhere in Britain,
some migrants undoubtedly favoured 'ethnic fade', distancing themselves from
all things Irish to effect the quickest route out of the Liverpool 'ghetto' into
economic success and assimilation.[49] This was the path followed by Robert
Cain, a humble migrant from Co. Cork turned self-made prosperous brewer
in Liverpool: increasing wealth led him to move away from Scotland Road to
become the Tory 'King of the Toxteths', in the process altering his place of birth
on official records to Liverpool, Lancashire.[50] There were others, however, who
pursued a different trajectory: having identified their best interests (or market
niche) in servicing the sizeable migrant community, they chose to accentuate
their Irishness, offering all kinds of goods and services to fellow expatriates. The
'commodification' of Irishness, to use the terminology of cultural studies, was
at a premium in what was in effect the capital of Ireland (and of Catholicism)
in England: here was the commercial equivalent of the cradle-to-grave spiritual
provision supplied by the Catholic Church. In Irish-Liverpool, as in other large
migrant 'enclaves', there was considerable internal stratification, but socio-
economic success was often legitimised through bids for ethnic leadership, both
cultural and political.[51]

---

48   NLI MS 32,483: Letter-book of Richard H. Sheil, 1850–56. *NP* 18 Apr. 1863.
49   Donald M. MacRaild, *Irish Migrants in Modern Britain, 1750–1922*, Basingstoke, 1999,
offers a timely critical perspective on orthodox assimilationist studies.
50   See Chris Routledge, *Cains: The Story of Liverpool in a Pint*, forthcoming, 2008.
51   Comparative research into large migrant communities throughout late-nineteenth-
century Europe has shown how ethnic associations 'tended to be related to social class,
to be bids for group leadership', see A.C. Hepburn, 'Ethnic identity and the city', in

Out of place in studies of the Irish in (small-town) Britain, the vast Liverpool-Irish 'colony', some 150,000 to 200,000 strong by the late nineteenth century, is perhaps best approached through comparison with large migrant communities overseas, enclaves within which 'ethnic' culture was not only retained but rewarded.[52] Some important differences, however, should be noted at the outset. In Irish Liverpool, there were no specific dietary, dress or linguistic requirements, the traditional consumer products of enclave economies.[53] 'Irishness' flourished without a specific language other than the local '*Patois*', a precursor of the distinctive scouse accent. Without designated ethnic badge products (other than specially imported shamrocks for St Patrick's Day), 'Irishness' was marketed as a cultural and political project in itself. As the chapters on cultural politics and leisure show, there was no place for such English misrepresentations as the 'stage Irishman', but there was a lucrative trade in 'authentic' images of Ireland and its people, depicted in dioramas, wax-works, lantern shows and music-hall 'spectacles' with casts of up to 100, the more sentimental the better ('I love old Ireland still' and 'The boat that brought me over' were particular concert favourites).[54] For cultural and literary theorists diaspora is posited as valorised space, a creative 'in-between' without secure *roots*, the point of departure for existential transnational *routes* crossing geographical, chronological and imaginative boundaries.[55] Possibly the case at individual artistic level, this was not how diaspora was experienced by the bulk of migrants in Irish Liverpool. As they adjusted to new surroundings, they displayed little relish for any 'interstitial' space or creative indeterminacy other than the delights of the vast entertainment sector in Liverpool, landfall of American popular culture. Although often articulated in the latest fashionable idiom such as blackface minstrelsy, simple nostalgia infused their literature,

---

M. Engman, F.W. Carter, A.C. Hepburn and C.G. Pooley, eds, *Ethnic Identity in Urban Europe*, Aldershot, 1992, pp.1–9.

[52] For a critical introduction to the 'enclave-economy hypothesis' of Alejandro Portes and colleagues, see J.M. Sanders and V. Nee, 'Limits of ethnic solidarity in the enclave economy', *American Sociological Review*, 52, 1987, pp.745–67.

[53] Diet has attracted much attention among American ethnic historians, see Donna Gabaccia, *We Are What We Eat: Ethnic Food and the Making of Americans*, London, 1998, and Hasia Diner, *Hungering for America: Italian, Irish and Jewish Foodways in the Age of Migration*, London, 2001.

[54] *LCH* 6 Oct. 1899.

[55] For a useful introduction to the difficult works of Homi Bhabha, Avtar Brah and other theorists, see John McCleod, *Beginning Postcolonialism*, Manchester, 2000, ch. 7. See also, Paul Gilroy, *The Black Atlantic: Modernity and Double Consciousness*, London, 1993.

balladry and popular entertainment, a packaged construction of memory of the old homeland, the heritage handed down to the second generation with mythic intensity.

From his newsagency and printing business in Byrom Street, John Denvir, a second-generation, upwardly mobile teetotal Irish-Liverpudlian, moved adroitly between Fenianism, cultural nationalism and electoral politics, promoting a canon of historical and literary texts, *Denvir's Monthly Irish Library*, which provided what Patrick O'Sullivan has described as 'a do-it-yourself how-to-be Irish kit, a portable identity, a way of being Irish outside Ireland'.[56] An ethnic impresario educated by the Catholic showman Father Nugent, Denvir also offered a series of 'Penny Irish National Concerts', exclusively Irish entertainment in vaunted superiority to the coarse vulgarities of the British music hall, delivered in accessible (often sentimental) manner without undue ideological or gaelic linguistic demands, a package which proved popular with second-generation Irish-Liverpudlians.[57] As secretary of the Catholic Club, Denvir, a founder member of the Home Rule Confederation (and later its national agent and organiser), hoped to carry the rich merchants and Liberal councillors into the Home Rule camp. Soon disabused by such 'anti-Irish Irishmen', he devoted his energies to securing the return of independent Irish National councillors.

Aided by some enthusiastic electioneering by a local priest, the first victory was secured in the Scotland Ward in 1875. Laurence Connolly, the first of the 48 Irish Nationalists who were to sit on the council between 1875 and 1922, had come to Liverpool in 1857 in connection with his brother's Dublin-based interests, but soon branched out into his own business as a fruit broker and commission merchant before moving into property speculation, gaining a fortune from resort development at New Brighton. Although ejected from the Catholic Club, the wealthy Connolly retained Liberal attitudes and attachments, shared with a number of others who joined him on the council benches as representatives of the Irish National Party (INP). Over the years, however, the INP was carried forward by a radicalising dynamic, driven as much by progressive change in the composition of its council members as by mounting frustration at the Liberals' failure to deliver Home Rule. On retirement from the council, members from established middle-class professions and occupations (doctors, lawyers and rich businessmen such as Connolly) tended to be replaced by those with a more popular style: butchers, shopkeepers, penny-a-week insurance collectors, undertakers and others who attended to the daily needs of

---

56   Patrick O'Sullivan, 'A portable identity', unpublished conference paper.
57   *Irish Programme* 19 Jan. and 3 May 1884, *Nationalist and Irish Programme* 6 Dec. 1884.

the Liverpool-Irish. When redistribution in the 1880s opened up the possibility of gaining one of the new Liverpool parliamentary seats, 'Dandy' Pat Byrne put himself forward as the local man made good. Having started work as a dock labourer, Byrne was a real rags-to-riches story, having acquired a string of public houses, a remarkable wardrobe, a fortune estimated at £40,000, a seat on the city council (where he championed the Irish poor) and parliamentary ambitions.[58] It took the personal intervention of Parnell to force him to withdraw his candidacy in favour of a carpetbag outsider, T.P. O'Connor, a national figure with the celebrity required to represent the Irish beyond the constituency, throughout the length and breadth of Britain.[59]

'Tay Pay' held the seat for over four decades, for the most part continuing to see his first priority as representing the Irish in Britain. However, his constituents were not neglected: his electoral committee, often meeting in the Morning Star, 'Dandy' Pat Byrne's most famous pub, operated as a political 'machine' ensuring the continued success of the INP at municipal level. Offering a form of what has been called 'Nat-Labism', a pragmatic blend of ethnic, confessional and class interests, the INP reached into parts beyond conventional 'Lib-Labism' elsewhere, seeking to ameliorate working and living conditions for the 'poor Irish'.[60] By the turn of the century, local-born INP councillors, second-generation Liverpool-born Irish such as the Harford brothers, prosperous retailers and wholesalers in cotton and cloth, outnumbered their Irish-born counterparts, after which, some commentators suggest, the party displayed less interest in the fate of Ireland than in the immediate needs of the local Catholic community in housing and employment.[61] This is a false distinction: the 'Nat-Labism' embraced by the younger generation of INP councillors was as ardent in commitment to Irish nationalism as to social reform, both policies exemplifying a decisive final rejection of Liberalism. Forthright in its independence from British political parties and unequivocal in its commitment to denominational education, extensive social reform and full-blown Irish nationalism, the INP under Austin Harford was the hegemonic

[58]   For biographical details of Byrne and all other INP councillors in Liverpool see the appendix in B. O'Connell, 'The Irish Nationalist Party in Liverpool, 1873–1922', unpublished MA thesis, University of Liverpool, 1971.

[59]   L.W. Brady, *T.P. O'Connor and the Liverpool Irish*, London, 1983, ch. 2.

[60]   The term 'Nat-Labism' was coined by Sam Davies in '"A stormy political career": P.J. Kelly and Irish Nationalist and Labour politics in Liverpool, 1891–1936', *THSLC*, 148, 1999, pp.147–89 (156).

[61]   O'Connell, 'The Irish Nationalist Party in Liverpool, 1873–1922', ch. 2; Waller, *Democracy and Sectarianism*, p.186.

political force in Edwardian Irish Liverpool, leaving little space or need for
class, confessional or gaelic alternatives, such as the Labour Party, the Catholic
Federation or Sinn Fein.

By the First World War, the Liverpool-Irish had consolidated their position
in working-class Liverpool, although the dominant Tory-Orange formation
continued to ensure the 'marginal privilege' of the Protestant worker.[62] As
is shown in Chapter 1, casualism still prevailed in waterfront labour markets,
but its effects were mitigated by a number of factors: the increasing number
of Liverpool-Irish who had risen to supervisory positions; the development of
work gangs, led by those with the 'knack', in which light tasks were found
for aged and incapacitated relatives and mates; and 'masculine' celebration of
the strength and independence of the Liverpool-Irish docker, unrestrained by
the time and work discipline of the factory hooter. In residential terms, the
'low Irish', a designation carrying topographical as well as socio-economic and
cultural connotations, remained huddled in low-lying 'squalid Liverpool', but,
as Chapter 2 attests, here too there were signs of improvement. INP councillors
in the north end stood forward to insist that demolition of insanitary property
be accompanied by adjacent re-housing schemes for the displaced 'poorest poor'.
Unlike the outer estates of later decades, pioneer pre-war re-housing in the
north end preserved the ethno-sectarian community spirit, infrastructure and
political allegiance of the slums.

Generational tensions, a dysfunctional feature of some migrant communities,
were held in check by the ready acculturation of the second-generation
Liverpool-born into the commemorative memory of the land of their forebears,
a sentimental portrayal of the 'old sod' promoted by religious and political
leaders, ethnic entrepreneurs and commercial impresarios. The educational
curriculum of Catholic schools has been condemned by sociologists for 'denationalising' the Liverpool-Irish, but a wider survey of Catholic activities
suggests quite the reverse.[63] Irishness was replenished in Liverpool by the
continuing influx of Irish priests, for many of whom the best testimony of
fidelity to the faith was commitment to the Irish national cause. 'There is no
more effective way of preserving their faith than by fostering their Irish spirit
and preventing it from being lost or obliterated under the influence of English
surroundings', a missionary priest averred in the 1890s: 'This is a task which

---

[62]   For the Tory 'common sense' of the Protestant working class, see Joan Smith, 'Class,
skill and sectarianism in Glasgow and Liverpool, 1880–1914', in R.J. Morris, ed., *Class,
Power and Social Structure in British Nineteenth-Century Towns*, Leicester, 1986, pp.158–215.
[63]   Mary Hickman, *Religion, Class and Identity: The State, the Catholic Church and the
Education of the Irish in Britain*, Aldershot, 1995, ch. 4 and 5.

Irish priests alone can accomplish.'[64] In the Liverpool context, Catholicism was not an alternative identity available to migrants and their descendants but an affirmation of their essential Irishness.[65]

As with other migrations, the Chicanos in Los Angeles for example, the Irish underwent considerable cultural adjustment in Liverpool but without significant upward and outward social mobility.[66] However, it would seem inappropriate to apply to the Liverpool-Irish what Don Akenson has caricatured as the 'gaelic-Catholic-disability variable', the exculpatory factor deployed by some scholars to account for migrant underperformance and disadvantage in the Irish diaspora.[67] Inhibited in economic performance and social adaptation by a residual pre-modern 'Gaelic world-view' discouraging individual initiative, Irish migrants retreated into defensive and aggrieved ethnic solidarity in which their displacement appeared as involuntary banishment rather than voluntary enterprise or self-improvement. There is little evidence of this 'exile motif' among the Liverpool-Irish. From the security and solidarity of their enclave, they ventured forth into inter-cultural contact and rivalry: by no means autarkic, ethnic provision was tried and tested in Liverpudlian sectarian competitiveness. A culture in itself, the flourishing of internal parish and league-based amateur sport, for example, reflected the dimensions and autonomy of the enclave, but it also facilitated wider civic contact, when the best of the Liverpool-Irish took on the best of the rest in city-wide competition. While 'Irish-Ireland' activists sought in vain to implant gaelic sports, the Liverpool-Irish preferred to perfect their talents in 'popular' sports and entertainment within internal leagues and parochial frameworks prior to the delight of beating the British in

[64] 'Among the Liverpool Irish. By a missionary priest', *Lyceum* Feb. 1894, pp.105–108. Pride of place in *The Second Book of Irish Poetry, Denvir's Penny Illustrated Irish Library no.4*, Liverpool, 1873, was accorded to original material written by Father P.W. Murphy of St Anthony's, Liverpool.

[65] For the importance of generational factors in the United States and the option of an identity as Catholic Americans, see T.J. Meagher, *Inventing Irish America: Generation, Class and Ethnic Identity in a New England City, 1880–1928*, Notre Dame, IN, 2001.

[66] George J. Sanchez, *Becoming Mexican American: Ethnicity, Culture and Identity in Chicano Los Angeles, 1900–1945*, New York, 1995

[67] D.H. Akenson, *The Irish Diaspora: A Primer*, Belfast, 1996, pp.237–42. His main target is Kerby A. Miller's major study of *Emigrants and Exiles: Ireland and the Irish Exodus to North America*, New York, 1985. For useful critical introductions to the controversy, see David Fitzpatrick, 'How Irish was the diaspora from Ireland?', *British Association for Irish Studies*, 25, 2001, pp.5–9, and John Belchem, 'The Irish diaspora: The complexities of mass migration', *Przeglad Polonijny*, 31, 2005, pp.87–98.

open competition at their own games. Strangely, the process stopped short at professional level: unlike the pattern in Glasgow and elsewhere, the support base for Liverpool's two professional soccer clubs defies ethno-sectarian analysis.

The dynamic of competitive (or parallel) rivalry in the provision of welfare, educational, leisure and sporting facilities has been unduly overlooked: studies of sectarianism in Liverpool have concentrated on head-on confrontation in the streets, the 'Pat-riot-ism' which, as Chapter 7 shows, vexed the local authorities.[68] After the fierce battles of the early Victorian decades, a pattern developed of ritualised annual clashes on key commemorative dates, accompanied by frequent minor skirmishes around disputed borderlands: direct invasions into 'enemy' territory, into well-defined enclaves, were comparatively rare and generally ill-advised. Huge outdoor Catholic processions with makeshift 'altars' constructed in the courts, specially spruced up for the occasion, were a new feature of street life, dating from the golden jubilee commemorations in the 1890s of the 'Famine' parishes. Attesting to a new Liverpool-based commemorative history in the making with its own sites of memory, these were open-air expressions of territorial pride and possession, occasions for celebration not provocation. Self-contained in Catholic slums, this festive culture of display caused no concern to the authorities until George Wise chose to re-direct the demagogic animus of ultra-Protestantism away from ritualism in the upper reaches of the Anglican church (and Tory party) to condemn the rampant Romanism flourishing 'illegally' on the streets of Liverpool. With brutal force, the ensuing sectarian riots clarified the boundaries between green and orange in Edwardian Liverpool.

By this time, however, another spatial division had arisen, setting a 'racialised' limit to the inter-cultural contact of the Liverpool-Irish. Still uncertain of their status and security, INP councillors and Liverpool-Irish trade union leaders took the lead in the Edwardian years in opposing the inflow of 'alien' Asiatic labour, the 'yellow peril'. Formerly contiguous with cosmopolitan 'sailortown' Liverpool, the north end was to become a kind of no-go territory for 'blacks' and 'aliens'. 'China town', 'dark town' and 'other alien quarters' were all located in the south end around Toxteth, the 'New Harlem of Liverpool', distant and apart from the 'Irish' north end.[69] At an individual level, contact doubtless continued, personified by Mary Ellen Grant,

---

[68]   The classic study is Frank Neal, *Sectarian Violence: The Liverpool Experience 1819–1914*, Manchester, 1988.

[69]   'Liverpool's coloured colonies', *Liverpool Echo* 6 June 1919; John Belchem, 'Whiteness and the Liverpool-Irish', *Journal of British Studies*, 44, 2005, pp.146–52.

the 'Connaught Nigger' with an Irish mother and West African father, the most notorious (and feared) of the female 'money lenders' in the Edwardian slums.[70] For the most part, the Liverpool-Irish settled for a 'low' whiteness, below British working-class norms, which shaded very readily into an intuitive and compensatory 'greenness'.

Habituated to what T.P. O'Connor described as their 'curious middle place',[71] the Liverpool-Irish of the inter-war decades conformed neither to the narrow representation of Irishness propounded by the new Irish Free State under the 'de Valera dispensation' nor to notions of Britishness which prevailed outside Liverpool in Baldwin's middle England. As economic depression deepened, they were to endure heightened levels of ethnic and sectarian prejudice, a blend of old attitudes and new fears fuelled by alarmist responses to the influx of numbers from the Irish Free State. Condemned as cheap labour and/or welfare scroungers, the new arrivals were ready scapegoats for Liverpool's worsening economic plight. Categorised in biological and cultural terms by eugenicists, the Irish were to encounter 'racial hibernophobia', but even so, as Chapter 12 shows, they fared considerably better than some other 'British subjects' in 'cosmopolitan' Liverpool. Although outside the United Kingdom, dominion status placed the Irish within the 'greater Britain' of the 'Old Commonwealth' alongside Canada, Australia and New Zealand, the pride of the British political establishment. Not always welcomed by the long-settled inhabitants of T.P. O'Connor's north end fiefdom, the new arrivals were able to take their place (albeit often lowly) in the 'white' majority, above the discrimination, institutional racism and enforced repatriation deployed against 'coloured' British subjects of otherwise similar legal status.

In resisting the growing clamour from Liverpool for immigration restrictions to match the quotas imposed by the United States, successive governments took solace in investigations undertaken by various civil servants, none of whom found evidence to substantiate the alarmist claims propounded by the city's leading politicians, clerics and pressure groups such as the Irish Immigration Investigation Bureau. Indeed, reports by the Ministry of Labour were soon highlighting the changing economic geography of migration as the 'second wave' of Irish migrants hastened through Liverpool to more promising and prosperous areas.

Denied replenishment from Ireland (other than the continued recruitment into the 1950s of Irish-trained priests), Liverpool was to lose its primacy among

---

[70] P. O'Mara, *The Autobiography of a Liverpool Irish Slummy*, London, 1934, pp.66–67.
[71] O'Connor, 'The Irish in Great Britain', p.32.

the Irish in Britain. In itself, this would not have mattered had the Liverpool-Irish been able to maintain their ethno-sectarian enclave. While the parent Irish Parliamentary Party collapsed in the early stages of the Irish 'revolution', the Nat-Labism of the INP had continued to resonate with Liverpool-Irish electors, seemingly offering (as Chapter 11 attests) the best local platform to secure post-war reconstruction and homes fit for heroes. The number of INP councillors was actually to increase until the Irish Civil War came to an end in 1923, after which the party spiralled out of existence as members defected to Labour, some directly and others via a brief detour into a short-lived Catholic Party. At the same time, the pace of cultural and spatial change worked against the retention of a specific Liverpool-Irish identity, undermining the framework of associational culture. Having struggled to adjust to the legal requirements of the Irish Settlement in the inter-war years, the network of ethnic and sectarian friendly societies (studied in Chapter 4), once the pride of Irish Liverpool, were to lose their rationale and identity when incorporated into the post-war welfare state. More serious still was the impact of major slum clearance schemes. Between the wars, some 140,000 people – 15 per cent of the total population of Liverpool – were re-housed, many in distant suburban estates without shops, schools, pubs or churches. There was little improvement over time as the housing committee operated a ban on second-generation houses, forcing the children of the new suburbanites to vacate the neighbourhood on marriage. Without kinship groups or adequate facilities, the new estates lacked the character, culture and welfare networks of the old slums.[72] All that remained was 'heritage', a mood of nostalgia in popular imaginings of 'the Liverpool That Was' before global trade declined, the empire disintegrated and the old slums were destroyed. Briefly embraced by Black Liverpool until, as Jacqueline Nassy Brown has noted, its history became as apart as its geography, this 'Merseypride' came to accord pride of place to the 'low Irish'.[73] Emblematic of the Liverpudlian struggle against adversity, misperception and misrepresentation, the Liverpool-Irish slummy was inscribed as the prototypical 'scouser'.

---

[72]   Madeline McKenna, 'The suburbanization of the working-class population of Liverpool between the wars', *Social History*, 16, 1991, pp.173–89.

[73]   Jacqueline Nassy Brown, *Dropping Anchor, Setting Sail: Geographies of Race in Black Liverpool*, Princeton, NJ, and Oxford, 2005, ch. 9.

While informed by theoretical and comparative perspectives on migration and ethnicity, the distinctive feature of this study is the depth and range of primary material consulted, archival research funded though the support of the British Academy and the Leverhulme Trust. In the developing mood of scepticism among historians about what has been labelled 'the "diaspora" diaspora – a dispersion of the meanings of the term in semantic, conceptual and disciplinary space', the need for evidence-based multi-generational study of migrant communities has become all the more important.[74] The process has not been without its frustrations. For example, the lack of complete runs of newspapers, the missing volumes (or those withheld for conservation purposes) seeming always to be those for particularly important years; the loss of key files, such as the papers of the Irish Immigration Investigation Bureau, seemingly stolen from the Liverpool Record Office; and the vain search for articles and pamphlets advertised in the press with such promising titles as John McArdle, 'The Irish In Liverpool' (1870), and John Hand 'The Irish in Liverpool: A retrospect' (1898) and his 'Ireland in Liverpool' (1906). These gaps notwithstanding, this study endeavours to provide a comprehensive source-based history of the Liverpool-Irish.

---

[74] Rogers Brubaker, 'The "diaspora" diaspora', *Ethnic and Racial Studies*, xxviii, 1, 2005, pp.1–19. See also the symposium, 'Perspectives on the Irish diaspora', in *Irish Economic and Social History*, 33, 2006, pp.35–58, with contributions by Enda Delaney, Kevin Kenny and Donald M. MacRaild.

Part One

1800—1914

1

Poor Paddy: The Irish in
the Liverpool Labour Market

A S ECONOMIC MIGRANTS, the Irish in nineteenth-century Liverpool experienced the kind of occupational disadvantage identified by 'segmented' or 'dual' labour market theory, discrimination normally applied to workers marked out by phenotypic difference.[1] The absence of any such marker notwithstanding, the Irish were labelled and stigmatised on arrival, victims of prejudice that hindered their prospects in the labour market. As 'poor Paddies' they were excluded from the 'primary sector' where relatively decent wages, labour conditions, job security and union membership applied, to be confined to a 'secondary sector' of low-paid, unprotected, dead-end jobs – on the docks, in adjacent processing and refining plants and on building sites. It was worse still for women, given the absence of textile factory employment in Liverpool and the general reluctance to employ the Irish as domestic servants, often advertised with the caveat, 'No Irish Need Apply' – in nineteenth-century Liverpool, with Welsh and country sources of supply for domestic labour, 'NINA' was a reality, not 'an urban myth of victimization'.[2] To make ends meet, Irish women were forced into the lowly chip, grit and oakum trades, or some other form of down-market 'basket' selling in Liverpool's notorious 'secondary economy' of the streets, the point of income (and consumption) for the least advantaged. Generalising from the Liverpool experience, George Cornewall

---

1   Sanchez, *Becoming Mexican American*, p.7. See also R.D. Barron and G.M. Norris, 'Sexual divisions and the dual labour market', in D.L. Barker and S. Allen, *Dependence and Exploitation in Work and Marriage*, New York, 1976.
2   'No Irish Need Apply! A servant's narrative', *Porcupine* 8 June 1861. See also the Liverpool correspondent of the *Drogheda Argus* on how 'No Irish Need Apply' was sounded from pulpit, platform and press, *Irish People* 12 Nov. 1864. In the United Sates, 'NINA' was an enduring 'urban legend', see Richard Jensen, '"No Irish Need Apply": A myth of victimization', *Journal of Social History*, 36, 2002, pp.405–29.

Lewis categorised the Irish poor in Britain in the early 1830s, a decade before the Famine influx, as 'an example of a less civilized population spreading themselves, as a kind of substratum, beneath a more civilized community: and, without excelling in any branch of industry, obtaining possession of all the lowest departments of manual labour'.[3]

Drawing upon unpublished census enumerators' books for the mid-nineteenth century, a statistical resource which conveniently spans the Famine influx, historical geographers have stressed the structural factors and constraints which precluded upward mobility. The Irish remained, in Iain Taylor's words, 'a large pool of unskilled casual labour, a proletariat who dominated the unskilled occupations at the bottom of the occupation and social hierarchy'. According to his estimates, 70 per cent of Irish household heads in the parish of Liverpool were 'labourers' in 1851.[4] Analysis of subsequent data registered little advance. By 1871, 57.4 per cent of Irish household heads in the much larger area of Liverpool borough were in semi-skilled or unskilled occupations: no less than 32.7 per cent of Irish household heads worked as dock and general labourers, while 34 per cent of Irishwomen household heads had no occupation. Comparative censual-based analysis confirmed the picture: all migrant groups in Liverpool were under-represented in the unskilled stratum, except the Irish; all migrant groups, except the Irish, were of a higher socio-economic status than the locally born.[5]

Adopting a broader time frame than previous studies, the analysis in this chapter offers a cultural approach, drawing attention to the role of ethnic agency. While clustered at the bottom of the labour market, migrants were by no means passive victims of prejudice. They were soon to formulate their own versions of Irishness, an ethnic affiliation which performed at first protective and defensive functions against disadvantage, disability and discrimination, but then became increasingly assertive. Building upon 'gang' systems of seasonal migration and various networks of regional and confessional allegiance, Irish workers developed a wider ethnic solidarity which gave them some influence within the otherwise free-for-all casualism of the waterfront labour markets. Through such solidarity, Irish workers acquired 'hands-on' control and supervision of certain 'niche' occupations in the 'unskilled' sector. These key jobs on the docks were to be retained while other forms

---

3   PP 1836 (40) XXXIV, p.iv.

4   Taylor, 'Black spot', pp.100–15.

5   Pooley, 'Migration, mobility and residential areas', p.75; Lowe, *Irish in Mid-Victorian Lancashire*, p.85. See also Papworth, 'Irish in Liverpool', *passim*.

of arduous and unpleasant labour (most notably in sweltering sugar refineries) were readily relinquished to newly arrived migrants from mainland Europe. This development, in line with experience elsewhere in the diaspora, lifted the Irish off the bottom of the labour market as other migrant groups slotted in below them. However, there were limits and constraints to this 'uplifting effect'.[6] Still uncertain of their status and security, the Irish took the lead in the Edwardian years in opposing the inflow of 'alien' Asiatic labour, the 'yellow peril'.

While ensuring their (lowly) place in the making of the white working class, the Liverpool-Irish did not abandon 'ethnic' affiliation in pursuit of 'racial' norms. Where choice allowed, they kept apart from the British and Protestant mainstream, enjoying the conviviality and mutuality of a vast and largely self-sufficient ethnic enclave economy. The 'commodification' of Irishness was at a premium in what was in effect the capital of Ireland (and of Catholicism) in England. Suitably packaged, Irish credentials offered the best marketing technique (or unique ethnic selling-point) for those offering all kinds of goods and services to their fellow, if generally less fortunate, expatriates. Here was the commercial equivalent, as it were, of the cradle-to-grave spiritual provision supplied by the Catholic Church. 'Poor Paddy', the focus of this chapter, was customer and compatriot of these 'Micks on the make on the Mersey', to adapt Roy Foster's terminology but without pejorative intent.[7] Barely discernible in census statistics, this upwardly mobile group can be charted through their growing ambitions for political and cultural leadership of the Liverpool-Irish, themes covered in later chapters.

Whatever the relative weighting of push and pull factors, migration flows tend to increase with improvements in transport links. The introduction of cheap steam navigation across the Irish Sea in the 1820s led to alarmist fears about an influx of professional beggars, benefit fraudsters and 'charity-hunters'.[8] As

---

6   For the operation of this 'uplifting effect' in the United States, see David Montgomery, 'The Irish and the American labor movement', in D.N. Doyle and O.D. Edwards, eds, *America and Ireland, 1776–1976*, Westport, CT, 1980, pp.205–18, here pp.206–209; and David Doyle, 'The Irish and American labour 1880–1920', *Soathar*, 1, 1975, pp.42–53.

7   Roy Foster, 'Marginal men and Micks on the make: The uses of Irish exile c. 1840–1922', in *Paddy and Mr. Punch*, London, 1995, pp.281–305.

8   PP 1836 (40) XXXIV, p.14.

Cornewall Lewis's investigation revealed, however, their numbers were dwarfed by economic migrants, work-seekers driven from Ireland by continuing post-war depression and the eventual implementation of the internal free market following the Act of Union. Viewed in historical hindsight, the decades before the Famine influx were a transitional period as well-established patterns of seasonal migration merged into longer sojourns and permanent settlement, leading to 49,639 Irish-born in Liverpool at the 1841 census, some 17.3 per cent of the population.

Some of the traditional seasonal flows had little impact on Liverpool other than as port of entry, as, for example, harvest workers from Connaught, distinctive in appearance, manner and deportment. 'The haymakers and reapers are generally Connaught mountaineers, and are extremely small feeble men', M.J. Whitty observed: 'they appear to be the remnant of the Celtic Irish; these seldom stop here, they go home after harvest'.[9] The agent of the Dublin Steam Packet Company noted that they were 'well-behaved and perfectly sober on board, both going and coming', in marked contrast to the cattle drovers who plied the waters on a regular basis, 'uniformly drunken' and 'very troublesome when on board'.[10] John Denvir remembered the Connaught harvesters 'filling the breadth of Prescot Street, as they left the town, marching up like an army on foot to the various parts of England they were bound for. This was before special cheap trains were run for harvestmen.'[11] Few harvesters, it seems, were tempted to prolong their stay. 'I am unable to hire a Connaught man', the builder Samuel Holme reported: 'he is always spoken of in terms of contempt by the others; he is discovered by them immediately, and they will persecute him till he quits. The other three provinces consider the Connaught men as a lower caste.'[12]

There was also a long-established pattern of seasonal migration from Ireland to brickfields and lime-works adjacent to Liverpool: 'The same men come over in the spring, work in the summer months, save money and go back in winter', another builder, John Johnson reported: 'I have known several instances where the sons and grandsons have followed the fathers in the trade.'[13] However, the Irish seem not to have participated in seasonal migration during the winter months. In this annual rural influx to the urban labour market, the Welsh were to the fore, due to the fact, the secretary of the Warehouse Porters Association

9   PP 1836 (40) XXXIV, p.21.
10   PP 1836 (40) XXXIV, p.9.
11   John Denvir, *The Life Story of an Old Rebel*, Dublin, 1910, p.35.
12   PP 1836 (40) XXXIV, p.29.
13   PP 1836 (40) XXXIV, p.30.

explained, 'that we have many Welsh warehousemen in Liverpool, who are very partial to their countrymen'.[14]

Alongside these seasonal migration streams, predominantly men only, the new cheap transport links facilitated family migration. In 1824, the Select Vestry drew attention to a new class of migrant pauper, 'the lower order of Irish, who, tempted by the facility of communication, and the prospect of obtaining employment in the manufacturing districts, resort hither with their wives and children in overwhelming numbers'. A 'mass of misery and wretchedness' on arrival, their condition deteriorated during the 'fruitless journey' into the 'interior' in search of work, and they returned to Liverpool in such a state as to test the compassion (and stretch the purse) of the Select Vestry. Rather than return to Ireland with their families, Cornewall Lewis reported, the distressed Irish were prepared to take 'any kind of employment, as hod-men, porters about the docks, etc, and become domiciled'. Liverpool was not only the port of entry but also the place of final refuge, 'a kind of terminus of all parts', bearing a disproportionate burden of relief expenditure (for which it repeatedly sought in vain for national assistance). The first report from the Commissioners on the Poor Laws acknowledged that Liverpool was 'a town peculiarly liable to an influx of labourers from Ireland; indeed, the natives of that country compose, at a moderate estimate, one-half of the common labourers in Liverpool'.[15]

As common labourers, the Irish displayed what Cornewall Lewis described as 'willingness, alacrity, and perseverance in the severest, the most irksome, and most disagreeable forms of coarse labour'.[16] While restricted to the lower echelons, they proved flexible and adaptable, qualities lacking in entrants to the urban labour market from the surrounding agricultural areas. 'English peasants do not readily adapt themselves to town work', M.J. Whitty, the Irish-born superintendent of the night watch, observed with some ethnic *schadenfreude*, noting how they ended up as night soil men: 'here we find the English monopolizing the most obnoxious and discreditable of all occupations'. Willing to tackle any task, the Irish were the much-needed 'auxiliaries or drudges of the steam-engine', praised for their industrial application by an

---

14   *Full Report of the Commission of Inquiry into the Subject of the Unemployed in the City of Liverpool*, Liverpool, 1894, p.38.

15   The 1824 Select Vestry report is cited in PP 1834 (44) XXVIII, First Report from the Commissioners on the Poor Laws, Appendix A, pp.912–17. See also PP 1836 (40) XXXIV, p.10, and PP 1878–79 (282) XII, Report on the Select Committee on Poor Removal.

16   The analysis in this and the following paragraph draws upon evidence presented to PP 1836 (40) XXXIV.

array of local soap and sugar manufacturers and by James Muspratt, father of
the British heavy-chemical industry, who left Dublin in 1822 to produce soda
by the Leblanc process on Merseyside. Samuel Holme, the builder and major
employer of Irish labour, underlined the economic benefits of the migrant
flow: 'I consider the Irish are of great value to the town: if it were not for the
influx of them, the almost unlimited number of them at our command, and
their willingness to do the dirtiest and meanest work, the wages of common
labour would rise considerably.' There was some debate as to whether the Irish
possessed specific physical attributes which enabled them 'to carry heavier
weights than the English', but most witnesses to Cornewall Lewis agreed
that they were simply doing the heavy work that others preferred not to do.
Holme provided the most extensive analysis, along with a table detailing the
occupations of 'about 7,500 Irish of the lowest sort employed in this town
and suburbs':

> I consider the Irish as usually more muscular than the English, and
> especially than the Welsh, more capable of doing the drudgery. I attribute
> their character of drudges partly to their muscular power, and partly to
> their condescending to do that which the national pride of an Englishman
> will not allow him to do ... The Irish are much employed as porters at the
> docks: the Welsh get the best places as porters, as there are more Welsh
> warehouseman, who employ the porters. At the chemical manufactories
> nearly all the dirty work is done by the Irish, under an overseer, who is
> generally not Irish. In soaperies and sugar-houses the common dirty work
> is usually done by them. All the low departments of industry are filled by
> the Irish. Of the labourers, of every description, more then a half – of the
> mechanics not more than a twelfth, at most – are Irish.

While acknowledging the economic benefits of this migrant inflow, employers
repudiated any suggestion that wage levels accounted for the poverty in which
many of the Irish in Liverpool lived. Cultural, ethnic and gender factors were
cited as the crucial factors. Bad economics in itself, the Irish penchant for
profligate conviviality and mutual assistance was aggravated by the inability of
Irish women to manage the family budget, a criticism which continued through
to the Edwardian period. The Irish, Holme observed critically, were 'very far
from living as well as the English on equal wages':

> I attribute their wretched way of living rather to their improvidence than
> to their drunkenness. In part, also, I attribute it to a foolish hospitality;
> for they are very kind to one another. They assist one another in sickness

Table 1.1 *Occupational analysis of the Irish in Liverpool in the early 1830s*

Occupation	Number	As percentage
Mechanics of various sorts	780	10.4
Brickmakers	270	3.6
Sugar-boilers	200	2.7
Masons' labourers	350	4.7
Bricklayers' labourers	850	11.3
Chemical works and soaperies etc.	600	8
Sawyers	80	1.1
Labourer employed in smithies, lime-kilns, plasterers' yards and by paviors	340	4.5
Lumpers around the docks who discharge vessels and re-load them	1700	22.7
Porters employed in warehousing goods etc.	1900	25.3
Coal-heavers and sundry other employments	430	5.7
Total	**7500**	

Source: Evidence of Samuel Holme: PP 1836 (40) XXXIV: Royal Commission on the Condition of the Poorer Classes in Ireland. Appendix G. The State of the Irish Poor in Great Britain, p.29.

and distress. Sometimes they send over money to their friends in Ireland. The Irish women in Liverpool are more improvident than the men, and bad domestic managers, and generally forestall their husbands' wages.

Similarly, the lack of upward mobility at the workplace was not for the want of opportunity. Rather, it reflected the aversion to formal training and apprenticeship whether in construction, warehousing or the merchant marine. Eschewing such discipline and mental application, the Irish remained deficient in 'practical ability' and 'mechanical capacity', hence incapable of 'work which requires skill or nicety in the execution'.

Attitudes towards the Irish hardened considerably during the Famine influx of the late 1840s. With heartless humour, satirical papers bemoaned the arrival of 'Irish Pauper, Esq. and family, attended by his suite, including Messrs. Fever, Starvation, Taxes, Impudence and Knavery, etc.' The *Liverpool Lion* chronicled Mr Dennis Bulgruddery's brazen prowess and blarney in cheating relief agencies, fraudulent begging, inner-city pig-keeping, heavy drinking and fisticuffs.[17] Rushton, the stipendiary magistrate, calculated that within 12 hours of disembarkation, the Famine Irish were to be 'found in one of three classes – paupers, vagrants, or thieves'.[18] According to his figures, 296,331 persons landed at Liverpool from Ireland between 13 January and 13 December 1847 of whom 116,000 were 'half naked and starving'.[19] Hard-pressed Liverpool rate-payers pleaded in vain for central government assistance while the local Poor Law authorities adopted 'crisis management'. An efficient new system of vetting and visiting curbed the number of fraudulent claims, while tough new regulations to facilitate prompt removal back to Ireland deterred genuine claimants. The proportionate amount spent on the Irish rose considerably in 1847–48, but as Frank Neal has shown, this was caused by earlier arrivals, unemployed Liverpool-Irish able to claim 'irremovable' status by the terms of the Five-Year Residency Act of 1846. As the presence of these long-stay Irish ensured low wages in the local labour market, Neal doubts whether they should be considered a net burden on rate-payer employers.[20] Nevertheless, the *Morning Chronicle* investigation of 'Labour and the Poor' in Liverpool in 1850 began by counting the cost of Irish in-migration in terms of mounting public expenditure on the poor law, police and public health:

> The town of Liverpool feels, through the sensitive medium of the pocket, that it has to pay a large price for the privilege of being the greatest port of the west, and that its advantages in being the outlet to America are nearly counterbalanced by the disadvantages in being the inlet from Ireland.[21]

When it subsequently sought to assess the downward impact on wage levels, the *Morning Chronicle* drew attention to the 'overwhelming numbers of utterly

17   'Unfashionable arrivals at the Clarence Dock', *Liverpool Lion* 11 Dec. 1847. 'Mr Dennis Bulgruddery's correspondence with his relations in Ireland' began in *Liverpool Lion* 8 May 1847.

18   Quoted in Canon Bennett, *Father Nugent of Liverpool*, Liverpool, 1949, p.38.

19   Cited in Neal, 'Liverpool, the Irish steamship companies and the Famine Irish', p.34.

20   Neal, 'Lancashire, the Famine Irish and the Poor Laws', pp.26–48. Frank Neal's definitive statistical analysis of the impact of the Famine influx on Liverpool has now been put in comparative perspective in his *Black '47: Britain and the Famine Irish*, Basingstoke, 1998.

21   'Labour and the Poor: Letter 1: The burdens upon towns – Irish pauperism', *Morning Chronicle* 20 May 1850.

superfluous Irishmen' attracted to the casual and overstocked waterfront labour markets:

> the subject is one which it is utterly impossible to bring to the test of figures, but the evil comprised in it is keenly felt by vast numbers of the labouring population – many of them Irish themselves – who might do tolerably well, were it not for the daily influx of raw and unskilled labourers, called 'Grecians', who think a shilling a day high wages, and who will often labour for 6d or 9d a day rather than not get a job. In fact, the labour market of Liverpool is cruelly overstocked; yet every week, and every day, the sixpenny deck passengers from Dublin and elsewhere pour in their multitudes, at the imminent risk of pauperizing of thousands of men who have hitherto managed to earn a decent subsistence.

Downward pressure on wages was at times compounded by the 'false economy' of the middlemen on the waterfront, lumpers, master porters and warehousemen, who readily took on 'the green hands – the "Grecians" – unskilled porters that are always coming over on the chance of work', altogether 'regardless of the waste and injury the Goods of the merchant sustain by this hurried and careless way of doing work'.[22] Although casual and unrestricted, dock labour was neither undifferentiated nor unskilled: there was a premium on work experience, proficiency and specialist know-how, useful adjuncts to stamina and strength. Those with the 'knack' – skills described by Jimmy Sexton, the dockers' leader, as combining the intelligence of a Cabinet Minister, the mechanical knowledge and resource of a skilled engineer and the agility and quick-wittedness of a ringtail monkey – were generally the first to find employment, able to exercise some control over the labour process.[23] Over time, a 'caste-system' developed as those with workplace specialist skills jealously guarded their 'niche' areas of expertise, enhancing their pride and position by acting as work gang leaders, distributing work to those in their 'network' with light tasks allocated to mates and relatives no longer capable of physical exertion. These 'networks', a form of primitive trade unionism, stretched across the water. Newly arrived migrants unaware of the 'goods', the latest secret Ribbonite grips and passwords, often

---

22   *Morning Chronicle* 27 May, 10 and 17 June 1850, letters 2, 4 and 5; 'To the Merchants and Brokers of Liverpool, 9 March 1848', posting-bill in HO 45/2410B.

23   James Sexton, *Sir James Sexton: Agitator. The Life of the Dockers' MP: An Autobiography*, London, 1936, p.67. See also Eric Taplin, *Liverpool Dockers and Seamen 1870–1890*, Hull, 1974, pp.7–10.

found themselves at a painful disadvantage within dock labour gangs, as John Denvir observed:

> more than one poor fellow coming fresh from Ireland to work at the Liverpool docks, and expecting to be at least civilly-treated by his fellow-workmen — who were, and are, mostly of his own nationality — has found himself cruelly deceived. If he did not know the grip, or the password, the heaviest part of the work would, somehow, be thrown upon him, while occasionally he would even receive bodily injury.[24]

Those unable to gain 'hands-on' experience on the docks looked to other opportunities within the open access waterfront to make ends meet. The theft of cotton and other goods reached unprecedented heights in 1848, for which the *Morning Chronicle* offered a ready explanation: 'The starving Irish that landed by thousands in a week on the quays of Liverpool could not resist the temptation thrust before them by the open and exposed state of the docks, and by the transit through the streets of countless wagons loaded with unprotected property.'[25] Here too 'gang' systems were apparently in operation: enterprising juveniles ran their own market in 'swag' scavenged from docks and warehouses, while women worked together at 'cotton-picking' from passing carts, concealing their booty in dresses 'with large receptacles or inner flounces'.[26] 'Cotton-stealing is a very clever and well-worked out system', Father Nugent informed a Select Committee of the House of Lords: 'they have means of giving order notes, and working the thing perfectly'. The collected booty was usually fenced through marine store dealers, a 'registered' trade for which the Irish, as John Denvir proudly recorded, displayed considerable aptitude. *Porcupine* ran an exposure of depredations 'about the docks and warehouses', charting the rags-to-riches career of Mr Joblott (not his real name), an Irish marine store dealer who had progressed from 'street pickings' gathered by his fellow countrywomen to illicit trade in whole bales of cotton (always with wrappers removed) obtained through salvage or more questionable means. Many of Liverpool's large fires, Nugent reported, were

---

24   Denvir, *Irish in Britain*, pp.127–31.

25   *Morning Chronicle* 27 May 1850, letter 2, headed 'The Liverpool Docks — their management and mismanagement, and their influence upon the social and moral condition of the poor'.

26   Martha Kanya-Forstner, 'The politics of survival: Irish women in outcast Liverpool 1850–1890', unpublished PhD thesis, University of Liverpool, 1997; M. Brogden, *The Police: Autonomy and Consent*, London, 1982, pp.43–73.

'simply started as the only means of covering up the robberies which have been perpetrated'.[27]

Whatever their role in criminal networks, marine store 'dealers' operated as the hub of a barter economy which, as Denvir noted, enabled them to 'develop large businesses in china and crockery ware, hardware of every kind, fur, wool, and every conceivable article of trade and commerce'.[28] They were a crucial point of recourse in the subsistence economy of poor migrant families. When times were hard, women purchased old rope from them to pick into oakum, selling it back to them for caulking of vessels at the very barest profit. Other labour of this lowly kind relied on direct selling. Women who pounded sandstone into grit to use in scouring door-steps hawked it by the halfpenny-worth on the streets. The chip trade, a matter of last resort, was a family affair: the men chopped up old boxes, the women tied the chips into bundles, and the children were sent out to sell them on the streets.[29] Most of Liverpool's so-called 'street arabs' were Irish, ragged children whose street-wise marketing skills embraced 'the commercial element without the commercial principle'.[30]

While the poor Irish were a visible (and often importunate) presence on the streets and waterfront, nationalist propagandists endeavoured to project a different image. In his report on the Liverpool-Irish to the Council of the Irish Confederation in Dublin in January 1848, George Smyth, a successful hat manufacturer in Paradise Street, calculated their numbers – 'including the children of Irish parents' – at upwards of 90,000 and stressed their economic contribution at every level:

The Irishmen in Liverpool perform nearly all the labour requiring great physical powers and endurance. Nine-tenths of the ships that arrive in this great port are discharged and loaded by them; and all the cargoes skilfully stowed. Out of 1,900 shipwrights 400 are Irish, or of Irish parents; and although Liverpool is a port rather for repairing than building vessels, there is one Irishman of the three or four master builders of the town, and many Irish foremen. In almost every branch of trade Irishmen, notwithstanding

27   Nugent's evidence, Third Report from the Select Committee of the House of Lords on Intemperance, PP 1877 (418) XI, qq.8194–346; Denvir, *Irish in Britain*, p.437; 'About the docks and warehouses', *Porcupine* 29 June 1871. See also the dubious exploits of 'Old Dan', an Irish marine store dealer in 'Tried for treason', the semi-fictional account of Fenianism in Liverpool serialised in *CT* 6 Aug 1870 onward.
28   Denvir, *Irish in Britain*, p.454.
29   *Morning Chronicle* 17 June 1850, letter 5 on the 'chip', 'grit' and 'oakum' trades.
30   'Entertainment in Aid of Destitute Street Boys', LM 2 Jan. 1867.

the many prejudices with which they have to contend, have risen to the highest promotion ... a large majority of the boot and shoemakers and tailors of the town are Irish, and I know that Irish skill is recognised in the various foundries. Many Irishmen are distinguished for their ability as architects, draftsmen [sic], and clerks of the works.[31]

Smyth's analysis offered an important reminder of an Irish presence above the unskilled sector, an indication of the various artisan and professional networks (ignored by Cornewall Lewis's focus on the 'Irish poor') which criss-crossed the Irish Sea: Dublin, Liverpool and Manchester formed an inner triangle within a wider circle of trades communication (and career development) from London to Glasgow, Belfast to Cork, Bristol to London. Don MacRaild's recent study of Orangeism draws attention to 'the idea of a northern British industrial zone, linking Ulster and lowland Scotland with northern England'.[32]

At critical times such as the Famine, however, trade mobility across the Irish Sea proved dysfunctional. Finding the 'honourable' trades overstocked, new journeymen arrivals from Ireland took whatever work was available in the unregulated 'slop' and 'sweated' sectors, producing shoddy goods for sailors, emigrants and the cheap ready-made market, competition which steadily eroded wage levels, standards and employment throughout the bespoke trade. The *Morning Chronicle* charted the downward spiral in the Liverpool tailoring trade:

The greater portion of the slop journeymen tailors in Liverpool seem to be Irishmen, who come over at a cheap rate in the steamboats. They are mostly in great distress when they arrive, and are therefore willing to work for the sweater, at the sweater's prices. Within the last few years the number of men employed on the premises of the master tailors has gradually diminished. The respectable master tailors as a body, complain that their trade is yearly falling off, and going into the hands of the show-shops and slop-sellers; and that the only means they have of competing with them is to lower the wages of their men.[33]

---

31   *Nation* 15 Jan. 1848. For a biographical sketch of Smyth, see 'Forgotten (Almost)', *United Irishman* 25 Feb. 1905, cutting in Clark Compendium, Diocese of Clogher Archives, Bishop's House, Monaghan (hereafter Clark Compendium), envelope D.
32   MacRaild, *Faith, Fraternity and Fighting*, p.290.
33   *Morning Chronicle* 24 June 1850, letter 6.

Table 1.2 *Occupational analysis of the Irish in Liverpool in the early 1870s*

Merchants, 1st class	300
Merchants, 2nd class, factors etc.	1500
Shopkeepers	3500
Clerks	3500
Stevedores, master porters and warehousemen	2500
Skilled artisans	15,000
Commercial assistants	2000
Professions	800
Market people and street sellers	2000
Miscellaneous, not living by manual labour	2000–3000
Unskilled manual labour	146,900 (= 81.7 per cent)
Total	**c. 180,000**

Source: Hugh Heinrick, 24 Sept. 1872, reprinted in Alan O'Day, ed., *A Survey of the Irish in England, 1872*, London, 1990, p.90.

Table 1.3 *Occupational analysis of the Irish in Liverpool in the early 1890s*

Dock labourers	458
Coal porters, heavers	72
General and other labourers	108
Watchmen, porters, messengers	27
Employed in gasworks	19
Carmen, carters	12
Sailors, ship-firemen, stokers	129
Artisans	71
Shopkeepers, dealers, publicans, hawkers	53
Other	51
Total	**1000**

Source: Census of England and Wales, 1891, vol. 4, General Report, p.62.

The high proportion of Irish-born tailors, some 57.5 per cent of the total identified in the sample from the 1851 parish enumeration books, should perhaps be considered a register of the impoverishment of the trade.[34]

In the early 1870s Hugh Heinrick sought to promote the Home Rule cause by pointing to the Irish contribution to the wider Liverpool economy. His

---

[34]   Taylor, 'Black spot', p.8.

occupational classification highlighted a significant mercantile, clerical and artisan presence, the 'one-fifth to one-sixth above the ranks of ordinary toil – a proportion which most strikingly exemplifies the intelligence, industry and good conduct of those who have risen, when we consider that all, or nearly all, had to force their way from the lowest ranks and against the most adverse odds'. Added to these were the 2500 Irish who had acquired key positions as stevedores, master porters and warehousemen on the waterfront. However, this still left some 80 per cent of Irish workers as unskilled manual labourers.[35]

With the rising numbers of Irish middlemen with hiring responsibilities, it is perhaps not surprising that labouring on the docks increasingly became an Irish speciality. 'There was no nationality could do the work along the docks like our people', Father Nugent proclaimed with pride.[36] The 'slapdash' analysis of 1000 adult males of Irish birth in Liverpool incorporated in the report of the 1891 census showed that the nearly half were dock labourers, over five times the proportion for the entire local workforce.[37]

By the late nineteenth century, dock labour, often punctuated by spells at sea, had become the characteristic Liverpool-Irish work pattern, handed down from father to son, and readily adopted by newer arrivals from across the water. Celebrated from personal experience in the novels of James Handley and George Garrett, men relished the independence of casual and maritime labour markets. This 'freedom' seemingly outweighed both the high risk of occupational injury, personified by Jimmy Sexton's disfigurement, and the lack of economic security, the pervasive motif of 'Irish slummy' literature. It was left to the women to balance domestic budgets against the odds. Having consolidated their position on the waterfront, the Irish seemed to have moved out of heavy, dirty and sweltering work in refining and processing, their places being taken in the 'modern Hades' by cheaper labour, the poorest economic migrants from Germany and Poland. Some Irish, however, continued to work in the refineries: J.G. Taggart, the 'first working-man's candidate to enter the City Council', was employed as a labourer in Tate's refinery when returned for the Vauxhall ward in 1888.[38]

---

35   Hugh Heinrick's survey is reprinted in Alan O'Day, ed., *A Survey of the Irish in England, 1872*, London, 1990.

36   *CT* 25 Apr. 1890.

37   David Fitzpatrick, 'The Irish in Britain, 1871–1921', in W.E. Vaughan, *New History of Ireland*, vol. 6: *Ireland under the Union II, 1870–1921*, Oxford, 2003, pp.653–702, here p.663.

38   *Mortality Sub-Committee. Report and Evidence*, Liverpool, 1866, p.237, drew attention to naked workers in sugar refineries; *Liverpool Forward* 1 Aug 1913. See also Taggart's obituary in *LCH* 18 Apr. 1925.

While the men consolidated their hold on the waterfront, Irishwomen remained on the streets, 'keeping body and soul together on tenpence a day', hawking fruit, fish, 'green stuff' and chips from their baskets. Catholic clergy were understanding of their 'habit of spending spare coppers in drink': '"Except that", said the priest, "as a rule they are good girls. They are chiefly Irish, and Irish girls don't often go wrong."' [39] Indeed, in the absence of other employment opportunities, the Society of St Vincent de Paul occasionally made grants to indigent women to establish them in the street-selling trade. Father Nugent introduced a system of rewards and Christmas treats (clothing, geese and coal) for 'basket-women' who 'could produce bank-books showing how they had saved some money during the previous twelve months'.[40] The fish-girls were particularly persistent and enterprising, paying weekly sums into a 'club' to cover the cost of regular fines for 'obstruction' – as in the case of Maria O'Donnell, Sarah Glynn, Margaret Ward, Mary Buck and Catherine M'Tague who threw salt and verbal abuse at non-purchasing passers-by in Sawney Pope Street.[41] Proud of her Irish descent (and regular in her attendance at mass at St Mary's), Annie Garvey, the 'Pier Head Squatter', was perhaps the best-known outdoor hawker: she spent over 40 years living alone in a hut on the Landing Stage where she sold apples and oranges every day until her death in 1914.[42]

With its absence of textile factories it was still 'not the "fashion" for girls to work' in Liverpool, but Amy Harrison's survey of 'women's industries' in 1904 revealed expanding opportunities in tobacco, soap, jam, confectionery and match factories, for 'the better class of industrial girls': lower down the pecking order, rope-making, sack mending and jute provided employment for 'the poorest class, a great proportion of whom are Irish'.[43] To the dismay of the priesthood, Irish women with more respectable occupations and higher social aspirations were often lost to the faith:

> The great body of our people being of the poorer labouring class, the more respectable Irish Catholic girl of the servant or shop-assistant class, not finding a desirable husband among her own people, yields to the prospect of comfort and a little grandeur, and without looking to the future grasps

39   *Squalid Liverpool: By a Special Commission*, Liverpool, 1883, p.42. See also *Mortality Sub-Committee. Report*, pp.252–55.

40   Bennett, *Father Nugent*, p.112.

41   'Police Intelligence', *DP* 9 Sept. 1865.

42   *LCH* 13 June 1914.

43   Amy Harrison, *Women's Industries in Liverpool: An Enquiry into the Economic Effects of Legislation Regulating the Labour of Women*, London, 1904.

at the Protestant's offer of marriage in opposition to the Church's law and without her sanction and blessing.[44]

Dismissing such upwardly mobile 'perverts', the Catholic Church preferred to champion the street-selling 'poor Irish' for their fidelity to the faith. 'They might be poor', Father Nugent averred, 'but the poor Catholic girl could do more for God by her sufferings, by the integrity of her character than many a high-born lady who was surrounded by every comfort and luxury.'[45] This blessing apparently extended to those who found marriage partners outside their ethnic group provided suitable 'conversion' preceded the nuptials. '"I'm a true Christian now, and mean to remain one"', Zaid, a well-known 'Asiatic' in Liverpool, assured a bemused Protestant evangelical missionary:

> "Yes", chimed in an Irish woman, with such a broad accent, from the land of Erin, that it made her declaration somewhat difficult to understand, "yes, he's a Christian now, and the priest who made him so says so; and I says to him, 'Sure and I won't marry you till you be a Christian, so long as my name's Driscol'". All this was true excepting what concerned Christianity. This worthy Romanist would marry none but a Christian; so the Arab consented to the *modus operandi* by which he was to be made one, and the priest sprinkled some water on his face, and pronounced him to be such, to the satisfaction of both.[46]

As in nationalist commentary, Catholic portrayal of the Irish in Liverpool was fundamentally ambivalent: celebration of the achievements of 'our people' was accompanied by inverse pride in the virtue to be found among those at the bottom of the socio-economic hierarchy. A point of sectarian honour, the extent of business success was tabulated with some precision:

> In proof of the business capacity we can point to the leading salesmen in the Liverpool Cattle Market, who are Irish Catholics; to the greatest importer of foreign meat in the kingdom, a Catholic Irishman; to one of the best known tug-owners, another; to a leading wholesale provision merchant and leading fruit merchant, both Irish Catholics; to the foremost cotton broker

---

44 'Among the Liverpool Irish. By a Missionary Priest', *Lyceum* Feb. 1894, pp.105–108.

45 'League Hall Reunion', *CT* 9 Jan. 1880.

46 Joseph Salter, *The Asiatic in England; Sketches of Sixteen Years' Work among Orientals*, London, 1873, p.232.

on 'Change, a Catholic of Irish descent; to the chief master porters, carters and stevedores connected with the docks who are Irish Catholics; and to doctors and lawyers having the largest and most lucrative practices, Irish Catholics also.[47]

In a speech to the Liverpool Celtic Literary Society in 1903, Thomas O'Hanlon called upon those who had 'succeeded' to establish a local Polytechnic, to be called the Irish Philanthropic and Patriotic Institution, where 'our poor people' ('sadly behindhand' in the 'mechanical and engineering crafts') could be given instruction in the trades, the value of which was so readily appreciated by the increasing numbers of 'foreign' migrants in the town:

> Whenever any job in the plumbing, glazing, or joinery line has to be done at our houses, we generally find some foreigner – perhaps a Pole or a Jew – come to do it ... It is quite evident that there must be something radically wrong somewhere – even apart from poverty – when we see poor foreigners, without perhaps one-tenth of the brains or physical adaptiveness of the poor Irish, carrying on the callings of artisans and tradesmen, while the vast majority of Irish have to be eking out a miserable existence in the lowest and most laborious slavery.[48]

Every encouragement was given to what Father Nugent called 'putting our Catholic boys to trades' in the hope of breaking the chain of deprivation as sons followed fathers into 'dead-end' jobs on the waterfront casual labour market, 'earning from the first a few shillings by mere drudgery and mean occupations'.[49] At the same time, however, there was proud appreciation of the achievements of Irish manual labour as 'hewers of wood and drawers of water to the rest of the community'.[50] Liverpool, John Denvir protested, was 'a "stony-hearted stepmother" to its Irish colony, which largely built its granite sea-walls, and for many years humbly did the laborious work on which the huge commerce of the port rested'.[51] A new series in the *Liverpool Catholic Herald*, 'Ireland in Liverpool', opened in praise of the Irishmen 'employed in taking up and re-laying the roads for the electric trams':

---

47   'Among the Liverpool Irish', p.106.
48   See the report of the lecture in *LCH* 6 and 13 Feb. 1903.
49   *CT* 28 July 1882.
50   *United Irishman* 18 Nov. 1876.
51   Denvir, *Life Story*, p.9.

It is, of course, only a repetition of the old fact – when Pat leaves home – through no fault of his own – he has to do the hewing of wood and drawing of water for the stranger … One cannot help admiring these fine specimens of Hibernians, these hardy sinewy sons of Irish fathers and mothers, and one cannot help feeling sorry that there is not work for their willing hands at home instead of in the hot and grimy streets of this Saxon city.[52]

As articulated in Liverpool, the Irish Home Rule project held out the prospect of improved working conditions, reducing the pressure on the local labour market by stemming the inflow. The Irish, T.P. O'Connor advised, should vote for candidates who would provide the opportunity for the Irish people 'to remain in Ireland, and to find work, not in the poison of Widnes, in the slums of Liverpool, or in the dockyards of Birkenhead, but on the green hills of Ireland'.[53]

While seeking to stem the emigrant outflow from Ireland, O'Connor and the municipal councillors of the Irish National Party stood forward to defend the 'poor Irish' already on Merseyside. The resonance of their 'Nat-Labism' was aided by a number of factors linked to the socio-economic structure of Irish Liverpool. First, a willingness to embrace all those linked by faith and nation, no matter how lowly: middle-class INP councillors defended basket women, ragged children, cotton-pickers and others who struggled to make ends meet on the streets against police prosecution and Protestant proselytisation.[54] Second, an understanding of the needs and culture of the Liverpool dockers, 'a body of Irishmen second to none in their patriotism'. While external observers and reformers concentrated on the evils of casualism and intemperance, the INP campaigned on the issue which really mattered to the dockers: safety at work.[55] The corner-stone of the 'Nat-Labism' alignment was the 'Dockers' Charter' of 1901, the culmination of a campaign by Sexton, the dockers' leader, with T.P. O'Connor acting as its energetic parliamentary champion, to extend the health and safety provisions of Factories and Workshop legislation to cover work on the docks, 'far and away the most dangerous employment in the

[52]   *LCH* 8 Sept. 1899.
[53]   'Irish Demonstration in Birkenhead', *LCH* 7 Aug. 1903.
[54]   Lynskey, solicitor and INP councillor, regarded it as a point of honour that he had never prosecuted a basket girl, see *LCH* 14 Apr. 1919.
[55]   See, for example, Eleanor Rathbone, *Report of an Inquiry into the Condition of Dock Labour at the Liverpool Docks*, Liverpool, 1904; and *How the Casual Labourer Lives. Report of the Liverpool Joint Research Committee on the Domestic Condition and Expenditure of the Families of Certain Liverpool Labourers*, Liverpool, 1909.

kingdom'.[56] O'Connor was aided by the solicitor and INP councillor George Lynskey, a leading specialist in labour and registration laws who carried an appeal through the House of Lords against the ruling depriving casual labourers of the benefits of the Compensation Acts.[57] Finally, the INP was aided by the emergence of a new lower middle-class leadership group, drawn from 'ethnic' publicans, shopkeepers and other service providers, traders in the enclave able to collapse socio-economic differences.

The petite bourgeoisie of Irish Liverpool has been largely lost from view: overlooked by contemporary social observers (and by historians) with their fixation on the 'poor Irish', they fell short of inclusion in the ethnosectarian contribution history of outstanding mercantile and professional success. However, there were already indications in the Cornwall Lewis inquiry of an emergent lower middle class, alert to the opportunities in the 'enclave economy', eager 'to rise to be small-shopkeepers, provision-vendors and public house keepers ... rather than large employers of labour where management or knowledge of mechanics is necessary'.[58] As the market grew, the Irish in Liverpool displayed what Denvir described (in a typical blend of prejudice and perception) as 'a remarkable aptitude for dealing':

> It is often noted that where an Irishman is steady and has got a good wife
> – for that is more than half the battle – he is frequently able to save enough
> to open a marine store ... a coal yard, or a small shop. By degrees, he gets
> on, for, as a rule, our people are more quick-witted in bargaining than
> even the Jews – the difference being that Moses sticks to all he gets, while
> Pat's often too generous nature frequently lets go easily what he has won
> so hardly.[59]

Newcomers were often keen to take advantage of purportedly lucrative trading opportunities in Liverpool, although they were not always aware of local conditions: John O'Hara was called before the magistrates for selling 'slink calf' in St James's market, considered fit for human consumption back in his native Sligo but not in Liverpool.[60] In the hope of raising sufficient funds for a stall, the O'Reilly sisters from Belfast targeted the Irish residents of Portland Place,

---

[56] 'Our Dock Labourers: Preventible [sic] Deaths', *Nationalist and Irish Programme* 29 Nov. 1884; *LCH* 28 June 1901.

[57] *Liverpool Review*, 26 Oct. 1901.

[58] PP (1836) 40, XXXIV, pp.8–41.

[59] Denvir, *Irish in Britain*, p.437.

[60] *DP* 1 May 1862.

Roscommon Street: claiming they were collecting 'for a death', they produced an array of begging letters (one of which was signed by the Sisters of Mercy of St Patrick's Convent of Our Lady of Mercy, Downpatrick) until apprehended by the police for obtaining money under false pretences.[61] The market in cheap second-hand clothing was the most ready point of access either in streets 'devoted to this business, such as Fontenoy Street'[62] or in St Martin's market, better known by its sobriquet 'Paddy's Market', where 'the refuse of the empire is bought and sold'. An indispensable resource for the adjacent poor Irish, it also attracted a cosmopolitan clientele of merchant seamen in port.[63]

At the other end of the scale, some market traders enjoyed considerable prosperity, particularly in the food markets. The most flamboyant was Thade Crowley, a Corkonian who became a successful pork butcher and leader of the local Hibernian society. Surrounded by banners, harps and shamrocks galore, Crowley marched at the head of the lodge on St Patrick's Day in proud display of both his socio-economic status and his ethnicity, dressed in 'buckskin breeches, top boots, green tabinet double-breasted waistcoat, bottle-green coat with brass buttons, and beaver hat'.[64] One of nine children, Father Nugent was the son of a first-generation Irish migrant who acquired substantial interests in the fruit, poultry and game business in St John's market and other outlets. Educated by the Irish Christian Brothers, Liverpool-born Thomas Burke, INP councillor and historian of Catholic Liverpool, owned a particularly lucrative poultry stall in St John's. Following in the footsteps of 'Kelly the Butterman' whose advertisements and charitable donations to Irish and Catholic causes figured prominently in the press in the 1860s, the most successful of the new entrants to the retail food business was probably John Hughes, a fervent Irish nationalist with gaelic cultural enthusiasms and republican political sympathies. Specialising in Limerick bacon and ham, Hughes arrived in Liverpool in the mid-1880s and soon developed (from his Bootle base) a huge grocery empire of some 60 retail shops which provided employment for local activists and 'cover' for Irish republicans on the run until sold to the Co-op after the First World War.[65]

For those who managed to set themselves up in a small retail business or public house, 'Irishness' often proved their best asset. This was certainly the case in the licensed trade, a notoriously competitive market. John McArdle

61   'Police Intelligence', *DP* 7 Oct. 1864.
62   Denvir, *Irish in Britain*, p.454.
63   Cooke, *Scotland Road*, pp.52–54.
64   Denvir, *Life Story*, pp.25–26.
65   Kelly, *Liverpool*, ch. 7.

who hosted a number of Irish societies at his Crosbie Street pub, famous for its Sunday night readings from *The Nation*, was an accomplished ethnic landlord who chose briefly to diversify into the grocery and provision trade to cater for the temperance fad in the Irish community following a visit by Father Mathew.[66] Jack Langan who ran the most famous 'Irish' pub, strategically positioned opposite Clarence Dock, enjoyed considerable fame and fortune (his estate was valued at over £20,000 on his death in 1846), appearing on the platform when his hero, Daniel O'Connell, visited the town.[67] No less remarkable was the rags-to-riches success a few decades later of 'Dandy' Pat Byrne, the 'scavenger's friend'. A poor migrant from Co. Wexford, Byrne started work as a dock labourer, before acquiring a string of public houses, a remarkable wardrobe, an INP seat on the town council and a considerable fortune.[68] The Morning Star Hotel, headquarters of his chain of pubs, was a favourite location for Liverpool-Irish 'politicking', frequently patronised by T.P. O'Connor's constituency committee.

In the absence of any specific dietary, dress or linguistic requirements (the traditional products of enclave economies), Irishness could be marketed as a cultural and political project in itself. As St Patrick's Day approached, a number of outlets offered specially imported 'Irish not "Queen's" Shamrock', available from specific counties: the first to sell out was always that grown on Daniel O'Connell's grave.[69] The *Liverpool Catholic Herald* offered a postal service from the Sisters of Charity in Ballaghaderin where 'peasant girls and boys pluck the treasured leaf from the swards and glens and valleys of Co. Mayo. The Sisters organise and direct the work, which provides occupations for many a humble home in Connaught at this trying season.'[70] Beyond such annual celebration, John Ignatius Cullen offered 'a large Assortment of Catholic Books and Works relating to Ireland' from his 'New Stationery and Catholic Book Depot' in Tithebarn Street opened in the 1860s.[71] Peter Murphy, a lifelong activist in the Irish Republican Brotherhood, financed the underground cause through the takings at the Irish Depot and Catholic Repository, 13 Scotland Place, 'opened expressly with the object of supplying the Irish people of this district with everything Irish they want', including 'Irish Literature and Pictures, Bog

66   Delegates in Liverpool since 1830, CO. 904/8 ff.79–80; Denvir, *Life Story*, pp.15–16.
67   Denvir, *Life Story*, pp.3–4 and 52; *LM* 19 June 1846.
68   Kelly, *Liverpool*, ch. 3
69   *DP* 18 Mar. 1886.
70   *LCH* 2 Mar. 1918.
71   *NP* 8 Feb. 1862.

Oak Jewellery and Ornaments'.[72] Nearby, at 55 Scotland Road, 'The Gael'
stocked 'only absolutely genuine Irish goods', supplying 'all humanity's many
wants in the clothing line, combining cheapness with quality, and affording the
purchaser the assurance that he is not merely getting good value for his money,
but doing a man's share to revive the prosperity of the land of his birth'.[73]
When 'The Gael' moved to 93 Scotland Road, the new premises incorporated
the well-known Irish tailors and outfitters Cahill and Carberry, whose stock
of 'the latest and best in IRISH MANUFACTURES' included 'the celebrated
"Wolfe Tone" and "Lord Edward" make in Shirts and Collars'.[74] Outside
commercial interests occasionally cashed in on 'Irishness', including the city's
most fashionable department store during the visit of the Abbey Theatre in
1906: 'THE DUTY OF IRISH LADIES / is to support the houses that stock
/ Irish Goods. The Bon Marche, Basnett / Street Liverpool has a magnificent
range of / the famous / KATHLENN NI HOULIHAN / Costume Clothes from
the mills, Co. Cork'.[75]

The Denvir brothers were perhaps the most effective ethnic entrepreneurs.
Based in Tithebarn Street, Bernard Denvir, 'a Catholic, Irish and General
Bookseller' (and also a highly placed Fenian) made it 'his *speciality* to keep
the works of every Irish writer that can be obtained, so that the lover of Irish
Literature can always be supplied at his establishment'.[76] From his newsagency
and printing business in Byrom Street (distribution point for O'Herlihy's inks
of Cork), his more famous brother John moved adroitly between Fenianism,
cultural nationalism and electoral politics, promoting a canon of historical
and literary texts, *Denvir's Monthly Irish Library*, which included a local trades
directory detailing 'From Whom to Buy Irish Goods': a typical listing included
booksellers, hoteliers, newsagents, poulterers, provision merchants, sculptors
(or ornamental masons), sweet sellers and tailors.[77] Dismayed by the whiggish
proclivities of the rich Irish merchants and Liberal councillors, Denvir devoted

---

[72]   *LCH* 3 Mar. 1899.

[73]   'Ireland by the Mersey', *LCH* 29 Mar. 1907.

[74]   See the front page advertisement in *Transport Worker*, Sept. 1911.

[75]   *LCH* 4 May 1906.

[76]   See the advertisement for B. Denvir's Irish Library, 55 Tithebarn Street, at the back
of John F. McArdle, *Catechism of Irish History*, Liverpool, 1873, issued under the imprint
'Denvir's Penny Library'.

[77]   Denvir's subsequent publications were interspersed with advertisements for Liverpool-
Irish businesses such as the 'funerals furnished to suit all classes, on the most economical
terms, and carried out in a truly Catholic spirit', offered by Thomas Maguire, 7 Mount
Pleasant in *Denvir's Penny National Irish Almanac for 1889*.

his energies to securing the return of independent Irish National councillors drawn from the lower social ranks, traders who could rally their ethno-confessional customer base to the independent Home Rule cause.

Over the years, the INP was carried forward by a radicalising dynamic, driven as much by progressive change in the composition of its council members as by mounting frustration at the Liberals' failure to deliver Home Rule. Members from established middle-class professions and occupations (the doctors, lawyers and rich businessmen celebrated in the early contribution histories) tended to be replaced by those with a more popular style: market traders, butchers, shopkeepers, penny-a-week insurance collectors, undertakers and others who had risen within the enclave by attending to the daily needs of the Liverpool-Irish. Remaining close to their constituents, INP councillors devoted considerable energy to improvements in housing and working conditions. Taggart, the first working man to be elected to the council, soon enjoyed considerable upward mobility himself, becoming an estate agent's collector and then acquiring his own business (and shares in Everton FC), but for most of his political career he remained 'an Irish Nationalist Labour representative' for whom 'all social and labour questions are part and parcel of Home Rule'. While his attempt to establish a municipal workshop on trade union conditions for the manufacture of clothing required by Corporation employers was heavily defeated, he was instrumental in securing the insertion of a fair wage clause in Corporation contracts and was frequently called upon to arbitrate in labour disputes.[78]

While Nat-Labism spread across the Irish enclave, independent labour struggled to implant itself in Liverpool. Trade unionism came late to maritime, dockland and casual labour markets, difficult settings in which organisation tended to develop in the wake of militant action and 'unofficial' strike waves. After the false dawn of the 1870s, the industrial militancy of the late 1880s marked a decisive advance towards permanent organisation, 'new unionism' aided by the mediation of Michael Davitt and the arrival of two other Irishmen, full-time leaders with considerable experience in labour (but not waterfront) organisation. Richard McGhee and Edward McHugh, disciples of Henry George, established the National Union of Dock Labourers (NUDL) and introduced the union button, more effective in restricting the labour supply than the old 'grips' and 'passwords'.[79] While the Society of St Vincent de Paul allocated grants to enable local Catholics to obtain the union badge, some Catholic

78   *CT* 27 Jan. 1888, and obituary in *LCH* 18 Apr. 1925.
79   Eric Taplin, 'Irish leaders and the Liverpool dockers: Richard McGhee and Edward McHugh', *Bulletin of the North West Labour History Society*, 9, 1983–84, pp.36–44.

clergy condemned the new leadership. Father Nugent mounted a sustained attack on free-thinking outsiders, 'Socialists and Communists, and men who did not believe in God or hell', agitators whose militancy threatened the very livelihood and identity of the Liverpool-Irish, now faced with the prospect of being 'shunted' out of *their* dockland labour market:

> Day by day the number of Irish dock labourers – and when he said Irish he meant Catholic, because they were practically one and the same – was becoming fewer ... They did not want anyone coming from any outside place, any wild, erratic man, or freethinker to lead them ... unless the Irish people in Liverpool became sober and used their reason and judgement, and stood firm to their religion, in ten years from this there would be very few Irishmen as master stevedores or men over gangs of labourers; for once the boss of a concern was anti-Irish, or had no sympathy with our people, or was narrow-minded, it would be difficult for them to get bread for their children, and have in their hands that labour which had been their special portion during the last thirty or thirty five years.[80]

McGhee and McHugh were ousted in 1893 after which the leadership of the NUDL was placed in local hands. Having started his working life on his parents' stall in the open market at nearby St Helens selling recycled umbrellas and cheap woollen caps, Jimmy Sexton, a heavy drinking ex-Fenian well known in local Irish nationalist and Catholic circles, was elected general secretary in 1893.[81] Circumstances were unpropitious: the union was losing members; branches were collapsing while employers were moving onto the counter-attack against new unionism in retreat. Surveillance reports for Special Branch noted that Sexton was not only no longer connected with secret societies but was also 'opposed to strikes if they can be avoided'.[82] Approvingly labelled as 'Catholic Labour' by the *Liverpool Catholic Herald*, Sexton was an able (and authoritarian) administrator who sought to sustain a strong dockers' union, fully recognised by employers so that disputes could be resolved and working conditions improved through negotiation and persuasion; similarly, he supported the Labour Party (but not its policy of secular education) in the hope of securing favourable legislation to better the standards and conditions of working people by constitutional means, working within the system. By no means an inspirational figure, often

---

[80]   *CT* 25 Apr. 1890.

[81]   Sexton, *Autobiography*, pp.20–22.

[82]   NAD, 3/716 CBS Précis Box 3, 12 Nov. 1901.

remote and patronising towards the membership with what he dismissed as their short-term and sectional interests, Sexton attracted little praise or affection for his calculated caution, but he succeeded where others failed in holding together a union of dockers. The success of the general transport strike in Liverpool in 1911 was not of his making, but the consequent concordat with employers on union recognition and working practices was more readily achieved and consolidated, Eric Taplin concludes, because of Sexton's work over the preceding years, permitting Liverpool to become the best-organised port in the country. The 'clearing house' scheme introduced in 1912 had limited effect in decasualising dock work, but it confirmed the union's control of access to the waterfront: indeed, it may have brought more benefits to the dockers than to employers.[83]

His teetotalism apart, Toxteth-born Jim Larkin seemed more in tune with the rank and file, following his dramatic metamorphosis from model foreman to militant and charismatic labour leader during the strike in 1905 at T. and J. Harrison, a large firm whose ships docked at the south end. Blessed with dazzling oratory and 'presence', Larkin was the very antithesis of Sexton in style, attitude and philosophy. However, as Sexton feared, the strike ended in complete and costly failure. Even so, it proved the making of Larkin, subsequently appointed national organiser for the NUDL, a post which conveniently took him away from Liverpool. Campaigning in Ireland, he was soon to part company with Sexton and the union as he sought to extend the benefits of organised labour beyond dock workers to include all unskilled labour. From his Irish base, Larkin, the socialist revolutionary, moved beyond trade union reformism, Home Rule and 'mere political reform', a trajectory which was to bring him into conflict with the mainstream 'Nat-Lab' movement in Liverpool.[84]

The leader who best exemplified the blend of ethnic, confessional and class loyalties was George Milligan, former barman, then quay porter and specialist checker for the White Star Line, an active member of the NUDL who played a vital role in organising non-union dockers in the north end, emerging as de facto deputy to Sexton after the successful strike of 1911. Milligan, indeed, became the vindicatory voice of the 'North-End Liverpool Dockers', a predominantly Irish groups of workers, the last to secure union recognition on the waterfront:

---

[83]   Eric Taplin, *The Dockers' Union: A Study of the National Union of Dock Labourers*, Leicester, 1986, ch. 5, 7 and 8.

[84]   Taplin, *Dockers' Union*, ch. 6.

They have been dubbed rabble and rebels and five-minutes Union men, etc. They have been charged with being unreasonable in their expectations and uncontrollable in their actions. We who know them best know the unfairness, the absolute calumny contained in these charges. The force of circumstances, the sheer weight of the great Western Ocean shipowners, has been responsible for their remaining outside the union. The Dockers' Union could be forced on the master porters and stevedores and smaller shipping companies, but not on the banded strength of the great Liner companies until – a week or two ago. And as to the character of the men, my honest opinion is that in the future they will be the cream of the Union.[85]

A devout Catholic and ardent defender of denominational education, Milligan was fervently anti-socialist but militant and fearless in defence of his fellow dockers' rights. He looked back beyond the 'new individualism' and the 'new materialism' of the Reformation to a medieval 'golden age' when 'the material welfare of the Church and of the worker fell together'. Here was the inspiration for modern organised labour: 'In these days, when trade unionism is being recognised as the only means left to the poor man for selling his labour at a fair price, I am quite sure this species of collective bargaining will be endorsed by the Catholic Church.'[86] Hence the priority was to 'Christianise the Labour Movement', to banish the twin evils of secularism and socialism. He was taken to task in the secular and socialist columns of *Liverpool Forward*, which vehemently repudiated his contention that the forward march of Labour was hindered by association with the Independent Labour Party and other socialist bodies.[87] Shortly afterwards, the Dublin transport strike led by Larkin prompted a major culture clash between Merseyside socialists and the Catholic labour movement.

Aided by James Connolly and Big Bill Haywood, Larkin's efforts to arouse sympathetic support in Liverpool were ridiculed in the local Catholic press, which noted the fawning preponderance of 'middle-class Socialists, Suffragettes, and curiosity mongers ... not overflowing with friendliness to sane trade unionism'. Sympathetic strikes, Milligan insisted, were 'not compatible' with 'the ethics of striking from a Catholic trade unionists point of view'. There was much contention over the welfare of children sent across

---

[85]   'The North-End Liverpool Dockers', *Transport Worker*, Aug. 1911.

[86]   Milligan, 'The Rights of Man', *LCH* 18 Oct. 1913.

[87]   *Liverpool Forward*, 18 and 25 Apr. 1913.

from Dublin to escape the privation of the strike. Much to the annoyance and concern of Liverpool Irish Catholics, they were jealously guarded by middle-class socialists in Wallasey, denied proper spiritual (and ethnic) guidance. While sympathising with the Dublin strikers, Austin Harford, leader of the INP members on the city council, did not conceal his fury:

> In advocating and fighting for the interests of labour he, in common with all Irish Nationalists, was as fully advanced as, if not more so than, those who claimed that Socialism was the only groove through which the condition of the working classes could be ameliorated. Whilst in the fullest sympathy with the Dublin strikers, he pulled up short and sharp at the outrageous policy of sending Dublin children into the non-Catholic and alien atmosphere on this side. He was aghast at the lack of true Catholic and Irish spirit shown by those responsible for the callous work, and his cry was, 'Hands off the Catholic young of Dublin!'

When the children were finally sent back, the opposing parties almost came to blows on the Liverpool landing stage, the socialists apparently insulting the Catholic priests in attendance while the Catholics drowned out the attempt to raise a cheer for Larkin.[88]

As this episode encapsulated, the terms Irish, Catholic and working-class had acquired synonymic force, strengthened in opposition to secular (often middle-class) socialism. By embracing this conjuncture, the INP was able to prevent a switch to Labour, to badge itself as *the* party of the Liverpool-Irish workers, committed to workers' rights, housing reform, denominational education and Irish independence. Beyond this potent blend of ethnic, confessional and class affiliation, however, was the looming issue of race and 'colour'.

At sea, there were commonplace clashes (part of the macho occupational culture, as it were) between 'Dublin Jack' and 'foreigners' like 'Dago Charlie'.[89] The hostility expressed towards the Chinese, an increasing presence in the merchant marine and in 'sailortown' Liverpool, was altogether different, poisoned by 'colour' prejudice and fantasy. The 'unguarded dumping' of 32

---

[88]   *LCH* 1 Nov. and 13 Dec. 1913, and 7 Feb. 1914. Equating socialist charity with Protestant proselytisation, Archbishop Walsh led the clerical opposition in Dublin to the original plan of the feminist-socialist Dora Montefiore to transport 300 children to a 'cleaner and more hopeful environment'; just 18 eventually arrived in Liverpool, see Lucy McDiarmid, *The Irish Art of Controversy*, Ithaca, NY, and London, 2005, ch. 4: 'Hunger and hysteria: The "Save the Dublin kiddies" campaign, October–November 1913'.

[89]   Sexton, *Autobiography*, p.40.

Chinese in Liverpool without the 'guarantees of employment' required by the new Aliens Act of 1905 prompted an hysterical 'Yellow Peril' reaction, fanned by labour leaders and councillors. Sexton was the most vociferous, deploying explicitly racist discourse to condemn the 'beastly' morals of the 'Chinaman': 'He comes here like an international octopus, spreading its tentacles everywhere, and he undermines and corrupts the morals, and pulls down the wages of the English people. (Shame).'[90] Prompted by Sexton, with ardent support from Austin Harford, the city council decided to appoint a commission to investigate Chinese settlements in Liverpool. Gratuitously prurient in parts, the findings repudiated the more sensationalist allegations of criminal, sexual and insanitary behaviour, but fears persisted that the Chinese were undermining wage levels.[91] For all its impeccable ILP socialist credentials, *Liverpool Forward* gave strong support to the efforts of the National Transport Workers Federation and National Seamen's and Firemen's Union (NSFU) to remove cheap Chinese or 'Ching-Ching' labour, a campaign intensified in the First World War as the double standards of 'flag-wagging' employers were soon exposed: 'When it comes to "business", patriotism takes a back seat. Liverpool men are too costly and Ching-Ching takes pride of place.'[92] In protecting the 'white' worker, 'Catholic' Labour and socialist Labour stood shoulder to shoulder.

Already to the fore in the making of the white working class, the INP and Catholic Labour leaders drew closer to the mainstream during the war while still retaining their separate and distinctive ethno-confessional infrastructure. For their ardent patriotism, upholding the virtues of what O'Connor described as the 'free' British Empire, 'founded on freedom, on free institutions, on the respect for nationality', Sexton was awarded a CBE and Milligan an OBE. A few years later, Milligan was appointed as the first president of the Society of Lovers of Old Liverpool, an exercise in social and political unity as the once great port city sought to come to terms with deepening post-war depression – the committee included T.P. O'Connor; Sir Leslie Scott, distinguished lawyer and

---

90   Quoted in Gregory B. Lee, *Troubadours, Trumpeters, Troubled Makers: Lyricism, Nationalism and Hybridity in China and its Others*, London, 1996, p.206.

91   *Report of the Commission Appointed by the City Council to inquire into the Chinese Settlements in Liverpool*, Liverpool, 1907. For analysis of the affair, see John Belchem and Donald M. MacRaild, 'Cosmopolitan Liverpool', in John Belchem, ed., *Liverpool 800: Culture, Character and History*, Liverpool, 2006, pp.370–74.

92   *Liverpool Forward* 27 March and 1 May 1914. See also Ken Lunn, 'The seamen's union and "foreign" workers on British and colonial shipping', *Bulletin of the Society for the Study of Labour History*, 53, 1988, pp.5–13.

Tory MP for Exchange; and Jack Hayes, the city's first Labour MP. As seaport Liverpool sought to diversify into factory-based industry, Milligan's popular and racy lectures to the Society looked back to the past. In this exercise in heritage, the free-spirited north end Liverpool-Irish docker, the former 'poor Paddy', was reconstructed as the iconic figure of happier times, symbolised by sartorial eccentricities, bizarre working habits and staggering drinking feats, not least the formerly obligatory 'three tides' of Saturday indulgence.[93] Here was a foundation figure of 'scouse' culture, an Irish contribution to the Merseypride which was to flourish in seemingly dialectical (and compensatory) response to economic adversity.

---

[93] 'Dockers in Toppers', *Liverpool Weekly Post* 6 June 1925, and other cuttings in Athenaeum, Liverpool: Gladstone Miscellaneous Pamphlets, 139.

2

'The Lowest Depth': The Spatial Dimensions of Irish Liverpool

H ISTORICAL GEOGRAPHERS have located the Irish in Liverpool at the bottom not only of the labour market but also of the residential hierarchy. Given their limited resources, the Irish tended to congregate around 'core-streets' in the city's two major working-class areas, close to the docks and the casual labour markets: the 'instant slum' of the north end with its purpose-built court housing, and the failed middle-class suburb of the south end, hastily 'made down' into overcrowded and cellared street housing. Over time, there was to be substantial concentration in the north end, extending out from the two pre-Famine 'clusters', the eastern half of Exchange and Vauxhall Wards, and behind the docks in Scotland Ward. By contrast, in the south end, where there were original 'clusters' between Park Lane and the docks, and between the Custom House and Derby Square, there was less coherence and increased fragmentation, accentuated by a growing Ulster Protestant presence. In the statistical terms of historical demography, these were not Irish ghettos. Outside the 'scale trap' of core streets such as Lace Street, Crosbie Street and Marybone ('as Irish as any part of Dublin'),[1] the index of segregation was not significantly high. The persistence rate was remarkably low (no more than 9 to 18 per cent, Colin Pooley has calculated, remained at the same address from one census to the next) as the Irish, lacking attachment to particular jobs or dwellings, favoured frequent short-distance movements within familiar territory. Overall, the size of Liverpool-Irish households was smaller than the average Liverpool household as they were often headed by a single parent and had fewer servants, but living conditions tended to be much worse because of high levels of multiple occupancy.[2]

---

1   *CT* 4 Nov. 1887.

2   Papworth, 'Irish in Liverpool', chs. 3, 4 and 10; Pooley, 'The residential segregation

Following the introduction of cheap transport across the Irish Sea, public health officials and social investigators had no hesitation in applying an ethnic label to the worst areas of the city, the 'squalid Liverpool' running along the low-lying westernmost strip from the Dingle to Sandhills, home to a population 'more dense than is to be found in any city of the civilised world'.[3] 'It is doubtful whether a town like Liverpool, which can be reached at a trifling expense by the most destitute of the Irish poor, will ever be as healthy as towns less accessible to that poverty-stricken people', Thomas Baines rued in his *History of the Commerce and Town of Liverpool*.[4] In a series of reports and publications in the early 1840s, ahead of the Famine influx, Dr Duncan castigated the Irish 'who inhabit the filthiest and worst-ventilated courts and cellars, who congregate the most numerously in dirty lodging-houses, who are the least cleanly in their habits, and the most apathetic about everything that befalls them'.[5] The critical factor was not material or environmental circumstance but 'racial' character:

It may be said that this is merely the result of their greater poverty, which deprives them of a proper supply of the necessaries of life, and compels them to select the most unhealthy (because the cheapest) localities as their places of residence. To a great extent this is true; but at the same time there appears to be, among the lowest class of Irish, such an innate indifference to filth, such a low standard of comfort, and such a *gregariousness*, as lead them, even when not driven by necessity, into the unhealthy localities where they are found to congregate; and which they render still more unhealthy by their recklessness and their peculiar habits.[6]

Unsuited to urban living, the 'low' Irish – a symbolic term with topographical and cultural connotations – were a contaminating presence responsible for

---

of migrant communities'; and Richard Dennis, *English Industrial Cities of the Nineteenth Century*, Cambridge, 1984, pp.39–41.

3   *Squalid Liverpool*, p.4.

4   Thomas Baines, *The History of the Commerce and Town of Liverpool, and of the Rise of the Manufacturing Industry in the Adjoining Counties*, London, 1852, pp.677–78.

5   W.H. Duncan, 'On the sanitary state of Liverpool', dated 31 Aug. 1840 in *Local Reports on the Sanitary Condition of the Labouring Population of England*, London, 1842, p.293.

6   W.H. Duncan, *Physical Causes of the High Mortality in Liverpool*, Liverpool, 1843, quoted in G. Kearns and P. Laxton, 'Ethnic groups as public health hazards: the Famine Irish in Liverpool and lazaretto politics', in E. Rodriguez-Ocana, ed., *The Politics of the Healthy Life: An International Perspective*, Sheffield, 2002, pp.13–40, here p.19.

Liverpool's notoriously high mortality rate, its unenviable reputation as the 'black spot on the Mersey':

> By their example and intercourse with others they are rapidly lowering the standard of comfort among their English neighbours, communicating their own vicious and apathetic habits, and fast extinguishing all sense of moral dignity, independence and self-respect ... I am persuaded that so long as the native inhabitants are exposed to the inroads of numerous hordes of uneducated Irish, spreading physical and moral contamination around them, it will be in vain to expect that any sanitary code can cause fever to disappear from Liverpool.[7]

Drastic interventionist social engineering became the order of the day, justified (in the face of laissez-faire sentiment and ratepayer retrenchment) through ethnic denigration of the Irish 'other', a 'contaminating' presence within the unreformed and unprotected 'social body'.[8] In the metaphoric logic of the diseased social body, the Irish in Liverpool embodied 'all the pathologies of violence, unreason and contagion that so obsessed the early Victorians'.[9]

Discursive shifts in the understanding of urban morphology, poverty and epidemiology notwithstanding, such attitudes towards the Irish persisted into the twentieth century. Edwardian progressives such as Frederic D'Aeth agonised over how to raise the 'low Irish' to the requisite standards (or 'national minimum') of responsible and healthy civic behaviour in the 'second city of empire':

> The Irish constitute a serious problem. They largely form the roughest and lowest element of the people, and are mainly settled in two poor districts in the north and south. Gay, irresponsible, idle, and quarrelsome, they seem by nature unfitted for the controlled life of a large town, which tends only to accentuate their failings. It seems impossible for them to adopt the restraints, the responsibilities, and the sense of corporate citizenship which should be the essential characteristics of the town dweller. They contribute abnormally to the work of the police court and fill the workhouses and

---

7   Duncan, 'On the sanitary state', pp.293–94.

8   Mary Poovey, 'Curing the "social body": James Kay and the Irish in Manchester', *Gender and History*, 5, 1993, pp.196–211; D.M. MacRaild, 'Irish immigration and the "Condition of England" question: The roots of an historiographical tradition', *Immigrants and Minorities*, 14, 1995, pp.67–85.

9   Scally, *Hidden Ireland*, p.206.

charitable institutions. They are the despair of the social reformer while they win his heart with their frolicsome humour.[10]

By this time, however, the allegedly 'feckless' Irish of the north end were proving themselves adept at laying claim to urban space. By the First World War, Liverpool, once notorious for the worst slums in Europe, had become the 'Mecca for housing experts', a transformation due, the *Liverpool Catholic Herald* noted with justifiable pride,

> to Irish Catholics who stirred up public opinion, made an end of the municipal creation of new slums more congested and more appalling than the old ones, and set on foot, and are still successfully carrying on, a scheme of municipal housing which has attracted the favourable attention of the leading authorities in Europe and America.[11]

As public health duly improved, the social problem was redefined: the cause for concern was no longer the death rate, but the high birth (and survival) rate among the Liverpool-Irish. As family size went into decline among the rest of the population, Protestant Liverpool began to fear being swamped by Catholics.

Housing reform notwithstanding, Scotland Road, 'the lowest depth', remained synonymous with 'poverty, vice and crime. Like a filthy fountain it sends forth its polluting streams to all parts of Liverpool, filling our streets with beggars, our workhouse with paupers, and our prisons with criminals.'[12] While praising the INP for its intervention in the north end, the local Catholic press sought to redirect the critical public gaze to 'darker' aspects of the urban morphology in the south end of the city with its 'lodging-houses for negro, lascar and other foreign seamen, mulatto children, drunken men and women, and street fights'.[13]

---

[10] Frederic G. D'Aeth, 'Liverpool', in Mrs Bernard Bosanquet, ed., *Social Conditions in Provincial Towns*, London, 1912, p.38.

[11] *LCH* 17 May 1913 and 11 April 1914.

[12] J. Allden Owles, *Recollections of Medical Missionary Work*, Glasgow, 1909, p.43, quoted in Matthew Vickers, 'Civic image and civic patriotism in Liverpool 1880–1914', unpublished DPhil thesis, University of Oxford, 2000, p.159.

[13] *Squalid Liverpool*, ch. 4; *LCH* 14 Feb. 1902.

Dr Duncan, the first Medical Officer of Health to be appointed in England, was at one and the same time a leading 'environmentalist' advocate of heavy expenditure on sanitary works and administration (costs which Liverpool Corporation with its vast income from dock dues could well afford) and an unrestrained 'moral' critic of the Irish. He was an influential force in promoting the Liverpool Sanitary Act 1846 to establish a pioneer public health service with powers to enter and inspect cellars and lodging-houses, as well as to clean and drain the exterior environment in what he described as 'the most unhealthy town in England'. Duncan, however, was not sanguine of ready improvement 'so long as the influx of destitute Irish is allowed to continue unchecked'. Refracted though the religious beliefs and sectarian considerations prevalent in Liverpool, Duncan's formulation of the 'problem' of the Irish undermined environmentalist sanitary agitation, drawing the public towards a 'moralistic contagionism'. In the 'calamitous' year of 'Black '47', Duncan described Liverpool as a 'City of the Plague'. As migrants flooded in and typhus spread, 'lazaretto politics' were the order of the day to contain 'Irish fever'.[14]

Liverpool became, in the words of the Registrar General's third quarterly report for 1847, 'the hospital and cemetery of Ireland'. Commandeered by the Select Vestry, warehouses near the docks were crammed to bursting with fever victims; four old prison hulks were requisitioned as floating hospitals in the Mersey; and the sick were to be excluded from wealthy districts. Every step was taken to prevent the spread of fever beyond the 'low Irish': at one point, no fewer than 88 per cent of sick persons under the care of the health authorities were Irish. The greatest incidence of death from fever, diarrhoea and dysentery occurred in Scotland, Vauxhall and Exchange in the north end and Great George in the south end, wards with large Irish-born populations – Frank Neal has calculated the number of such Irish deaths as at least 5500 in 1847. In Lace Street alone there were some 472 deaths, one third of all the inhabitants. Ten Catholic 'martyr' priests fell victim to the fever while tending to their sick flock, as did a similar number of doctors and the Revd John Johns, the Unitarian domestic missionary.[15]

Given the high levels of overcrowding in the low-lying residential areas along the waterfront, typhus remained a constant threat – these were the

---

14   Kearns and Laxton, 'Ethnic groups as public health hazards'.
15   Neal, *Black '47*, ch. 5.

areas too where the cholera epidemic of 1848–49 took hold, its ravages being confined, Duncan reported, 'to the destitute population in the lower districts of the town'.[16] Once the crisis had passed, however, the authorities paid scant attention to sanitary reform: instead, they sought to rectify Liverpool's 'black spot' image through lavish schemes of civic ornament and grandeur, urban 'boosterism' befitting the 'second metropolis'.[17] As criticism mounted of these mistaken priorities, the local press commissioned investigative explorations into 'the real condition of the Liverpool poor'. Having ventured into the nether world below the boundary of spatial segregation, journalists sent alarming reports from fetid courts and cellars, areas of pestilence and death 'as much unknown and as little understood as the hut of the Esquimaux is to the African savage'.[18] As the death-rate began to rise alarmingly in the 1860s, scientists warned of the 'national danger' of mortality in Liverpool with its low-lying 'fever districts'. Spatial segregation, the *Quarterly Journal of Science* cautioned, had bred a false sense of security among those living in the wealthy residential areas, built upon the sandstone ridge above the 'nursery of fever below ... where the thousands of poor Irish and the hundreds of emigrants lie huddled together like sheep in a fold'. The central commercial districts were far more vulnerable, however, 'surrounded by a feeble cordon separating them from typhus and other diseases (resulting from over-crowding, drunkenness, and every other kind of vice)'.[19]

Panic returned in 1865 and 1866 as a three-pronged epidemic – cattle plague, typhus and cholera – propelled the death rate up to over 57 per thousand. Starting with denigration of their 'wild' cattle and drovers, the Irish were held increasingly accountable for the escalating crisis.[20] Drawing a convenient distinction between typhoid and typhus, the *Report of the Sub-Committee on the Causes of the Excessive Mortality of the Town* refused to accord blame to the local authorities. Whatever the criticisms, sanitary reform had proved sufficient to reduce deaths from typhoid to a minimum: no such intervention,

---

16   Quoted in Gallman, *Receiving Erin's Children*, p.97.

17   'Another royal statue in Liverpool', *DP* 22 Oct. 1866.

18   'The real condition of the Liverpool poor. From our own Commissioner', *DP* 31 Oct., 6, 9, 15 and 23 Nov. 1865. See also 'The untruthful boasts of the Health Committee', *Porcupine* 21 Oct. 1865.

19   'The mortality of Liverpool and its national danger', *Quarterly Journal of Science*, 3, 1866, pp.311–23 (315–16).

20   'The Liverpool cattle trade', *DP* 5 Sept. 1866; Report from the Committee on the Transit of Animals by Sea and Land, PP 1870 (116) LXI, evidence of Lloyd, qq.586–677.

however, could contain typhus, the Irish fever. Trench, the Medical Officer of
Health, suggested that 'nationality' accounted for

> those personal habits and that indigence which I believe has more to do with
> typhus than mere external physical causes ... there are streets so open and
> so free from glaring physical defects of construction, that I could not include
> them in my presentment to the Grand Jury, and yet such streets, because
> of their being inhabited by poor Irish, are the foci of typhus.

Shearer, the Medical Officer to the Toxteth Board of Guardians, who was allegedly
'in the habit of reading the Bible to Roman Catholic patients receiving relief',[21]
was more emphatic: the Irish were 'of naturally improvident and filthy habits ...
We have a vast work to do to break this large section of the population off from
their native ideas of health and cleanliness, the rustic *hygiene*, in short.'[22] Similar
factors were also held accountable for the spread of cholera in 1866. Originally
restricted to German and other emigrant ships (a public health hazard of a global
port city like Liverpool), cholera took hold on land in Bispham Street, 'inhabited
by the lowest of the Irish population, and situated in the worst part of what may
be justly described as the chief fever district of the parish'. To Trench's horror,
relatives of the first victim refused to allow the immediate removal and burial
of the body, and insisted on holding a wake – 'one of those shameful carousals
which, to the disgrace of the enlightened progress and advanced civilization
of the nineteenth century, still linger, as dregs of ancient manners, among the
funereal customs of the Irish peasantry'. Before the month was out, 48 persons
living within a radius of 150 yards of the wake had died of cholera.[23]

The Irish continued to be portrayed as barbarously primitive into the 1880s
when 'squalid Liverpool' vied with 'Outcast London' as the focus for social
concern. In a masterly study, Gareth Stedman Jones has shown how housing
discourse in the capital shifted from demoralisation to degeneration. Poverty
was no longer pauperism in disguise: the savage and brutalised condition of the
casual poor was perceived as the result of long exposure to the degenerating
conditions of city life.[24] In 'squalid Liverpool', Scotland Road was a particular
scandal, an affront to late-Victorian standards of health, decency and order:

---

21   *DP* 24 Jan. 1862.

22   *Mortality Sub-Committee*, pp.9–46 and 95–117.

23   PP 1867–68 (4072) XXXVII, Report of the Cholera Epidemic of 1866 in England,
pp.229–32.

24   Gareth Stedman Jones, *Outcast London: A Study in the Relationship between Classes in
Victorian Society*, Harmondsworth, 1976, ch. 16.

It is inhabited by the very lowest and worst population in the whole city. Disorder is perpetual, and disease is never absent. Sometimes whole streets are blockaded against the police, and then a pandemonium of violence proceeds unchecked. Every Saturday and Sunday, throughout the whole district, the inhabitants give themselves up to a drunken orgie, and never a week passes but some shocking crime of violence is perpetrated.

The new environmentalism stretched back over the generations and across the Irish Sea to account for such unacceptable and 'uncivilised' behaviour:

These people are what the conditions of their environment have made them ... The wretches you see in Scotland-road inherit probably the proclivities of a dozen generations of degradation. Many of them come from Ireland, and bitterly has the sister country repaid us for centuries of wrong inflicted by our hands. Her poor, ground down from year to year to lower and lower depths of poverty, at length are driven by hunger from the sterile heaths and mountain sides, to find and to intensify in our great cities a squalor worse than they originally experienced. But the blame is not theirs. They have been born to ugliness and destitution, and with predispositions to vice transmitted from many a savage, ignorant ancestor.[25]

Infused with hostility and prejudice, the new environmentalism had important policy implications. In Ireland, the 'eternal Paddy' was best left to 'home-rule' himself, having failed to appreciate 'anglicised' solutions to grievances and problems;[26] in 'the lowest depth' of squalid Liverpool, however, there was to be active interventionism to demolish insanitary property colonised by the Irish, the breeding ground of disease, crime and disorder.

Liverpool, in fact, had pioneered compulsory purchase in legislation in 1864, but little had been achieved in the face of difficulties over compensation, betterment and development rights. Although welcome in itself, the new momentum from the 1880s made matters worse. In the absence of re-housing provision at a suitable location (close to casual labour markets) and at affordable rents (calculated by Forwood at no more than three shillings per week), the demolition ordered by the Insanitary Property Committee simply intensified

---

25 *Squalid Liverpool*, p.77.
26 Michael de Nie, *The Eternal Paddy: Irish Identity and the British Press, 1798–1882*, Madison, WI, and London, 2004, pp.267–77.

over-crowding in adjacent areas, creating new slums.[27] Such 'improvements' added to fears, already aroused by railway clearances and the northward expansion of the docks, of the spread of the 'low Irish'. At the Commission of inquiry into unemployment in 1894, H.E. Williams, an expert witness on rents, reported on the deterioration of housing between Great Homer Street and Scotland Road vacated by respectable inhabitants 'filtering-up' to be replaced by what he described as

> very bad indeed, bad class of tenants ... the low Irish from the bottom parts of the city, court houses and cellars, etc ... this particular place has become a city of chip merchants, donkey owners, pigeon breeders and all kinds of ruffians of all shades. In some streets, doors, stairs, and floors, become the spoil of the chip merchants, lead piping and iron removed to marine store dealers, and we all ask where are the police!![28]

The reports of the St Vincent de Paul Society at St Francis Xavier's, Everton, whose resources were to be stretched by new arrivals, present a more sympathetic picture of those displaced:

> A great number of poor families have migrated from the lower parts of the town to this end, in consequence of the extensive clearances made by the Corporation and the Railway Companies. They, for the most part, consist of unskilled labourers and widows, with, as a rule, a pretty large number of children each, to provide for, and any one who knows the present state of the labour market in Liverpool can form some idea of the destitution and want these unfortunate people very often suffer; our funds, therefore, are nearly all expended on provisions. Frequently, however, we assist persons to start a little business by granting them small sums of money.[29]

As Catholic charities struggled to cope with urban poverty, a new generation of INP activists, led by the Harford brothers, former pupils at St Francis Xavier's, stood forward to demand improved housing conditions. Beginning in 1898, the campaign for 'betterment of the district' started in seemingly negative and internecine manner, calling for an end to demolition and the replacement of INP councillors, venal politicians in league with 'the big bugs and moneyed

27   Waller, *Democracy and Sectarianism*, pp.87–88.
28   *Commission of Inquiry into the Subject of the Unemployed*, pp.101–102.
29   *Xaverian* May 1887.

snobs of the gilded chamber ... making a bit out of insanitary property, the tramways, or anything else that offered'. Viewed by the Harford brothers, the clearances undertaken by the Insanitary Property Committee constituted a co-ordinated attack on the economic, religious and political coherence of the Irish enclave (and hence of the future of the INP), 'beggaring our churches and schools and scattering the people to other districts, where the associations of an alien religion are bound to do incalculable harm'. Dwellings were replaced by 'warehouses, public-houses and mills for the capitalist, the brewer and the speculator', along with the re-location of mortuaries, refuse 'destructors', tanneries and stables, noxious health hazards unwelcome elsewhere in town: this 'unhousing of the labouring classes' was undermining the customer base of traders and shopkeepers (and Catholic churches). Demolition was driven by crude political advantage, 'confined almost entirely to those districts in which there is what some consider an inconvenient superfluity of a certain class of voters'. The Tories, it seemed, 'want to wring the Scotland Division from the Nationalist representation, and the most feasible means of achieving that end appears to be the eviction of the Irish voters through the destruction of "insanitary property"'. Having gained a seat on the council, Austin Harford had the temerity to challenge the great 'Tay Pay' himself at the general election of 1900 (until John Redmond, leader of the Irish Parliamentary Party, prevailed upon him to withdraw):

> Could anyone tell him what Mr O'Connor had done for the division? The demolition of insanitary property had gone on, but the people had not been re-housed. They were now in a position that unless they were careful in a short time their stronghold would be taken by the Tory party.[30]

Somewhat chastened, O'Connor hastily befriended Harford to adopt a 'Nat-Lab' position on housing and social reform. Looking back, he acknowledged the lesson he had leant in Liverpool-style gerrymandering: 'Their opponents had endeavoured to transform a Nationalist stronghold into a Tory stronghold by the demolition of property, and he was convinced that even the ablest leaders of Tammany in New York could learn something from the Tory wire-pullers of Liverpool.'[31]

---

[30] LCH 27 Jan. 1899 to 28 Sept. 1900. LCH 5 May 1899 dates the beginning of the campaign to October 1898. Unfortunately the holdings of LCH at Colindale do not start until 1899.

[31] LCH 1 July 1904.

Harford continued to oppose 'wholesale demolitions', encouraging the hapless tenants of Whitley Street in 1902 to take direct action to defend the roof over their heads: they were eventually evicted by being 'smoked out'.[32] Increasingly, however, he concentrated his efforts (with the support of other INP councillors such as Flynn and O'Shea) on making 'the Re-housing of the Labouring Classes a practical question', by insisting that each presentment to the Council should be accompanied by 'a scheme for the rehousing of the persons who will be dispossessed by the demolition of the insanitary houses'. Soon after his motion was accepted (after initial opposition and defeat), he was elected to the new Housing Committee which replaced the Insanitary Property Committee.[33] Its most energetic member, Harford quickly developed expertise in the provision of housing for the 'poorest poor', while safeguarding the political interests of the INP by opposing any attempt to 'utilise the Housing Committee as a political weapon for the destruction of the Catholic and Irish vote in the centre of the city'. He refused to endorse plans to re-house those dispossessed in the Scotland and Exchange Divisions 'not in the demolition areas and in the vicinity of their work, but four or five miles away on the extreme boundary of the city'.[34] Furthermore, he sought an alternative to 'workhouse-like' tenement blocks, previously advocated by Forwood in his pioneer (and short-lived) proposals in the 1880s for affordable municipal housing close to work. Speaking on return from a housing conference in Liège (one of several such European engagements), Harford noted that 'no city in Europe had gone so far as Liverpool in the practical direction of "housing the poorest poor"', but, he insisted, 'more comprehensive operations of housing the people generally must be taken up, with the block tenement system altogether discarded in favour of single houses'.[35] The much-praised 'self-contained' flats and cottages of the Bevington Street scheme apart, however, municipal provision remained predominantly tenement in form, but with design modifications to ensure single defensible space. Liverpool pioneered new-look blocks designed 'as far away from the tenement appearance as possible', with individual front doors opening onto a balcony.[36] While applauded at European congresses, as in Vienna in 1910, municipal housing in Liverpool still fell short of Harford's ideal:

---

[32]   *LCH* 8 and 15 Aug. 1902.

[33]   *LCH* 12 Oct. 1900 to 5 Apr. 1901.

[34]   *LCH* 5 Oct. 1907.

[35]   A.B. Forwood, *The Dwellings of the Industrious Classes in the Diocese of Liverpool and How to Improve Them*, Liverpool, 1883; *LCH* 8 Sept. 1905.

[36]   S.D. Adshead and P. Abercrombie, eds, *Liverpool Town Planning and Housing Exhibition and Conference, 1914*, Liverpool, 1914, pp.118–28.

We are convinced that all housing schemes ought to contain ordinary clothes-washing conveniences, such as boiler with hot and cold water supply, baths, in at least a proportionate number to the population of each area or block of dwellings, more playgrounds with gymnasia for children, the cultivation of plants and flowers among the people, the planting of trees wherever possible, the opening of reading rooms and libraries, and lectures and exhibitions from time to time in the reading rooms on hygiene and domestic economy (including cooking).[37]

Harford's commitment to wholesale housing reform – his determination to make 'slumdom' a word of the past in Liverpool [38] – gained much approval in the Catholic and nationalist community. His election as deputy chairman of the Housing Committee in 1907 was hailed in the local Catholic press as 'An Irish Victory', Harford being, as T.P. O'Connor observed, 'Liverpool by birth and training, but Irish by race'. At a special banquet in Harford's honour, John Redmond, the Irish leader, praised the work he had done already in connection with

the great question of the housing of the working classes ... probably the greatest of their social problems, the problem that lay at the root of the temperance question, and the question of public health, and at the root of almost all those questions which concerned the social well-being and the happiness of the people.[39]

By shifting the emphasis from slum-dwellers to the slums themselves, Harford and the INP provided a timely counterweight to the anti-Irish moralism which still prevailed in liberal and professional quarters. Although much reduced, the death rate continued to tell against Liverpool in league tables of civic health. Echoing his predecessors, Dr Hope, the Medical Officer of Health, persisted in blaming drink, dirty habits and incompetent domestic budgeting, failings which placed the Irish in Liverpool below the standards of Edwardian citizenship and civic responsibility.[40]

---

[37] *LCH* 22 Oct. 1910.

[38] *LCH* 1 Mar. 1913.

[39] *LCH* 30 Nov. to 7 Dec. 1907.

[40] Vickers, 'Civic image', ch. 6. Hope incurred the wrath of Sexton (and others) when he attributed a rise in infant mortality to the general transport strike of 1911, see 'How poor children died' and 'Truth about the strike', *Liverpool Weekly Mercury* 21 and 28 Oct. 1911.

'Bright homes and healthy people were the things they were striving after', Harford informed a keen-to-learn visiting delegation from Keighley in 1913: 'The cost of one Dreadnought would clear away all the slums of Liverpool and convert it almost into a garden city'.[41] On the eve of the First World War, Harford and the INP could take pride in their record on the Housing Committee: of the 22,000 insanitary court houses noted in the 1860s, only 2771 remained and these were scheduled to disappear along with 5646 others 'which though less objectionable, are of an antiquated, undesirable and unhealthy type'; having belatedly acknowledged the need to provide re-housing in the 1890s, the Corporation in 1914 was responsible for 2721 dwellings and 10,223 inhabitants. None but the dispossessed were allowed to become Council tenants. In areas where the Housing Committee had been active, there was a remarkable improvement in the death rate 'whilst those breaches of the law which may be traced to overcrowding and bad environment have considerably decreased'. All in all, the improvement in health, crime and rental receipts was 'a striking testimony to the moral character of the tenants'.[42]

Local socialists, however, were unimpressed. Unable to break the electoral hold of the INP in the north end, they criticised the nationalists for 'their one great scheme of "Re-housing the Poorest of the Poor"' conducted at the expense of a campaign against poverty itself.[43] Socialists were incredulous of the self-enclosed horizons, the 'mental and physical starvation', of 'Irish slummies' whose lives (even when re-housed) extended no further than 'the sad blot called Paddy's Market'. A correspondent to the *Liverpool Forward* described his impressions of 'A Day in the Slums':

> what appalled me most was not the open ashpits, not the endless gin shops, not the beautiful and costly Roman Catholic churches, not the stuffed and broken windows, not the stinking refuse in the gutters, but the grave content amongst a people who are living their lives without knowing what life is.[44]

The Catholic press, by contrast, applauded the faith and mutuality which held the community together: 'Next to the splendid faith of the Irish poor, which keeps them from falling into the terrible depths of degradation and despair

---

41   *LCH* 1 Mar. 1913.

42   *LCH* 1 Aug. 1914.

43   'Why Liverpool is unhealthy', *Liverpool Forward* 30 May 1913.

44   'A day in the slums', *Liverpool Forward* 1 June 1912.

attained by so many of their neighbours of other nationalities, it is grand to witness their sympathy and generosity to each other.'[45] With the establishment of the Catholic School for Mothers to lessen the infant mortality rate (one-third of the children born in Liverpool were Catholic but only one-quarter of the children reaching school age were Catholic), Archbishop Whiteside was confident 'the Church in Liverpool would go ahead fast'.[46] To the alarm of Protestants, Whiteside repeatedly praised his co-religionists for their fecundity when 'race suicide' was otherwise advancing rapidly in England, 'due, it is to be feared, in the main to the terrible sin of criminal sterility'.[47]

By the early twentieth century, the 'low Irish' had adjusted in various ways to urban living, although militant cultural nationalists, advocates of Sinn Fein, believed much remained to be done through 'a non-political and non-sectarian Irish society of social workers in Liverpool to improve the conditions of slum life'.[48] As conditions began to improve in the north end, the Catholic press sought to deflect attention away from the proverbial binge-drinking and violent disorder of Scotland Road, 'unrivalled in this town and surpassed in few, if any others, for poverty, vice and crime'.[49] In a series which brought new meaning to the sobriquet 'black spot on the Mersey', the Liverpool Catholic Herald drew attention to the 'no-go' cosmopolitan area around Mill Street and Beaufort Street in Toxteth, characterised by 'lodging-houses for negro, lascar and other foreign seamen, mulatto children, drunken men and women, and street fights. These streets are not considered desirable beats by the police, many of whom have come to grief in the perambulations therein.'[50] Studies of sectarian violence have highlighted disputed borders (particularly along and around Netherfield Road) between 'green' and 'orange', but the inviolable boundary which kept 'black' distant and apart awaits investigation. In 'cosmopolitan' Edwardian Liverpool, 'China town', 'dark town' and 'other alien quarters' were all located at some distance from the north end, the territory of the Irish.[51]

---

45   LCH 7 Feb. 1902.
46   LCH 23 May 1914.
47   LCH 22 Feb. 1913.
48   Anon., The Liverpool Irishman, or Annals of the Irish Colony in Liverpool, n.p., 1909, p.6.
49   Owles, Recollections, p.43.
50   'Black spot on the Mersey', LCH 10 Jan. to 14 Feb. 1902.
51   'Liverpool's coloured colonies', Liverpool Echo 6 June 1919.

3

The Holy Sanctity of Poverty: Welfare, Charity and the Sacred Irish Poor

MATTHEW GALLMAN's recent comparative study of Liverpool and Philadelphia highlighted a significant difference in the 'host' response to the Irish Famine influx. Where the city of brotherly love relied on voluntarism, the 'black spot on the Mersey' pioneered a number of public initiatives in poor relief, public health, policing and other areas of urban policy, some of which were already in place before the Famine crisis.[1] This public interventionism, however, added significantly to the weight of the local Protestant establishment, prompting fears that relief and assistance – even for such special cases as the blind – would be accompanied by attempts at proselytisation.[2] Hence Catholics in Liverpool campaigned persistently for pluralist religious provision at public expense within the workhouses, industrial schools and other 'pauper' institutions, increasingly inhabited by disproportionately large numbers of poor Irish Catholics. As the ruling Tory-Anglican-Orange formation strenuously opposed any such provision of 'Rome on the rates', Catholics duly pooled their limited resources to construct their own 'welfare' institutions. Although generally staffed by religious orders, this expanding institutional infrastructure was a substantial financial burden beyond the not inconsiderable sums necessarily expended on the foundational parochial structure of mission chapels. However, the competitive logic of sectarianism offered some compensation: it was a source of double pride, for instance, that housekeeping costs were lower but overall

---

1   Gallman, *Receiving Erin's Children*.

2   *Report of the Investigation of the Treatment of Roman Catholics in the Liverpool School for the Blind. Reprinted from the 'Liverpool Mail' of February 11, 1841*, Liverpool, 1841.

expenditure higher in Catholic female orphanages.[3] Proposing the toast 'Our Catholic Charities and Institutions' at the annual dinner of the Catholic Club in 1866, J. Neale-Lomax challenged the Protestants to match the 'array of institutions' upheld by the poor Catholics themselves:

> He felt it a glory to belong to a Church that would take care of the destitute ... Eleven out of every twenty who filled the workhouses and hospitals and other places were Catholics. Of the upper classes of Liverpool only one or two were Catholics, and of those who lived in £20 houses one in ten were Catholics; so that it rested upon those who were Catholics to do individually what they could to assist in maintaining the institutions.[4]

Similar competitiveness prevailed in charitable provision, where as Neale-Lomax noted with pride, the Catholics 'held, if not more, at least as many public charities as all the other denominations put together'. There were pronounced sectarian differences in the philosophy and operation of the voluntary sector. Excluded from municipal power, the wealthy Unitarian liberal elite stood forward to apply business acumen, scientific rationality and trained professionalism to Protestant philanthropic provision in Liverpool. 'There was an evil worse than suffering, worse even than death, and that was demoralisation', William Rathbone averred, adding that in a large town like Liverpool 'the danger was not in giving too little, but in giving too much, and thereby bringing about the very evil of mendicancy'.[5] Having curbed the growth of indiscriminate charitable provision, the 'deformation of the gift', the Central Relief Society pioneered the practice of 'scientific charity'.[6] While lacking an equivalent wealthy donor base, the Catholics continued with traditional 'alms-giving', convinced of its superior welfare and spiritual benefits. Protestant charity, the *Catholic Institute Magazine* critically observed, 'proceeds with a fixity of system, a calm calculation of practical results, a rigid economy of good works, which utterly destroy to Catholic eyes all that in Charity is most beautiful and most holy'.[7] Catholic charities relied on 'the magic of the poor man's penny', building up resources from below to help those at the very

---

3   'Catholic female orphanage', *DP* 12 Feb. 1862.
4   *LM* 23 Mar. 1866.
5   *DP* 5 Dec. 1866.
6   W. Grisewood, *The Poor of Liverpool and What is to be Done for Them*, Liverpool, 1899.
7   'Liverpool Catholic charities: No. 1', *Catholic Institute Magazine*, Jan. 1856.

bottom, 'the thousands of homeless, moneyless, raimentless, foodless creatures that call the Catholic Church their mother in Liverpool'.[8]

Construction of this institutional and charitable provision, a welfare state apart, was accompanied by a culture of poverty in which 'the ancient Catholic virtue of Holy Poverty' became the proud hallmark of being genuinely Irish. Just as some Irish-Australians chose to eschew the Australian narrative ethic of individual material advancement in favour of the communality, solidarity and charity benefits available only at the bottom of the social, but not the spiritual, scale,[9] so some Irish Liverpudlians exercised the same 'rational choice' (or what in today's management speak might be considered a perverse incentive), preferring to remain on charity as 'poor Irish'.

The Liverpool welfare burden, however, was a case apart, accentuated by its role as world seaport and human trans-shipment depot. A pioneer exercise in refuge for the 'houseless poor' (one of several Liverpool 'firsts' in social policy), night asylums were established on a temporary basis during the winters of 1816, 1820, 1821, 1822 and 1829, providing shelter for shipwrecked, stranded, castaway, robbed, sick or destitute sailors who lacked any claim on the parish or call upon local charities. They were soon adapted to cater for new arrivals, the 'low Irish' migrants, with permanent provision of nightly refuge for those on the streets, 'establishments which, by affording shelter to the most destitute and wretched of the human species, materially diminish the temptation to commit depredation'.[10] As trans-shipment port and central hub of the Irish diaspora, Liverpool had to cope disproportionately with its casualties, 'the residuum of the Irish – that is, those cases who had not "wing" enough, when they came from Ireland to carry them across the Atlantic'.[11] Friend and showman of the poor on the streets, Father Nugent was ready for the challenge: 'I want the poor people with me, I want the very poorest of the poor, in order that I may throw some ray of comfort and consolation across the path of their troubled lives.'[12]

[8]   'Church-going in Liverpool', *Catholic Institute Magazine*, Nov. 1855.

[9]   Patrick O'Farrell, *The Irish in Australia*, Kensington, NSW, 1986, p.299.

[10]   *Appeal to the Public. Description of the Liverpool Permanent Night Asylum for the Houseless Poor*, Liverpool, n.d. [1830?].

[11]   *LCH* 27 Jan. 1905.

[12]   *CT* 29 Oct. 1886.

The introduction of cheap steam navigation across the Irish Sea in the 1820s drew attention to Liverpool's pivotal position in relief provision, adding to the disproportionate burden of charities such as the Dispensaries offering 'extensive, immediate and efficacious relief ... to all classes of the poor, without regard to age, sex, country, religious denomination, or any distinction whatever'. The mathematics of the operation, the Committee noted in 1825, stretched resources to the limit: 'the supporters of the Charity only form 1–200th part of the population of Liverpool; whilst one-fifth of the whole town yearly receives its relief'.[13] 'It is impossible to behold such a mass of misery and wretchedness without feelings of compassion', the Select Vestry noted in its annual report of 1824 as the number of arrivals increased, 'yet to administer relief indiscrim-inately is only to hold out encouragement to others, and ultimately to increase the evil'.[14] In the first annual report of the Liverpool District Provident Society in 1830, the committee was taken to task 'for relieving so many of the Irish poor'.[15] They faced mounting criticism the following year, but insisted they were powerless to reverse 'the fearful discrepancy between the numbers of Irish applicants and those of other countries':

> Out of 11,303 relieved, 8069 have been from Ireland. Heavy as this burthen must be, it appears unavoidable. Many had by long residence gained a charitable settlement; many were women and children left by their husbands to casual charity; and so long as the Irish poor are situated as at present, this charge upon the funds of the Society cannot, it is feared, be much diminished.[16]

Where the mendicity department of the Provident Society sought to restrict 'the promiscuous and more particularly the *pecuniary* relief of street beggars'

---

13   Liverpool Dispensaries, *Report of the Committee of the Liverpool Dispensaries, for the Year 1825*, Liverpool, 1826, pp.4–5.

14   Quoted in PP 1834 (44) XXVIII Appendix A, p.914.

15   Liverpool District Provident Society, *The First Annual Report of the Liverpool District Provident Society, for the Year 1830, with the Rules of the Society and a List of Subscribers*, Liverpool, 1831.

16   Liverpool District Provident Society, *The Second Annual Report of the Liverpool District Provident Society, for the year 1831*, Liverpool, 1832.

through the issue of soup tickets, the Catholic Benevolent Society, the oldest Catholic charity in Liverpool, guarded against fraud and deception via the good offices of the local clergy: 'No imposition can be practised here, as, according to the fundamental rule of the Society, no relief can be granted but at the recommendation of the Clergymen, to whom the situation of the object is perfectly known.' Even so, its limited resources were soon spent. Moribund by the early 1840s, the Society was revived in 1850 to cope with the aftermath of the Famine influx, including those unable to progress beyond Liverpool, 'the arrival from Ireland of many persons who intended to emigrate, but who were stricken down by sickness and want, and were thus compelled to remain'.[17]

At the very beginning of 'Black '47' Alfred Austin, Assistant Poor Law Commissioner for the North West, went to Liverpool to investigate the exponential increase in claims for relief. While harshly critical of 'child borrowing' and other fraudulent practices by the applicants (including those waiting trans-shipment to America and Australia), Austin also drew attention to the extent of charitable provision:

> The extremely wretched appearance of most of the Irish immigrants strongly excites the compassionate feelings of the Inhabitants of Liverpool; and an indiscriminate almsgiving has been the consequence. Every street swarms with Irish beggars; and their gains is at once an inducement to them to continue the profitable pursuit of Mendicancy, and an invitation to fresh numbers to come over from Ireland to Liverpool to participate in the profit.[18]

Supported by the press, the authorities and charitable agencies applied 'crisis management', introducing strict new systems to curb undue relief and misplaced charity.[19] By contrast, the Catholic Church began a long-term process of adjustment, according priority to the needs of 'the poor of the sister country, who are living among us and under our own eyes'. 'These are a portion of that flock', Bishop Brown (1840–56) acknowledged to his clergy, 'for which I and you have to be answerable to the Divine Lord of the Vineyard.'[20]

Brown's successor, the Lancastrian recusant Bishop Goss (1856–72),

---

17   RCLv Box 56, Account book of the Liverpool Catholic Benevolent Society 1816–43; LVRO, 361 CAT, Liverpool Catholic Benefit Society Minute Book, 1850–58. See also, 'The Catholic Benevolent Society', *Porcupine* 2 Mar. 1867.

18   HO45/1080B, Ireland: Potato disease, distress, disturbances and relief, 1845–48.

19   Neal, 'Lancashire, the Famine Irish and the Poor Laws', pp.26–48.

20   RCLv Box 40, Brown 'To the clergy only', 23 May 1853.

described himself as 'a real John Bull', but there was a distinct 'hibernicisation' at parochial level.[21] The Church readily embraced Irish idioms and personnel in its philanthropic, associational and pastoral provision, markedly ahead of similar developments in Glasgow where the appointment of Irish priests, and other forms of 'Irishness', were at first strongly resisted.[22] Father Francis Murphy struck the appropriate chord at the opening of St Augustine's, Great Howard Street, in 1848, applauding the mission 'to erect a temple close to the spot where the heart-broken exile, flying from his own loved, but misgoverned land, just places his foot on a friendly shore'.[23] The cost of building (and maintaining) an adequate mission framework for the Irish influx – there were only four Catholic chapels in 1832 – was a constant drain on limited resources. 'In most of the other Diocesses [sic] of England', Bishop Brown noted with ill-concealed envy, 'there is a greater number of extensive landed proprietors <u>Catholics</u> than in this Diocess [sic].'[24] Church provision depended on the goodwill of Irish merchants, prepared to donate money, resources and time. Pending proper premises, warehouses were used (as in the 1840s and 1850s in the 'District of St Vincent of Paul' in the south end) as places of worship – this was a variant on earlier practice when the original Edmund Street chapel, destroyed by a Hanoverian mob in 1746, was rebuilt under the disguise of a warehouse by the Irish merchant Henry Pippard.[25] Commercial business skills were put to use in organising subscription schemes and weekly penny collections for church building, a method pioneered by a group of newly arrived Irish merchants in the south end where the first mission church, appropriately named St Patrick's, opened for worship in 1824. Thereafter the focus of attention switched to the north end, where most new (Catholic) Irish arrivals were to settle. St Anthony's, a small chapel built by French refugees, was rebuilt in the early 1830s through the efforts of a subscription committee assisted by local Hibernian Societies and by a Ladies' Society 'established for the purpose of providing whatever is requisite

---

21   P. Doyle, 'Bishop Goss of Liverpool (1856–1872) and the importance of being English', in S. Mews, ed., *Studies in Church History 18: Religion and National Identity*, Oxford, 1982, pp.433–47 (442).
22   M.J. Mitchell, *The Irish in the West of Scotland 1797–1848*, Edinburgh, 1998, pp.116–30 and 236–43.
23   Ryan Dye, 'The Irish flood: Famine, philanthropy and the emergence of duelling Catholic identities, 1845–1865', *THSLC*, 150, 2001, pp.97–120 (104).
24   RCLv Box 40, Brown 'To the clergy only', 23 May 1853.
25   J.A. Klapas, 'Geographical aspects of religious change in Victorian Liverpool, 1837–1901', unpublished MA thesis, University of Liverpool, 1977, p.24.

and becoming for the service of the altar, and the decoration of the chapel'.[26] By 1870, there were 18 Catholic parishes in Liverpool served by 64 priests; by 1900, according to the calculations in John Smyth's study of 'Catholicity in Liverpool' for the *Liverpool Catholic Herald*, there were 34 churches and chapels, a seminary, four religious orders of men, 19 convents and several refuges in the city, within which 130 priests ministered to 150,000 Catholics.[27] With 16 parishes clustered in the Scotland, Vauxhall and Everton areas by 1914,[28] the pattern of new church building, almost invariably serviced by Irish priests (All Hallowe's College, Dublin, was a main source of supply), encouraged further residential propinquity, giving spatial meaning and protection to the hyphenated identity of the Liverpool-Irish. Great Homer Street was the acknowledged boundary between Catholic and Protestant Liverpool with the most partisan Orange district running north of Netherfield Road. Other borders were less clearly defined: they were to witness considerable sectarian violence, a form of ritualised territorial skirmishing. The foolhardy Salvation Army apart, direct invasions into 'enemy' territory, well-defined enclaves, were comparatively rare and generally ill-advised.[29]

Prevention of 'leakage' from the faith was the over-riding consideration, the obligation to win back the negligent and lapsed to a proper observance of their religion. Having left Ireland before its 'devotional revolution', migrants (particularly those from the vast and under-resourced parishes of the 'wild west') were unacquainted with the discipline of Tridentine conformism, the high standard of practice among the small indigenous Catholic community.[30] Writing from Birkenhead in 1848, the Rev. Dr Miley lamented the spiritual deprivation of Famine migrants:

> From the clergy and the nuns one hears the most heart-rendering accounts, not so much of the physical privations and miseries of every sort which

---

[26]   RCLv Box 40, Relation Status Missiorum in Diocesi Liverpolitana, and Box 28 for more material on St Anthony's.

[27]   *LCH* 1 June 1900. The growth of the Catholic parochial and institutional network can be charted through the *Catholic Family Annual and Almanac for the Diocese of Liverpool*.

[28]   Frank Boyce, 'From Victorian "Little Ireland" to heritage trail: Catholicism, community and change in Liverpool's docklands', in R. Swift and S. Gilley, eds, *The Irish in Victorian Britain: The Local Dimension*, Dublin, 1999, pp.277–97, here pp.282–83.

[29]   Norman H. Murdoch, 'From militancy to social mission: The Salvation Army and street disturbances in Liverpool, 1879–1887', in John Belchem, ed., *Popular Politics, Riot and Labour: Essays in Liverpool History*, Liverpool, 1992, pp.160–72.

[30]   *LM* 25 Jan. 1866.

form the ordinary lot of these exiles, but of the deplorable effects which
the woes of the last seasons seem to have had in almost utterly destroying
the religious instincts of the Irish in England ... mass is neglected by
multitudes, all kinds of profligacy, cursing and blasphemy in particular have
fearfully increased within that period. There are in Liverpool alone a great
many thousands who are said to have abandoned every religious practice
with the exception of abstaining on Fridays.[31]

More alarming still, the parlous socio-economic plight of arrivals from Ireland
made them continually vulnerable to Protestant proselytisation through
dependence upon charitable and poor law agencies with their over-zealous
'scripture readers'.[32] For example, in the dire distress caused by the severe
winter weather (and unwonted easterly winds) of February 1855, Irish Catholics
took relief wherever they could get it: indeed, they constituted 78 per cent
of the cases relieved by the District Provident Society and 82 per cent of the
applicants for poor relief.[33] The figures for those arrested in the February bread
riots were no less instructive: 64 of the 84 men arrested were Irish-born, and
19 of the 22 women arrested.[34]

From the early 1850s, local Catholic merchants, led by the Co. Wexford-
born woollen draper James Whitty, mounted a sustained campaign in the Select
Vestry and on the Council for Catholic religious provision in the workhouse and
other public institutions. The *Lancashire Free Press*, the first local Catholic paper
published in the north, offered wholehearted support: 'Let Catholics have the
full and free benefit of the British Constitution, which had its origins in Catholic
times – let Catholic prisoners and paupers have free access to their priests – let
us have complete religious equality.' [35] A room was set aside for Catholic services
in the Brownlow Hill workhouse (where Wilkie, the governor, calculated the
number of Irish as one-half of the inmates), following concerns that those
allowed out to attend mass in the nearby chapel had been abusing their weekly
Sunday excursions with theft, drink and other rowdiness. It was not until the

---

[31]   Dublin Diocesan Archives, Archdeacon Hamilton Papers. Dr Miley, Birkenhead, to
Hamilton, 26 Oct. 1848.

[32]   *LFP* 3 Mar. 1860.

[33]   C.L. Scott, 'A comparative re-examination of Anglo-Irish relations in nineteenth-
century Manchester, Liverpool and Newcastle-upon-Tyne', unpublished PhD thesis,
University of Durham, 1998, p.36.

[34]   Kanya-Forstner, 'The politics of survival', p.28.

[35]   *LFP* 28 Jan. 1860.

end of 1880, however, after he had been ministering to inmates for 13 years, that Rev. O'Donnell was accorded payment by the Select Vestry.[36]

In the absence of any subvention from the rates, Richard Sheil underwrote the cost of providing a Catholic chaplain at the Kirkdale Industrial Schools, where from 1845 'at risk' pauper children were given instruction in the trades. A communicant at the 'fashionable' parish of St Oswald's, Sheil took delight in arranging elite charity functions within the social 'season', an opportunity to mix with the recusant gentry from in and around Liverpool, but he found other aspects of his considerable fund-raising and charitable work more tiresome:

> The entire task of collecting subscriptions for the maintenance of the Catholic Chaplain to the industrial schools has been allowed to fall upon me and as you will easily conceive this circumstance not only causes very serious inconvenience to me but is also attended with much danger to the charity, for nothing but the great stagnation of business could have enabled me to spare the amount of time which I have already devoted to going about in search of subscriptions.[37]

Despite the growing preponderance of Catholic pupils – there were 451 Catholic and 344 Protestant children in the schools in 1862 – the Select Vestry repeatedly rejected proposals for the appointment of at least one Catholic teacher. In the absence of adequate religious instruction within the schools, Catholic merchants and professionals, including James Whitty, Sheil's associate C.J. Corbally, the solicitor John Yates (a Lancastrian convert), and the corn merchant and commanding officer of the 64th (Liverpool Irish) Lancashire Rifle Volunteers, Colonel Bidwill, joined forces in the Workhouse Catholic Children's Fund to find suitable placements for Catholic children on completion of their training at Kirkdale. Unless places were found, 'certain perversion awaits them', the committee rued as it condemned 'the alarming amount of proselytism that had been going on for years, by placing the poor Catholic children in the hands of Protestants'. Taking advantage of the 1866 Industrial Schools Act, the Catholics purchased a former hospital from the West Derby Union to establish their own

---

36 'The Select Vestry and the Catholic difficulty', *DP* 1 Dec. 1880.
37 NLI, MS 32,483 Sheil Letter-book, f.392 to President of the Irish Catholic Club, 19 Dec. 1854. For the 'elite' at St Oswald's, see Dublin Diocesan Archives: Cullen Papers, 353/2/101, Fr McGinity to Dr Cullen, 3 Dec. 1852.

facility, St George's Industrial School at 29 Everton Crescent, initially under the control of the Irish Christian Brothers.[38]

Industrial Schools were part of an ever-expanding network of provision to deal with a pronounced Liverpool problem, the 'army of "street arabs" who infest our thoroughfares, fill our gaols, increase our taxes, spread disease, and drive policemen and philanthropists to despair'.[39] According to police figures in the 1860s, of the 48,782 children aged between five and 14 not attending school, some 25,000 roamed the streets, the 'school' of crime and vice, 'where the girl scarce in her teens is degraded into a fallen outcast, the youth to a felon, to gaol, and finally to penal servitude'.[40] 'No other town in the Kingdom tolerates upon its streets such masses of uncovered, ignorant and destitute children', Father Nugent protested: 'Need we be surprised at the recent increase of juvenile crime in Liverpool?'[41] 'We were not prepared for the exodus which came from Ireland', Nugent conceded, 'and now we are punished by the children of those parents who came from Ireland, and who have grown up in ignorance and neglect'.[42] Members of the St Vincent de Paul Society (SVP) probed more deeply, assessing parental neglect against the inadequate casual earnings and high mortality rate among adult dock labourers, and the irregular budgetary conduct of seafaring fathers who

> go away for a long time and leave little or no provision for their families in their absence, and when they come back many of them get paid large sums which they spend in riotous living, not remembering the weary months during which their families will have to eke out their existence during the next voyage.[43]

As the first president of the Liverpool Catholic Reformatory Association, Nugent was convinced that he could reform and redeem Irish youths 'flung into the vortex of Liverpool low-life'.[44] Other leading Catholics, however, wished to dispose altogether of the troublesome youths: Bishop Goss favoured

---

[38]   *NP* 14 June 1862; *Porcupine* 12 July 1862; *DP* 3 July 1861, 6 July 1864, 23 Oct. and 14 Nov. 1866; and *LM* 20 Feb. 1866.

[39]   *Porcupine* 13 Apr. 1867.

[40]   The police reports for 1867–68 were highlighted in Liverpool Society for the Prevention of Cruelty to Children, *First Annual Report, 1884*, Liverpool, 1884.

[41]   Letter from Father Nugent. *DP* 10 Nov. 1865.

[42]   PP 1877 (418) XI, q.8314.

[43]   'Our boys', *Xaverian* Sept. 1892.

[44]   'Reformatories', *Catholic Institute Magazine*, Sept. 1856.

their emigration, while M.J. Whitty, editor of the *Daily Post*, advocated their transportation to India to serve in the harsh discipline of the forces.[45] At first, Nugent sent the young offenders out of the depraved city for reformation in a distant Cistercian facility, but soon abandoned the experiment:

> Hitherto a fatal mistake has been made by sending so large a number of boys to Agricultural Reformatories. How few townsmen ever, either through choice or necessity, betake themselves to agricultural labour. The class of boys committed to reformatories have been accustomed to the streets of Liverpool from their childhood; they have their respective avocations, either begging, stealing or trading, and though young, theirs has been a life of continuous excitement, and Liverpool's busy streets, quays, docks, ships and river are indelibly stamped upon their minds ... In land reformatories the boys were always thinking of the sights of Liverpool, but on board ship they saw the Cunard and other vessels coming up or going down the river, and there was something constantly to excite their interest.[46]

Moored in the Mersey alongside the 'Akbar', already requisitioned through the largesse of Liverpool shipowners and merchants to provide a rigorous (and Protestant) regime of appropriate nautical discipline and training, the 'Clarence' was brought into service in 1864, providing instruction in seamanship, carpentering, shoemaking, tailoring and other trades while religious instruction and practice was in the hands of a chaplain appointed by the Bishop of Shrewsbury. Under pressure from Protestant militants, the Council suddenly withheld the set-up grant, previously agreed on the same terms as for the 'Akbar'. In the midst of the ensuing and unseemly financial dispute (in which Catholics itemised their extra burdens as they were compelled both to subsidise Anglican establishments and to finance their own facilities), Nugent was censured for favouring the criminal above the destitute. A serial controversialist, he responded by exposing the lack of any provision for Catholic instruction on board the 'Indefatigable', a training ship for 'poor and destitute, but honest boys'. Under pressure, the committee of Protestant philanthropists reluctantly agreed to amend the policy, having been informed by Raffles, the stipendiary magistrate, that 'his opinion was that three-fourths of the boys wandering about Liverpool belonged to the

---

45   *DP* 16 July and 4 Dec. 1866; *LM* 4 Mar. 1867.
46   Quoted in Bennett, *Father Nugent*, p.53.

Roman Catholic faith, and he thought that provision should be made for them in an institution which professed to be for the good of the town'.[47]

Nugent's mission to 'Save the Boy' was comprehensive in scope, extending beyond institutional care to sheltered accommodation available on leaving Industrial School or reformatory. His Association of Providence for the Protection of Orphan and Destitute Boys came into being in Dan Lowery's old theatre in Bevington Bush in 1864, promoted in what was to become signature style with popular entertainment and showmanship. A year later, multi-purpose premises were opened in Soho Street (subsequently relocated to more spacious accommodation in St Anne Street), combining a night shelter and refuge for homeless boys ('Nobody's Children'), together with facilities for workplace training: a printing office, paper-bag factory, and shop for tailoring and shoe-making. Funded by concerts, entertainments and popular penny-a-week collection schemes (the target being a million pennies), the Association of Providence provided 97,881 suppers and 7743 nights' lodging in its first five years.[48] While keeping boys off the streets at night, the aim was to rescue and reform, to give a new image and pride to the 'low Irish':

> I want to make honest, upright men of these lads, to give them self-respect
> and independence, instead of leaving them to ask people to 'buy a box of
> fusees', degrading themselves, and making the Irish people spurned and
> despised by their fellow townsmen. Irishmen should educate their children
> and then instead of being behind they will be abreast of society, and by
> gaining self-respect they will hold that position to which by education, good
> habits and good manners, they will be entitled.[49]

Nugent's penchant for publicity was regarded in some Catholic quarters as counter-productive, keeping the 'problem' Irish too much in the forefront of the public eye.[50] By the mid-1860s, amid growing discussion of parliamentary reform, franchise extension and the redistribution of seats, members of the Catholic middle class, proud of their advance since the Famine years, were looking for political recognition. Their aspiration to secure the proposed third seat for Liverpool for one of their own kind exemplified the equitable citizenship to which Catholics, one-third of the population, felt they were

---

[47]   *DP* 14 Nov. and 7 Dec. 1865; *LM* 10 Feb. 1865 and 8 Mar. and 7 June 1866; *Porcupine* 31 Mar. 1866.

[48]   For recollections of the early history of the Association, see *CT* 25 Feb. 1887.

[49]   *DP* 10 Oct. 1865.

[50]   See, for example, *DP* 4 Dec. 1866.

entitled by virtue of their contribution to Liverpool's progress and prosperity. Much to the detriment of the case, however, the Irish presence in workhouses, industrial schools, prisons and other such institutions was disproportionately much higher. 'Over and over again it has been incontestably shown', *Porcupine* reported, 'that the Irish people form the predominating element in our prisons and our poorhouses. Over and over again it has been proved beyond the shadow of doubt that the irreconcilable, untameable "rough" element in our midst is almost exclusively Irish.'[51] It was these 'casualty statistics' which Nugent chose to broadcast when appointed in 1863 as Catholic chaplain to Walton Gaol.

Among the first under the Prison Ministers Act of 1863, Nugent's appointment by the magistrates at an annual salary of £300 was not without controversy: indeed, the Council tried to persuade the Home Office to rescind the arrangement. Between 1864 and 1879 no fewer than 65 per cent of all those committed to the gaol were Roman Catholic, 8 out of 10 of whom were Irish-born or the children of Irish-born parents.[52] When 'first appointed', Nugent reported in 1877, 'the Irish-born prisoners exceeded the number of Liverpool-born prisoners, but now the Liverpool-born prisoners exceeds the number of those born in Ireland'.[53] The disproportionate Catholic preponderance was accentuated among women, no strangers to pubs, 'houses of bad character' (of which there were 1313 in 1866) or prison: it was a matter of shame, Nugent remonstrated, that Liverpool was 'the only prison in the world where the females exceed the males'. Between 1864 and 1876, the number of female Catholic committals (50,389) averaged 54.1 per cent of the total Catholic committals (93,139). Of the 8543 Catholics under Nugent's charge in 1877, 3882 were male and 4571 female of whom only 648 were first-time offenders.[54] Here was the legacy, Nugent rued, of the Famine influx:

> As a reason for the large proportion of Catholic prisoners, he said that from
> '46 to '50 a very large Irish population was poured into Liverpool; that

51   *Porcupine* 18 Aug. 1877.

52   HO45/9572/78351C, Catholic Chaplaincy at Liverpool Prison, 1878–89. Significantly, green labels were placed over the cells occupied by Catholics, see *CT* 14 May 1870.

53   PP 1877(418)XI, q.8198.

54   'Major Greig's story of crime in Liverpool', *DP* 20 Nov. 1866; 'Catholic female criminals', *CT* 29 Jan. 1870. Commenting on Nugent's annual report for 1876–77, the *Times* was appalled by the 'absolute preponderance of females – a state of things which is altogether without parallel in the rest of the world, though, unhappily, it is chronic in Liverpool', see 'Liverpool's Black-Book', *Times* 26 Nov. 1877. See also Neal, 'Criminal profile'.

Table 3.1 *Committals to Liverpool Borough Gaol, 1864–78*

Year	Total commitments	No. of Roman Catholic commitments	Roman Catholic commitments as %
1864	9913	5786	58
1865	7477	4243	57
1866	7746	4375	56
1867	8876	5419	61
1868	8909	5531	62
1869	10,530	6707	64
1870	12,719	8391	66
1871	11,724	7713	66
1872	13,723	9023	66
1873	12,420	8322	67
1874	13,239	9022	68
1875	13,683	9397	69
1876	13,313	9310	70
1877	12,285	8453	69
1878	15,420	10,596	69
Total	**171,977**	**112,288**	**65**

Source: National Archives: HO45/9572/78351C Catholic Chaplaincy at Liverpool Prison, 1878–89.

this was not the well-to-do class, or even skilled labourers or mechanics, but the poorest and the most ignorant and destitute class. Again, as Liverpool increased in its docks and commerce the criminal class found it better ground to work upon than at home. The poverty of Ireland did not afford the same market and the same facilities for crime; and as regards prostitution, there was in Ireland, a much stronger public opinion against it than in England.[55]

Most prisoners were convicted for drunken, disorderly and dissolute behaviour (the infamous Irish 'rows') or for the petty crime which flourished on the waterfront ('thieving along the line of the docks') and in the secondary economy of the streets. Nugent calculated that 9 out of 10 prisoners under his

[55] Nugent's evidence to the Prison Ministers' Committee reported in *CT* 14 May 1870.

care owed their imprisonment directly or indirectly to drink; and that '75 per cent of all the money that comes dishonestly is spent in drink', with barmen acting as the 'bankers of thieves'.[56] As police court reports attest, some were Liverpool 'characters', as, for example, John Sheridan who 'was in the habit of soliciting charity at the doors of different Catholic chapels in the town with the proceeds from which he got drunk'. When brought before the court (for the umpteenth time) for being drunk and disorderly in Marybone between 9 and 10 in the morning, Sheridan insisted with characteristic grandiloquence that the arresting officer was 'a gigantic uncultivated barbarian, an unscrupulous falsifier of fact, and had assaulted him in the most unconstitutional way, as he was proceeding along the street, in a decent, orderly manner as a well-conducted citizen should do'.[57] There were a few 'professional' criminals, but no major network of Irish-controlled 'organised' crime. Known as 'Brockle Jack', John McNulty of Sawney Pope Street was the most notorious fence in the 1860s, by which time nearby Ben Jonson Street, previously the market for poachers selling game, had become the regional fencing nexus for 'watches, jewellery and articles of that kind' acquired by criminals who 'worked' Chester and North Wales.[58] Nothing was sacrosanct, however: having arrived in Liverpool, John Donolly, a 'man on the road', took to stealing cushions from St Nicholas's, Copperas Hill, and other Catholic chapels and selling them to a saddler at Prescot.[59]

The Irish nationalist press was scandalised by the publicity surrounding Nugent's first annual report which revealed that 'more than 60 percent of the law-breaking prostitutes of Protestant Liverpool are our own countrywomen'.[60] Subsequent investigation underlined the transmogrification from unquestioned virtue in Catholic Ireland to moral degradation on the streets of Liverpool

---

[56]   See Nugent's evidence to *Mortality Sub-Committee* and to PP 1877(418)XI. The Liverpool-Irish were 'never targeted overtly as a "crimogenic" group for reasons of racial or ethnic identity, despite their impressive showing in mid-Victorian statistics', J.K. Walton, M Blinkhorn, C. Pooley, D. Tidswell and M.J. Winstanley, 'Crime, migration and social change in north-west England and the Basque country, c. 1870–1930', *British Journal of Criminology*, 39, 1999, pp.108–109.

[57]   'Police intelligence', *DP* 28 Mar. 1862.

[58]   *DP* 12 May 1862; *Mortality Sub-Committee*, p.197.

[59]   'Police intelligence', *DP* 4 Mar. 1862.

[60]   'The special dispensation', *Irish People* 12 Nov. 1864. For an interesting discussion of ethnic, gender and class factors, see Martha Kanya-Forstner, 'Defining womanhood: Irish women and the Catholic Church in Victorian Liverpool', in Donald M. MacRaild, ed., *Great Famine and Beyond*, pp.168–88.

– 'from a state little lower than the angels they had descended to a condition below that of the brute'.[61] In the absence of factory or other regular employment, drink and low entertainment hastened the fall, after which Irish women had recourse to their niche labour market, servicing 'black' sailors in a network of streets in the north end 'known by various names, the least objectionable, perhaps, of which, is "Blackman's Alley"':

> It is well known that Irish women in their own country are, even amidst very unfavourable surroundings, a most virtuous class, and yet they furnished the largest proportion of prostitutes in this city … they have generally belonged to the lowest and most degraded class of prostitutes, living in brothels situated in the very worst streets of the borough, and resorted to by the numerous negroes always present in Liverpool as ships' cooks, stewards, seamen and labourers. The condition of these women, both physical and moral, is deplorable, and their reclamation is a prospect of which the most hopeful might despair.[62]

Removal from Liverpool was the only solution. Following quickly in the pioneer footsteps of the Protestant scheme of Miss Rye, Nugent arranged for 'at risk' Irish girls and young women to be shipped to Canada, virgin territory where they could reclaim their native virtue and faith.[63]

By the late nineteenth century, broader schemes of infant and juvenile emigration were promoted by leading philanthropists across the sectarian divide. Louisa Birt's Liverpool Sheltering Home was the fashionable leading agency in the field, strongly supported by the evangelical Ryle, Liverpool's first Anglican bishop.[64] Not to be outpaced, the Catholic Children's Protection Society (patronised by Catholic aristocratic and gentry families throughout the land) opened rival premises at 99 Shaw Street, where 'rescued' children were similarly prepared for emigration: by June 1886 some 605 children had been sent to Canada to be acculturated and placed through the offices of the

---

61   *CT* 11 Feb. 1881.

62   F.W. Lowndes, *The Extension of the Contagious Diseases Acts to Liverpool and Other Seaports Practically Considered*, Liverpool, 1876, p.31, and *Prostitution and Venereal Diseases in Liverpool*, London, 1886, pp.3–4.

63   See Nugent's evidence in Report from the Select Committee of the House of Lords on the law relating to the protection of young girls, PP 1882 (344) XIII, qq.90–178.

64   I.D. Farley, 'J.C. Ryle – Episcopal evangelist. A study in late-Victorian evangelicalism', unpublished PhD thesis, University of Durham, 1988, pp.152–53.

Hotel Dieu in Kingston, Ontario.[65] Underlying the competitive rivalry were fears of proselytisation, exaggerated by rumours of kidnapping and capture. As allegations intensified, a hapless Catholic named Malony, a single father with three children in the Liverpool Sheltering Home, endeavoured to secure their release:

> Two strong ill looking Irishmen came with him evidently prepared to use force in taking them out. Of course these two men were not allowed to come inside the Home. Malony was called in; he said he did not want to take the Children out, but that the Priests & Roman Catholics amongst whom he dwelt cursed him & consigned him to Purgatory & Hell forever, if he did not take them out of this Protestant Institution.[66]

During the 1890s, when the Liberals briefly came to power through a campaign for 'social purity', there was a renewed emphasis on the provision of night shelters and refuges to curb prostitution and intemperance. Not to be outpaced by Protestant initiatives, Nugent came out of semi-retirement with a new slogan: 'Rescue the Fallen'.[67] He took a model lodging-house in Limekiln Lane and transformed it into St Saviour's Refuge 'to meet the urgent want then occasioned by the local police crusade against immoral houses, whereby large numbers of unfortunate women of this class were thrown destitute and houseless on the streets'. Tended by nuns, the inmates were given immediate shelter prior to being transferred for long-term penitent work in the laundries of one of the local Homes of the Good Shepherd.[68] Soon afterwards, Nugent launched a new fund-raising project to build a 'House of Providence' to 'lessen the crime of child murder, by providing an asylum of unmarried mothers and their infants'.[69] The opening of the House of Good Counsel, Dingle, in 1904 symbolised, the *Liverpool Catholic Herald* observed, the 'marked success' of Nugent's 'rescue work resulting from his intimate experience of the undercurrents of life'.[70]

The 'social purity' campaign was a passing fad. Juvenile street-trading, however, the issue which prompted the formation of the Society for the

---

[65] *CT* 10 June and 23 Sept. 1881, 3 Feb. 1882, 4 June 1886 and 2 Sept. 1887. See also *Xaverian* Aug. 1887.

[66] UL: D715 Records of the Liverpool Sheltering Home, Mar. 1876.

[67] *CT* 12 Feb. and 4 Nov. 1892.

[68] *LCH* 17 June 1904.

[69] *LCH* 21 June 1901.

[70] *LCH* 29 July 1904.

Prevention of Cruelty to Children in 1883, remained a constant concern.[71] Immured in a culture of selling, begging and thieving, youths on the streets were condemned by the Commission of Inquiry into the Unemployed in Liverpool in the 1890s as apprentice members of 'Class B', predisposed against the morality and discipline of steady work.[72] Stirred by such criticism, Father Berry launched a major Nugent-style initiative to rescue and reform 'Our Boys', ranging from night shelters and boys' homes across the city offering street-trading lads supper, bed and breakfast at one penny each, to training homes for cases referred from the Police Courts which would 'civilize and tame street arabs and turn them into industrious citizens'. Despite lobbying by Bishop Whiteside and INP councillors such as Austin Harford, no public funding was forthcoming. Father Berry's Homes were soon forced to cut back, concentrating resources on the SVP Home for Working Boys in Shaw Street where street-trading boys unable to support themselves from their earnings could 'sleep in comfort and be taught to say their morning and night prayers'.[73] By this time, the Corporation had been granted 'exceptional' powers to introduce a licence or 'badge' scheme to regulate street trading by children, following the acknowledgement by the Chief Inspector of Reformatories in his 1896 report that 'there is no town which contains so difficult a population as that of Liverpool'. The original proposal included the provision of accommodation in Corporation-approved lodgings 'in the case of children having reckless, drunken parents or guardians, or living in bad conditions'. As this raised fears of proselytisation, Lynskey, Harford, Taggart and other INP councillors moved an amendment 'That the child reside in lodgings under the control of a person of the same religious belief as the child approved by the Corporation'. In a characteristic display of sectarian feeling, the amendment was defeated by a large majority. Dismayed by the bickering, the Home Office refused to sanction any provision for accommodation. The result of Tory partisanship on the Council, Thomas Burke rued, had been 'to nullify to a great extent the hopes of the promoters of those novel regulations'. Some 64 per cent of the first applications for licences, 550 out of 860, came from Catholic children.[74]

Under Bishop Whiteside (1894–1921), the 'Bishop with a trowel in his

---

[71]   Liverpool Society for the Prevention of Cruelty to Children, *First Annual Report*.

[72]   *Full Report of the Commission of Inquiry into the Subject of the Unemployed*.

[73]   Canon Bennett, 'The story of Father Berry's homes', *Cathedral Record*, 19, 1949, pp.149–52; *Xaverian* July 1892; *LCH* 18 July 1904 and 4 June 1910.

[74]   HO45/10172/B27657, Children: Liverpool City: Street Trading by Children; Byelaws 1899–1905; Thomas Burke, 'The street-trading children of Liverpool', *Contemporary Review*, 78, 1900, pp.720–26.

hand',[75] the Catholics sought to complete their infrastructure of parochial provision and institutional care. 'No Irish land-grabber could stand comparison with Archbishop Whiteside', Cardinal Logue quipped when attending the opening of another new church, St Sebastian at Fairfield.[76] Looking beyond the criminal (tended by the recently formed Liverpool and County Police Courts Catholic Aid Society) to the welfare of the destitute, Whiteside sought to remove every Catholic child from the workhouses though the provision of poor law schools.[77] At speeches to inaugurate new facilities, Whiteside proudly charted the growth of 'Catholic Liverpool', beginning with the construction of mission churches and schools, 'but in recent times another work had been undertaken – that of the rescue of the fallen, and of those in danger'.[78] Opening a new chapel in 1908 at the Homes at Everton Crescent run by the Sisters of Charity (which ranged from accommodation for 'respectable servants out of place' to a night refuge for vulnerable girls), the Bishop noted that there were

> over thirty institutions founded for the work of alleviating all manner of human misery and poverty, comprising seven industrial schools, three reformatories, four poor-law schools, one blind asylum, three refuges for the aged poor, seven institutions for looking after waifs and strays, and other places, including the group of Homes at Everton Crescent.[79]

When he returned to open a new extension at Everton Crescent in 1912 as the newly elevated Archbishop, he highlighted the work of the 37 institutions keeping about 4000 children and young persons out of danger, of which 17 institutions (responsible for 2500) received some government funding, the remaining 20 being entirely voluntary.[80]

The extent of Catholic rescue and welfare provision for the Liverpool-Irish was remarkable, all the more so in the absence of a wealthy resource base. Within the institutions themselves, the Little Sisters of the Poor, recent arrivals from a French order, were perhaps the most saintly and street-wise in balancing the books. Preferring rather 'the regular weekly pennies of the people, to the occasional pounds of the well-to-do', the Sisters covered the building costs and capital expenditure for their home for the infirm elderly in Belmont Grove.

---

75   *LCH* 24 Feb. 1912.
76   *LCH* 24 Jan. 1914.
77   *LCH* 25 June 1910.
78   *LCH* 23 Nov. 1912.
79   *LCH* 8 Aug. 1908.
80   *LCH* 23 Nov. 1912.

Food was obtained by systematic daily begging trips in a sombre black van to city centre hotels, restaurants and refreshment rooms as well as collecting scraps from St John's Market, the best pickings being given to the inmates (some 138 in 1887) before the 15 Sisters allowed themselves anything to eat.[81]

The impressive expansion notwithstanding, there were already indications before the First World War of difficulties ahead. Sectarian animosities aside, continued public funding for Catholic institutions could not be assured given new approaches to social policy (these were the years of 'Liberal Welfare' reforms) and heightened 'national minimum' standards of inspection. The findings of the Royal Commission on the Care and Control of the Feeble-Minded in 1905 made disturbing reading: the numbers of the 'feeble-minded', the level of the death-rate and the incidence of recidivism were all considerably higher in Catholic industrial schools and reformatories than in Protestant institutions.[82] Within a few years of the Children Act of 1908 Whiteside was expressing concern at 'uneconomic' occupancy rates in some Catholic institutions:

> There had been a sort of honourable understanding between the Catholic body in Liverpool and the city authorities that while the former had gone to the expense of providing money for building various institutions for boys and girls, it was understood the authorities would keep them well supplied with children ... For the past five or six years Catholic institutions had to complain of this shortage that was going on. It looked as though a policy was being followed to, if possible, deplete the industrial schools.[83]

With some foreboding, Whiteside was concerned that responsibility for such institutions would pass from the Home Office to the Department of Education with its 'faddist' inspectors (on a matter of principle, the Irish Christian Brothers had earlier withdrawn from Liverpool, refusing to submit to such external inspection).[84] At local authority level, the Education Committee was thrown into sectarian turmoil when INP councillors protested at the excessive cost of improvements following remarks by the Medical Officer of Health about the 'filthy' state of Catholic schools. Lengthy legal disputes followed as to whether the local authority should contribute to the cost of furnishing schools built with Catholic funds.[85] While praising what had been achieved by 'the

---

[81] 'Little sisters of the poor', *Liverpool Review*, 15 Oct. 1887, p.11.

[82] *LCH* 27 Jan. 1905.

[83] *LCH* 20 July 1912.

[84] Thomas Burke, *Catholic History of Liverpool*, Liverpool, 1910, p.196.

[85] *LCH* 17 Feb. 1905 and 18 Jan. 1913.

pence of the poor' in establishing a network of elementary schools – since the 1860s it had been a proud boast that 'there was not a part of the town which was distant more than a quarter of a mile from a Catholic school'[86] – T.P. O'Connor acknowledged the 'quality deficit' of denominational Catholic education:

> Honest religious conviction was the very salt of the life of any nation, and it was through such conviction that Catholics preferred their own, poor, and often squalid schools wherein they were taught their own faith, to the well-endowed, well-equipped schools they might have used during the past thirty-five years.[87]

As well as ongoing political battles to defend denominational education (which on occasion led to alliance with Tory Anglicans to the despair of the INP), Catholics would have to raise standards in the post-war years to qualify for public assistance or risk their schools being listed as 'condemned'.

Underpinning the institutions was a comprehensive network of parish-based provision, a flourishing local *Vereinskatholizismus*, to use the German term for the multiplication of organisations designed to meet the special needs – spiritual, economic and recreational – of every identifiable group within the Catholic population.[88] Established in Liverpool in 1845, the SVP served as a 'General Purposes Society' (in Catholic Glaswegian fashion), granting generous relief in case of need and where there was proof of minimal religious observance.[89] The best-documented study of the Society relates to St Mary's, Highfield Street, a parish established in the eighteenth century close to the business quarter to serve the small Catholic population, but then overwhelmed by the Famine influx of poor Irish immigrants into what became the 'most squalid part' of town.[90] In 'succouring the really deserving poor', the SVP gave immediate relief on the

---

[86]   Canon Walmsley's speech at Liverpool Catholic Club, *LM* 17 Mar. 1865.

[87]   *LCH* 6 Oct. 1905.

[88]   H. McLeod, 'Building the "Catholic ghetto": Catholic organizations 1870–1914', in W.J. Sheils and D. Wood, *Studies in Church History: Voluntary Religion*, Oxford, 1986, pp.411–44.

[89]   Bernard Aspinwall, 'The welfare state within the state: the Saint Vincent de Paul Society in Glasgow, 1848–1920', in Sheils and Wood, *Voluntary Religion*, pp.445–59.

[90]   John Davies, 'Parish charity: The work of the Society of St Vincent de Paul, St Mary's,

understanding, later articulated by Whiteside, that it was better to relieve a few 'imposters' than to reject a genuine case through zealous scrutiny.[91] There was little resentment when investigation was undertaken by one's own kind, such as the humble 'plain clothes' home visitors from the SVP, or by the likes of burly Barney, a proud member of Father Nugent's teetotal League of the Holy Cross, in charge of the funds of the Dock Labourers Committee:

> If he does not know his man, he probes and tests him with an ingenuity worthy of an Old Bailey lawyer. These men, who work the charity themselves, for their fellows, we may even say for their fellow-sufferers, for they are poor enough themselves, have no intention of being imposed upon, and their work is done with a business-like order and unfailing intelligence which many a more ambitious charity might with advantage imitate.[92]

Here there were major differences from Protestant 'scientific charity' with its rigid division between fund management and direct contact with the poor. Lowly individuals themselves, members of the SVP continued to raise funds, make policy decisions and distribute relief in person.

'Nominal' Catholics as most of them were (only 43 per cent attended Mass regularly in 1865),[93] the Liverpool-Irish maintained an exalted notion of their own religion and a sovereign contempt for the 'haythen' by whom they were surrounded. This loyalty owed much to the resident priest, a respected and revered figure based in an adjacent humble abode, who displayed none of the condescending censoriousness of the Protestant clergy and other 'visitors to the poor'.[94] Denuded of 'wealth and worldly position', the Catholic clergy 'belonged to what was really and truly the church of the poor'.[95] In a manner Protestants

---

Highfield Street, Liverpool, 1867–68', *North West Catholic History*, 17, 1990, pp.37–46 (37).

[91]   L. Feehan, 'Charitable effort, statutory authorities and the poor in Liverpool c. 1850–1914', unpublished PhD thesis, University of Liverpool, 1987, p.57.

[92]   Hugh Farrie, *Toiling Liverpool*, Liverpool, 1886, ch. 5.

[93]   Dye, 'The Irish flood', p.106.

[94]   R. Samuel, 'The Roman Catholic Church and the Irish poor', in R. Swift and S. Gilley, *Irish in Victorian City*, London, 1985, pp.267–300 (277). For an interesting comparison, stressing the key role of 'nominal' Catholics, see W. Sloan, 'Religious affiliation and the immigrant experience: Catholic Irish and Protestant Highlanders in Glasgow, 1830–50', in T.M. Devine, ed., *Irish Immigrants and Scottish Society in the Nineteenth and Twentieth Centuries*, Edinburgh, 1991, pp.67–90.

[95]   Speech by John Yates at St Mary's Catholic Young Men's Society, *DP* 20 Nov. 1861.

admired but could not emulate, the Catholic priest served as 'the parson, the policeman, the doctor, the nurse, the relieving officer, the nuisance inspector, and the school board inspector all in one'.[96] The Catholic parish operated as spiritual and welfare centre. Penny banks (another of Nugent's enthusiasms) and special 'clubs' for the poor aided those who could not afford weekly subscriptions (and insignia) to the various confraternities, sodalities, guilds and societies. As in Dundee, another area of high Irish in-migration, the Catholic Church created 'an entire way of life based upon the parish church, school and church-hall', reinforced by cradle-to-grave care within a Catholic 'micro welfare-state' mainly administered by Irish nuns.[97] The centre of associational life, particularly for women (and the girls of the Children of Mary), the Catholic parish co-existed in complementary rivalry with the local pub where Irishness was given a more masculine expression in tontines, friendly societies and other networks which continued the old secret and bibulous Ribbonite traditions and practices.

George Wise, the Protestant demagogue, was far from impressed by Catholic welfare provision, claiming it was not the Catholic Church but Lee Jones and his League of Well-Doers (formerly the Liverpool Food and Betterment Association) who provided the 'social salvation' of 'the Scotland Road area'. While most of the recipients (but not the donors) of his Limekiln Lane-based charity were Catholic, Lee Jones refused to be drawn into sectarian points-scoring, insisting that he 'helped the poorest poor from the standpoint of character, not for one moment from the standpoint of creed'.[98] A stern critic of the 'new philanthropy' of professional social work, he found much to praise in the humble 'hands-on' practice of the SVP and Catholic priests – and sought to emulate Nugent in providing entertainment (free open-air concerts in courts and alleys) as well as charity. While some priests were dismayed by his relative inattention to the evils of intemperance, the local Catholic press agreed with Lee Jones that 'drink has very little to do with the appalling poverty in our midst, most of which is due to low wages, scarcity of work, early marriages, and sickness or death of bread-winner'.[99]

Although prepared to work alongside Lee Jones – the choir at St Sylvester's

---

[96]   *Squalid Liverpool*, p.38.
[97]   McLeod, 'Building the "Catholic ghetto"'; Frank Boyce, 'Irish Catholicism in Liverpool: The 1920s and 1930s', in John Belchem and Patrick Buckland, eds, *The Irish in British Labour History*, Liverpool, 1993, pp.277–97, here p. 296.
[98]   *LCH* 3 Dec. 1910.
[99]   *LCH* 7 Feb. 1902, 1 Feb. 1907.

were the pioneer performers at his open-air concerts[100] – Catholics otherwise jealously guarded their independence and self-sufficiency. Where Anglican and Nonconformist agencies came together in coordinated effort in philanthropy, 'scientific charity' and social work, Catholics kept apart, determined to look after their own. *Porcupine* was critically incredulous of this

> rock of irreconcilability ... upon which in Liverpool many schemes of physical and moral improvement have been constantly wrecked ... The Catholics forget the thousand and one good things which men of all creeds are equally interested in obtaining, and which impinge in no way upon religious belief. There is no sectarian patent for fresh air, clean dwellings, sobriety and thriftiness.[101]

Welfare was a competitive imperative, a matter of confessional honour and pride in the prevalent sectarian rivalry. The SVP developed a Catholic niche, taking on cases overlooked by the Central Relief Society, with its focus on the 'respectable', and the Distress Committee which, in providing relief through work, inevitably favoured the 'able-bodied'.[102] Beyond this extensive provision, however, there was no distinctive Catholic social philosophy or social movement, 'European' features which took root on the Clyde, but not on the Mersey.[103] Furthermore, broad though it was, Catholic welfare was neither comprehensive nor inclusive. The workhouse and other official institutions loom large in Pat O'Mara's autobiography of a 'Liverpool Irish Slummy' – as do pawnshops and money-lenders, the infamous 'Fish and Money' people, who relied less upon collateral than upon their reputation for administering physical beatings to recalcitrant debtors. Accepting the Catholic Church's teachings on marriage, O'Mara's much-abused mother was unable to turn to the priest and the parish at times of greatest need, when compelled to leave her drunken and violent husband.[104]

---

100 *LCH* 30 June 1899.

101 *Porcupine* 1 May 1875.

102 'The Society of St Vincent de Paul and civic life', *Xaverian* Dec. 1909.

103 T. Gallagher, 'The Catholic Irish in Scotland: In search of identity', in T.M. Devine, ed., *Irish Immigrants and Scottish Society in the Nineteenth and Twentieth Centuries*, Edinburgh, 1991, pp.19–43, and B. Aspinwall, 'The Catholic Irish and wealth in Glasgow', in Devine, ed., *Irish Immigrants and Scottish Society*, pp.91–115.

104 O'Mara, *Liverpool Irish Slummy*. Margaret Hopley, a registered money-lender, sent the O'Briens (Martha and Sarah Ann) to sort out defaulters, see *Liverpool Weekly Mercury* 20 May 1911.

Beyond the parish and the priest, the Irish in Edwardian Liverpool had their own political party to attend to their welfare needs. Reconfigured to embrace 'Nat-Labism', the INP came to the forefront not only in issues of safety at work and housing but also in enhanced poor relief provision, taking advantage of reform of the Vestry in the 1890s. Sensitive to language and stigma, the INP put pressure on the Select Vestry to 'cease official use of the word "pauper" and to substitute for it "persons in receipt of relief"'.[105] In areas of Irish Liverpool under INP control, poor law relief 'discretion' was subsequently applied in 'generous' fashion. Eleanor Rathbone was scathing of such flagrant confessional favouritism in her 1913 *Report on the Condition of Widows under the Poor Law*:

> The Orangeman or Welsh Nonconformist of Everton or Kirkdale cannot be expected to relish the knowledge that if misfortune and an untimely death should oblige his widow and children to appeal for help, they will in all probability receive just half as much out of the public purse as they would have done if they had been Irish Roman Catholics living in a slum near the Vauxhall Road.[106]

Reinforced in their ethnic identity through lengthy and bitter struggles over charity and social provision, the 'low Irish' seemed to be turning things to their own advantage on the eve of the First World War. Eligible for charitable 'handouts' beyond those on offer across the confessional divide, the 'poorest poor' were also beginning to exploit the benefits of ethno-sectarian 'machine' politics.

---

[105] *LCH* 9 Mar. 1912.

[106] Eleanor Rathbone, *Report on the Condition of Widows under the Poor Law in Liverpool*, n.p., 1913, pp.24–33.

4

Faith and Fatherland:
Ethno-Sectarian Collective Mutuality

Although privileged in historical studies, 'top-down' institutional and charitable provision needs to be assessed in wider context, taking account of the various networks, formal and otherwise, by which migrants themselves adjusted to new surroundings. Working through family links, social connections and regional solidarities, many arrived in Liverpool through chain migration, with those already at destination helping newcomers (in classic 'moving European' fashion) to find jobs and housing, thereby protecting them from disorientation, dislocation and anomic behaviour.[1] Unknown arrivals who lacked such support mechanisms had to integrate themselves into street or court networks of mutual aid. Invariably run by women, those who gave expected to become recipients themselves when the wheel of fortune, or the family cycle, took a turn for the worse. Newcomers to the north end courts were quickly welcomed and enlisted, as an interviewee reported to Hugh Shimmin:

> Why, before my wife had got her furniture put into any sort of order, she had been visited by half the women in the court – in a friendly way, of course. One and all wished her good luck; some wanted to borrow pans and mugs, some wished her to join them in a subscription to bury a child that was dead in the top house; others that had joined for a little sup of drink, wished her to taste with them; some wanted her to subscribe to a raffle for a fat pig, which had been fed in the cellar where it now was.[2]

---

1   For a useful comparative and 'systemic' perspective on migration, see Leslie Page Moch, *Moving Europeans: Migration in Western Europe since 1650*, Bloomington, IN, 1992, in particular pp.16–18 and 103–60.
2   Quoted in H. Shimmin, 'The courts at Christmas time', in J. Walton and A. Wilcox,

Instrumental in making ends meet, such female networks were by no means devoid of bibulous conviviality, good cheer and personal indulgence, as evinced by the Monday 'tea party' following the obligatory weekly visit to the pawnshop to pledge the Sunday best:

> On these occasions there appeared to be no lack of meat or drink, and immediately after the arrival of each visitor a little girl would be sent off to the grog shop for spirits ... There was generally a great bustle to get all indications of the tea party cleared off before the time at which the husbands might be expected home – that is supposing them to be at work – and the women separated with very loud protestations of friendship for each other.[3]

In more formal networks of collective mutuality, however, conviviality tended to be a male preserve.

Based on ethnic and/or religious affiliation, pub- and parish-based associations of collective mutuality reached into parts beyond the remit either of the craft-dominated organised labour movement (a class apart from the casualism of the waterfront) or of industrial insurance. For profit-driven insurance companies, the Liverpool 'fever-dens' quickly became 'no-go' territory. Having endured 'fearful loss', the Prudential promptly pulled out of Irish Liverpool: 'it was only the low Irish, the very worst class of all', the manager explained to the Royal Commission in 1873, 'that we do not take, who, in my opinion, are not genuine Irishmen; they are outcasts'.[4] No such exclusions applied to specifically Irish networks, whether run by nationalist activists, Catholic clergy or ethnic entrepreneurs. By focusing on three episodes in the development of Liverpool-Irish mutuality – the Ribbonite networks of the pre-Famine decades, the collecting burial societies of Fenian times, and the friendly societies of the Home Rule period – this chapter will give an indication of the changing range of provision. It will also highlight tensions between competing and sometimes complementary political, clerical and commercial formulations of Irishness as the basis for collective affiliation and mutual support.

---

eds, *Low Life and Moral Improvement in Mid-Victorian England: Liverpool through the Journalism of Hugh Shimmin*, Leicester, 1991, p.156.

3   H. Shimmin, 'The social condition of the people', in Walton and Wilcox, eds, *Low Life and Moral Improvement*, p.111.

4   PP 1873 (842) XXII, RCFBS, 3rd Report, evidence of Harben, qq.25,920–26,082.

Characterised by secrecy and ritual – an occult culture of constantly changing signs and passwords known as the 'goods' – Ribbonism was multi-functional and morally ambiguous, a blend of Catholic 'Defender' nationalism, Whiteboy agrarian redress, primitive trade unionism and criminal protection racket. Implanted in England, with Liverpool as the hub, Ribbonism moved away from the underground (and underworld) towards the collective mutuality and associational culture of the Ancient Order of Hibernians, protecting and safeguarding those united by commitment to 'Faith and Fatherland'.[5] Thus, the secret network that provided 'political' sanctuary for members in flight from the Irish authorities also offered 'tramping' benefits to itinerant migrant workers. 'The lower Classes are very fond of belonging to these Bodies', the Commissioner of Dublin Police reported to a Select Committee of the House of Lords: 'A Person going over to Liverpool without a Farthing in his Pocket very soon meets with a Man whom he calls a Brother, who will give him Three-pence or Sixpence.'[6]

There is evidence of Ribbonism extending across the Irish Sea in the early 1820s, on the eve of the introduction of cheap steam navigation, in the informers' reports summarised by Major Sirr, the Dublin police magistrate. Although the picture was somewhat confusing, it would seem that this was a period of major reorganisation, as the Dublin leaders, having abandoned plans for simultaneous insurrection with the English radicals – a scheme premised on a revolutionary outcome of the Queen Caroline Affair – sought to consolidate links not only with Ulster but with their compatriots in Britain. In June 1821, at a meeting chaired by Michael Keenan, a coal-porter with a reputation for toughness, a certain Fullinsby was appointed as special envoy to England: 'Keenan gave Fullinsby six tests and desired him to bring over the people of Liverpool and Manchester into Union with Dublin'.[7] An unhappy chapter of events ensued, typical of the confusion, suspicion and treachery which tended to prevail when secret societies extended from their base. Fullinsby was received in Liverpool by Campbell and Doogan: the former, a publican in Dickens Street, had close

5   John Belchem, '"Freedom and Friendship to Ireland": Ribbonism in early nineteenth-century Liverpool', *International Review of Social History*, 39, 1994, pp.33–56.
6   PP 1839 (486) XII, Report from the Select Committee of the House of Lords appointed to enquire into the state of Ireland in respect of crime, q.5018.
7   TCD, Sirr Diaries, MS N4/6 f.88.

links with Ribbon activity in Ulster, travelling to Armagh every quarter, presumably to receive the 'goods'; the latter, a Dublin-born boot and shoe maker, was master of the Ribbon lodge which met in Campbell's pub, and was also apparently an expert in disguise. Having infiltrated a local Orange Order meeting, Doogan spotted one of the spies who had tailed Fullinsby across the Irish Sea. Suspicions soon fell on Fullinsby himself – there were rumours that he was a Protestant, his attendance at Mass notwithstanding, and that he wished to tell the Liverpool authorities 'the whole secret'. Campbell made a special trip to Dublin to express his concern, but what happened thereafter is impossible to disentangle. Reorganisation, however, was finally effected in February 1822 with the establishment of a national board, for which purpose Liverpool was considered an integral part of Ireland itself: listed as one of the nine committees 'in the North', it was entitled to send two delegates.[8] Shortly afterwards, Keenan and the other Dublin leaders were convicted for administering an unlawful oath, mainly on the evidence of the police informer Coffey.[9]

These trials brought an end to the first peak of Ribbon activity and to the hope of organisational unity. Henceforward, Ribbonism was split into separate Ulster- and Leinster-based societies – the Northern Union, or Sons of the Shamrock, and the Irish Sons of Freedom – both of whom contested for the allegiance of the Liverpool-Irish in the face of opposition from the Catholic Church. In accordance with a solemn Interdict of February 1831, Catholic clergy refused the sacraments to any known member of an organisation bound by secret oath.[10] Under the formidable leadership of 'Captain' Rice, the Northern Union subsequently concealed its operations behind the façade of clerically approved benefit societies, such as the Liverpool Hibernian Benevolent Burial Society, established in 1834, the model for the expansion of Catholic collective mutuality throughout the Irish diaspora. Official histories of the Ancient Order of Hibernians acknowledge its pioneer status, praising its 'divine precepts' of charity and devotion, together with its public declaration of allegiance to the monarch, constitution and Catholic Church.[11] As new societies were formed,

---

8   Sirr Diaries ff.118 and 126; and N4/7 ff.36 and 106.

9   *A Report of the Trial of Michael Keenan for Administering an Unlawful Oath*, Dublin, 1822; *A Report of the Trial of Edward Browne and others for administering and of Laurence Woods for Taking an Unlawful Oath*, Dublin, 1822.

10   G.P. Connolly, 'The Catholic Church and the first Manchester and Salford trade unions in the age of the industrial revolution', *Transactions of the Lancashire and Cheshire Antiquarian Society*, 135, 1985, pp.132–33.

11   T.F. McGrath, *History of the Ancient Order of Hibernians*, Cleveland, OH, 1898, pp.51–55; Wayne G. Broehl, Jr, *The Molly Maguires*, Cambridge, MA, 1964, pp.32–33.

the Hibernians underlined their clerical and constitutional loyalty by public disavowal of any connection with 'any illegal or excommunicated society in Ireland':

> The sole object of the Hibernian Society in England is to assist its Members in sickness and distress, and bury them when dead ... no society in Ireland or elsewhere, has or shall have so long as such society shall be proscribed by the pastors of the church, any voice or influence in the government of our society, or the management of its finances.[12]

Such public proclamations notwithstanding, Hibernian societies acted as convenient cover, preserving the link, an informer revealed, between English lodges and the Northern Union:

> A form of declaration has been adopted for the members at Liverpool, which begins by disclaiming all connexion with any societies in Ireland using secret signs and passwords; but this, like the article in the old declaration or oath of the Societies here, promising allegiance to the King or Queen, is only intended as a blind. The promise of allegiance was always 'turned down' and not read, when a member was admitted – and the present disclaimer is to be treated in the same way.[13]

This subterfuge, however, was but the first step to full admission to the secret lodges, each consisting of a 'parish' master, two committee men, a treasurer and 36 members:

> Much precaution is used in the introduction of members, none but Roman Catholics being admissible; and a report list, with the name, age and residence, the parish and county where each candidate comes from, must be read out in each body, and afterwards in the General Committee of the Town ... each must be passed in two or more bodies and afterwards approved by the General Committee.[14]

There were at least 30 active branches (some well in excess of 36 strong) by the mid-1830s, despite persistent efforts by the clergy to eradicate oath-bound

---

12   Handbill, St Patrick's Hibernian Benevolent Society, CO 904/7 f.149.
13   CO 904/7 ff.465–70.
14   Extracts from communications from the informant A.B., CO 904/8 ff.309–10.

activity. 'The clergy here this several years past', the Liverpool president of the rival Irish Sons of Freedom later reported to Dublin, 'were violently opposed against Irishmen on this side of the Channel holding a communication with Ireland. These Hibernians or Widgeons had recourse to every open artifice to deceive the clergy but God help them they were deceiving themselves when they would go to confession.' Under threat of denial of the sacraments, some Northern Unionists withdrew altogether; others alternated in attendance, according to conscience and need, between church and lodge; and certain sections of the leadership contemplated a range of exculpatory options, even severance of the offending link with Ireland. There was much internal dissension (and increased friction between the rival networks) when the Hibernians gave serious consideration to 'dropping Ireland ... of complying with the Bishops declaration and setting up shop for themselves confining their system, as they say, to England alone'.[15]

Radiating from Liverpool across the industrial districts, the Northern Union functioned as a form of affiliated friendly society for migrant workers, supplementing the informal mechanisms of chain migration by a tramping network of relief and assistance, irrespective of skill or trade. Basic cover was provided at modest cost, normally 1s for admission and a quarterly payment of either 3d or 6d. Sickness and death benefits were left to the discretion of the local branch or lodge: tramp relief, however, was distributed out of the 'box' (held at local headquarters – in Liverpool, the Grapes Inn, Grayson Street) through the highest local officer, the 'county delegate', and charged quarterly upon each branch. Elected by the branch officers at the quarterly meeting of the general committee, the 'delegate' was entrusted to attend the quarterly General Board of Erin or 'market' in Ireland to receive the 'goods', the latest signs and passwords, the correct version of which had to appear on the card or certificate presented by tramps seeking relief. The delegate's expenses in attending the General Board had the first call on funds, followed by relief and assistance for arrested or fugitive members in Ireland, leaving the remainder for benefit payments.[16]

By operating in secret without such cover, the Irish Sons of Freedom avoided, or so its leaders believed, the duplicity, deception and financial corruption inherent in the dual-layer Northern Union – indeed, they accused

---

[15]   NAD, Frazer MS 43, Transcript of the books written in short hand found on the person of Richard Jones on the 1st October 1839, no. 42: Wilson, Liverpool 4 May 1838.

[16]   Extracts from communications of the informant A.B., CO 904/8 ff.309–17; statement of John O'Brien, 3 Nov. 1841, HO 45/184.

Rice of debasing Ribbonism into a venal protection racket. Smaller in scale, the Liverpool branch of the Irish Sons of Freedom operated from headquarters in George Carrick's Hibernian Tavern in Newton Hill Street, where much of the administration was left to the local 'president', equivalent in rank and role to the county delegate, but elected by all members. Members paid 6d quarterly into the county fund, which was used to send the president to the quarterly board, to relieve tramps, to pay counsel for members of the friendship in jail, and to assist friends 'injured by opponents'. Within a few months of his election as president in 1838, William Wilson, a painter and decorator, complained of the disproportionate burdens of office, for which he received no expenses. On top of his onerous responsibilities for tramp relief, he had to

> attend the general meeting, take reports, read letters, in effect do the whole work of the society ... Every Sunday night either 3 or 4 of our bodies meet, they require my attendance every Monday night. I have to attend at Mr Carrick see the money forthcoming, receipt the Stewards books, see the sick money paid.[17]

Wilson's brief tenure of office, chronicled in detail in the shorthand books kept by Richard Jones, the national secretary, seized on his arrest in a major round-up in Dublin in October 1839, was full of controversy. A complex struggle for power had begun earlier when Thomas Jones, a recent arrival from Co. Kildare, was ousted from the Liverpool presidency in 1837 on discovery that he had joined the Oddfellows.[18] His replacement, Kennedy, ruled against such dual membership, but was voted out of office soon afterwards for reasons which remain unclear. Kennedy, however, retained the confidence and ear of the Dublin leadership to whom he continually traduced Wilson, his duly elected successor. Ratification of Wilson's position, indeed, was delayed pending thorough investigation of his background – including detailed questioning of his old Dublin landlady about his attendance record at Mass – and a special 'mission' to Liverpool by Jones and Andrew Dardis, the national president, in which they attempted to run an alternative candidate.[19] Thereafter, they established a relationship of mutual respect, symbolised by signing their correspondence with the current password, 'Freedom and

---

17   Jones transcript, no. 80: Wilson, 22 Aug. 1838.
18   Jones transcript, no. 12: Thomas Jones, 24 Mar. 1838.
19   Jones transcript, nos. 1–6, 14, 20 and 38.

Friendship to Ireland'.[20] Wilson, however, lost local support as members queried the cost of his ambitious plans to institute a united framework of Ribbonite self-sufficiency, free from clerical interference or friendly society competition:

> Any good rules I propose I cannot get them carried into effect to meet the wants of distressed tramps. I proposed that each member should pay 1d per month that it be lodged in the hands of Mr Carrick and according as any distressed friend would come and apply to me for assistance for me to give a note to Carrick for the price of his bed and supper. Carrick to keep all these dockets and get credit for nothing at the quarterly settlement but what he could provide a docket for ... all we could get to pay was 22 men ... all my labour was in vain in introducing good discipline among them, they are all generals and no privates.[21]

Where Jones's seized papers offer illuminating insight into the operation of the Irish Sons of Freedom in Liverpool, details of the Northern Union can be gleaned from the reports of a shady intelligence network operated by those seeking financial gain at the movement's expense. Having failed in trade, E. Rorke moved in with his Liverpool mistress to exploit his old mercantile contacts with Irish connections, eliciting information which he then sold to the authorities. His main informant, P.H. McGloin, a respectable young businessman, employed by wool merchants on a salary of £100 p.a., later claimed that until approached by Rorke, he had 'taken very little part in the thing, because being in a respectable situation and having business to attend to, it was against his interest to spend his nights in attending meetings and "boozing", which the Officers of the Society must do'. In the aftermath of the major round-up of Ribbon leaders in Ireland in 1839, McGloin learnt of Rorke's disreputable morals and excessive middleman's commission. Having gained assurance that he would not be called as a witness himself, McGloin negotiated a direct deal with the authorities in Dublin Castle: 'He was formerly a Delegate, and might now take an office which would put him in possession of all their secrets. When he comes to Dublin he

---

20   Jones transcript, nos. 48: Wilson, 25 May, and 49, Dardis and Jones, 28 May 1838. Tramps had to produce printed cards or certificates bearing the initial letters of the password. Others used after FAFTI, include GUAI, General Union among Irishmen, and FNDO, Fear Not Danger Over, adopted by a cruel irony on 30 Sept. 1838, the day before Jones's arrest.

21   Jones transcript, no. 80: Wilson, 22 Aug. 1838. His wife died soon after he was elected president, see no. 38: Wilson, 2 May 1838.

has to transact business (in trade) with a Delegate and would have many facilities of gaining extensive information.'[22] Plagued by informers, the networks were also exploited by criminal elements. The main port of entry, Liverpool was the first place of refuge for Irishmen on the run, including bankrupts, criminals and disreputable members of the 'friendship' such as Robert McDonnell.[23] After being discovered selling the 'goods' for his own profit, McDonnell, a brogue maker, had turned to embezzlement and other crime before fleeing to Liverpool where he tried to defraud a local tontine by faking his own death. Counterfeiting and other crimes followed (including 'dilapidating and gutting the house he occupied in Liverpool') until he discovered his true vocation as a Protestant preacher in Sheffield.[24]

Given its nodal location, Liverpool figured prominently in the ill-fated unity discussions between the rival networks in 1838, providing a 'neutral' venue away from regional rivalry, and offering a ready-made communications network: 'as all persons going on tramp to England would have to call in Liverpool, they would be able to send word to all parts of Ireland'.[25] These advantages, however, were outweighed by the financial demands on the local branches in the main port of entry: like the poor relief authorities and charitable agencies, collective mutuality in Liverpool was under disproportionate strain. While the cost of relieving fugitives seems to have been spread throughout the national networks, Liverpool bore the expense of aiding distressed members – economic migrants rather than political refugees – passing through the port. In the Leinster network, Wilson did what he could for tramps out of his own meagre pocket: 'I have nothing to depend upon but my hand. I have to support a helpless and motherless family and when a distressed friend comes my heart relents.' As numbers increased inexorably, there were rumours within the Irish Sons of Freedom that 'the Men of Liverpool were on the point of charging the Country a certain sum for the <u>Renewals</u> and that they did not assist <u>tramps</u>'.[26] The Northern Union experienced similar difficulties, compounded by the withdrawal of 'respectable tradesmen' and funds in the wake of arrests in Ireland in 1839. The number of branches, McGloin reported, fell from 30

---

22   Matheson's report to Drummond on his interview with McGloin in Dublin, CO 904/7 ff.465–70.

23   A freelance informer kept a close watch for fugitive criminals and bankrupts, see NAD, Outrage Papers, Co. Cavan, 1839, 23994C, enclosing a letter from 'A Friend', Gt Homer Street, Liverpool.

24   Statement of John Kelly, CO 904/7 ff.77–92.

25   Jones transcript, no. 75: Jones, 6 Aug. 1838.

26   Jones transcript, no. 49: Dardis and Jones to Wilson, 28 May 1838.

to 20; funeral processions became less lavish; and the relief fund, previously assessed on the branches quarterly, 'got into disuse in toto', ending the standard arrangement by which tramps holding 'regular certificates' were given a bed for the night and a payment of 1s 6d. As 'respectable tradesmen' quit the general committee, the Liverpool lodges of the Northern Union were left in the hands of 'labourers, warehousemen, and lumpers and varied only by an occasional publican', without the necessary funds to serve as reception and assistance centre for migrant members.[27]

In organisational terms, Ribbonism was a minority movement, strongest among migrants from Ulster and adjoining counties, but its sectarian mentality helped to construct a wider sense of national identity and affiliation in pre-Famine Irish Liverpool in which Catholic and Irish became synonymous. Having imported their fierce sectarian loyalty, Ribbonmen from the north were to rally their fellow countrymen and co-religionists against the hereditary enemy, the Orangemen. In 1842, by which time the movement was past its peak, Head Constable Whitty calculated that there were still 13 Ribbon pubs in Liverpool, although most were 'used only as houses of resort, for ordinary rather than special communication'.[28] At some Irish pubs, however, an old faction-fighting culture still prevailed, as at the alehouse in Sawney Pope Street, venue of the Molly Maguires. In this Liverpudlian manifestation, the Mollies were sworn to give mutual help, an insult to one 'being taken as an insult to all, for which is sought satisfaction'.[29]

Collecting burial societies have been dismissed as the weakest engines of thrift in Victorian Britain, exploiting the economic irrationality and lack of self-discipline among 'lower levels' of the working class. Where artisans and skilled workers insured and improved themselves through a participatory, self-governing friendly society culture, those lower down the scale saved only for an ostentatious funeral, assured at excessive expense through dependence upon weekly home visits by street-wise, ambitious

---

27   CO 904/8 ff.82–89.

28   Whitty's report, 2 Apr. 1842, CO 904/9 ff.210–15.

29   *Liverpool Journal* 17 Apr. 1858, quoted in Anne Bryson, 'Riot and its control in Liverpool, 1815–1860', unpublished MPhil thesis, Open University, 1989. For the American version, see the classic study by Kevin Kenny, *Making Sense of the Molly Maguires*, New York and Oxford, 1998.

and unaccountable collectors, the 'penny-a-week death hunters'.[30] Gender
and ethnic factors accentuated the contrast. Unlike the pub, hall, lodge
or other 'associational' meeting place, home was the woman's domain. 'It
is the mother who transacts the business with the collector', Sir Edward
Brabrook observed, 'and saves up and pays to him a few pence which insure
her own and her husband and children's funeral money.'[31] In the absence of
shareholders (as in industrial assurance) or of proper regulation by members
(as in friendly societies), misappropriation and malpractice prevailed, most
notably in Liverpool where, the historian of working-class self-help bemoans,
there were 'many Irish migrants, some illiterate, and open to fraud and
exploitation by the collectors'.[32] Such 'nefarious doings' were not entirely
one-way: 'a regular trade was being done by wretched women', the former
medical officer to the Liverpool Infirmary for Children reported to the first
annual meeting of the Society for the Prevention of Cruelty to Children,
'insuring children under false names'.[33] This is the critical backcloth against
which to assess the United Assurance and Burial Society of St Patrick, better
known as St Patrick's Burial Society, the most successful but ultimately the
most infamous of the Liverpool-based collecting societies.[34] With the blessing
of the parish, the sponsorship of the pub and the enterprise of its network
of weekly collectors on commission, the Society mobilised Irish and Catholic
resources, originally in Liverpool but soon throughout the United Kingdom,
ensuring a final promise of independence, dignity and pride for the 'low
Irish', a proper funeral without recourse to patronising (and proselytising)
philanthropy or the pauperising indignities of the Poor Law.

---

30   L. Ginsberg, 'Industrial Life Assurance', in W.A. Robson, ed., *Social Security*, London,
1948, pp.261–88; Bentley B. Gilbert, *The Evolution of National Insurance*, London, 1966,
pp.318–22; P.H.J.H. Gosden, *Self-Help: Voluntary Associations in the Nineteenth Century*,
London, 1973, ch. 5. For a recent reassessment, see Paul Johnson, *Saving and Spending:
The Working-Class Economy in Britain 1870–1939*, Oxford, 1985; and Marcel van der Linden,
'Introduction' in Van der Linden, ed., *Social Security Mutualism: The Comparative History of
Mutual Benefit Societies*, Berne, 1996, pp.11–33.
31   Sir Edward William Brabrook, *Provident Societies and Industrial Welfare*, London, 1898,
p.78.
32   Eric Hopkins, *Working-Class Self-Help in Nineteenth-Century England*, London, 1995,
p.38.
33   Liverpool Society for the Prevention of Cruelty to Children, *First Annual Report*,
p.17.
34   For a full study, see John Belchem, 'Priests, publicans and the Irish poor: Ethnic
enterprise and migrant networks in mid-nineteenth century Liverpool', *Immigrants and
Minorities*, 23, 2005, pp.207–31.

Opened for worship in 1827, St Patrick's, the first mission chapel in Liverpool's south end, was itself a pioneering venture in 'penny collections'. Collectors made 'a weekly round amongst the Catholic population for small alms towards the building of the Church', a much-repeated exercise in subsequent decades as the Catholic Church, in the absence of local recusant wealth, struggled to finance its ever-expanding building programme.[35] A few years after St Patrick's opened, its pastor, Rev. Dr Murphy (subsequently Bishop of Adelaide), adopted the subscription principle to establish a 'purgatorial society'. Masses would be said for the dead and a decent burial assured through modest weekly contribution to St Patrick's Assurance and Friendly Burial Society. There were narrow actuarial and geographical limits: restricted to Catholics resident in the vicinity, members were admitted only between the ages of 18 to 40, paying a weekly contribution of 1½d for a death benefit of £4, later raised to £5. Even so, the impact of the influx from Famine-struck Ireland proved disastrous: funds were soon exhausted as mortality soared through 'Irish fever' and the Society moved into debt. A meeting was called at St Patrick's school-room in July 1849 at which it was proposed to dissolve the Society. From the floor, John Treacy, formerly a day labourer in the Irish ordinance survey, voiced his opposition:

> I observed the resolution was discreditable to them as Catholics and Irishmen. They asked what I advised and I replied, 'Go to work like men and do as your neighbours. Do they make such Societies prosper? Why cannot you do the same?' I was then asked if I would have the courage to undertake the management, and I answered rather than it should be said that my co-religionists and countrymen were incapable of managing an institution of the sort I would do what I could.[36]

Under Treacy's entrepreneurial management, the Society enjoyed remarkable growth and commercial success. Reconstituted with a mere 151 members, the Society secured registration under Friendly Society legislation within a few months, the expenses being paid out of Treacy's own pocket. Thenceforth, members were admitted 'from the period of birth up to 40 years on a payment of 1d instead of 1½d per week, and on certain other terms; and the period of entrance was extended to 70 years'. In little more than a decade, the Society

35   RCLv Box 40, 'Relatio Status Missiorum in Diocesi Liverpolitana'; 'The Collectors of St Vincent of Paul's Church', *NP* 4 Jan. 1862.

36   John Treacy, *Mr John Treacy's Reply to Mr S.B. Harper*, Liverpool, 1863, p.7.

had acquired a national membership in excess of 100,000 (with branches 'in all the large towns of England, Scotland and Ireland') and over £20,000 in funds.[37] Thenceforth there was further rapid expansion and a short-lived extension into sickness insurance (where fraudulent claims were harder to detect). Absorption of smaller, less successful Catholic burial societies (including a large London-based assurance society under the patronage of Cardinal Wiseman) brought economies of scale, aided by Treacy's readiness to poach successful collectors (and their books) from other societies.[38]

'The prosperous condition of St Patrick's Burial Society must be a matter of exultation to the Catholic body', the *Lancashire Free Press* proclaimed in January 1860, attributing its success to two factors: Treacy's extensive use of collectors on commission ('the grand secret of its success') and the continued patronage of Catholic clergy:

> So long as it enjoys the confidence and co-operation of the Clergy it is certain to 'go on and prosper' ... It is now so firmly established, and so many individuals are interested in its progress and prosperity, that the idea of its ever failing cannot be contemplated ... It is destined to be as enduring as the faith planted by the great apostle whose name it bears.[39]

Within a few years, however, the society was mired in legal disputes – by 1865 there were six separate actions at law and a Chancery suit – in which Treacy and the collectors were accused of systematically defrauding 200,000 poor Irish in Britain of their savings and benefits. In a dramatic reversal, Treacy found himself denounced and disowned by Father Nugent and other local Catholic leaders, once fervent in support of his success, but now as anxious to dissociate themselves from the corruption and sleaze of the St Patrick's Burial Society as from the secrecy and violence of Fenianism.

The legal campaign to expose Treacy's 'gross mismanagement' was begun by Hugh Caraher, a local customs officer and president of St Mary's Christian Doctrine Confraternity. Irish by birth, Caraher held that the 'distinguishing trait in the national character was undying love and veneration to their pastors and their faith'.[40] Having organised a highly successful collecting system in his

---

37   'St Patrick's Assurance and Burial Society', *LFP* 28 Jan. 1860; Treacy, *Reply*, pp.1–9.
38   'The St Patrick's Assurance Sick and Burial Society: Misrepresentation corrected', *DP* 16 Jan. 1863.
39   'St Patrick's Assurance and Burial Society', *LFP* 28 Jan. 1860. See also the glowing report of the annual meeting of the Society in *LFP* 21 Jan. 1860.
40   *NP* 22 Feb. 1862.

parish to raise funds to aid the beleaguered Pope against the temporal advance
of Italian nationalism, Caraher had been put forward to serve on the committee
of the St Patrick's Burial Society, but on appointment was amazed to find his
services were not required. Appalled by the lack of accountability (or even of
committee meetings), he wrote to Rev. Phelan, parish priest of St Patrick's and
President and Treasurer of the Society, in the 'interests of the poor Catholics,
who have invested their money in the society', calling upon him to 'put a stop to
the carryings on of the secretary' who ran the Society in cavalier and profligate
manner.[41] Nothing came of his complaints other than his sudden expulsion
from the Society, a decision he challenged in the courts in the autumn of 1864,
thereby beginning the complex, protracted and fruitless series of actions against
Treacy's 'gross mismanagement'.

Running parallel with the court actions were a series of public meetings,
tempestuous affairs where rival camps ultimately came to blows, belying the
image of mid-Victorian respectability on such indoor occasions. Treacy could
always rely on carrying the day, the audience being 'packed' not with members
(too poor and distant to attend) but with agents and collectors from out of town
who acted (without any legal authority) as their representatives, supplemented
by local roughs hired through 'foremen' on Liverpool street corners.[42] At one
particularly rumbustious meeting, Nugent was heckled and forced to withdraw
– 'Shame, Father Nugent; you are in a wrong cause' – unable to submit
a resolution that 'the Liverpool Catholic clergy here present express their
disapprobation of the past management of the society, and that it has not now,
nor for some years has had, their patronage'.[43] When 'Nujint' quit the hall at
'The Matin' av the Members av St Pathrick's', *Porcupine* reported in brogue,
'some av the boys wanted more room to foight in, an' wint down shtairs, an'
the gintlemn got tired av blagaardin.' [44]

Where Rev. Phelan, the poor parish priest who drew a salary for his work
in promoting the Society, was penitent and apologetic during the court actions,
Treacy gave no ground whatsoever. Having saved 'the Burial Society from
itself being buried', he continued to place himself above either criticism or the

---

[41]   RCFBS, Caraher's evidence, qq.20,504–20,614; 'St Mary's Christian Doctrine
Confraternity: Annual soiree' and 'Sympathy with Pope: Great meeting at St Mary's', *LFP*
4 Feb. and 24 Mar. 1860.

[42]   RCFBS, qq.20,737–20,739.

[43]   'St Patrick's Sick and Burial Society: Uproarious meeting', *LM* 9 Aug. 1865; letters
from Canons Walmsley and O'Reilly in *LM* 10 and 11 Aug. 1865.

[44]   *Porcupine* 12 Aug. 1865.

law, the inadequacies of which were ably exploited by Nordon, his solicitor.[45] Unrestrained by the courts, 'Mister Thrasey' was not to be dislodged either from control of the Society 'machine' (he could always rely on strong-arm supporters to see off opposition) or the popular affection of its poor members. In part, this continued tenure can be explained in technical terms. Friendly society legislation proved inadequate and/or inappropriate as a means of legal redress, a deficiency compounded by frequent change in the Society's rules (and in its title): 'there were almost as many different sets of rules as years that the society had been in existence. It would confuse Philadelphia to find a lawyer who could say what the rules were.'[46] Beyond the law, Treacy's power base depended first and foremost on 'a troop of friends' and 'a bulwark of his relations' – within the Society the 'principal parties' were 'all related to Treacy; they were either cousins, or married to his nieces, or were brothers-in-law'.[47] The network of old friends and drinking partners was headed by Edward Doran and William Judge. Doran was accorded the contract to print the rules, collection books and other stationery 'with great disregard to expense', and served on the committee, a sinecure also enjoyed by a number of Merseyside publicans, including Francis M'Donald at whose Cheapside premises Treacy was alleged to be 'a large private customer'.[48] Judge was a very old friend: a cobbler by trade, he was appointed vice-president in 1849, agent for Bootle (receiving a salary, 2½ per cent on the gross sum collected by the district collectors, and rent-free accommodation) and on the death of Dr Campion in 1863, medical inspector for the Society![49] When the Society was in its 'infant state', Treacy and Judge encouraged collectors to sell their books to supplement their 25 per cent commission: the practice developed into a lucrative source of income with books in Manchester changing hands for £400 and in Liverpool for over £500. Provided they remained loyal to Treacy, collectors could expect a good living and the prospect of advancement within a management structure which accounted for 46 per cent of the Society's

[45] *Porcupine* 4 Feb. 1865.
[46] RCFBS, Second Report, PP 1872(514–1)XXVI, q.20,645. There are six different sets of rules, each approved by Tidd Pratt, in the volume labelled *Liverpool United Assurance Society* in the British Library. The title changes from United Assurance and Burial Society of St Patrick's (1832–57), to United Assurance Sick and Burial Society of St Patrick (1858–68), to United Assurance Society of St Patrick (1868–69), and finally, until its demise in 1885, United Assurance Society.
[47] RCFBS, q.20,611. 'St Patrick's Sick and Burial Society: Alleged gross mismanagement', *LM* 17 Dec. 1864.
[48] The allegation was refuted by M'Donald, see his letter in *LM* 17 Dec. 1864.
[49] See Judge's evidence to RCFBS, qq.20,136–20,382.

income.[50] 'Many collectors', the *Lancashire Free Press* observed approvingly, 'have made a position for themselves, and are amongst the most worthy and respected of our Catholic fellow citizens'.[51] Treacy himself was a rags-to-riches role model. Having come to Liverpool as a day-labourer with 'nothing', he confessed in the legal actions to being 'middling': his salary, originally 8 shillings a week, was now £400 per year; he lived in a house built by the Society; had sent two of his daughters to be educated privately in Belgium; owned property in Scotland Road (six houses bought for £900); and had £1200 vested in mortgages, while his savings amounted to between £200 and £300.[52] His health failed, however, during the course of the legal actions and he died a few months later.

'A perfect martyr to the society', Treacy was revered in death, his legacy being upheld by a corps of relatives, friends, collectors, agents and publicans (including his Fenian brother-in-law, Martin Clarke), Irishmen who took inverse pride in their class and ethnic status: 'They belonged to the humble and poor, and shame on the men who had begun the litigation, by which the society had lost to the extent of £6000.' Poor, humble and Irish, they had 'gained a victory over those men who had been the means of bringing poor Treacy to the grave ... Oh, might Jesus have mercy upon his soul for he had gone to the grave with a broken heart.'[53] The continuation of Treacy's autocratic management style by his closest cronies, however, cut across the ambitions of collectors and publicans who aspired to office, thus precipitating a further and final round of litigation and turbulent meetings. In a veritable coup d'état, two publicans, John McCormick and Patrick Birnie, packed the AGM at Hope Hall in August 1868 with their supporters.[54] They then hired a public house in Duke Street a few doors away from the Society's offices and issued advertisements 'holding themselves out as being authorised to receive the subscriptions of members'. Pending satisfaction in the courts, the matter was literally fought out in a series of meetings, further evidence *Porcupine* reported of 'the irrepressible combativeness of your true-born Paddy'.[55] The worst violence occurred when the two sides – or Irish factions, as they were reported in the press – advertised meetings at the same venue, Prince Patrick Hall, on the same day. At first, assaults were simply verbal: 'One old Irish crone made herself specially prominent. She got upon a form, and after

---

[50]   See the evidence of Hamilton, the Manchester district manager, RCFBS, qq.19,210–19,356. See also 'Burial Societies', *Porcupine* 26 Sept. 1868.

[51]   'St Patrick's Assurance and Burial Society', *LFP* 28 Jan. 1860.

[52]   See the reports of Treacy's libel actins in *LM* and *DP* 18 Aug. 1865.

[53]   'St Patrick's Burial Society: Disorderly meeting', *LM* 16 Mar. 1866.

[54]   'St Patrick's Burial Society again: Uproarious proceedings', *LM* 29 Aug. 1868.

[55]   'More about Burial Societies', *Porcupine* 5 Sept. 1868.

wringing her hands and uttering a loud and plaintive "Ochone!" poured forth a volley of anathemas against those who "were taking away the money from the poor ould women and the helpless orphans".' Then they became physical: 'A band of men rushed from the body of the hall, scrambled upon the platform, and then a desperate struggle ensued for supremacy. A powerful old Irishman led on the assault and his war-cry made the hall ring again.' As the fighting became general, the despairing manager of the hall turned off the gas: 'This was no doubt done with the best intention; but it led to indescribable confusion ... a regular "free fight" in semi-darkness took place.' Press reporters, the 'only non-combatants present', were fortunate to escape unharmed from 'one of the most disreputable disturbances that has taken place in connection with the very disreputable history of Liverpool friendly societies'.[56] Bruised and bloodied, the rival camps abandoned direct confrontation but otherwise yielded no ground. When the case finally came before the County Court, Sergeant Wheeler pledged to call the special attention of the Registrar of Friendly Societies to the most unsatisfactory rules of the Society which gave 'a freehold office to the officers of the society, and made them irremovable and independent of the members. He thought that was very wrong. When this Augean stable would be cleansed, and these societies put in proper shape, he did not know.' [57]

In 1871, by which time Baldwin, the president, had absconded to America with over £500 of funds, members of the Royal Commission on Friendly and Benefit Societies (1870–74) spent a week in Liverpool collecting evidence. By far the most damning revelations concerned what was now known simply as the United Assurance Society, still the fourth-largest burial society in the country with over 140,000 members and £15,000 in funds.[58] 'We are living in an atmosphere of fraud – possibly of murder', *Porcupine* expostulated: 'a depth of wickedness has been disclosed, an account of dishonesty has been unveiled, that quite throws ordinary villainy into the shade'.[59] New legislation in 1875, however, failed to protect the poor members. Complacency still prevailed in the upper echelons: at the 51st annual meeting, John Denvir, the leading Irish nationalist and a trustee of the Society, rejected any criticism of the management committee and 'regretted the hostile and carping spirit in which several gentlemen from London appeared to have come to the meeting'.[60] By the time Ludlow, the new Registrar, eventually despatched his chief clerk to Liverpool

---

56 'St Patrick's Assurance Society: Terrible fighting at a meeting', *LM* 21 Sept. 1868.
57 'Troubles of St Patrick's Burial Society', *LM* 30 Oct. 1868.
58 PP 1874 (916) XXIII, RCFBS, 4th Report, p.civ.
59 'The Commission on Friendly Societies', *Porcupine* 18 Nov. 1871.
60 'The United Assurance Society', *Irish Programme* 7 June 1884.

in 1885 to take out a summons, the offices in Duke Street were shut up and the officers had left for America. 'What became of the society, except that it vanished out of sight, I believe nobody knows', Tompkins reported. According to the *Fenian Memories* of Dr Mark Ryan, the business was transferred to Pearl Assurance, the originators of which included prominent supporters of Home Rule.[61]

Once the Catholic hierarchy had removed its patronage and support, the Society was run by ethnic entrepreneurs who stood forward to reassure poor members, appealing to their ethnicity rather than their faith. Accentuating the 'Irishness' of the Society, they ran it as a machine which looked less to the respectability (or religion) of the members than to their assurance of an adequately funded Irish 'wake', transplanted as the Liverpool 'buster', a great guzzle which often continued, *Porcupine* despaired, in heavy sessions in public houses, run by officers of the burial societies, conveniently situated in the path of returning mourners.[62] Having witnessed an Irish Sunday funeral, Shimmin was a harsh critic of the sabbatarian desecration and financial cost involved:

> Since the Burial Societies got a-head, most funerals are 'busters'. They go in for a spree, a feed, a guzzle, winding up with long pipes, long yarns, and, very often a row ... Had his funeral been held on a week day, and could his wife have been kept out of the traps for spending money which the burial club people laid for her, she might have had something to start the world with. As it was, the first thing after the great funeral spree was a collection for the widow![63]

---

61   See the evidence of Tompkins and Sutton in Report from the Select Committee on Friendly Societies, PP 1888 (389) XII. From Police Court reports it seems that after Walker had sought to dissolve the Society and negotiate a deal favourable to the collectors for transfer to the Royal Liver, members were offered membership of the Liverpool Victoria 'though with a considerable reduction of benefits', *Times* 23 May, 9 and 17 July 1885. According to Mark Ryan, however the St Patrick's Burial Society 'afterwards became the Pearl Insurance Society', for whom he worked as medical examiner, see Mark Ryan, *Fenian Memories*, Dublin, 1946, pp.48 and 58. Advertisements for respectable and energetic collectors for Pearl Assurance appeared regularly in *LCH*. The annual report of Pearl figured prominently in *Denvir's Penny National Irish Almanac for 1889*, Liverpool, n.d.

62   *Porcupine* 16 June 1866.

63   'Sunday Funerals', *Porcupine* 28 April 1866. The preponderance of such funerals following the opening of the Anfield Park Cemetery prompted a censorious *Report on Sunday Funerals by the Executive Committee of the Burial Board for the Parish of Liverpool*, Liverpool, 1866.

Irishness of this order was not only condemned by the Catholic church – which for once welcomed Protestant philanthropic intervention through the generous donation of Robert Hutchinson towards the cost of constructing a mortuary chapel in the north end [64] – but was also censured by Irish members of the professions in Liverpool. The campaign initiated by the devout Caraher was carried forward by lawyers with political ambitions, most notably Dr Commins, co-founder of the Home Rule Confederation. Home rule was predicated on self-reform, the eradication of the old 'Irish' ways and means, whether secret, violent, criminal or crude. Purging the excesses of the St Patrick's Burial Society – and the associated 'peasant' culture of wakes – was a useful apprenticeship (and necessary preliminary) for the new political project.[65]

The pre-eminent Irish organisation in Liverpool throughout the Home Rule period, embodying (as its motto proclaimed) 'Nationality, Unity and Benevolence', was the Irish National Foresters (INF), an association which offered the full range of properly audited friendly society benefits along with an ethnically accentuated open culture of display and parade. Founded by members expelled from the Ancient Order of Foresters for 'political' participation in an amnesty demonstration for political prisoners in Dublin in 1877, the new society, restricted to those of Irish birth or descent, prompted unduly alarmist fears in Special Branch reports: with its secret rituals, the INF afforded 'a very tempting opening' to the Fenians 'for the propagation of their designs'.[66]

The first English branch was formed in Ardwick in 1878 and soon spread

---

[64] Among the many articles on Irish wakes, see 'Correspondence between Dr Trench and Robert Hutchinson, Esq', *DP* 9 Nov. 1865; 'Burying the dead', *DP* 3 July 1866; 'New Roman Catholic mortuary chapel', *DP* 12 Dec. 1866; building work was abruptly terminated following Hutchinson's 'unfortunate failure' in business but was later resumed thanks to a public subscription organised by Dr Trench. 'It is a somewhat singular fact that although the mortuary chapel will be almost exclusively used by Roman Catholics, the entire money raised for its completion has been contributed by Protestants', see 'The mortuary chapel for Liverpool', *LM* 12 Nov. 1870.

[65] For defence of the Irish wake in Liverpool in the cholera epidemics of earlier decades, see Michael Durey, 'The survival of an Irish culture in Britain, 1800–45', *Historical Studies*, 20, 1982, pp.14–35.

[66] CO 904/16 f.51 memo 'explanatory of the origin and political tendency of the Irish National Foresters' Organization'.

throughout Greater Manchester; the Liverpool District, however, was not established until some years later in 1889. There was steady progress thereafter, with some considerable acceleration in the early years of the twentieth century. However, the INF in Liverpool never reached the levels of popular membership attained in Glasgow and the west of Scotland. What was impressive about the INF in Liverpool was less its overall size than its ability to unite seemingly divergent strands and to provide national leadership of the Order. While offering an efficient agency of collective mutuality (£10,494 was paid out in sick and funeral benefits between 1891 and 1910), the INF facilitated an enduring 'new departure' of Irish nationalists in Liverpool of almost every hue.[67]

From the outset, the INF enjoyed the blessing of the Catholic Church, although strictly speaking it was a 'non-sectarian Society which admits into the ranks Irishmen and Irishwomen, no matter in what country they toil or at what altar they kneel'.[68] Church parades, led by the Harp of Erin Fife and Drum Band, were a monthly focus of INF activity in Liverpool, 'members from all the male branches wearing the Robert Emmet Costume, and lady Foresters in their white dresses, cloaks of green and gold and plumed hats'. Such was their popularity that steps had to be taken to prevent unauthorised bands and collectors from appending themselves to the proceedings. Sometimes the Sunday outings involved ferry trips or specially chartered trains to carry the resplendent Foresters to the outer reaches of Merseyside.[69] Then there were the annual Whit outings and the 'Irish Children's Pleasant Days' – Holywell and its shrine was a favoured destination – at which mass was celebrated outdoors by crowds of 1000 to 2000, followed by sports with prizes including 'a handsome cup and medals of Irish design and manufacture', promoted for the benefit of the juvenile sections otherwise at risk 'from contaminating and denationalising surroundings, and giving them opportunity for realising the obligations and privileges of a separate nationality'.[70] The great highlight of the 1903 INF Convention, held in Liverpool, was the church parade, in full green and gold regalia, from St George's Hall to St Alban's. Here in what was 'practically

---

[67]   *LCH* 5 Dec. 1902 and 17 July 1903. NLI holds annual printed reports for 1899–1902, 1907–10 and 1919–22. For the INF in Scotland, where it was the 'primary Irish organisation' in the late nineteenth and early twentieth centuries, and remained important until the Second World War, see Joseph Bradley, 'Wearing the green: A history of nationalist demonstrations among the diaspora in Scotland', in T.G. Fraser, *The Irish Parading Tradition*, Basingstoke, 2000, pp.111–28, here pp.114–15.

[68]   *Thirty-Third Annual Convention: Navan, 2–4 August 1910*, p.55.

[69]   *LCH* 14 Apr. 1905 and 1 June 1912.

[70]   *LCH* 8 and 29 June, 7 Sept. and 28 Dec. 1906, 13 June and 28 Sept. 1907.

a wholly Catholic district, situated at the north end of the city', they were greeted by Father O'Byrne, for whom commitment to nation and faith were mutually reinforcing: 'he would beg the young Irish emigrant to England to join the nearest branch of the Foresters after they had made the acquaintance of their parish church. Thus they would safeguard within their hearts the idea of nationhood, and foster and make keener their devotion to their holy faith.'[71]

By this time the INF was thriving in Liverpool. 'Week after week', the *Liverpool Catholic Herald* reported in May 1904, 'we find ourselves called upon to record the opening of new branches, the strengthening of old ones, the establishment of juvenile sections, the formation of branches for ladies, and, more hopeful still, the growing interest of the clergy in the work'.[72] In recognition of the expansion, a new banner was commissioned, composed entirely of Irish materials, 'worthy of one of the most progressive Districts in the Order'.[73] To promote the national cause, all printing was sent to Ireland (until this proved too expensive in 1910), branch funds were invested in Irish securities and everything possible was done to promote the Irish economy.[74] When James Moran, long-serving secretary of the English Central Branch (based at 93 Scotland Road), completed an annual term as Grand High Chief Ranger of the Order in 1913, he was presented with a roll-top desk and a handsome illuminated address, designed and executed in Ireland, a case of Irish-manufactured cutlery being at the same time presented to Mrs Moran.[75] Local members proudly proclaimed their affiliation in press advertisements: Patrick J. Mullooly, INF, landlord of the Throstle's Nest, Scotland Road, offered 'Special Old Irish'.[76] Under the heading, 'Irishmen and Catholics Support Your Own', W. Fagan, INF, a tailor in Scotland Road, advertised special terms for Foresters' uniforms made from Irish cloth.[77]

In its promotion of Irish culture, as of Irish-made goods, the INF stopped short of fundamentalist 'Irish-Irish' rigour and autarkic self-sufficiency. When the United Irish League of Great Britain held its convention in Liverpool in 1903, the INF sponsored a Gaelic Athletic Festival and Feis at Aintree, but such one-off occasions apart it relied on conventional sports and athletics to attract

---

[71]   *LCH* 7 Aug. 1903.

[72]   *LCH* 27 May 1905.

[73]   *LCH* 13 Apr. 1906 and 20 Aug. 1910.

[74]   *LCH* 14 June 1907, 1 Jan. and 24 Dec. 1910.

[75]   *LCH* 26 July 1913.

[76]   *LCH* 1 Jan. 1910.

[77]   *LCH* 6 July 1900.

the crowds, not least to its annual Whit outings.[78] Similarly, while pride of place in parades was accorded to the fife and drum, most new branches (like societies across the ethnic spectrum) formed brass bands: the first parade of the Catholic Defence Association in 1910 was accompanied by a brass band provided by the INF.[79] Gaelic vigilantes were frequently to complain at the 'Killarney'-type 'stage Irish' entertainment which intruded at INF gatherings, including a concert with 'a decidedly stagey "jig" and a "Highland fling" ... out of place at an emphatically Irish entertainment'.[80] By no means averse to linguistic retrieval – at the 1901 convention, indeed, it was Liverpool District which proposed a motion that 'the salutation in entering a meeting of the Order as well as the welcome be in Irish'[81] – the INF in Liverpool promoted the use of Irish in a manner short of the highbrow exclusivist thrust of the Gaelic League. While criticised by purists, this non-doctrinaire (and convivial) approach to 'Irish' culture may well account for the popularity and success of the INF in Liverpool.

Whenever T.P. O'Connor was in town or some other Irish notable, whether it be John Redmond, the parliamentary leader, Joe Devlin, the Belfast Catholic nationalist leader, the Lord Mayor of Dublin, or a revered Fenian veteran such as O'Donovan Rossa, the INF provided a suitably sartorial guard of honour.[82] Constitutionally 'non-political' as well as non-sectarian, the INF was able to effect an overarching nationalist unity. The INF, Alderman Purcell of the INP explained, was

> a society wherein Irishmen of all Shades of Opinion could come together for mutual help ... without interfering with the work properly belonging to the political societies, they would be fostering the spirit of intense patriotism, becoming even better Irishmen than before, and helping each other on the social scale.[83]

Membership extended from prominent INP aldermen, councillors and members of the Select Vestry through Irish Republican Brotherhood (IRB) 'suspects'

---

78   *LCH* 7 Aug. 1903.

79   *LCH* 30 Apr. 1910.

80   *LCH* 30 Nov. and 28 Dec. 1906.

81   Irish National Foresters, *Report of the Twenty-fourth Annual Convention, Newry 1901*, Dublin, 1901, p.92.

82   See, for examples, *LCH* 20 Mar. 1903, 24 Mar. 1905, 16 Nov. 1906 and 22 Mar. 1907.

83   *LCH* 1 May 1903.

1. The main point of disembarkation, Clarence Dock was recommended as a visitor attraction in the years before the Famine influx, the Irish packets providing much amusement as they discharged their 'freight of bipeds, old and young, holding converse in jargon that would be difficult to interpret; whilst the rest of the deck will be crowded with a medley of sheep, pigs and oxen'. (LVRO)

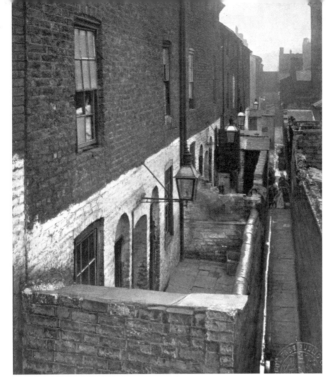

2. Back-to-back court housing around Lace Street photographed in 1899. Lace Street was notorious as one of the most insanitary areas of 'squalid Liverpool': one-third of its inhabitants died during the 'Irish fever' of 1847. (LVRO)

SALTNEY ST. MAR 8. 1920

3. Overshadowed by the newly constructed tobacco warehouse at Stanley Dock, Saltney Street offered 'safe' territory within the north end Liverpool-Irish enclave. Denied access to a city centre public hall, Maud Gonne, 'the Irish Joan of Arc', held an open-air rally in the street to condemn enlistment in the British army during the Boer War. The Gaelic League held their first open-air concert in Liverpool at number 6 court, Saltney Street. (LVRO)

4. On the distant walls of this photograph of number 2 court, Mount View, one of a series of slum pictures taken by Richard Brown in the early twentieth century, it is just possible to discern a slogan proclaiming the allegiance of the court: 'God Bless the Pope'. (LVRO)

5. Starting appropriately from Waterford House, an early twentieth-century (and rather tranquil) view along Scotland Road, the great artery of the Irish north end of Liverpool, 'unrivalled in this town and surpassed in few, for poverty, vice and crime'. (LVRO)

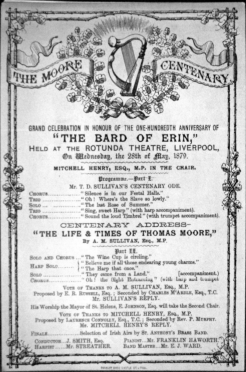

6 and 7. The 'People's Palace of Entertainment', the Rotunda in Scotland Road catered especially for the local Liverpool-Irish. The latest 'Irish' shows and spectacles on tour from Dublin shared the stage with the ever-popular Irish melodramas of Dion Boucicault and Hubert O'Grady. In May 1879 it was the venue for the centenary celebrations in honour of Thomas Moore, 'The Bard of Erin', with music by T.D. Sullivan and a special address by his brother and former editor of *The Nation*, A.M. Sullivan, MP, an ever-popular guest in Liverpool. (LVRO)

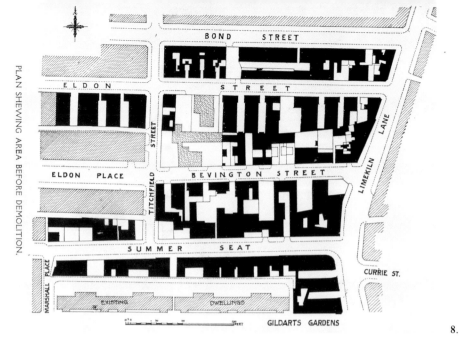

PLAN SHEWING AREA BEFORE DEMOLITION.

BOND STREET

ELDON STREET

TITCHFIELD STREET

ELDON PLACE

BEVINGTON STREET

LIMEKILN LANE

SUMMER SEAT

MARSHALL PLACE

CURRIE ST.

EXISTING DWELLINGS

GILDARTS GARDENS

8.

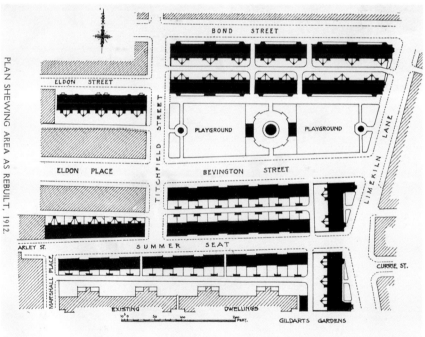

PLAN SHEWING AREA AS REBUILT. 1912.

BOND STREET

ELDON STREET

TITCHFIELD STREET

PLAYGROUND   PLAYGROUND

ELDON PLACE

BEVINGTON STREET

LIMEKILN LANE

ARLEY ST.

SUMMER SEAT

MARSHALL PLACE

CURRIE ST.

EXISTING DWELLINGS

GILDARTS GARDENS

9.

8–11. Liverpool's reputation as the most progressive housing authority in Britain before the First World War owed much to the efforts of Austin Harford, leader of the Irish Nationalists on the city council, and to the success of the Bevington Street scheme with its 'self-contained' cottages and flats and open spaces. The new buildings facing Limekiln Lane, however, were in tenement form but with design modifications (individual front doors opening on to balconies) to ensure single defensible space. (LVRO, except 11, Crosby Library)

10.

11.

12. Thomas Burke, an Irish Nationalist member of the city council and the historian of *Catholic Liverpool*, was also an accomplished photographer. His studies of Irish street-sellers (or 'Mary Ellens'), include a number of shots taken at the rag market near Fox Street, forerunner of the famous Paddy's Market. (LVRO)

13. A characteristically posed photograph by Richard Eastham from around 1902 depicting slum children outside the rooms of the Food and Betterment Association in Limekiln Lane. Given this location, it is not surprising that most recipients of this charity, forerunner of the League of Well-Doers, were Liverpool-Irish. (LVRO)

14. Through their stock and premises, marine stores, such as this depicted here in Athol Street, offered a number of services, not always strictly legal, to complement the 'secondary economy' of the streets on which many poor Liverpool-Irish depended. The Liverpool-Irish, John Denvir recorded, displayed considerable aptitude for such 'dealing'. (LVRO)

15. One of the many Irish street characters who 'performed' for a living on the streets, this disabled man and his dog, photographed by Richard Eastham in 1901, worked the pitch outside the door of the Empire Theatre. (LVRO)

16. The first mission church in the south end, appropriately named St Patrick's, opened for worship in 1827. Built in classical style, it was financed by 'penny collections' among poor Irish Catholics. (LVRO)

17–18. The 'mother church' of the north end, St Anthony's, a small chapel built by French refugees, was rebuilt in the early 1830s in the newly fashionable Gothic style, to cope with the increasing numbers of Irish migrants clustered around Scotland Road. Beneath the church with its impressive interior a vaulted crypt provided over 600 burial spaces.
(altar, Joe McLoughlin; crypt, Graeme Dunne)

19. One of the 'famine churches' opened in 1848, St Augustine's was built as 'a temple close to the spot where the heart-broken exile, flying from his own loved, but misgoverned land, just places his foot on a friendly shore'. As the population declined amid urban redevelopment a century or so later, the church (as depicted here in the 1970s) was used as a builder's warehouse prior to demolition in 1997. (© NTPL/E. Chambré Hardman Collection)

20. Mass at Holy Cross, another of the 'famine' missions founded in 1848, was said in a room over a cowhouse in Standish Street until the church, depicted in this watercolour by Herdman, opened in 1860 under the charge of the Oblate Brothers. (LVRO)

21–22. In 1933, in the depth of inter-war depression, the foundation stone was laid amid great ceremony for 'a great House of God in the metropolis of Northern Catholicity'. Designed by Lutyens, the proposed cathedral, located on the former workhouse site on Brownlow Hill, was an extravagant prestige project to symbolise the Catholic contribution to Liverpool. Only the crypt was completed before funds ran out. Construction work on Gibberd's radically different 'Paddy's Wigwam' design began in the early 1960s. (LVRO)

21.

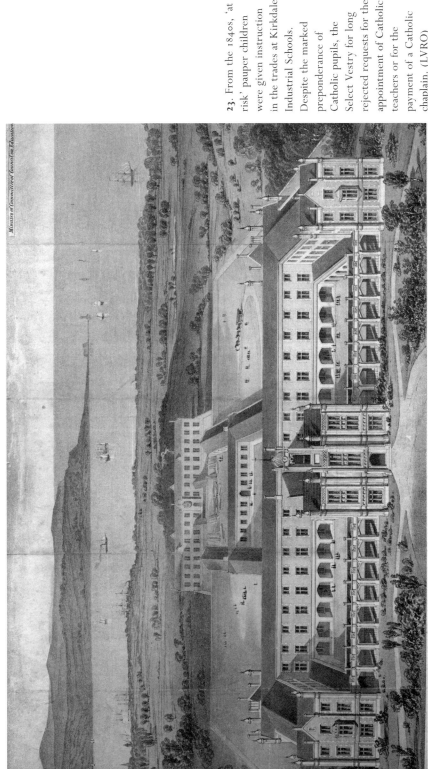

22

Minutes of Committee of Council on Education

23. From the 1840s, 'at risk' pauper children were given instruction in the trades at Kirkdale Industrial Schools. Despite the marked preponderance of Catholic pupils, the Select Vestry for long rejected requests for the appointment of Catholic teachers or for the payment of a Catholic chaplain. (LVRO)

24. By teaching seamanship and other skills, the *Clarence*, a Catholic reformatory for young offenders, sought to take account of the special needs of local troublesome youths. Such advantages notwithstanding, the facility was prone to bouts of mutinous indiscipline and outbreaks of fire, as on this occasion in 1884. (LVRO)

under surveillance by Special Branch in its reports on the 'revolutionary underground' to ethnic publicans like Hugh O'Donnell, successor to Dandy Pat Byrne as landlord of the Morning Star, a member of the Gaelic League, and an acquaintance of Dr Mark Ryan, the IRB leader in London.[84] Most members, police reports noted, 'are strong Nationalists, but not of the secret society type, as they did not hob nob with the extreme set in Dublin'.[85] In 1902 Peter Murphy of the Irish Depot and Catholic Repository in Scotland Road, the leading IRB activist in Liverpool and a member of INF branch '98, and P.J. Daly, fruiterer, tobacconist, INP councillor for the North Scotland ward and treasurer of the Liverpool District INF, were both nominated for the office of Grand High Chief Ranger – the Harp of Erin Fife and Drum Band accompanied Daly on his victory parade through the north end.[86]

The INF hastily invented a tradition of anniversaries and memorials, the cultural base which facilitated the display of unity. The sacred high point of the year for the INF in Liverpool was the anniversary commemoration of the Manchester Martyrs – Allen, Larkin and O'Brien – the 'noble-hearted three' hanged at Salford gaol on 23 November 1867 on insecure and unsafe evidence for the murder of a policeman during a Fenian rescue operation.[87] Commenced in 1898, the magnificent memorial to the martyrs in St Joseph's cemetery, Moston (now much vandalised), was the work of John Geraghty, sculptor and monumental mason, who was also commissioned for the memorial cross at St Patrick's to mark the 50th anniversary of the 'martyr priests' of 1847, heroic victims of 'Irish fever'.[88] An INP councillor in Bootle, where he was subsequently a leading force in the successful campaign against incorporation into Liverpool, Geraghty was also a member of the local 'inner circle' of the Amnesty Association, described in Special Branch reports as 'merely a blind for organising the IRB', and Grand High Chief Ranger of the INF in 1897.[89] Special Branch estimates of the crowds at the unveiling ceremony, held in inclement weather (a 'perfect hurricane of rain') in August 1900, ranged from 6000 to 20,000, three-quarters of whom wore INF regalia and 'displayed a good

---

[84]   For O'Donnell's manifold Irish activities, see *LCH* 27 Aug. and 5 Oct. 1897; 5 Feb. 1898; and 7 and 21 Sept. 1900. He also owned a hotel in Donegal.

[85]   CBS Précis Box 2, 1 Aug. 1898.

[86]   *LCH* 31 Oct. 1902.

[87]   *LCH* 30 Nov. 1900.

[88]   *CT* 7 Oct. 1898.

[89]   CBS Précis Box 1, 23 Jan. 1895 and 29 Jan. 1897. See also the obituary in *LCH* 29 Mar. 1913.

deal of military order and discipline'.[90] Thereafter, the anniversary itself was marked by an annual medley of special processions with black feathers worn in the headgear (another innovation of the 'progressive' Father McFadden branch which had already introduced the carrying of pikes at regular INF processions), Irish concerts, and 'demonstrations' with honoured guests from across the Irish Sea.[91] Commemorations had to be abandoned in 1909, however, in the wake of the worst sectarian violence in Liverpool's history, 'a perfect epidemic of terror'.

Despite its registration as a non-sectarian and non-political friendly society, the INF was included in the list of societies restricted by new regulations for street meetings and processions drawn up by the 'Peace Conference' chaired by the Earl of Derby following further sectarian disturbances during the 'general' strike of 1911 (see chapter 7 below). This was rather ironic as the INF now faced serious competition from explicitly sectarian agencies of collective mutuality seeking registration as 'approved societies' under the terms of the National Insurance Act. There was some delay in the INF gaining registration itself as it insisted on 'suiting the special requirements of the Order and making State Insurance subsidiary to nationality': thousands of non-Irish Catholic applicants were apparently rejected as the INF continued to restrict membership to those of Irish birth or descent.[92] 'As a Forester myself for many years, I am glad your officials are taking steps to secure for your members the benefits of the Act', Austin Harford opined, as Liverpool became the headquarters for the Central Council of the INF under the National Insurance scheme: 'Every Irishman who values the history, traditions and aspirations if his country should today, more than ever, associate himself with Irish societies like the Foresters, which besides being national, is one in which democratic ideals and true brotherhood are marked features.'[93] By this time, however, there were alternatives on offer: the new National Catholic Benefit and Thrift Society and – a more serious threat to the INF – the revivified Ancient Order of Hibernians (AOH).

Many INF members resented the Catholic Church jumping on the bandwagon. 'Until the Insurance Act came on the carpet, and the assistance of the State and the employers was forthcoming, there had been no similar attempt to organise Catholics in one great body', T. Phelan complained: 'He

---

90   CBS Précis Box 2, 6 Aug. 1900.

91   *LCH* 27 July 1900.

92   *LCH* 13 and 20 July, and 2 Nov. 1912.

93   *LCH* 8 June 1912. Harford was initiated into the '98 branch in Sept. 1900, see *LCH* 14 Sept. 1900.

thought that Irish National Forestry, which gave benefits in the past which no other body would give, had a claim on all Irishmen prior to that of any other organisation.'[94] While conscious of the needs of non-Irish members of the flock, Bishop Whiteside was diplomatic and conciliatory in his pronouncements on the INF: 'No pressure must be used by any one to get people to join the Catholic societies. The main point was that Catholics should remain true to the Church, and that could be done as well in the Irish National Foresters as in any other society.'[95]

Restricted to Irish Catholics, the revival of the AOH with its Ribbonite links and heritage was a far more serious challenge to the pre-eminence of the INF. Having been through interminable factional disputes and schisms in the United States, the main wing of the AOH had become associated with constitutional ways and means by the end of the nineteenth century, and had even acquired Papal approval. While jealously defending its culture of passwords and signs, the proud heritage of heroic struggle in the 'dark days' of the past, the now respectable AOH insisted it was 'not oath-bound, and admitted the Catholic clergy to all its deliberations, and, therefore, in no sense could it be termed secret'.[96] Although it progressed rapidly in Catholic Belfast in the wake of unity discussions around the Board of Erin in 1905, the AOH was completely overshadowed by the INF in Liverpool until the implementation of the National Insurance Act, when it began an aggressive advertising campaign:

> The Society being the oldest, and numerically strongest, Catholic Society in Ireland, England, Scotland and Wales, is enabled to give equal Benefits (better in most cases) to any other Society. Irish Men and Women who believe that Irishmen are capable of managing their own affairs should join the A.O.H. The Society is managed by Themselves for Themselves. The only Catholic Society that stands for God and Country.[97]

In 1912 there was just one division in Merseyside, but by early 1913 there were nine divisions in Liverpool and five in Birkenhead and New Ferry, with a number of special seamen's sections for Irish Catholic crew members of vessels

---

94   *LCH* 6 Jan. 1912.

95   *LCH* 17 Feb. 1912.

96   *LCH* 8 June 1912. For the re-branding of the AOH in America, see Kevin Kenny, 'The Molly Maguires and the Catholic Church', *Labor History*, 36, 1995, pp.345–76; and for its appeal in Belfast, see A.C. Hepburn, *A Past Apart: Studies in the History of Catholic Belfast 1850–1950*, Belfast, 1996, ch. 9.

97   *LCH* 15 June 1912.

such as the *Mauretania, Lusitania, Carmonia* and *Adriatic*. Previously identified
with the INF, Father O'Byrne (and several other Catholic clergy) welcomed
the advance of the explicitly Catholic AOH. P.J. Kelly, a collector for the
Royal Liver Friendly Society, future INP councillor and President of the Irish
Self Determination League, came to prominence through promotion of the
AOH, 'the only Catholic and National friendly society in the world'. 'The first
principle of membership of the Order', he noted approvingly, 'was practical
Catholicity.' [98] Other advocates stressed 'the many advantages the Order
possessed over mere collecting and distributing societies ... the wide scope of
its energies, its literary department, unemployment register, foreign bureau,
and social activity'.[99]

Although the AOH was catching up fast, the INF remained the pre-eminent
organisation in pre-war Irish Liverpool. Appropriately, it took the lead in co-
ordinating the 'Liverpool Irishmen's Demonstration' as a counter to Carson's
monster Unionist 'Ulster Day' in 1912 held, in accordance with the new
regulations on processions, out of the city centre in Sheil Park. 'No Irishman
was worthy of the name unless he belonged to some Irish organisation', Harford
proclaimed as he rallied forces for the final stages of the Home Rule campaign:
'The man who merely shouted for Ireland was of no use ... They were there as
Irish Nationalists to show what the spirit of Irish Nationality was in Liverpool.' [100]
A few weeks later the anniversary commemoration for the Manchester Martyrs
was another great rallying occasion in support of the recently passed Home
Rule bill. The *Liverpool Catholic Herald* calculated the numbers from the various
societies on parade: the INF 8000; the Catholic Defence Association (formed
after the riots of 1909) 5000; the AOH 3000; the Gaelic League 300 and the
Gaelic Athletic Association 200.[101] From its pivotal base in Liverpool, the INF
looked forward to safeguarding a brave new world of Irish Home Rule:

> Irish Exiles! With the passage of Home Rule the chief reason for the
> existence of Irish political clubs ceases. They have done good work. Who
> are to be their successors? The Irish National Foresters is the only Society in
> England for the administration of the Insurance Act benefits that can speak
> for the whole Irish nation. Remember, the greatest bulwark for Ireland is a
> strong Irish organisation in England. Are you doing your share? [102]

---

98   *LCH* 3 and 10 May 1913.
99   *LCH* 18 May 1912.
100   *LCH* 12 Oct. 1912.
101   *LCH* 30 Nov. 1912.
102   *LCH* 15 June 1912.

5

Electoral Politics: Towards Home Rule

E LECTORAL POLITICS in Irish Liverpool underwent a diverse (at times bewildering) range of hyphenated political allegiance before the consolidation of 'Nat-Labism' in the years before the First World War. Taking account of recurrent socio-economic, generational and other tensions within a large migrant enclave over time, this chapter endeavours to chart the convoluted route, nearly but never entirely completed, from grateful dependence upon the Liberals to defiant 'Home Rule' political independence. Alternative forms of extra-parliamentary nationalist politics, from the Confederates through the Fenians to the IRB, are considered in the next chapter.

The Liberal alignment had a venerable past stretching back to the campaigning days of Daniel O'Connell, the 'Liberator'. In seeking emancipation, Catholics identified with the Liberal project of civil and religious liberty, but this was called into question by subsequent defence of denominational education. On this recurrent point of tension, Catholics drew away from the Liberals and their increasingly vociferous Nonconformist secularist activists towards expedient clericalist alliance with Tory Anglicans. Similarly with Repeal of the Act of Union, there was a strong initial Liberal link, but the relationship was to be strained by subsequent elaboration of a distinctive form of Irish nationalism: faith-based and compatible with Catholic ultramontanism, it was anathema to British Liberal norms. Gladstonian Home Rule restored the old alignment but the Liberals' failure to deliver on the project strained the patience of the INP.

The INP developed into an efficient Parnellite electoral machine in Liverpool, able to challenge the Liberals and gain control of the north end of the city. A range of key supporters ensured a decent turn-out at the polls, the restrictive franchise and registration requirements which limited the party's electoral base among the 'poor Irish' notwithstanding: Irish lawyers, adept at adding names to the electoral register; sympathetic priests, well versed in marshalling the vote at School Board elections; ambitious publicans and ethnic entrepreneurs, keen to progress to political prominence by rallying their customer base; and militant activists prepared to undertake the routine slog of electoral politics in the hope of seeing their cherished policies implemented. There were structural and cultural limitations, however, to further advance. Parliamentary constituencies and municipal wards were rigid geo-political categories – the Liverpool-Irish enclave had no such precise spatial boundaries. Outside the 'majority wards' of the north end there was no prospect of Irish electoral success other than through some form of proportional representation. However, the persistent call for 'equitable citizenship' for the Catholic Irish, generally estimated between a quarter and a third of the overall population, tended to be counter-productive, leading to endless rehearsal of the disproportionate Irish presence in criminal and 'casualty' statistics, factors which called into question Irish qualification for full British citizenship.

Within its own confines in the Scotland Division (T.P. O'Connor's personal parliamentary fiefdom for some four decades), the smooth operation of the electoral machine was interrupted at times of tension between hard-working militant activists out in the wards and the moderate representatives whose election they secured, pragmatic residual Liberals once in the council chamber. Structural stress was accentuated by factors of generation, provenance and socio-economic status. From 1898 local-born INP councillors (second-generation Liverpool-born Irish like the Harford brothers) outnumbered their Irish-born counterparts after which the party purportedly displayed less interest in the fate of Ireland than in the immediate needs of the local Catholic community in housing and employment. This is a false distinction. The Nat-Labism embraced by the younger generation of INP councillors (drawn for the most part from lower social ranks than their predecessors) was as ardent in commitment to Irish nationalism as to social reform, both policies exemplifying a final rejection of Liberalism. Forthright in its independence from British political parties and committed to denominational education, extensive social reform and full-blown Irish nationalism, the INP under Austin Harford was the hegemonic political force in Edwardian Irish Liverpool, leaving little space or need for class, confessional or gaelic alternatives, such as the Labour Party, the Catholic Federation or Sinn Fein.

The pursuit of civil and religious liberty linked the local Liberal (predominantly Unitarian) elite, English Catholics of recusant and gentry stock from in and around Liverpool, and the increasing number of Catholic arrivals from Ireland. There were already stresses and strains, however, following Daniel O'Connell's success in securing Catholic Emancipation in 1829. To the dismay of 'respectable' commercial opinion (Liberal, Catholic and otherwise), the 'low Irish' were keen to follow 'the Liberator' into campaigns to repeal the Act of Union. 'Dan's first appearance in Liverpool', the *Times* reported ruefully in January 1836, was accompanied by unwelcome boisterousness on the streets in the 'low parts of the town':

> bands of music, flags, banners, etc belonging to the Hibernian clubs, were instantly brought into action and, parading through the populous parts of the town, a large concourse of persons, chiefly Irish, was speedily collected together, and the town thrown into confusion, to the great annoyance of the respectable portion of the community, and the hindrance of business.[1]

Such politics of disorder were disowned by socially exclusive and politically conservative resident recusant Catholics. Determined not to jeopardise their newly emancipated status, these 'Catholic Protectors', as Ryan Dye categorises them, regarded repeal as 'too political, too proletarian, and too Irish for their support'. These concerns were accentuated considerably among the local clergy, terrified by the prospect of something far more objectionable among their newly arrived migrant parishioners: secret, oath-bound 'Ribbonite' forms of Irish nationalism. Unable to eradicate Ribbonism by proscription, priests sought to outbid its mutual and welfare functions through concerted efforts to shift the focus of migrant associational culture from the pub to the parish. The new clerically controlled Catholic societies soon sought a place in St Patrick's Day parades, marching behind the Hibernian Societies whose Ribbonite members wore their shamrocks in distinctive manner as instructed by their 'Boards' and who remained to the fore in the inevitable clashes with Orangemen at the end of proceedings. When the magistrates called for a ban on the procession in 1845 in an effort to curb sectarian violence, the clergy and their societies readily complied. The Hibernian Societies, however, marched in proud defiance only

---

1   *Times* 29 Jan. 1836.

to find the doors first of St Patrick's then of St Anthony's closed firmly against them. Thenceforth, Ryan Dye maintains, the Irish in Liverpool faced a stark political choice, normally determined he suggests on socio-economic lines: they could either join the Catholic Protectors in pursuit of spiritual and social respectability (the default middle-class option) or else embrace Irish nationalism (the 'low Irish' preference).[2]

Richard Sheil, the leading Irish Catholic merchant in Liverpool, seemingly personified the first approach. Elected on a Liberal ticket in Scotland Ward in 1835, he was for long the only Catholic member of the Town Council. A founder member of the (aptly named) Protector Society (1839) and first President of the Catholic Club (1844), he sought to defend and promote Catholic interests through electoral registration and by adoption of modern Tridentine norms of religious observance, ahead of the 'devotional revolution' yet to reach Ireland. Established as a counterweight to Hugh McNeile's Protestant Association in the fierce controversy over the schools issue – in 1841 the Tories brought an end to the Liberals' 'crucial experiment' of non-denominational public education – the Catholic Club under Sheil's presidency brought together prosperous middle-class Catholics, Irish and otherwise, in continuing support of Liberal candidates drawn from Unitarian and progressive ranks within the mercantile elite.[3] A pillar of mercantile respectability, Sheil acquired the 'solid and practical character of Englishmen', but he did not conceal his 'rich, mellifluous brogue' or his Irishness:

> Ireland has not a son who loves his country better … He is ever to be found at the head of any movement which, in his opinion, is calculated to promote her political or religious welfare, and his enthusiasm on such occasions shows with what heartiness and zeal he espouses the cause of Ireland.[4]

His assimilationist profile notwithstanding, what mattered to Sheil was not making the Irish British but keeping the Irish Catholic, a priority which was to add further strain to the liberal alliance in the wake of the Famine influx. After

---

2   Ryan Dye, 'Catholic protectionism or Irish nationalism? Religion and politics in Liverpool, 1829–1845', *Journal of British Studies*, 40, 2001, pp.357–90; Head Constable Dowling's report, 18 Mar. 1842 in CO 904/9, ff.203–206.

3   The Protector Society introduced an innovative instalment system of rate-paying qualification until declared invalid, see Brady, *T.P. O'Connor*, pp.27–28; J. Murphy, *The Religious Problem in English Education: The Crucial Experiment*, Liverpool, 1959.

4   H. Shimmin, *Pen-and-Ink Sketches of Liverpool Town Councillors*, Liverpool, 1866, pp.87–91. See also the obituary notice in *Porcupine* 4 Mar. 1871.

the political events of 1848 – when there were real fears of major diversionary activity in Liverpool to assist revolution in Ireland – the local liberal press added its weight to the volume of anti-Irish prejudice. There was a further hardening of attitudes on discovery that charitable funds, intended for the Irish poor, were diverted to assist the reinstallation of the Pope in Rome.[5] Denounced as 'Papal aggression', the restoration of the Catholic hierarchy in England in 1850 strained relations to breaking point: 'the smouldering fires of strife have been rekindled; party cries that were nearly forgotten have been raised again with greater vigour than ever; passions that have nothing to do with religion are taking up her colours, and professing her name'.[6]

Stunned by Liberal hostility, Sheil and other prominent Catholics sought to improve the Irish image in Liverpool. Particular attention was accorded to the promotion of upward social mobility among Liverpool-Irish youths. Having introduced the refined indoor soirée to replace the boisterous street procession on St Patrick's Day, Father Nugent took advantage of the intervals between performances to lecture the audience, drawing 'the attention of young men to the various openings which were constantly occurring in the customs and in the mercantile and marine services of this country, urging that by enterprise and energy they might obtain situations of trust and respectability'.[7] New post-elementary educational facilities were opened, supplementing the Jesuit provision at St Francis Xavier's, for the benefit of the middle classes, 'the bone and sinew of Catholicity in this town'. An extension of the Catholic Middle School established in Rodney Street in 1851, Nugent's Catholic Institute (which boasted 'Classical' and 'Commercial' sections) moved into new premises in Hope Street in 1853, opened with some ceremony by Cardinal Wiseman. Under the motto, 'Religion first, Literature next', the Institute broadcast its facilities and achievements through its own literary journal:

> Here was the Catholic Institute of Liverpool, with its Oratorian services, Confraternities, its Company of St Philip; its three priests; its body of twelve professors; its High school, Middle school and Night school;

---

5   *LM* 1 and 11 Aug. 1848; *Jones* (a satirical periodical) 10 Mar., 5 May and 14 July 1849.

6   Liverpool Domestic Mission Society, *Report Presented at the Fourteenth Annual General Meeting of the Liverpool Domestic Mission Society, by their Minister to the Poor*, Liverpool, 1851, pp.19–21.

7   *LM* 19 Mar. 1861. For the move indoors in celebrations of St Patrick's Day elsewhere in the diaspora, see M. Cronin and D. Adair, *The Wearing of the Green: A History of St Patrick's Day*, London, 2002, p.60.

its weekly Lectures, its Reading Room, News Room, and Library; its Gymnasium; and above all its serried phalanx of young men, who make its hall their pleasure, their home, and their safeguard.[8]

Further encouragement in the path of respectability and upward mobility was offered by the network of Catholic Young Men's Societies (CYMS). Established in Limerick in 1849 by the Rev. Dr O'Brien, the CYMS enjoyed rapid growth in Liverpool in the 1850s. There were eight branches in 1860 with 2700 members, assembled in St George's Hall for their first annual soirée to hear Lord Edward Howard, the leading lay Catholic in the country, calling upon them to become 'more thrifty, more frugal, more sober – so their ranks might number a far larger middle-class than they at present did'.[9] Here was 'the admirable basis' for the organisation of other associations 'calculated to advance the moral and material welfare of the Catholic people', as the *Lancashire Free Press* noted:

> Wherever the Young Men's Society is in active operation, and its principles and practices energetically carried out, it will be found that the Society of St Vincent de Paul and the Christian Doctrine Confraternity are also in prosperous condition – that tontine societies, benefit clubs, and in some instances, building societies, are established, for the purpose of promoting those habits of industry and frugality without which the great majority of our people cannot expect to raise themselves from the humble position in which they have been placed by centuries of misrule and oppression.[10]

Through the CYMS and its associational culture (with competitive league competitions quickly established in activities ranging from debating to billiards), Irish Catholic young men could enjoy 'all the advantages which the wealthy and great possess in their magnificent club-rooms. The wealthiest aristocrat of the land cannot have more intellectual enjoyments by resorting to the Carlton, than the working man of Liverpool who frequents the room of the Young Men's Society.'[11] The training ground in debating and other skills for future INP city councillors, the CYMS continued to prosper but the hopes attached to the

---

[8]   *Catholic Institute Magazine*, Oct. 1855; *LFP* 21 Jan. 1860; Bennett, *Father Nugent*, ch. 2; Burke, *Catholic History*, p.111.

[9]   *LM* 18 Jan. 1865.

[10]   *LFP* 10 Mar. 1860.

[11]   *LFP* 10 Mar. 1860.

formation of a Central Council in Liverpool in 1860, the construction of a local Catholic Working Men's College, were not to be fulfilled.

Beyond the confessional framework, the enhanced concern for status and respectability was embedded in the Liverpool Irish Rifle Volunteer Corps (64th LRV), known as the 'Irish Brigade'. As Anglo-French relations deteriorated in the 'invasion scare' of 1859, Liverpool raised the first Volunteer battalion, beginning the permanent revival of the volunteer movement in Britain. The Liverpool-Irish were quick to participate, forming their corps (soon one of the largest in the town) early in 1860. Its leading officers were Daniel Powell and Peter Silvester Bidwill, merchants in the Liverpool corn trade and prominent members of the reconstituted Catholic Club; inevitably, Nugent was appointed chaplain to the unit. In line with other Rifle Volunteers, the 64th LRV, Simon Jones notes, 'provided an opportunity for social advancement, both for the moneyed middle class to prove that as Volunteer officers they aspired to a pseudo gentry status, and as an opportunity for the skilled worker in the ranks to demonstrate his increased standing'.[12] Subsequent events in Europe, however, were soon to draw attention to Catholic apartness. As it became clear that Italian nationalism and the temporal power of the papacy could not coexist, the Liverpool-Irish stood outside the union of sentiment over Italy which brought the great Victorian Liberal party into being.

In rallying to support the 'holy father in his "present difficulties"', Irish Liverpool condemned Victor Emmanuel and Cavour as 'the Henry the Eighth and Cromwell of Sardinia'. Following a fund-raising meeting at the Catholic Institute where 'there was no baragon jacket but mine', Felix Brennan opened a collection fund on the waterfront:

> I worked on the Public Works at the time that the Holy Father's generous aid relieved many a hungry stomach, now thirteen years ago in poor and persecuted Ireland. How are we now to act? I am only a dock labourer myself with six children. I will cheerfully give a day's wages.[13]

There was consternation and outrage in local liberal circles at such support for ultramontanism, 'that curse of Europe': 'even the strongest-kneed Liberals are occasionally pulled up very short, and made very uncomfortable, by the

---

12   Simon Jones, 'Fenianism in the Liverpool Irish Rifle Volunteers', unpublished MA thesis, University of Liverpool, 1997. See also Helen McCartney, *Citizen Soldiers: The Liverpool Territorials in the First World War*, Cambridge, 2005, p.17.

13   *LFP* 24 Mar. 1860.

ultramontane and other enormities of the Roman Catholic Church', *Porcupine*
observed.[14] Anathema to advocates of liberal nationalism, ultramontanism
was by no means incompatible, however, with other inflexions of nationalism.
Indeed, it encouraged a specifically confessional formulation of the Irish national
cause. Prompted by the plebiscites to legitimise the annexation of Tuscany,
Parma, Emilia, Modena and the Romagna by the kingdom of Piedmont-
Sardinia, the Irish National Petition Campaign of 1860 (which included 23,577
signatures from Liverpool) marked a rapprochement between nationalists and
the church on Merseyside:

> we tender our warmest and best thanks to the Catholic clergy of Liverpool
> and Birkenhead who have afforded every facility and aided to obtain the
> signatures of our countrymen at the various chapels to the petition for
> Home Rule: and we are, therefore determined as Catholics ever to uphold
> that golden link of affection and attachment as laymen to our venerated
> clergymen and the head of our church, even should the sacrifice of our
> lives be required.[15]

Thenceforth, the local Catholic press extolled the virtues of Catholic
Irish nationalism. The most ardent support came (as is often the case in
fundamentalist ideological propagation) from a marginal 'outsider', S.B. Harper,
editor of the *Northern Press* (later renamed the *Catholic Times*), which, thanks
to the intervention of Nugent and a loan from John Treacy of the St Patrick's
Burial Society, replaced the collapsed *Lancashire Free Press*. Transplanted from
Scotland, Harper, an 'honorary' Irishman, had all the ardour of a convert
from Anglicanism. Ultramontane to the core, his platform was nevertheless
Irish nationalist, launched (in a pre-emptive exercise against the local Fenians)
with a free print of T.B. McManus, on the occasion of the translation of the
Confederate's remains from California to Ireland. The tragic hero of the
'revolution' of 1848, McManus, a wealthy Liverpool-Irish businessman who had
'staked his life and suffered temporal ruin and exile in behalf of his country', was
an object lesson in glorious failure – and a suitable counterweight to Garibaldi,
characterised by Harper as an 'illiterate freebooter' flattered by 'bigot' Liberal
adulation. In canonising McManus, Harper deployed a recurring trope of
constitutional nationalism in which 'honest and honourable' physical force
(but not random terror) was legitimised and memorialised in defeat. McManus

14   *Porcupine* 20 July and 18 Oct. 1862.
15   *Liverpool Weekly Mercury* 1 Sept. 1860; *Irishman* 13 Apr. 1861.

was to be revered not as role model for active imitation but as martyr symbol of Irish grievances. These wrongs were best addressed, Harper insisted, by a reconstructed O'Connellite mobilisation firmly under clerical control, an exclusive form of Catholic nationalism, religious not racial, constitutional not Fenian:

> there are two ideas of nationality: one which inspires infidels and revolutionists in their attack on the Pope, and another of which fidelity to the Church is an essential element ... What identifies the nationality the most, what gives it its form and shape and individuality, is its religion ... Hence the true nationality of Ireland consists − not in her being Celtic, for she is not so except in part − but in her being Catholic. This is the determining feature of her nationality.[16]

The local clergy added their support. 'Elsewhere there seemed to be an alienation between nationality and the Church but it was not so in Ireland', Father Walsh averred: 'Elsewhere to be a nationalist was to be an infidel; but in Ireland to be a lover of true freedom was to be a good Catholic.'[17]

Harper's fundamentalist views, however, perturbed a number of leading lay Irish Catholics in Liverpool. They were anxious to restore links with the Liberals, an urgent priority as the *Liverpool Mercury* 'the organ of Protestant Liberals has become more bitterly antagonistic to Catholics and their creed than the organs of Orangeism'.[18] In an effort to mend fences, M.J. Whitty, Catholic editor of the *Daily Post*, propounded an ecumenical and pluralist approach, duly ridiculed by Harper as 'kind of pic-nic omnibus, without a conductor'.[19] The hapless Whitty, *Porcupine* observed, 'is accused by the *Mercury* of being a Roman Catholic; he is denounced by the *Northern Press* for not being one'.[20] Divisions widened after Harper all but applauded the Birkenhead Catholics who went on the rampage (in the absence of adequate policing) in October 1862, outraged by provocative bright orange advertisements for a pro-Garibaldi meeting. Previously sympathetic to Catholic 'civil and religious liberty' claims

---

16   This analysis is based on the incomplete (and only extant?) run of *NP* held at the Newspaper Library, Colindale, which covers the period 4 Jan. to 6 Dec. 1862. The editorial 'Nationality' in 19 Apr. 1862 is followed by a reprint of the foundation article on 'The meaning of the honour paid to the remains of M'Manus'.
17   *NP* 1 Feb. 1862.
18   *NP* 2 Aug. 1862.
19   *NP* 25 Jan. 1862.
20   *Porcupine* 28 June 1862.

for equitable treatment in prisons, workhouses and the like, *Porcupine* withdrew support after this 'Reign of the Shillelagh' when 'Murty Mulligan' became 'the dictator of Birkenhead'.[21] A useful barometer of liberal opinion, *Porcupine* moved into outright opposition when two members of the Catholic Club, James Whitty and John Yates, having joined Richard Sheil on the Town Council as Liberals, chose to denigrate Garibaldi in the council chamber: 'It has come to this: – Roman Catholics are liberal so long as they have to secure anything from Protestant Governments. They are advocates of despotism at all other times.'[22]

There was little prospect of reconciliation as Liberals came under increasing pressure from Nonconformist faddists and activists. Even so, Catholics still cherished the hope of working with the Liberals to secure the additional third seat for Liverpool, promised in forthcoming parliamentary reform to facilitate 'minority representation', for one of their own faith. Such direct parliamentary representation had long been the ambition of James Whitty, the 'Daniel O'Connell of Liverpool', who founded the Irish Catholic Club in 1851 with the aim of returning a Catholic MP (on a Liberal ticket) within 20 years. Around 1860, it seems, the Irish Catholic Club subsumed the original Catholic Club of 1844 but (somewhat confusingly) decided to take its name.[23] The Club's annual dinner at a local hotel, accompanied by wines 'of that *recherché* character for which the cellars of the Adelphi enjoy a more than local celebrity', was an occasion to display the requisite political respectability, in Bidwill's words from the chair in 1862, 'to give offence to no party, and from our position as citizens to be moderate in all our acts, at the same time consistent'.[24] The following year, he outlined the Catholic case for greater participation, noting that 'their co-religionists numbered one-third of the whole population (cheers). As in proportion to their numbers the Catholics bore their share of the public burdens, it could not be considered unfair if they sought a due representation in our local and parliamentary institutions.' James Whitty frequently drew attention to the statistical force of Catholic claims as 'one-third of the whole public body'.[25] Speaking at Nugent's St Patrick's Day soirée in 1865, J.B. Aspinall, subsequently the first Catholic Recorder of Liverpool, followed the numerical logic through to the possibilities offered by imminent parliamentary reform: 'The Catholics comprised one-third of the population of the town and

21   *Porcupine* 18 Oct. 1862.
22   *Porcupine* 16 Apr. 1864.
23   *LFP* 4 Feb. 1860.
24   *DP* 19 Mar. 1862.
25   *DP* 20 Mar. 1863.

they should make it their business to insist, as a matter of right, that one at least of the three members, which Liverpool was to have under the operation of the new Reform Bill, should be a Catholic.'[26]

With their eyes set on gaining the minority parliamentary seat for one of their own, prominent Irish Catholics in the 1860s repudiated any connection with unconstitutional or disreputable inflexions of 'Irishness', whether separatist, secret or violent forms of nationalism, or the sleaze and corruption surrounding the St Patrick's Burial Society. Nor was there any support for non-sectarian Irish initiatives. When Dr Andrew Commins, a barrister on the Northern Circuit, prominent in the St Patrick's Burial Society litigation, established the Irish Patriotic Society in 1862, 'an associated body capable of giving expression to their opinion as Irishmen, apart from religious sectarianism', he was taken to task in the Catholic press for 'dubbing the Church, the fidelity of the Irish people to which is their greatest glory, a sect'.[27] Far more vehement criticism was directed against oath-bound nationalist conspiracy, the 'secret society' tradition carried forward by the National Brotherhood of St Patrick (NBSP) into Fenianism. It was this Irish addiction to politics and conspiracy, carried across the Irish Sea, which, Father Porter rued, precluded Catholic advance in 'this country':

> they do not leave Irishism behind them when they come to it, and set themselves to rise in the world in order that the Church might share the glory of their position in the state. Instead of that, the Irishrie will meddle in politics, will hate England, and will form political organizations. But the most dangerous of Irish organizations are secret societies – most of all, the Fenian.[28]

After the collapse of Fenianism, however, things altered dramatically, part of the wider 'transformation in the British–Irish relationship' in the 1860s.[29] Commins stepped forward to lead the Home Rule challenge. Born in Ballybeg, Co. Carlow, Dr Commins had enjoyed a brilliant student career, first at Queen's

---

26 *LFP* 24 Mar. 1860.

27 *NP* 31 May and 7 June 1862.

28 *Irish People* 29 Apr. 1865.

29 See the editor's introduction in Peter Gray, ed., *Victoria's Ireland? Irishness and Britishness, 1837–1901*, Dublin, 2004, p.9. The 'British–Irish relationship' needs to be considered alongside contemporary discussions of citizenship, see Catherine Hall, Keith McClelland and Jane Rendall, *Defining the Victorian Nation: Class, Race, Gender and the Reform Act of 1867*, Cambridge, 2000.

College, Cork, then at London University, prior to taking up his legal practice in Liverpool, writing poetry, promoting Cobdenite financial reform and pursuing other interests – 'there was a general belief amongst Liverpool Irishmen', John Denvir observed, 'that he knew *everything*'. Closely involved in the formation and launch of Isaac Butt's Home Government Association in Dublin in 1870, founder and chair of its first British-based branch in Liverpool in January 1872, Commins emerged as 'the leading figure in the struggle for Home Rule in Great Britain' to become president of the Home Rule Confederation (HRC), and 'a household word wherever there is an Irishman'.[30] The new movement for Home Rule drew upon political realignments as Fenianism, previously feared as a serious threat of violent revolution, underwent reassessment and reformulation. Quickly rehabilitated into constitutional nationalism, Fenianism was a spent but inspirational force, another poignant symbol of Irish grievances, personified by its political prisoners whom Butt had defended and whose amnesty he now championed.[31] At the same time, Gladstone's electoral victory in Britain suggested a new Liberal commitment to Ireland, much to the delight of the president of the Catholic Club: 'there were now at the lead of the Government men with large hearts and minds filled with a determination to redress the wrongs of Irishmen'.[32]

For all the promise of these realignments, however, creed and country soon began to pull in opposite directions. In their determination to defend denominational education, some Catholics (in true 'Protector' spirit) were drawn towards the Tories, 'mysteriously reminded', *Porcupine* noted with incredulity, 'of some remote and recondite connexion between the abstract principles of Toryism and those of the Roman Catholic Church'.[33] At the same time, the more ardent Irish nationalists, dismayed by the lack of progress, sought to force the pace of the Home Rule movement to the discomfiture of moderates in Dublin and 'Catholic Whigs' in Liverpool.

As the 'capital of Catholic England', Liverpool rallied the faithful (not just the local Irish) against the 1870 Education Bill at a series of monster meetings, graced by the 'time-honoured house of Norfolk'.[34] Once again *Porcupine* was incredulous of the Catholic stance against Liberal 'progressive' legislation, as

---

30   *UI* 23 Sept. 1876; Denvir, *Life Story*, pp.171–72. On Commins' retirement, *LCH* 10 May 1913 reviewed his lengthy political career.
31   R.V. Comerford, *The Fenians in Context: Irish Politics and Society 1848–82*, Dublin, 1998, pp.170–71.
32   *LM* 18 Mar. 1870.
33   *Porcupine* 1 Feb. 1873.
34   *CT* 10 Sept. 1870.

it ridiculed the 'uncompromising denominationalism' of Bishop Goss and his successor Bishop O'Reilly:

> It seems strange that so acute a body of men as the Roman Catholic priesthood comprises cannot perceive that this undisguised admission of the fear of instruction, even in indifferent matters, not given by teachers selected by themselves affords a powerful weapon to their opponents. One would hardly have thought that heresy lurked in the alphabet, or the copy-book, or the multiplication table ... they are stirred to active exertion only because they fear unbiassed intelligence more than unreflecting ignorance.[35]

Unable to prevent the passage of the Act, Catholics subsequently struggled to ensure due implementation of Clause 25 which permitted the School Board to pay the fees of poor children attending denominational schools. Protestants protested angrily at this ill-considered concession to 'Romanists' who were 'not ratepayers, but rate receivers and consumers'. Catholics, Dr Hakes of the Church Association warned, 'were instructed in such a way as only to fit them for jails or workhouses'.[36]

The electoral consequences of the 1870 Act were readily apparent in the municipal by-election in Exchange Ward in 1871 when a substantial Catholic swing to the Tories ensured the defeat of the Liberal candidate Stitt, an opponent of Clause 25 and of the use of the (Catholic) Douai Bible in schools (offences compounded by his approval of placing a statue of the Revd Hugh McNeile in St George's Hall). Detailed scrutiny of the returns for the victorious Tory candidate, Armstrong, revealed that the new sectarian politics operated through an unwelcome import from across the Atlantic, Tammany-style 'machine' manipulation:

> Upon looking over the list of streets where the poorest Catholic voters reside *all* the votes are polled for Armstrong. This shows what use may be made in skilful, and unscrupulous hands of Mr Disraeli's 'residuum'. Here is the system adopted in New York, and which has led there to such disastrous results.[37]

---

35 *Porcupine* 5 Nov. 1870.
36 Waller, *Democracy and Sectarianism*, pp.28–30; Neil Collins, *Politics and Elections in Nineteenth-Century Liverpool*, Aldershot, 1994, ch. 6.
37 *Porcupine* 4 Nov. 1871.

The Catholic clergy, indeed, quickly developed considerable expertise in electoral matters. At the 1873 School Board elections, priests converted schools into committee rooms and held classes for 'illiterates' to instruct them (most successfully) in the compound complexities of the cumulative voting system (the five official Catholic candidates easily topped the poll for the 15 available seats).[38]

At the parliamentary by-election in 1873, however, the old Liberal alliance was patched together in the vain hope of capturing one of the Tory seats, vacant on the death of Samuel Graves, the first Irishman to serve as mayor of Liverpool (1860–61). Charles Russell, the most distinguished of the Liverpool-based Irish lawyers on the Northern Circuit (he took silk in 1872), declined the nomination of the Catholic Club, pledging his loyalty to Caine, the Liberal candidate, and to Gladstone's policies on Ireland and free trade. Having quizzed the Baptist Caine over education, a deputation from the Catholic Club reluctantly accorded him their support only because it had become apparent that Torr, the Tory candidate, had 'succumbed to the Orange Party'. Under Nugent's guidance, the Catholic Temperance Union also came out for Caine, a noted teetotaller, but also expressed a preference for Torr's education policy. There was similar lukewarm endorsement from Commins who initially put his own name forward on a devolution platform – 'I think that the Imperial legislature is overloaded, but that it might easily get rid of the most onerous and vexatious part of its burden by relegating to an Irish Federal parliament, the management of exclusively Irish affairs' – but withdrew when Caine offered to give Home Rule 'his best consideration'.[39]

By now, other nationalists were impatient for independent action at the polls at least at municipal level. As secretary of the Catholic Registration Association established by the Catholic Club in 1873, John Denvir (who had accompanied Commins to the opening meeting of the Home Government Association in Dublin in 1870 and was a fellow founding member of the HRC) became aware of the potential of the Irish vote.[40] Soon disabused of his hopes of carrying the rich merchants and Liberal councillors of the Catholic Club into the Home Rule camp, Denvir devoted his energies to securing the return of independent Irish

---

38   O'Connell, 'Irish Nationalist Party', p.179.

39   See the newspaper cuttings and other items in UL: Rathbone Papers RPIX scrapbook 9.21; *Porcupine* 1 Feb. 1873.

40   Home Government Association, *Report of the Inaugural Public Meeting of the Home Government Association*, Dublin, 1870. Three thousand new voters were registered in the first year, O'Connell, 'Irish Nationalist Party', p.135.

National councillors on the Home Rule platform propounded by his new weekly newspaper, the *United Irishman*:

> Ireland ruled by a sovereign Irish Parliament, Ireland free and independent from Malin Head to Cape Clear, and from the Irish Channel to the Atlantic, – this is the HOME RULE which must be *the essential condition of every Federal arrangement and every Imperial connection*.[41]

In promoting the candidature of Laurence Connolly in Scotland Ward in 1875, Denvir was concerned with the tactical promotion of national issues not the amelioration of local grievances:

> Ireland, even with a majority of her members pledged to Home Rule, is outvoted in the British Government; it naturally follows that if the battle is to be won at all, it must be in Great Britain where the Irish element may be looked upon as the advanced guard of the national movement. Now, there is no town in Great Britain where the Irish element is stronger than in Liverpool. Consequently, it is right that there the banner of Home Rule should be first raised on England's soil ... In the first place, a candidate elected to the Council on Home Rule principles will give stability to the movement in Liverpool, and in the next it will be a trial of strength for a Parliamentary contest in the same town when the occasion arises. There is every reason to believe that the Irish element is so strong in Liverpool that it could carry one of the three members, providing of course that due prudence were exercised in the selection of a candidate.[42]

As it was, Connolly's success in 1875 on 'the Catholic, Irish, and Home Rule platform' owed as much to Catholic as to explicitly nationalist support.

The first of the 48 Irish Nationalists who were to sit on the council between 1875 and 1922, Connolly had come to Liverpool in 1857 in connection with his brother's Dublin-based interests, but soon branched out into his own business as a fruit broker and commission merchant before moving into property speculation, gaining a fortune from resort development at New Brighton. While disavowed by the 'notables' of the Catholic Club, Connolly enjoyed the energetic support of a local priest (and accomplished canvasser) Father McGrath, while young lads

---

[41] *UI* 23 Sept. 1876.
[42] See the letter from Denvir and Alexander Bligh, 'A Home Ruler for a Liverpool Ward!', *CT* 22 Oct. 1875.

from Father Nugent's Boys' Refuge distributed handbills to rally the Catholic vote. Speaking after his victory, Connolly admitted he had come forward 'as the champion of Catholics first, and "Home Rule for Ireland" afterwards ... He certainly was not ashamed, nor was he now ashamed, to proclaim himself a Catholic first, and secondly a "Home Ruler".' [43]

Connolly's victory over the Welsh Calvinist Methodist William Williams, the highly regarded sitting Liberal member, broke the mould. The *Daily Post* spoke of 'the beginning of a new era both for Irishmen and Catholics in Liverpool'. [44] The real breakthrough, however, came in the following year, when three more INP councillors ('not the less – but rather more – good Catholics because they are good Irishmen') were elected to seats previously held by Catholic Club members. The first, Charles McArdle, originally from Castleblayney, Co. Monaghan, subsequently a wealthy cotton broker in Liverpool and 'veteran' of Nugent's Catholic Total Abstinence League, was returned unopposed, having been nominated by the HRC but without Catholic Club approval, for the Vauxhall Ward at a by-election following the death of the 'Catholic Whig' James Whitty. The last of the old generation of Catholic 'Protectors' linked to the Liberals, Whitty's demise marked the end of an era. The 'czar of the Catholic Club', he was in his later years, Denvir regretted, 'a stumbling block in the way of the Irish national cause'. [45] When the Catholic Club, now under the control of 'half a dozen anti-Irish nobodies' proposed to expel McArdle, Denvir gave vent to the pent-up anger:

> The political power of this body has of late years been gradually leaving it, and indeed it at present has no existence beyond the name. The wire-pullers, a small group of would-be respectables who keep it alive, have for a long time past taken every opportunity of thwarting and opposing the popular will if it was not directed by them. This opposition gradually assumed the shape of anti-Irishism, and the great bulk of the Catholic people of Liverpool, being Irish, soon refused to brook this insolence, and in a short time scouted the assumption of the clique to speak in the name of the Catholic people. Frenzied at seeing their power going, for it was ever on the shoulders of the Irish people these respectable *Catholics* climbed into social position, they became reckless, and now, like a drowning man

---

43   *CT* 5 Nov. 1875. Connolly left a bequest in his will to start a fund for a Catholic cathedral in Liverpool, see *LCH* 23 May 1908.

44   *DP* 1 Nov. 1875.

45   *UI* 10 Feb. 1877. See also *LCH* 18 Oct. 1901.

they are only hastening final destruction by their frantic and exhaustive struggles.[46]

There was considerable acrimony in the autumn municipal elections when two leading figures from the HRC – Commins and Dr Alexander Murray Bligh, a medical practitioner with a special interest in 'sanitary science', born in Co. Galway and trained in Dublin – ousted the sitting Liberal members, the Catholic 'anti-Irishmen' who previously represented Vauxhall and Scotland wards. A passionate exponent of Home Rule, Bligh exposed the 'shoneenism and anti-Irishism' of John McArdle, Charles's Liberal cousin, but, in order to ensure victory, he found it necessary to reassure the Scotland ward electors of his own confessional allegiance: 'He was born a Catholic, reared a Catholic, educated a Catholic, and was a Catholic today'.[47] In Vauxhall, Commins' victory was no less hard won over the 64th LRV commander, P.S. Bidwill, 'an Irishman by birth, and a Catholic; but one who, at the same time, has refused to identify himself with the national aspirations of the great bulk of his constituents'. In his victory speech Commins (who had recently chaired the HRC convention in Dublin which adopted the policy of 'obstruction') ridiculed the serried ranks of opposition parties: 'They had had Tory sugar; they had Whig currant jelly; they had the Orange Lodges; and the Catholic Club ... They had fought them all, and they had beaten them all.'[48] Parnell, on return from a trip to America, happened to be passing through Liverpool to take pride of place in the festivities celebrating the victories secured by 'the patriotic men of Scotland and Vauxhall Wards'.[49] At the HRC conference in Liverpool the following year, 1877 Parnell replaced Butt as president, the first major step towards gaining the parliamentary leadership.[50]

Dispute and confusion continued to prevail, however, until Parnell was finally able to assert his unchallenged authority. In the interim, the local party was riven by tension between hard-working 'militant' activists in the wards and 'moderate' elected representatives. A generic structural weakness of electoral parties, this division was accentuated in the Liverpool INP, Bernard O'Connell suggests, by factors of age (at 40 Denvir was the aged Nestor of the militants) and of socio-economic status (the initial group of middle-aged

---

[46]   *UI* 23 and 30 Sept. 1876, and 3 Feb. 1877.

[47]   *UI* 14 and 21 Oct. 1876.

[48]   *UI* 4 Nov. 1876.

[49]   *UI* 18 Nov. 1876.

[50]   Parnell also took pride of place at a monster open-air demonstration outside St George's Hall in 1879, see *Times* 1 Dec. 1879, and Denvir, *Irish in Britain*, pp. 285–86.

councillors being rich merchants or distinguished professionals with doctoral qualifications).[51] Enthused by the social radicalism of Davitt's Land League and the uncompromising politics of Parnellite obstruction, the 'Denvirites' or 'irreconcilables' waited in vain for those whose election they had secured to initiate the 'new departure' in Liverpool. There were indications of a new spirit among the wider community – at the local livestock markets, Irish merchants and butchers refused to handle cattle and sheep sent across the Irish Sea from 'boycotted' estates[52] – but there seemed no change in the council chamber despite the arrival of the 'Connollyites'. All links with the Catholic Club had been broken but, in the absence of any practicable or meaningful political alternative, Connolly and his handful of Home Rule colleagues, categorised by the ruling Tory party as 'men seditious to the Queen and traitors to their country', were in no position to jettison the Liberal alliance. Given that the Tories retained power only through their accumulated advantage in aldermanic seats, the necessary first consideration was to prevent any Tory gains through splits in the 'progressive' Liberal and Nationalist vote. Thus, council members of the two parties quickly developed procedures (often bypassing the nationalist activists) for the selection of candidates in certain wards and divisions: in 1877, for example, the Liberals stood aside in the Scotland ward, ensuring an easy win over the Tories for the ('moderate') Home Ruler and resident of Liscard Castle on the Wirral, Patrick de Lacy Garton, a wholesale fish dealer with large herring fleets at Howth and Kinsale.[53]

Militant discontent grew as Rathbone, the minority Liberal MP, refused to pledge himself to Home Rule, to support an amnesty for Fenian prisoners, or to retract his disparaging parliamentary remarks about 'the burden of pauperism and crime' in Liverpool being 'more than half imposed upon them by the Irish population'.[54] When the Liberals endeavoured vainly to gain a second seat at the by-election in 1880 following the death of the Tory Torr, their candidate Ramsay proved more pliant, agreeing under pressure from militants (who had toyed with running the veteran A.M. Sullivan as an independent candidate) to vote for an inquiry into a separate Irish parliament. Commins, leader of the INP councillors, came up with 'a neutral form of words ... which Lord Ramsay can repeat, meaning one thing and the Home Rulers can repeat, meaning another'. In the general election shortly afterwards, Ramsay was returned unopposed as

51   The analysis here draws heavily upon O'Connell, 'Irish Nationalist Party', ch. 2.
52   *DP* 21 Dec. 1880.
53   O'Connell, 'Irish Nationalist Party', p.137.
54   UL, Rathbone Papers IX scrapbook 9.21, items dated 19 May 1877 and 3 Aug 1878; Rathbone's speech, 2 July 1878, *Parliamentary Debates*, ccxll, cols 672–73.

the minority member, the hapless Rathbone being despatched (unexpectedly without success) to South West Lancashire while Commins' political skills were rewarded (and his local prestige enhanced) by being returned as MP for Roscommon, to be followed by a number of other prominent Irish Liverpudlians encouraged to stand for Irish seats by Parnell.[55] Ramsay's subsequent elevation to the Lords on his father's death led to another by-election as the Tories refused to recognise any proprietary right of the Liberals to the minority seat. When Plimsoll, the Liberal candidate, declined to meet members of the Liverpool branch of the Land League, the militant Home Rulers campaigned actively against him, while the moderates absented themselves from his unsuccessful campaign. The one branch of the HRC which went against the official policy of abstention and supported the hapless Plimsoll was dissolved by the Central Council, the local power-base of the activist militants.[56]

The loss of Liberal parliamentary representation was a blow, but there were compensations for the moderates at municipal level. The Liberal alliance was reaffirmed during Garton's campaign to secure re-election in Scotland Ward in 1880, 'a fight in a great measure against their old foe – the Orange Toryism of Liverpool'. Having stood aside again, the Liberals were lauded as fair and honest in speeches by the moderate notables, Commins, Bligh, McArdle and Parsons, with A.M Sullivan putting in another celebrity appearance. Speaking after his success, 'a great victory for Liberalism, Home Rule and Ireland', Garton looked to the Liberals to extend their fair play policy to Ireland itself:

> Let them remember this, that the Liberals had been their best friends (hear, hear). But he would say this, that if the Liberals or Tories attempted to lay hands upon their people or their leaders for legitimately asserting their rights, then the Irish people would meet, as they had never done before, in their might and protest against coercion, whether it came from Liberal or Tory.[57]

To the ire of the activist militants, Garton and his colleagues failed to live up to their words. They chose to support Samuel Smith, 'the Whig coercion candidate', at the parliamentary by-election in December 1882, an act of 'treachery and hypocrisy' compounded by defiance of Parnell's instructions to

---

55   J.P. Rossi, 'Home rule and the Liverpool by-election of 1880', *Irish Historical Studies*, 19, 1974–75, pp.156–68.
56   O'Connell, 'Irish Nationalist Party', pp.48–52.
57   *DP* 1 and 2 Nov. 1880.

abstain. Denvir and the militants of the Central Council were outraged by the behaviour of these 'Anglicized Irish Catholics' who

> profess to believe in Parnell, and cheer his name with fervour, and yet when he issues a recommendation to them to remain neutral or adopt any other course, they invariably show that their almost superstitious belief in Liberalism is too strong for them, and they disobey the man whom they pretend to regard as their leader.[58]

Thenceforth there was open and unseemly civil war: branches were purged, the Central Council dissolved, and rival candidates put forward in the Irish wards at the municipal elections in 1883 and 1884. The two militant candidates, Denvir and Dandy Pat Byrne, went down to heavy defeats in 1883, prompting the Liberal *Liverpool Review*, no friend of Home Rule, to dismiss the 'irreconcilable vote' as 'a mere turnip's head bogey of which in future it would be the extreme of imbecility to be frightened'.[59] The following year, however, Byrne scored a notable victory in Vauxhall over Charles McArdle, demonised in Denvir's *Nationalist and Irish Programme* as 'both a traitor and a hypocrite for he at that moment had on his address that he was a follower of Charles Stewart Parnell, whereas he had publicly and notoriously disobeyed him'.[60] Far more was at stake, however, than party discipline and loyalty to the esteemed national leader.

Radicalised in opposition to the indolence and insider dealing of the Commins clique – 'a "ring" of men of wealth and social position' – the militants were driven not only by ardent nationalism but also by a commitment to social reform. The 'scavenger's friend', Dandy Pat Byrne, the dock labourer turned publican with a social conscience (and aversion to moralistic Liberal teetotallers), stood far apart in education, background, occupation and policy from Commins and his clique, 'the small knot of Whig "nominal Home Rulers" who have too long posed as leaders in Liverpool'. To the fury of Byrne and his colleagues, it was this exclusive clique which charmed and hoodwinked the national executive of the INLGB through manipulation of certain local branches ('fraudulent' malpractice which ensured Connolly's unopposed return in 1884) and by puffed-up promotion of spurious organisations such as the Liverpool Election

---

58   O'Connell, 'Irish Nationalist Party', pp.55–56; Waller, *Democracy and Sectarianism*, p.36.

59   *Liverpool Review* 2 Nov. 1883.

60   *Nationalist and Irish Programme* 1 Nov. 1884.

Committee (no more than a private clique of Commins and colleagues whose meetings were unknown even to the manager of the hotel in which they were purportedly held). Furthermore, the clique precluded any discussion of much-needed social reform. Byrne's advocacy of sanitary and other social reform in the November 1883 elections was drowned out in a concerted attack on those 'who fatten and prosper on agitation'. When Byrne had the vulgar audacity to stand again in 1884, Commins advised him to attend elementary school to learn some manners and acquire some literacy. The denigration continued in the council chamber. Having dismissed Dandy Pat's promotion of the claims of the poor as 'ridiculous philanthropy ... simply clap-trap for dishonest purposes', Commins appealed for police intervention to eject the infuriated Byrne.[61]

Applauded by Denvir for having 'fed the starving labourers and their families by the thousands', Byrne was an early precursor of the radicalising dynamic which was eventually to lead to Edwardian 'Nat-Labism'.[62] The INP was to be driven forward as much by progressive change in the composition of its council members as by mounting frustration at the Liberals' failure to deliver Home Rule. On retirement from the council, members from established middle-class professions and occupations (doctors, lawyers and rich businessmen like Connolly who vacated the council in 1885 on becoming MP for South Longford) tended to be replaced by those with a more popular style, publicans, butchers, shopkeepers, penny-a-week insurance collectors, undertakers and others who attended to the daily needs of the Liverpool-Irish. When redistribution in the 1880s opened up the possibility of the INP gaining one of the new Liverpool parliamentary seats, Byrne proudly put himself forward as the local man made good. Here he overplayed his hand, coming into conflict with Parnell's intentions: he duly forfeited the support of Denvir and the local militants.

Parnell wished to secure maximum advantage from the new electoral arrangements and to bring an end to the civil war in Liverpool. In July an 'Irish National Conference' met in Liverpool and sat until 3am to work out the appropriate strategy. Irish electors throughout the country were to hold aloof from support of any English party, casting their votes as instructed by Parnell and executive of INLGB; Justin McCarthy was invited to stand in Liverpool Exchange, an initiative designed to mend local fences; and special care was to be taken in selecting a candidate for Liverpool Scotland, the one English

---

[61]   See *Irish Programme* 19 Jan. to 23 Aug. 1884, after which it changed its title to *Nationalist and Irish Programme*, running until 7 Feb. 1885. See also O'Connell, 'Irish Nationalist Party', pp.60–62, and Waller, *Democracy and Sectarianism*, p.39.

[62]   *Nationalist and Irish Programme* 1 Nov. 1884.

constituency within their grasp, as he would be the representative of the Irish throughout Great Britain, over 2 million strong:

> we believe that a candidate for this the largest Irish constituency in the world should be chosen from the front rank of the Irish Parliamentary party, and that Mr Parnell and the Executive of the National League of Great Britain be requested to recommend an Irish candidate from their own ranks.[63]

Until called away to contest Derry, McCarthy worked hard to effect reconciliation, fondly recalling his earlier days in Liverpool, subsequently described rather disparagingly in his autobiography as a 'stepping-stone on my way to London'. The president of the INLGB, T.P. O'Connor, yet to be announced as the candidate for Liverpool Scotland, made a decisive personal intervention:

> The executive are glad to be able to announce that, after many failures, the president of the organisation was able by a personal visit to Liverpool to establish a *modus vivendi* between different sections of Irishmen in Liverpool, and to start, after a painful interregnum, once gain the great work for Ireland which that important city has so long performed.[64]

One sticking point remained. Dandy Pat had yet to withdraw his candidature, 'a violation of the unity of the Irish party, and utterly unworthy of a loyal supporter of Mr Parnell'.[65]

In the end, it was Parnell himself who prevailed upon Byrne to withdraw in favour of O'Connor, a carpetbag outsider but a truly national figure (a talented journalist and popular biographer) with the celebrity required to represent the Irish beyond the constituency.[66] The injunction to support O'Connor was clear, but otherwise there was some difficulty and confusion in understanding Parnell's local intentions. After McCarthy's departure, he had put his own name forward for Exchange but then withdrew (not in time to save

---

[63]   *United Ireland* 4 July 1885.

[64]   'The Irish National League of Great Britain: Convention in Glasgow', *United Ireland* 7 Nov. 1885.

[65]   *United Ireland* 18 July and 15 Aug. 1885; *Liverpool Irish Herald* 31 Oct. 1885 (seemingly the only extant issue). See also the press cuttings in NAD 3/714 Irish National League Box 6.

[66]   Brady, *T.P. O'Connor*, ch. 2.

his deposit), advising perplexed constituents to vote for the Liberal candidate, Captain O'Shea (husband of his mistress), in contradiction to his instructions elsewhere.[67] Misunderstandings were put aside, however, in celebration of O'Connor's emphatic victory in the Scotland Division and the overall 'hung' national result, an outcome which served to confirm Parnell's credentials as a master political strategist.

With T.P. O'Connor displaying no interest in local affairs and with Parnell in unassailable (and dictatorial) charge of the national party, the history of the INP in Liverpool in subsequent years has been described as 'eventless'. While expanding its framework to 14 branches, the Liverpool organisation operated simply, O'Connell notes, as 'an efficient, locally powerful cog in a national electioneering machine'. The smooth operation continued despite the turmoil of Parnell's divorce crisis in 1890–91. There was a brief display of militancy among the ranks of the Liverpool Parnell Leadership Club. Loyal to the disgraced leader in the face of otherwise pervasive censure, members were characterised by youth, intense hostility to the Liberals, interest in social reform and, in the wake of the recent dock strike, general sympathy for the 'labour cause' (although as Special Branch reports averred, there was no equivalent in Liverpool of the Parnellite links with Socialists in Glasgow).[68] The new radicalism, however, was unable to survive the shattering blow of Parnell's death in October 1891. In Ireland, the movement was henceforth riven with emasculating division within and between Parnellite and anti-Parnellite factions, but in Liverpool all branches of the INLGB followed the majority anti-Parnellite line. Electoral efficiency was duly preserved in what was otherwise a period of local torpor: the INP gained two aldermanic seats in 1892; polled well in Select Vestry elections in 1894 (the Kerryman John O'Shea's introduction to public life); and benefited from ward boundary changes which, however, brought an end to the Liberals' brief tenure of municipal power (in which the INP had served as junior partner) between 1892 and 1895.

The Liberal defeat prompted one of the Parnellite 'young Turks' prominent in the Amnesty Association, the insurance agent P.J. Kelly, to mount an independent challenge. Drawing attention to unemployment and poor housing, he stood against the official INP candidate O. O'Hara, undisputed 'king' of the Irish egg trade, in the new South Scotland ward in 1896. The machine was duly

---

67   NLI MS 15,516 Parnell to Patrick O'Brien (his agent in Liverpool) 17 May, 23 Nov. and 27 Dec. 1885; *United Ireland* 28 Nov. 1885.
68   O'Connell, 'Irish Nationalist Party', pp.63–68 and 152; Sam Davies, 'P.J. Kelly', p.149; CO 904/16. See the report on the Irish National League in CO 904/16.

mobilised to ensure his defeat: armed with a letter from T.P. O'Connor asking all true nationalists to 'vote solid' for O'Hara, Lynskey informed the electors that O'Hara had the 'unanimous and undivided support of the clergymen in the ward'. Nominated again in 1897, Kelly stood aside in 1898 to allow Frank Harford a clear run against Lynskey, the local INP leader and acknowledged expert in electoral and labour law.[69]

For all his useful legal attributes, 'Jubilee Jeremy' Lynskey, one of four INP councillors attached to the office of Irish-born solicitor W. Madden, was adjudged insufficiently attentive to his constituents' needs. A prominent figure at Town Hall receptions and imperial celebration, he ran the local party in autocratic manner. The proponent of party discipline, he led the 21-strong Liverpool delegation – an indication of the city's proud pivotal role in the Irish diaspora – to the Irish Race Convention in Dublin in 1896, hoping to call the warring Irish to order:

> In every movement, whether constitutional or otherwise, the Irishmen of Liverpool have been in the forefront of it. We look upon it as the Capital of Ireland in England. We come here today to deliver one message, and speaking the unanimous voice of the Irish people of that city, I say that we come here for the purpose of supporting, maintaining, and helping majority rule and discipline in the Irish party ... dissension has paralysed our action in England ... dissension has deprived us of the support of men that ought to be in our ranks.[70]

Following the failure of the Convention to effect any rapprochement, there was a marked 'degeneracy' in the 'local National movement in Liverpool'. Lynskey and his fellow 'Jubilee Mutton-eaters' continued to associate with Liberals but kept apart from nationalist 'extremists' and their plans to mark the centenary of the 1798 rising.[71] To ardent Irish nationalists, Lynskey and his clique stood condemned as an 'old gang of sycophants, Whigs, and West Britons'.[72]

The challenge to Lynskey in 1898 needs to be set in both Irish and local context. Boosted by the centenary celebrations, there were signs in Ireland of a revived 'new departure', with a renewed stress on social reform and hopes of political unity through the newly formed United Irish League (UIL). As

---

[69] Davies, 'P.J. Kelly', pp.149–52.

[70] *History and Album of the Irish Race Convention*, Dublin, 1897, pp.303–304.

[71] CBS Précis Box 1, 10 May 1897.

[72] *LCH* 10 Feb. 1899.

they sought to implant the new nationalist spirit in Liverpool, Harford and his supporters were no less determined to reverse the woeful neglect of the Irish wards in the city, shamelessly unprotected by INP councillors. A former legal adviser to Parnell, Lynskey successfully objected to Harford's nomination in 1898 on a technicality, but this disqualification was subsequently over-ruled, prompting a by-election between the two candidates in April 1899. Harford scored a sensational victory thanks to strenuous canvassing by the 'low Irish' – the Basket Women and Street Traders Defence Association were particularly prominent – and the powerful rhetoric of his brother, Austin: 'They had been called factionists, but he would impress upon them all that the principle upon which they had banded themselves together was for the betterment of the district and to in some way, mitigate the evils caused by the past and present neglect of their representatives.'[73]

In the course of challenging Lynskey, the Harford brothers established a rival organisation to the INP, the Irish National Association (INA), which gave shape and structure to emergent 'Nat-Labism'. The INA offered a programme of ardent commitment to Irish nationalism, social reform and political independence; a structure premised on local control; and an outreach package of popular Irish culture and entertainment, all endorsed by Charles Diamond's influential *Liverpool Catholic Herald*.[74] Where Liverpool had been backward in the 1798 centenary celebrations, the Harford brothers ensured it was at the very forefront of commemorations for the Manchester Martyrs: accomplished amateur performers, they offered songs and recitations at the various ceremonies marking the construction and unveiling of the Moston memorial – at all such events thereafter, Frank was in great demand for his poignant rendition of Irish ballads.[75] Soon after its formation, the INA put on a series of popular Irish concerts in the north end, 'a refreshing departure from the ridiculous jingo doggerel so prevalent at social and political entertainments at the present time', including 'an exposition of Irish dancing (so rarely seen in these days)'.[76] On the electoral front, the INA moved quickly to broaden its challenge, putting up candidates in Select Vestry elections 'to look after the welfare of the poor'. To ensure a ready rapport between the INA and the electors, it was agreed that all branch officers should be rate-payers in the ward.[77]

[73] *LCH* 7 and 21 Apr. 1899. O'Connell, 'Irish Nationalist Party', p. 79.
[74] Unfortunately the holdings of *LCH* at the Newspaper Library, Colindale, do not start until no. 370, 6 Jan. 1899.
[75] *LCH* 15 Dec. 1899 and 29 Nov. 1901.
[76] *LCH* 24 Feb. and 24 Nov. 1899.
[77] *LCH* 9 June 1899.

By the time Austin joined his brother on the council, having gained election for South Scotland in November 1899, a number of INP members, led by Taggart, its first 'working-class' councillor, were arguing for internal reorganisation to head off the INA challenge. These local disputes over what the *Liverpool Catholic Herald* condemned as 'bossism and mal-administration' fed into wider discussion of organisational reform to facilitate the reunification of the Irish Parliamentary Party and the extension of the UIL to Britain. There were hopes that the UIL in Liverpool would be a brand new start, not simply a renaming of the discredited INL, a 'thing of the past' which had put 'Liberals and anti-Irishmen and jingoes in the City Council, instead of good Irishmen'.[78] As it was, the veteran Dr Commins took the chair at the great demonstration at the Adelphi Theatre in March 1900 to proclaim the reunification of the Irish Parliamentary Party under the banner of the UIL. This was another occasion for some Liverpool-Irish Merseypride, reported under the headline 'What Liverpool says today Ireland will echo to-morrow':

> It was here in Liverpool that the late Mr Parnell first assumed, by the unanimous wish of his audience, the reins of office, in the shape of the chairmanship of the Home Rule Confederation. It is only right, therefore, that the reunion of the Irish Parliamentary Party should receive its first public endorsement at the hands of the people of this city … The voice and action of Ireland in Liverpool is bound to command respectful attention wherever and whenever it is directed, and so it is that we here in this great Irish centre, undertake grave responsibilities in connection with the national movement.[79]

Underneath the surface, however, tensions continued. To Austin Harford's fury, the organisers had refused to recognise the INA and its officers in its official invitations and had even contemplated excluding reporters from the *Liverpool Catholic Herald*. The new unity notwithstanding, Harford resolved to challenge 'Tay Pay' at the next general election.[80]

Harford brought a series of charges against O'Connor, the absentee MP who lacked 'a single achievement' for his constituents during his lengthy 'stewardship'. The 'dilettante purveyor of the small talk and boudoir gossip of London society', O'Connor stood accused of metropolitan high living at the

---

[78]   *LCH* 23 and 30 June and 15 Dec. 1899.

[79]   *LCH* 30 Mar. 1900.

[80]   *LCH* 2, 16 and 30 Mar. 1900.

expense of any concern for working, housing and spiritual conditions in the Scotland Division. An ardent Catholic, Harford condemned the 'wriggling' attitude towards denominational education and 'protested most strongly at the conduct of Mr O'Connor in championing in the House of Commons the retention on stage of plays of obscene tendencies'. With populist fervour, he exposed the derisory nature of O'Connor's support, financial and otherwise, for the Liverpool dockers during the great strike of 1890, while spending 'hundreds and thousands of pounds on society functions'.[81] Cultural nationalists across the Irish Sea applauded the exposure of the 'Member for Blarney', representative of the last remaining 'pocket borough':

> For 16 years the Scotland Division has been practically disfranchised ... a local Tory or Liberal would have been a better choice than the successful carpet-bagger who has simply used his seat as a jumping off-place in his nest-feathering career. For the purpose of this one-sided arrangement, the foolish Irishmen of Liverpool, in addition to their self-effacement, have been at the expense of maintaining a costly organisation to ensure his safe return.[82]

There were few other endorsements, however, of Harford's vilification of Tay Pay. Speaking for the INP, Dr Bligh 'marvelled at the effrontery of Mr Harford, whom none in Liverpool had ever heard of during the struggles of the past ten to fifteen years, coming forward to oppose a well-tried Nationalist as Mr O'Connor'. Amid the Boer War 'khaki–ism' of the day, the foolish presumption of this 'mushroom politician', it was widely feared, would serve only to benefit the Tories by splitting the Irish vote.[83]

As his correspondence with John Dillon reveals, O'Connor was furious at having to spend time (and his own money) in Liverpool to defend his seat, 'an infernal nuisance', when he should have been directing national operations in the otherwise propitious context of a reunified Irish parliamentary party.[84] 'Instead of being at his desk in London, he had to come down to Liverpool', he protested at the opening meeting of his campaign, 'not to face a Tory, but a candidate whose cause was treason to Ireland. (Applause).' There was the occasional rhetorical gesture to the local audience, but O'Connor persisted

---

[81] *LCH* 28 Sept. 1900.

[82] *United Irishman* 1 Sept. 1900.

[83] *LCH* 28 Sept. 1900.

[84] TCD John Dillon Paper 6740–44: T.P. O'Connor correspondence, 24 Sept. to 24 Dec. 1900.

in stressing national imperatives, placing himself (as ever) above municipal considerations:

> There were some seafaring people present, and what would they think if their crew were to put the captain in the stockhole, instead of on the bridge (Loud applause) ... When Parnellite and anti-Parnellite were meeting each other in friendly embrace, when dissension was dying, the torch of discord was introduced for the first time into Scotland Division, and instead of being an example, as it always was, it was a shameful exhibition of discord (Loud applause). Alluding to municipal differences, he said he had always held that it was not his business to interfere in such matters.[85]

As the acrimony intensified, John Redmond, leader of the reunited Irish Parliamentary Party, sent a telegram to Harford: 'My urgent advice is to retire for the sake of Ireland.' Harford duly complied, but O'Connor, now itching for a fight, displayed no gratitude.[86] 'Redmond's interference here was very curious', he wrote to Dillon:

> It was taken without any previous consultation with me: and really instead of doing me good, was calculated to get my enemies decently out of their hole. If Harford go to the poll, I shall beat him and the Tory handsomely. Even those who have been behind Harford in the fight with Lynskey, are with me now. I shall have to come down and settle the fellow and his gang at the Municipal election for they are the Healys of Liverpool. I cannot help thinking that if things go all right in Ireland, we are at the beginning of a big movement in Liverpool and England generally. You can fancy how I feel at being tied down here while the great fight in which I might have been of so much service is going on in Ireland.[87]

Having secured his parliamentary seat, O'Connor admitted that his 'troubles in Liverpool' were not yet over:

> The gang which raised the rival gang to mine, while thoroughly beaten by me, is yet so powerful municipally – through the weakness of others and the disappearance of the organisation – that they still have to be reckoned

---

85   *LCH* 28 Sept. 1900.

86   *LCH* 5 Oct. 1900.

87   Dillon Papers, O'Connor to Dillon, 28 Sept. 1900.

with. And one of the very worst agencies in producing division in Liverpool and in assailing me, is Diamond's paper.

Unwilling to spend more of his time and money in Liverpool, the exhausted O'Connor decided against a return visit, preferring to recuperate in Paris (he loved the Latin Quarter 'almost as much as if I were a young student', he reported to Dillon).[88] At the municipal elections, the INA candidate, John O'Shea, a local tea-dealer of humble means, won a handsome victory over the official nationalist candidate in South Scotland on a platform of 'Nat-Labism': 'he would see that the Council should build houses for the people on the various plots and spaces now vacant, and he would do everything in his power to forward the interests of the Irish and Catholic people who were so much neglected'. Hailed by the *Liverpool Catholic Herald* as 'the final defeat of Lynskeyism',[89] O'Shea's victory added to O'Connor's disaffection with politics at a complex time in his commercial and publishing life. 'Do you think Sexton would be induced to take my seat at Liverpool in case I gave it up?', he asked Dillon.[90]

Within a matter of months, however, a remarkable rapprochement (unfortunately unrecorded in the Dillon correspondence) was effected: the INA moved into the mainstream of the local UIL; Harford became chair of its central council (a return to the structure favoured by the activists of the early 1880s); and a rejuvenated O'Connor, the 'best-dressed man in town', was seen regularly in Liverpool, the star of constituency and community events stage-managed by Harford and reported with lavish approval in Diamond's *Liverpool Catholic Herald*. In the first of four visits in 1901, O'Connor toured the north end, addressing open-air demonstrations in Eldon Street, Latimer Street, Athol Street and Regent Street, thenceforth a much-favoured means of charming his constituents. He still insisted that he 'never intervened personally in the local struggles in Liverpool', but stressed the paramount need for unity: 'It was vain to act up the principle that they could have one organisation in Ireland, and two in Liverpool.' In a symbolic new departure, he then attended a meeting of the Executive of the NUDL, at which he agreed to take parliamentary charge of amendments to the Factory and Workshops Bill submitted by Sexton, to reduce the 'terrible level' of accidents at the docks, 'far and away the most dangerous employment in the kingdom'.[91]

---

88   Dillon Papers, O'Connor to Dillon, 15 and 28 Oct. and 8 Nov. 1900.
89   *LCH* 26 Oct. and 9 Dec. 1900.
90   Dillon Papers, O'Connor to Dillon, 24 Nov. 1900.
91   *LCH* 28 June 1901.

With Harford at his side, O'Connor returned to Liverpool in August to present the prizes at the Irish Athletic Festival and Gaelic Re-union at Greenwich Park, Aintree – he subsequently donated the major prize at this annual event, the O'Connor Challenge Shield. Adapting to local Merseypride, he again took the opportunity to seek union: 'when there was unity throughout the world there should be unity in Liverpool. Liverpool would hold the vanguard in the fight to right Ireland's wrongs.'[92] A few weeks later, the INA transformed itself into the South Scotland branch of the UIL, trusting 'to accomplish inside the ranks of that organisation what it was unable to carry out constituted as a separate body'.[93] With Harford and O'Shea at the forefront, housing was the first priority: 'as far as Liverpool was concerned the cause of Faith and Fatherland depended upon the Irish working classes and, therefore the representatives of the several Irish districts should consider the housing question, and it alone, of the utmost importance'.[94] Ireland itself was not forgotten in this 'Nat-Labism' formulation: in launching itself to the public, the new South Scotland branch was the first organisation to hire the popular entertainment package offered by the *Liverpool Catholic Herald*, a lantern lecture on the 'Beauties of Ireland', the finest slides ever shown in Liverpool, interspersed with music and songs 'intrinsically Irish and National in every particular', followed by Irish jig and reel dancing.[95]

O'Connor returned in October to be lauded by dockers for his efforts to ensure 'for the first time in our history we shall have effective control over all plant and machinery, gear, gangways and ladders', and to campaign in support of Frank Harford and other INP candidates at the municipal elections, hailed by the *Liverpool Catholic Herald* as the symbolic 'Close of the Era of Division and Discord'.[96] He was back again in November at the head of torchlight processions and open-air demonstrations to celebrate electoral success, including the first INP seat in the south end won by the Harfordite J.A. Kelly, a barge owner and stevedore. No longer the absentee MP, the dapper O'Connor enjoyed a ready rapport with his constituents. 'Mr O'Connor is so lovable because he is so human', the *Liverpool Review* acknowledged: 'The sense of sympathy in the man is heightened by the charm of his voice, his accent, his style.'[97]

The relationship became closer in subsequent years: in 1903, for example, O'Connor's Merseyside engagements included chairing the profit-sharing

---

92   *LCH* 9 Aug. 1901.

93   *LCH* 30 Aug. and 13 Sept. 1901.

94   *LCH* 15 Aug. 1902.

95   *LCH* 18 Oct. 1901.

96   *LCH* 11 Oct. 1901.

97   *LCH* 8 Nov. 1901; *Liverpool Review* 12 Oct. 1901.

meeting of W.P. Hartley's employees in January; joining Redmond on the stage at the St Patrick's Day celebrations at the Hippodrome; presiding over the annual UILGB convention in May; presenting the prizes at the Irish Athletic Festival at Greenwich Park in August followed by a series of open-air meetings on both sides of the Mersey; and a lecture on 'Parliament and its Personalities' at the Philharmonic Hall in November (when he and Harford were elected vice-presidents of the Liverpool Dickens Fellowship). 'The more the people knew of Mr O'Connor', councillor Taggart observed at the UILGB convention, 'the more they revered him.' 'The dockers owed more to Mr O'Connor than to any other living man', Sexton declared at the August meetings: 'He had won them their Labour Charter'. With suitable 'Nat-Labism' inflexion, O'Connor's speeches now squared the circle, showing the local relevance of Irish priorities:

> To his mind, the real tragedy of Ireland was the tragedy of the Irish who had left Ireland, and not those who remained. For that reason they must vote for the policy of the party which would keep the Irish at home, and not perpetuate the tragedy, the monument of which he saw around him in the houses of the Scotland Division ... he would not have lived in vain if the electors of the Scotland Division would remember what he has assisted to do on behalf of their class.[98]

Following his unanimous election as chair of the central council of the UIL in Liverpool, Harford brought what O'Connor praised as 'sirocco-like' energy to local organisation in a bid to secure for the party the balance of power in the council chamber.[99] Speakers from the Central Council were sent round the branch network, every branch was visited (and vetted) by Harford himself, while he promoted and chaired major demonstrations, beginning on St Patrick's Day, 1903, held at large venues such as the Hippodrome (and later, Liverpool Stadium), with major parliamentary figures and revered former Fenians (most notably, the reprieved Manchester Martyr, O'Meagher Condon) as crowd-pulling attractions, with the INF in all their regalia providing the guard of honour.[100] For some of the old clique, however, Harford was moving too quickly. An ill-tempered dispute, reminiscent of the controversies of the early 1880s, developed when the Michael Davitt branch in St Anne's Ward insisted on its right to select its own candidate. Harford reacted angrily: 'Once the

---

98   *LCH* 16 Jan., 20 Mar., 29 May, 5 June, 7 Aug., and 6 Nov. 1903.
99   *Xaverian* Sept. 1906.
100 *LCH* 30 Jan. and 20 Mar. 1903, 23 Nov. 1907, and 20 Mar. and 2 Oct. 1909.

Central Council fails to be a guiding power and protector of Irish Nationalism, the confidence of the people in it ceases, and a branch, acting in isolation, is likely to be an object for the scheming ambitions, and possibly the corrupting influences of self-seeking persons.' When the branch proved obdurate, Harford resigned in a fit of pique, with J.F. Sullivan, the branch president, taking over as chair of the Central Council:

> Mr Harford is too young in Irish politics to have learned that no good purpose is served by the publication of our differences ... To my mind Mr Harford has adopted a most childish attitude in regard to the Central Council, and one which leads me to think his is a policy of rule or wreck.[101]

In the end, however, Harford emerged with his power base strengthened: after some concern about a return to time-serving 'cliqueism', the Central Council was abolished to be replaced by the Liverpool and District Committee under Harford's unquestioned chairmanship.[102]

As party leader, Harford soon came to understand the need for pragmatic compromise. Along with his brother Frank, the slate of INP candidates in the 1904 municipal contests included his old adversary Lynskey and J. Clancy, a former 'hotel boots', now the owner of a substantial tobacconist business, whose politics lay 'between the Nationalist heaven and the Liberal earth'.[103] Relations with the Liberals remained flexible and contingent, but there was to be no accommodation with new political formations, whether class-based or confessional. Harford ensured that Labour failed to gain a foothold among Liverpool-Irish voters. Despite a big campaigning effort by Labour leaders, John Hill, secretary of the boilermakers union, polled poorly at the parliamentary by-election in Kirkdale in 1907, for which the *Liverpool Catholic Herald* had a ready explanation: 'too much Socialism, too little Home Rule, and too little religious teaching'.[104] Against the advice of George Milligan, the leading Catholic Labourite, Labour decided to run Joseph Cleary, secretary of the Warehouse Workers union, in a head-on challenge with the INP in a by-election in Great George Ward in 1913. Educated (like the Harford brothers) at St Francis Xavier's, the INP candidate, T.P. Maguire, 'a Liberal solicitor masquerading as a Nationalist', had impeccable Catholic credentials: his siblings included a Jesuit

---

101   *LCH* 5 and 12 Feb. 1904.
102   *LCH* 25 May 1906.
103   Waller, *Democracy and Sectarianism*, p. 216.
104   *LCH* 5 Oct. 1907; Waller, *Democracy and Sectarianism*, pp. 233–34.

priest and a nun of the Community of the Faithful Companions of Jesus, whose convent in the ward was renown for charitable and educational work. Cleary polled a derisory 72 votes.[105]

Although an ardent Catholic, Harford faced criticism from co-religionists claiming that the INP should do more to defend their faith and their schools, under ever more vehement attack by Protestant demagogues such as George Wise, Nonconformist Liberals and godless socialists. An early pointer to the Edwardian constitutional crisis, Liberal proposals to remove funding from denominational schools prompted some Catholics to vote Tory in 1906, a swing which Harford was resolved to reverse. Having previously criticised O'Connor for 'wriggling' on this very issue, he took steps to enhance Tay Pay's image as defender of the faith, making sure his Liverpool schedule included opening bazaars, fetes and other fund-raising events at local Catholic schools.[106] At the general election of 1910, O'Connor condemned Tory attempts to attract Catholic votes on the schools issue as 'one of the most impudent pieces of double-faced duplicity'. 'Every Irishman base enough to vote for a Tory candidate sells his country, his faith and his manhood', his election address proclaimed.[107] Interviewed by the *Liverpool Catholic Herald*, Harford rammed the point home: 'the future fight may be safely left once again in the hands of the Irish Party, who are the real Catholic Party, representing not only a Catholic nation, but the Catholics of this country as well. They are the sheet anchor for Catholic matters.'[108] This was a standing rebuke not only to Tory Catholics but also to the Salford-based Catholic Federation, seemingly prepared to sacrifice Home Rule to defend denominational schools. The main propagandist of 'Nat-Labism', the *Liverpool Catholic Herald* was harshly critical of the political ineptitude of the Federation and the new Catholic Labour League. For Catholics outside the 'citadel of Irish Nationality in the Scotland Division of England's greatest commercial capital', the best advice was to work within existing parties and unions: 'Any attempt to form a Catholic Party at this moment is in our opinion not calculated to serve Catholic interests but to harm them.'[109]

---

[105]   *Liverpool Forward* 21 Nov. 1913; *LCH* 22 Nov. 1913.

[106]   See, for example, O'Connor at the opening of St Anthony's School's bazaar in *LCH* 6 Oct. 1905.

[107]   *LCH* 15 Jan. 1910.

[108]   *LCH* 11 Dec. 1909.

[109]   *LCH* 15 Jan. and 9 Apr. 1910; P. Doyle, 'The Catholic Federation 1906–29', in Sheils and Wood, *Voluntary Religion*, pp.461–75. See also Steven Fielding, *Class and Ethnicity: Irish Catholics in England, 1880–1939*, Buckingham, 1903, pp.113–17.

As well as seeking to satisfy class and confessional interests within the INP, Harford struggled to appease those agitating for votes for women. There was fury in Catholic circles about a sensational report, subsequently retracted, that activists for women's suffrage were working in league with the Wiseites to free Catholic nuns from 'slavery'. Harford mounted the platform at a meeting in St Martin's Hall in a vain effort to secure a 'fair hearing' for speakers from the Women's Freedom League, but was forced to withdraw. The *Liverpool Catholic Herald* was convinced that the fury and abuse directed against him had been carefully orchestrated:

> In various quarters the opinion was freely expressed that the attack on Mr Harford had been organised by persons anxious to discredit the Catholic cause, split the Catholic ranks, destroy other influence of the United Irish League and introduce into Liverpool an organisation, the existence of which in other parts of Lancashire has not been beneficial either to Catholic or Irish interests.[110]

While charting an electoral path through the frequently competing demands of class, confessional and gender interests and allegiances, Harford was always prominent at the key events in the nationalist calendar of commemoration and celebration, appropriating the heritage of heroic physical force for the Home Rule cause. He was particularly active in events to mark the centenary of Emmet's rising in 1903, joining the torchlight procession through the north end, addressing the crowds on the plateau in front of St George's Hall, leading the delegation to Dublin which, Special Branch reported, 'assembled at Scotland Road and were escorted to the railway station by some thousands of Scotland Road roughs, yelling children and drunken women', and, on his return, attending a special INF church parade.[111] In 1907 he chaired a meeting in support of a memorial at Enniscorthy to honour the priests and people who fell on the battlefields of Wexford in 1798.[112] 'The heritage bequeathed by the men of '67, '48, and '98 was that they must stand fast to the Irish cause', he proclaimed from one of the three platforms outside St Sylvester's to greet the procession, 38,000 strong and two miles long, which he mobilised to mark the anniversary of the Manchester Martyrs in 1912, an enormous demonstration of strength to counter Carson's Ulster Demonstration day in Sheil Park a few weeks previously:

---

110   *LCH* 30 Oct. 1909.

111   *LCH* 25 Sept. and 2 Oct. 1903; CBS Précis Box 3, 21 Sept. 1903.

112   *LCH* 26 Apr. 1907.

The impelling feature of the '67 movement was to point out to Parnell that the Parliamentary movement was the only way to success for Ireland. It was their pride and pleasure to see that the great constitutional movement which Parnell had moulded was, through his efforts and those of his successors, leading them into the Promised Land, and that they were nearing the end of the struggle for Ireland.[113]

There was to be no relaxation in the efforts of the INP in Liverpool, however, for whom Harford envisioned a long-term future beyond Home Rule:

There was, he said, no city in the world where the Irish needed to be more active in the face of great difficulties than Liverpool, where the Orange Party concocted and built their policies, and where the pace was set against Ireland. It was necessary that the Irish people of Liverpool should concoct and build a counter-policy. Personally, he thought it would be a calamity if the Irish ranks in Liverpool, which had done so much for Catholic and Irish causes, were allowed to be broken and their people to become voters for the Tory, Liberal and Labour Parties.[114]

As the battle for Home Rule appeared to have been won on the eve of the First World War, Harford and O'Connor took pride in their joint achievements. Over the years, they had come to respect each other's talents and attributes. No longer the carpetbagger, O'Connor was greeted by Harford in Liverpool on return from one of his regular fund-raising trips to the United States (an esteem factor of his international standing in the diaspora), as a 'great warrior in the cause of Ireland, one who was looked upon as one of Liverpool's own belonging'.[115] Shortly afterwards, at the ceremony to present Harford with a portrait in honour of his achievements, reflecting what Redmond described as 'three special virtues' – Harford's 'love of religion, love of country, and love of the welfare of his fellow-citizens' – O'Connor repaid the compliment with another appropriation:

Mr Harford was Liverpool by birth and training, but Irish by race (Hear, hear). Mr Harford belonged to that second generation of the Irish people who had grown up in English cities, but who, if they were at all distinguished

113 *LCH* 30 Nov. 1912.
114 *LCH* 7 Feb. 1914.
115 *LCH* 16 Nov. 1906.

from their countrymen at home, were distinguished by the fact that their patriotism and love of their motherland, despite distance, were as ardent as those of any whose fathers had never left Ireland's shores (Hear, hear).[116]

Working partners in the campaign, Harford and O'Connor applauded Liverpool's contribution to the cause. 'When the history of the Home Rule fight was completed', Harford opined at the St Patrick's Day celebrations in 1913, 'one of the most impressive chapters would tell of the extraordinary fidelity, the Unflinching and Dogged Fidelity of the Liverpool Irish to the sacred cause of their Motherland. The reward was now well in sight. (Applause).' With the Home Rule Bill having passed its third reading, O'Connor hailed the 'victory for Ireland' but added with his characteristic imperial pride that 'it was not a defeat for England; it was a victory above all others for the British Empire, to whose unity and security and whose honour it would add much'.[117] When war broke out, O'Connor was one of the most powerful voices in recruiting troops to fight for king and empire, while Harford rallied the Irish professional and commercial classes, along with representatives from the various Irish organisations in the city, to form a Liverpool-Irish National Volunteer Force for home defence to render assistance to civil and military authorities, a duty 'made the easier and the more obligatory by the fact that there was now taking place the longed-for act of reconciliation between England and Ireland for the granting of Home Rule'.[118]

While delivering workplace protection, improved housing, enhanced relief payments and other social reforms, the constitutional Home Rule perspectives of the INP brought the Liverpool-Irish political class into mainstream politics. Harford progressed rapidly onto the magisterial bench (1906), the vice-chairmanship of the Housing Committee (1907) and, in 1914, elevation to aldermanic status – appropriately enough his unopposed replacement as councillor for South Scotland was P.J. Kelly, the Parnellite 'young Turk' who had pointed the way to 'Nat-Labism' in the early 1890s.[119] One prize eluded Harford, an indication of deeply entrenched sectarian attitudes in Liverpool: Liverpool-Irish Catholics were not considered eligible for the post of lord mayor, the city's first citizen.[120]

---

116   *LCH* 7 Dec. 1907.
117   *LCH* 22 Mar. 1913.
118   *LCH* 29 Aug. 1914.
119   *LCH* 11 July 1914.
120   *LCH* 13 Nov. 1909.

6

Extra-Parliamentary Politics:
The American Connection

I N EXTRA-PARLIAMENTARY as in constitutional inflexion, Liverpool was the pivot of Irish politics in Britain. A cause of much concern to the authorities, there were persistent fears of violent disturbance and commercial catastrophe, in particular the destruction of shipping and warehouses, either in simultaneous support of a 'rising' in Ireland or as a diversion to hinder the despatch of troop reinforcements across the Irish Sea. The hub of the wider Irish diaspora, Liverpool was also the first point of contact for returning Irish-Americans with their 'republican spirit and military science'.[1] The source of funds and arms for separatist physical force endeavour, Irish America also supplied the requisite accentuated anti-British sentiment. 'I have been speaking to persons recently returned from America who tell me that there is a very strong feeling of enmity amongst all classes of the Irish against the British Government' one of the Dublin police officers stationed in Liverpool to keep watch on trans-Atlantic shipping reported: 'That the emigration caused by eviction, the sufferings, deaths, and hardships during the voyage, the disappointments and heartburnings on the other side, are all laid to the charge of the Government ... for imaginary causes or otherwise a very bad feeling exists among the Irish.'[2]

This chapter examines three episodes which illustrate the critical but changing nature of this American connection. The Confederates of 1848 were emboldened by the prospect of the arrival of an Irish Brigade from New York but waited in vain. As if by amends, Liverpool became the centre of operations for the 'Irish-Yankee' officers of the Fenian army, battle-trained in the American Civil War. These were the years of greatest anxiety for the authorities, their fears

---

1   John Belchem, 'Republican spirit and military science: The "Irish Brigade" and Irish-American nationalism in 1848', *Irish Historical Studies*, 29, 1994, pp.44–65.

2   NAD, 3/715/1 Police Reports Box 4, Head Constable McHale, 18 Sept. 1865.

compounded by the increasing traffic in hazardous materials such as petroleum and 'American Burning Fluids', and the recent relaxation of old restrictions prohibiting the use of fire and lights on ships in port.[3] Where Fenianism was an exercise in co-operation with considerable popular resonance throughout Irish Liverpool, the dynamite campaign of the 1880s was conducted by Irish-Americans in isolation, without the sanction or approval of the local Irish by then well attuned to electoral pursuit of Home Rule.

While the rich merchants of the Catholic Club chose not to deviate from constitutional (and Liberal) norms, others in the Liverpool-Irish enclave were drawn beyond the 'moral force' ways and means of Daniel O'Connell to support Ireland's cause. Two groups were particularly prominent: those whose commercial interests still centred on the Irish Sea, which took them regularly across to Famine-ridden Ireland, and those whose professional practices brought them into everyday contact with the Liverpool-Irish community. Terence Bellew McManus, leader of the Irish Confederates in Liverpool in 1848 and one of the more heroic participants in the ill-fated Ballingarry rising, was a forwarding and commissioning agent prominent in the Irish trade who passed £1.5 million in goods a year. An Ulster-Catholic by birth, he was a friend of Charles Gavan Duffy from early business days together in Monaghan.[4] McManus was assisted by his second cousin, Dr Patrick Murphy, whose professional duties had brought him into direct contact with the Famine influx. In recognition of his heroic exertions, Murphy was invited to preside at a meeting in February 1848 to raise a memorial to the monks of St Benedict who had given up their lives in the typhus epidemic, the 'Irish fever', of 1847.[5] Significantly, two other members of the medical profession, Francis O'Donnell and Lawrence Reynolds, were among the most militant of the Liverpool Confederates in 1848.

Convinced of the efficacy of physical force by events in revolutionary Europe, 'the springtime of the peoples', the middle-class leadership cadre readily embraced direct action and duly prepared to assist nationalist revolution

3   LVRO, 352POL2/2, Reports of the Head Constable to the Watch Committee, 7 Apr. 1862.

4   T.G. McAllister, *Terence Bellew McManus 1811(?)–1861*, Maynooth, 1972; Charles Gavan Duffy, *My Life in Two Hemispheres*, 2 vols, London, 1898, vol. 1, pp. 277–78; Diocese of Clogher Archives, Bishop's House, Monaghan: Clark Compendium, envelope D f.636.

5   Burke, *Catholic History*, p.95.

across the Irish Sea.[6] Delegates from John Mitchel's Irish Confederation, the militant wing of 'Young Ireland', were received at James Lennon's Temperance Hotel in Houghton Street, regarded by J.D. Balfe, a high-placed informer, as the centre of insurrectionary planning. After Mitchel's arrest and conviction in May, McManus promised the junta in Dublin that come the day of the rising his fellow Liverpool Confederates would seize a couple of the largest Irish steamers in Liverpool, load them with arms and ammunition taken from Chester Castle, and proceed to Ireland. As a diversionary ploy, the port of Liverpool was to be crippled by setting blaze at low tide to quayside cotton warehouses, 'filled with material as inflammatory as the dried grass of a prairie'. To this end, the Liverpool Confederates – eschewing O'Connellite restraint and Chartist open agitation – developed in para-military fashion, revivifying the Ribbonite culture of secrecy (alas not immune to turncoats and informers) to establish a network of armed clubs in sympathetic pubs, temperance hotels and private houses. Reaching out to enrol the 'low Irish', this organisational expansion was co-ordinated by James Laffin, a tailor, using James Ord's temperance coffee-house, venue of the Roman Catholic Total Abstinence Benevolent Society, as his operational base.[7]

Alarmed by the rapid spread of the clubs, the local authorities placed the town under a state of siege. A specially appointed committee of magistrates reported that some 30 to 40 secret clubs were in existence by early July – I have succeeded in identifying 23 of them (see Table 6.1) – each capable of assembling 2000 to 4000 armed men, unannounced on the streets. Armed insurrection in Liverpool was 'very probable and indeed almost certain if there be an Insurrection in Ireland ... though a political, might (in the outset) be the ostensible motive – the real one would soon appear; a triumphant armed mob in a rich town would not respect property or life'.[8] A number of emergency measures were taken, establishing a pattern to be repeated during Fenian and other points of tension: the police force was hurriedly expanded (at the expense of usual standards as 'it was found impracticable to take the usual precautions for enquiry into the Characters of the Candidates'); some 12,000 special constables

---

[6] For a full account, see John Belchem, 'Liverpool in the year of revolution: The political and associational culture of the Irish immigrant community in 1848', in Belchem, ed., *Popular Politics, Riot and Labour: Essays in Liverpool History 1790–1940*, Liverpool, 1992, pp.68–97.

[7] Takashi Koseki, 'John Donnellan Balfe and 1848: A note on a Confederate Informer', *Saothar*, 23, 1998, pp.25–32.

[8] Report of the Committee of Magistrates appointed at a General Meeting of Magistrates held on the 8th of July 1848, HO45/2410B.

were sworn in (one of their batons was displayed at the Historical Exhibition of Liverpool Antiquities in 1907); military reinforcements were despatched to a vast tented camp at Everton (financial responsibility for which was later a matter of considerable controversy); and, in the absence of a suitable warship, armed marines were put aboard the *Redwing*, a government tender boat on the Mersey.[9] Throughout the 'anticipated disturbances', John Bramley-Moore, Tory chairman of the Dock Committee and the incoming mayor, had 'a bed placed in the Albert Dock Warehouses that he might be ready for any emergency'.[10]

Within hours of the introduction of the Habeas Corpus Suspension Bill in Ireland on 22 July, the mayor, magistrates and other leading citizens petitioned for its provisions to be extended to Liverpool, where there were fears of a rising that very night.[11] William Rathbone, a celebrated Liberal, explained the circumstances to his daughter:

> 100,000 Irish in Liverpool unemployed, and Chartists to join, are fearful materials for mischief ... our open docks and warehouses leave us much at the mercy of the incendiary ... The English law is defective, we cannot search for arms when we know where they are; we cannot incarcerate the leaders, though preaching rebellion or virtually such, though not legally; nor can we enter the houses where clubs we know meet, and the most inflammatory and rebellious language is used; yet Liverpool is the high road to and from Ireland, a post which a general would say the country's safety required to be guarded; yet her majesty's Ministers leave us very much to ourselves, and in some degree tie our hands by their reserve.[12]

Frustrated by Whitehall, the local authorities set legal objections aside to raid club premises. By chance, they stumbled across the Confederate minute book, a detailed record of committee membership and meetings. With its leaders in flight and most of its weapons seized – the major arms cache included 500 cutlasses and some canisters of gunpowder concealed in a cellar [13] – Confederate

9   Horsfall, 25 to 26 July, HO45/2410B. See also 1848, pp.154–55.
10   'The Mayor at the Albert Dock warehouses', *Jones*, 18 Nov. 1848.
11   C.B. Banning, Post Office, Liverpool, 22 July, and Horsfall, 24 July, HO45/2410B. LM 25 July and 1 Aug. 1848, for the counter-petition of those who thought suspension would be 'an unnecessary interference with the liberty of the subject ... an indelible stain on the town of Liverpool'.
12   W. Rathbone to Mrs Paget, 23 July 1848, quoted in Emily A. Rathbone, ed., *Records of the Rathbone Family*, Edinburgh, 1913, pp.223–24.
13   Horsfall, 3 Aug., HO45/2410B.

Table 6.1 *Irish Confederate Clubs in Liverpool and Birkenhead, 1848*

Name	Venue	Officer/Delegate
Liverpool		
1 Bermuda	Gt Howard Street	—
2 Oliver Bond	46 Naylor Street	—
3 Brian Boru	40 Gilbert Street	Patrick O'Hanlon
4 Byrne	—	—
5 Connaught Rangers	Addison Street	—
6 Davis (formerly Faugh a Ballagh)	—	Peter Ryan
7 Emmet	32 Rose Place	—
8 Lord Edward	—	—
9 Erin's Hope	—	—
10 Felon's Brigade	—	—
11 Felon's Hope	Ord's Temperance Hotel	Murphy
12 Bagenal Harvey	Bevington Bush	Dr O'Donnell
13 Liberator	Newsham Street	—
14 John Mitchel	47 Thomas Street	Ferrell and Perkins
15 Roger O'Moore	—	—
16 Owen Roe O'Neill	Ord's Temperance Hotel	Williamson
17 William Orr	—	—
18 Hamilton Rowan	—	—
19 St Patrick	New Bird Street	Martin Boshell
20 Sarsfield	—	Edward Murphy
21 Tom Steele	—	John Clifford
22 Wolfe Tone	—	—
23 '82 Club, Liverpool	—	T.B. McManus
	Eldon Place	—
	52 Hurst Street	—
	Milton Street	Dr Reynolds
	Limekiln Lane	Matthew Somers
	Dublin Street	Matthew Somers
Birkenhead		
John Frost	—	—
John Mitchel	Davis Street	Robert Hopper

Source: Reprinted from John Belchem (ed.), *Popular Politics, Riot and Labour: Essays in Liverpool History, 1790–1940* (Liverpool, 1992), p. 96.

conspiracy was rendered powerless on the eve of the Irish rising. Bitterly disappointed, McManus (who had previously chartered three steamers to be on standby ready to sail to Wexford) made personal amends at Ballingarry, where the 'rising' collapsed in Widow McCormack's cabbage patch, proving himself 'the boldest fellow among the entire body of insurgents'.[14]

The authorities remained on the alert, alarmed by intelligence reports from New York pointing ominously to Liverpool as the landing-stage for the first squads of the 'Irish Brigade', prototype Fenians with an officer corps drilled in the American militia, the latest firearms technology (including Colt revolvers) to supplement the native pike, and battle-hardened veterans of the Mexican War.[15] A couple of members of the advanced guard of the Brigade were spotted in Liverpool, tailed to Dublin, arrested and held without charge. Throughout the summer, the Liverpool authorities eagerly awaited the opportunity to apprehend the squads on arrival in British waters. When the *John R. Skiddy*, reportedly carrying the first contingent, crossed the bar, the mayor telegraphed her master and despatched three detectives by steam-tug to board and search the vessel off Crosby lightship. 'We have had a very rigid enquiry instituted', the mayor reported to the Home Office, 'and there does not appear to be any person of a suspicious or even of a questionable character on board ... or any supply of either arms or ammunition'.[16] Thereafter, Horsfall adopted a less conspicuous approach: two specially trained local police officers were stationed at the docks along with a detective from the Dublin force to watch all American arrivals; and work began on a special telegraph link to hasten communication with Clarendon in Dublin, with whom Horsfall was already in direct correspondence.[17] Occasionally, some suspicious types were spotted, as for example the 'two athletic Tipperary men', on the *Columbus*, 'whose conversation during the Passage shewed them to be interested in Irish affairs': they were kept under surveillance by a police officer as they crossed to Dublin. Most arrivals, however, were either old, infirm or lowly, 'that order of persons who appear incapable of taking any but the most subordinate part in a seditious or rebellious movement'. By the end of September, Horsfall began to doubt whether 'anything is to be apprehended of any arrivals from America worthy

---

[14]   For McManus's own narrative of events, see Denis Gwynn, *Young Ireland and 1848*, Cork, 1949, Appendix 3.

[15]   For a full account, see Belchem, 'Republican spirit and military science'.

[16]   Horsfall, 2 Aug. 1848, HO 45/2410B. See also, 'Non-arrival of the American Irish Brigade', *Isle of Man Times* 12 Aug. 1848.

[17]   Horsfall's daily reports, 3–18 Aug. 1848, HO 45/2410B. Bodleian Library, Oxford: Clarendon Papers, Box 16: Horsfall, 18 Aug. 1848.

of consideration'.[18] It was not until March 1849, however, that Head Constable Dowling felt sufficient confidence in the restoration of tranquillity to dispense with the 55 additional officers (30 warehouse guards and 25 'armed Patrols on the outskirts') hastily added to the force when alarm was at its height.[19]

There was a distinct hardening of attitudes as Britain emerged unscathed from the revolutions of 1848, having withstood not simply the Chartists but also the challenge of 'the savage Celt on one side, and the flighty Gaul on the other'.[20] Perry Curtis Jr. has charted the 'emergence of a bestialized or demonized Paddy, bent on murder and mayhem, in cartoons after the rather farcical rebellion of 1848'.[21] As prejudice intensified, the Irish in Liverpool withdrew (at least temporarily) from identification with physical force nationalism. Efforts were expended (as the next chapter shows) on cultural projects of national regeneration, such as the National Brotherhood of St Patrick (NBSP), offering open and respectable educational and recreational facilities away from the pub and any association with oath-bound secrecy, bibulous excess and precipitate violence. As the Catholic Church feared, however, the NBSP also provided convenient cover for Fenian advance.

The NBSP was launched in Liverpool in 1861 at a fund-raising meeting in the Concert Hall for the funeral of the exiled McManus in Dublin, following the translation of his remains from California, a prototype exercise in stage-managed political/funereal art which brought the Irish Republican Brotherhood (IRB) to public attention.[22] For the more militant members of the NBSP in Liverpool McManus was far more than a martyr symbol of Irish grievances: he was the inspirational role model for emulative action. 'They believed in the doctrine of 1848', Patrick Justin O'Byrne averred at the opening of a new branch across the Mersey in Birkenhead:

> that a great boon is worth a great sacrifice, and that the emancipation of our country, being a great good, is worth more than one drop of blood: aye, that in any attempt to crown our country with the laurels of freedom,

---

[18]   Horsfall, 22, 23 and 25 Sept. 1848, HO 45/2410B.
[19]   LVRO, Watch Committee 352 MIN/WAT 1/4, ff.614–48, Dowling's statistical returns for 1848.
[20]   'The Saxon, the Celt, and the Gaul', *Economist* 29 Apr. 1848.
[21]   L. Perry Curtis, Jr., *Apes and Angels: The Irishman in Victorian Caricature*, Washington, DC, 1997, p.xxii.
[22]   *Irishman* 4 May, 1 June, 6 and 20 July 1861.

the leaves would look none the worse for being sprinkled with the blood of the enemy (great applause).[23]

Toasting 'Ireland a nation, redeemed and regenerated' at the St Patrick's Day dinner in 1863, O'Byrne sought to rally 'such a body of Nationalists as would put to the blush those who came to Liverpool, made their fortunes, and swore allegiance to the constitution of England'.[24] By this time, George Archdeacon, leader of the Manchester Confederates in 1848, had returned from America to provide the requisite leadership for a nationalist programme of 'unconditional independence': 'No repeal humbug, no sham tenant right; the food of Ireland for the Irish people, Irish resources fully developed, commerce unrestrained, close alliance with our Transatlantic brethren, and total independence.'[25] Having opened a newsagency in Bidder Street where he operated as local agent for the *Irish People*, Archdeacon was appointed president of the Liverpool Central District Branch of NSBP, and then became the 'head centre' of Liverpool Fenianism until arrested in September 1865 on a Dublin warrant for high treason. He was described by Head Constable Greig as 'almost of the lowest order', a troublesome individual who 'has been engaged in every uneasy movement in Ireland or elsewhere since 1848'.[26]

Archdeacon apart, Greig was unaware of any significant Fenian presence in autumn 1865, although this is the period generally acknowledged by commentators and historians as the most propitious opportunity for Fenian insurgency. Greig, indeed, was curtly dismissive of alarmist reports which reached the Home Office by other channels of drilling, arms-running and other sinister activities in Liverpool. There were sensational claims that Liverpool had been 'selected by the head authorities of the Fenians in America and Ireland as the "centre" of the brotherhood in England'.[27] The entrepôt for shipment of arms to Dublin, Liverpool was the headquarters from which 'emissaries are spread all over the district, who collect money, appoint agents, and enrol adherents'. Pending the arrival of 'officers' from America, the leading role was taken by waterfront workers who had worked their way up to supervisory positions on the docks: 'the management of the affairs of the Fenian body in Liverpool is chiefly confined to Irishmen of low origin and defective education, who in the capacity of lumpers, master porters, and cotton dealers have

23   *Irishman* 24 June 1862.
24   *Irishman* 4 Apr. 1863.
25   *Irishman* 8 Aug. and 10 Oct. 1863.
26   LVRO, 352POL2/3, 26 Sept. 1865. See also *DP* 25 Sept. 1865.
27   *Bulwark* 1 Apr. 1865.

secured for themselves a comfortable worldly position'.[28] In the aftermath of Archdeacon's arrest, and under direct instruction from the Home Office, Greig rather begrudgingly submitted a full report:

> seeing that Liverpool has been represented as the great hotbed of such persons, he has caused the most diligent inquiry to be made by his most intelligent officers, following up every representation made, and found them entirely without the smallest foundation ... It is the Head Constable's thorough conviction that there is no ground for thinking that there is any Fenian organization in Liverpool, and further he believes that there are very few persons holding such opinions.[29]

Greig was a proponent of what W.J. Lowe has labelled 'vigilant moderation': ever aware of the need to preserve public order, he was determined not to inflame the local situation by heavy-handedness or provocative over-reaction.[30] A prickly individual, not prepared to have his judgement questioned, he reacted angrily whenever the Home Office gave credence to alarmist reports received via Dublin Castle from Irish police (RIC) stationed in Liverpool to spot the arrival of 'suspects' at the docks:

> Doubtless the Irish Officers, who are stationed here, principally to watch these persons, transmit to their Government every matter, however trifling it may be, coming under their observation, whereas the course I have adopted since September 1865, when I first received a communication from the Home Office relative to the Conspiracy has been to transmit nothing which would give needless ground for alarm.[31]

These competing reporting mechanisms, and the frequent tension between the various authorities, add to the difficulty in assessing the strength and composition of Liverpool Fenianism.

Judged on the basis of informers' reports, most of the local leaders or 'centres' were publicans or worked in artisan trades as tailors, shoemakers, painters, plasterers and joiners – there is no evidence from Liverpool, however,

---

28   *Irish Times* 5 Sept. 1865 citing *Sheffield Daily Telegraph*.
29   LVRO, 352POL2/3, 26 Sept. 1865.
30   W.J. Lowe, 'Lancashire Fenianism', *THSLC*, 126, 1977, pp.156–85, here p.158.
31   LVRO, 352POL2/5, 5 Feb. 1869. For RIC officers, see Lowe 'Lancashire Fenianism', p.162.

of the linkage to the broader working-class radical republicanism highlighted in John Newsinger's account of Fenianism in mid-Victorian Britain.[32] The absence of a mercantile and professional leadership cadre in Liverpool equivalent to that of the Confederates in 1848 was a matter of concern to the Fenian hierarchy. At an early secret council meeting in Liverpool described in 'Tried for Treason', John McArdle's part historical record, part fictional account of Liverpool Fenianism serialised in the *Catholic Times*, James Stephens, the Chief Organizer of the Irish Republic, bemoaned the absence of leaders 'risen out of the ranks of manual labour', ready to 'risk their creditable positions and lucrative situations in the furtherance of the cause': 'We shall not want for the bone and sinew when the time does come for action; but the more brains we can get the better. We require men to plan, and direct, and temper energy with judgment.'[33] According to the local press, numbers of young men, 'some occupying very respectable positions', were enticed 'to join the conspiracy', only to discover (too late) that Stephens's aim 'was lucre, not liberty'.[34] For the most part, the middle-class presence in Liverpool Fenianism comprised second-generation bored or rebellious young sons of successful Liverpool-Irish merchants, such as John Ryan, alias Captain O'Doherty, educated by the Christian Brothers at the Catholic Institute along with John Denvir.[35]

Estimates of the numbers of sworn members of the rank and file range from 12,000 to 30,000, the upper figure covering the Merseyside sub-region.[36] One of the most reliable informers, known as 'the sworn Fenian', claimed there were 'about 200 Centres in this District which includes Birkenhead, Bootle and the outer Townships, each centre being supposed to have nine nines [81] in his circle'.[37] Liverpool was the operational focus: Saturday nights were particularly busy in Fenian pubs in Fontenoy Street, 'navvies and others come in from all parts of the surrounding districts Hale Prescot etc'.[38] Beyond the membership of the secret cellular structure was a yet wider circle of sympathetic support: it was this ethnic protective environment that rendered the movement so dangerous to the authorities. 'There is scarcely an Irishman in Liverpool who is not a sympathizer in the movement, whilst many are sworn members of the Brotherhood and contribute money according to their means, some

32   John Newsinger, *Fenianism in Mid-Victorian Britain*, London, 1994.
33   'Tried for Treason', ch. 4, *CT* 24 Sept. 1870.
34   *LM* 26 June 1867.
35   Ryan, *Fenian Memories*, p.12.
36   HO45/7799, Fenianism, Supt. Ryan, 5 Mar. 1866.
37   LVRO, 352POL2/4, 24 Sept. 1867.
38   LVRO, 352POL2/4, 15 Dec. 1866.

one shilling others half a crown a week', John Wilson reported, utilising his links in the tailoring trade to transfer his informing activities from Dublin to Liverpool, adding that he had 'heard from several members of the Organization that they intend to fire the warehouses along the line of Docks'.[39] Irish women were actively involved in promoting the cause. Mrs Johnson and Mrs Mullins were brought before the police court for a street brawl started by Mullins when Johnson was forced to withhold payment of her weekly Fenian shilling, her irate husband, an Englishman, having just learnt of the arrangement.[40]

Such was the resonance of Fenianism that the drunk and disorderly adopted the cause, at least when in their cups: in a typical display of such bravado, John Grady, a young labourer from Harrison Street, Marybone, inebriated after a Sunday evening wake, brandished an old cavalry sword in the streets shouting out that he was a Fenian and would stand by the Fenian flag.[41] Perhaps the most resolute was Patrick Byrnes, a fireman on the Cork steamers: having disembarked and strengthened his resolve with alcohol, he knocked over Police Constable 456 in Dublin Street, proudly proclaiming, 'I'll stand six months for the sake of my Fenian brotherhood.'[42] When the police went to a pub in Great Crosshall Street following a tip-off about a prize fight, they were attacked by drunken customers led by John Lynch, a licensed hawker, who defiantly declared: 'I am a Fenian. This a Fenian meeting and you have no right to come in here.'[43]

Strict security applied in the network of pubs where the real business of Fenianism was conducted, generally in upstairs rooms with quick exits. Plain-clothes police, whatever their disguise, were unable to hoodwink savvy doormen such as 'the Sentinel' deployed outside James Galoin's pub at Strand Street, Canning Dock.[44] No fewer than eight scouts were posted outside and around Joseph Willis's pub in Richmond Row when Frank Kerr, Liverpool head centre in 1869 and a member of the Supreme Council, met other leading Fenians, the key discussion, however, being transferred to the outside urinal, beyond the earshot of the turncoat informer.[45] Bar staff, such as Boyd, the manager at Lowry's in Scotland Road, and a Fenian sworn in by Kerr, ensured complete security: when he changed jobs to work in Moss and Co. Vaults, the

---

[39]   LVRO, 352POL2/4, 19 Nov. 1866.

[40]   *LM* 24 Mar. 1866.

[41]   *LM* 23 Feb. 1866.

[42]   *DP* 10 Oct. 1865.

[43]   *LM* 16 Apr. 1866.

[44]   NAD, Fenian Papers R Series 4892R, 8 Nov. 1869.

[45]   NAD, Fenian Papers R Series 5179R, 6 Dec. 1869.

local circle meetings moved with him.[46] On rare occasions, however, bar staff were prepared to give information to the police: to supplement income from his boot and shoe shop, Bradley worked behind the bar at the California Vaults, Gerard Street, where he took a dim view of Fenian meetings, 'a dodge to get money out of the poor deluded creatures'.[47] In some instances, pub owners were genuinely oblivious of the nature of the meetings, simply providing facilities on a commercial basis, as was the case with Rose Lennon of Jackson Street until disabused by the local police who, much to the annoyance of the Home Office, promptly threatened to close her establishment:

> It is practically impossible to prevent the Fenians from assembling; and it is most important that their meeting places should be known to the Police, so as to enable them by quiet observation and secret enquiry to ascertain the names and become familiar with the persons, of such as are most active in the movement and also to learn of the arrival of any foreign agents or emissaries. When therefore the Police discover a Fenian rendezvous, it might be more discreet, especially when, as in this case, the proprietor of the house is free from any suspicion of abetting the conspirators, not to take any action that would drive them elsewhere, unless for some definite purpose, as for instance to make an arrest or to attempt a seizure of documents or arms.[48]

Unable to penetrate the security cordon to implant their own agents and spies, the authorities had to depend for the most part on intelligence provided by turncoat informers. Most useful of all was the information provided from within the officer corps, by impoverished and/or foolhardy 'Irish-Yankee' officers, instantly recognisable by their American square-toed boots.[49] Having arrived in some style in January and February 1866, 'well-dressed and well supplied with funds', travelling first class to avoid suspicion at the landing stage, they were reduced to penury (and boredom) as they languished (not always in weekly receipt of half-pay) in pubs and boarding houses waiting to take command come the rising.[50] Peter Oakes, a former lieutenant in the Federal Army, and commissioned as a Fenian officer by John O'Mahony, was the first

---

46   NAD, Fenian Papers R Series 5019R, 24 Nov. 1869.

47   LVRO, 352POL2/5, 9 Nov. 1869.

48   LVRO, 352POL2/5, letter to Mayor, 6 Aug. 1869.

49   *Nationalist* 6 Dec. 1884.

50   *LM* 13 Jan 1866. HO45/7799, 15 Sept. 1866.

to offer his services to Head Constable Clear of the RIC stationed in Liverpool, in the hope of securing a paid safe passage to Canada. In a series of interviews in September 1866, Oakes provided graphic details of the parlous plight of a dozen or more American officers, by then 'almost starving' in lodging houses (Mrs Skuce's in Blackstone Street and Mrs Blackmore's in Salisbury Street) and in the two main Fenian pubs: Lambert's beerhouse in Lord Nelson Street where Captain O'Rourke, the Fenian paymaster in England, was staying under the alias Beecher, and Austin Gibbons' pub in Richmond Row where the landlord's Fenian sympathies were boundless. The American officers, Oakes reported, 'are indebted to Gibbons a large sum of money, which he advanced, credit was given for board lodging and drink ad libitum'. Avis Gibbons, the landlord's wife, was treasurer of the local Ladies Committee which held raffles in the pub (watches were a favourite prize) in aid of families of Fenian prisoners.[51]

The most disturbing revelation concerned 'Fenian fire', the concealment in the roof of Mrs Blackmore's lodging house of 'a large quantity of combustibles for the purpose of setting fire to the city'. Some 55 glass jars of liquid phosphorous were discovered in the ensuing police raid, specifically intended (according to information later received) to destroy shipping in the Liverpool docks prior to the rising in Ireland. By this time, however, Mrs Blackmore's American tenants, whose rent was apparently paid by Gibbons, had already 'skedaddled' from the *refugium peccatorum*, taking flight a few days earlier on learning of the arrest of a leading Fenian (with a bewildering number of aliases) across the Mersey at Seacombe.[52] Some seven or eight 'Irish Yankees', described as 'dirty and repulsive' in appearance, were encountered in subsequent police raids on five other premises mentioned by Oakes, 'but the result arrived at was only the finding of a few treasonable songs and some drill books'.[53]

Soon after Oakes, another Federal army veteran offered his services to the police, the infamous John Joseph Corydon, the villain of 'Tried for Treason', an adventurer who revelled in treachery and deception.[54] Acting upon his information, the police seized a cartload of arms (addressed like the 'liquid

---

51 LVRO, 352POL2/4, 7 and 11 Sept. 1866; Lowe, 'Lancashire Fenianism', p.159.
52 LVRO, 352POL2/4, 7 and 26 Sept. 1866; *DP* 8 Sept. 1866. For the arrest of head centre 'Baynes' at Seacombe, see *DP* 17 Aug. 1866.
53 LVRO, 352POL2/4, 13 Sept. 1866. HO45/7799, 15 Sept. 1866, first report by Inspector Detective Williamson, one of the experienced officers sent from London to assist the local police 'in endeavouring to make further discoveries in relation to the treasonable plans which are apparently entertained by persons in Liverpool and are perhaps on the point of execution', see letter to Mayor, 13 Sept. 1866.
54 Lowe, 'Lancashire Fenianism', p.160.

fire' at Salisbury Street to 'Mr Brooks, Liverpool') containing 47 rifles, 38 bayonets and 10 canisters each containing 80 sticks of pure phosphorous, as it was being taken from College Lane by four men: Charles Campbell and William Carey, Fenian suspects recently released from Mountjoy prison in Dublin; Captain Michael O'Brien, an Irish-American officer destined to become one of the Manchester Martyrs; and a young local labourer, Patrick Keeley, who at first evaded arrest but was subsequently apprehended at Gibbons' pub.[55] The case against the four focused on the rifles, most of which were apparently government property belonging to the London Irish and Tower Hamlets Volunteers. Despatched to Liverpool to check the cache, an inebriated Sergeant Cox (not an Irishman the report pointed out) inadvertently lost the register of arms book along with other belongings during a visit to a brothel in the company of a Lime Street prostitute. In the absence of definitive proof that they had knowingly moved government property, the four were discharged.[56]

By this time, alarmist rumours were rife, every one of which Greig was now compelled to investigate, wasting time and resources, for example, in a wild-goose chase for a specially designed coffin with ventilating apparatus, intended to provide James Stephens with safe sanctuary 'in case of urgent need', when it would be transferred to the vaults beneath St Patrick's Church.[57] Of more concern were the ever-increasing reports of Fenian infiltration of the 64th LRV, Liverpool's 'Irish Brigade', allegedly a 'hotbed of Fenianism', Colonel Bidwill's strident proscription of any connection with oath-bound secret societies, bibulous conspiracy and militant nationalism notwithstanding. Members of the Volunteers were spotted sporting their uniforms at such Fenian venues as Archdeacon's newsagents shop and Gibbons' pub – it later emerged that the head centre who replaced Archdeacon after his arrest was Arthur Anderson, bugle major of the 64th LRV.[58] Following an undercover investigation by the Commander of Northern District in December 1866, it was decided to remove some of the corps' armaments for safe keeping to the military store at Chester (a nice irony given subsequent events).[59] Simon Jones concludes his balanced survey of the 64th LRV by dismissing claims of widespread Fenian penetration as 'exaggeration characteristic of intelligence gathered in public houses ... of the desire by paid informers to please their paymasters with the information

---

55   LVRO, 352POL2/4, 22 and 26 Sept. 1866.
56   HO45/7799, 8 and 12 Oct. 1866. *DP* 18 Dec. 1866.
57   LVRO, 352POL2/4, 7 Dec. 1866.
58   LVRO, 352POL2/4, 7 and 11 Sept. 1866. HO45/7799, 18 Oct. 1866. NAD, Habeas Corpus Suspension Act index entry on Arthur Anderson.
59   HO45/7799, 5, 17 and 29 Dec. 1866.

which justified their existence'.[60] Such judicious scepticism should doubtless be extended to similar 'information' obtained by RIC officers in Liverpool and now held in the National Archives in Dublin, detailing the initiation procedures conducted by Big Bill Walsh, a sergeant in the 64th LRV and leader of the Fenian circle at the Seven Stars pub, Regent Road, opposite Bramley Moore dock:

> when a man joins the corps it must be ascertained whether he is a Fenian, if he is not, efforts are made to induce him to join, if he resists, he is forced to resign or made drunk in order to come under Colonel Bidwill's notice and thus procure his expulsion from the corps.[61]

Given the extent of false rumours and exaggerated reports, Greig had 'no faith' in Corydon's sensational claim about an imminent arms raid on Chester Castle by Fenians drawn from across the north-west region, but just in case he wisely decided to alert the local authorities who in turn ensured the rapid despatch of troop reinforcements from London. Had the raid succeeded, the train tracks were to be torn up and the telegraph wires cut: a carefully planned exercise by John Denvir and others, enabling the newly armed contingents to reach Holyhead and the Irish Sea boats unimpeded. When the news first broke in Liverpool on 11 February, it was considered a hoax, an assessment soon abandoned as Sir James Picton recorded in his diary:

> it would be a queer hoax which could concentrate fifteen hundred to two thousand Irish roughs on one point, many of them armed with revolvers and ball cartridge. A little more brains, a little more audacity, and the affair might have been serious. No Irish insurrection would be complete without the inevitable Government spy and informer, who is as essential to the plot as a chorus to a Greek play.

Betrayed by Corydon, Fenians 'from distant towns' retreated from Chester, many to seek refuge in Liverpool prior to being despatched to Ireland by small craft from Runcorn, Garston and other 'out-ports' where surveillance was less intense.[62]

---

[60] Jones, 'Fenianism', p.47.

[61] NAD, Fenian Papers R Series, 5076R.

[62] LVRO, 352POL2/4, 11, 12 and 14 Feb. 1867; *DP* 12 and 13 Feb. 1867; Denvir, *Life Story*, p.83; J.A. Picton, *Sir James A. Picton: A Biography*, London, 1891, p.302; NAD, Fenian Papers F Series, Box 3, 16 and 20 Feb. 1867

Although the Fenian rising in Ireland in early March collapsed apace, alarmism in Liverpool reached staggering new heights as St Patrick's Day approached. There was every expectation that on the night of 16 March the local Fenians would seize all Irish-bound vessels, set fire to all other shipping in the docks, and then sail for the Irish south coast. The chairman of the Docks and Harbour Board, the director of the gasworks, the collector of customs, the engineer of the water works, the superintendent of the local railway stations and the borough engineer were all duly instructed to take extra security measures. At an emergency meeting in the mayor's room, attended by the Adjutant General of Northern District, it was decided to call out the enrolled pensioners, despatch three companies of infantry, and station 300 extra marines on the HMS *Donegal* moored in ready proximity to the iron-clad HMS *Clyde* off Princes landing stage. In the event, all passed peaceably, prompting *Porcupine* to offer some critical reflections on the 'theatric tomfoolery' and 'ludicrous exhibition we made of ourselves on St Patrick's Eve'. Greig reported that he

> never believed that any large body of men would show, but the great apprehension on my mind was, that a number of men disposing of themselves in small parties, might set fire to shipping, or warehouse property, not only for the sake of destruction, but to draw the Police to those points and whilst so engaged make a general attack on property in the Town.[63]

Reassuring reports were subsequently received from the informers. Corydon passed on information 'learnt from Gibbons, the medium through whom the Fenians in this town receive instructions', to the effect that 'the business in Ireland was "dead", that there would be no more disturbances there, that all who can will try and get off to America and join Roberts in his invasion of Canada'.[64] As the 'Yankee' officers left, Inspector Horn reported that he could

> neither trace nor hear of any revival of the organisation of the Brotherhood in Liverpool. At the various places known as the Fenian Rendezvous here, there was an entire absence of any known Fenians, and at the principal Rendezvous, there was not a person in the house, except the landlady.[65]

---

63   LVRO, 352POL2/4, 12–19 Mar. 1867; HO45/7799, 13 Mar. 1867; HO41/20 Disturbance Entry Book, 14 Mar. 1867; *LM* 15 and 16 Mar. 1867; *Porcupine* 23 Mar. 1867; Denvir, *Irish in Britain*, p.229.
64   NAD, Fenian Papers F Series, Box 4, 3 Apr. 1867.
65   LVRO, 352POL2/4, 7 June 1867.

Within a few months, however, alarmism returned, prompted by the sensational rescue of Thomas Kelly and Timothy Deasy from a police van in Manchester during which Police Sergeant Brett was accidentally shot dead.

Armed for the first time with Colt revolvers, the police undertook exhaustive searches for Kelly and Deasy, even opening coffins at railway stations ('nothing is left undone and observation incessant', Greig reported), followed by a round-up of suspects 'calculated to discourage the "body" in Liverpool'. The haul included James Chambers, the head centre who had replaced the disgraced Anderson (drunk at the time of the Chester raid, but subsequently redeemed through active service in Ireland) and two recently recruited informers, quickly discharged to continue their trade undetected. Although lacking the qualifications of their American officer predecessors (Corydon had been a trained medical officer with the Federal army), Greig's latest clutch of informers – including 'barman Jack' and an illiterate shoemaker with 'a very retentive memory of persons, places and circumstances' – provided detailed information of frenzied activities at 'the place', Rossiter's beerhouse in Adlington Street, the new main Fenian rendezvous.[66]

Throughout the ensuing legal proceedings in Manchester from the opening of the Special Commission in October to the execution of Allen, Larkin and O'Brien on 23 November (when 25 extra police patrols were deployed), Liverpool was put on high alert. As in March, gunboats were moored off the landing stage, additional marines were drafted to HMS *Donegal*, and in the absence of adequate local barracks, a regiment of infantry was accommodated on board two of Messrs McIver's steamships. To the relief of the undercover reporter despatched by the *Liverpool Mercury* to the Fenian haunts around Marybone on the night of the executions, a mood of quiet resignation prevailed among the customers, 'that class of men who are known as "loafers", and women who earn a living by hawking fish or chips'. '"Ochone, my poor ould country"', proclaimed an old Irishwoman, pint pot in hand, while a man with flute struck up Erin-go-Bragh, and the inevitable raffle for funds was held.[67]

In place of secret plotting in pubs, posters appeared announcing a great funeral procession on 15 December from Scotland Road to St Patrick's Church in honour of the Manchester Martyrs. A dock labourer arrested for posting the notices was described in press reports in the stock terms of pejorative Irish caricature:

---

66   LVRO: 352POL2/4, 24 Sept. to 12 Oct. 1867; *LM* 12 Oct. 1867.
67   HO45/7799 Box 2, 9, 11, 17 and 19 Oct. 1867; HO41/20, 10 Oct. 1867; *LM* 22 and 25 Nov. 1867.

his physiognomy was marked by an expression which would lead to the involuntary desire to be some distance from him on a dark night in an unfrequented place; and his garments, which may have been once new, showed that the exchequer of the Fenian republic, when it succeeded in having a being, would speedily be called into requisition to furnish him with better.[68]

The authorities feared the worst, as the Orange Order, previously compliant with regulations against 'party political' processions within the borough, announced plans for a counter procession in honour of Sergeant Brett. 'Liverpool is a very exceptional place owing to the Orange element prevailing', the mayor explained to the Home Office, justifying his decision to issue a special proclamation to prohibit the funeral procession (outside the remit of the 1852 regulations) on the grounds of a likely breach of the peace. The mayor's proclamation, rapidly endorsed by a pastoral from Bishop Goss, persuaded the Orange Order to abandon its confrontational plans. The Fenians, however, resolved to continue, re-routing the procession to the outskirts of the borough, with no party emblems allowed: mourners were to assemble in Sheil Road, wearing crape tied with green ribbon on their left arm. Having issued a ban on the procession, the county magistrates joined the Liverpool authorities in a co-ordinated mobilisation of the forces of order, reminiscent of events (and the rainy weather) in London on 10 April 1848, 'the Waterloo of peace and order'. On 15 December, in the wake of news of the Clerkenwell explosion, some 800 Liverpool police occupied the ground supported by 350 county police from Blackburn, Bolton and Southport, 130 pensioners stationed in Newsham House, and a troop of the 14th Hussars at the ready in the neighbourhood. On behalf of the Fenians, A.J. O'Shea issued a last-minute handbill abandoning the procession, but, even so, significant crowds (estimates vary from 3000 to 40,000) braved the wet weather to gather in Sheil Road in vain hope of 'a row'.[69]

The peaceable outcome of 15 December 1867 was a matter of huge relief to the Catholic Church, the respectable Irish merchants of the Catholic Club, the officers of the 64th LRV, and the broader Liberal-Catholic-Irish alliance. In the Liberal press, abandonment of the procession became the test-case of the rationality and loyalty of the Liverpool-Irish, their chance to disassociate

---

68   *LM* 12 Dec. 1867.
69   HO45/9472/A19903 Disturbances: Prohibition of Orange Processions in Liverpool and Scotland, 1867–73, 10 and 13 Dec. 1867. LVRO, 352POL2/5, 3 and 9 Dec. 1867; *LM* 11–14, and 16 Dec. 1867.

themselves from Fenian folly. From the outset, Liberal newspapers had sought to distinguish genuine Irish grievance from Fenian villainy, a distinction undermined, however, by recourse to stereotype in characterising the latter. Ireland would 'continue in the bad odour she is now held in all over the civilized world', the *Daily Post* averred, unless Fenianism were defeated:

> The genius of her people, the splendour of their intellects, their wonderful energies, their skill, their patience, their endurance, their wit, their piety, their benevolence, fail to give them a fair estimate in the opinion of mankind, because fools, like ye, Fenians, contrive ever and anon to do something so villainously absurd as cannot be described in any other way than by saying 'it is Irish'.[70]

On the eve of the proposed procession, the *Liverpool Mercury* called upon the Liverpool-Irish, citizens of the United Kingdom, to keep apart from the Fenian few:

> In this town they form a large community. They are invested with the same rights and privileges as English citizens. They are free to go and come at their will; the labour market is equally open to them as to any one else; they have full scope for their enterprise, their industry, and their ingenuity. No one desires to see this condition of things altered. And yet it is impossible for even the Irish themselves not to recognise the fact that by joining in Fenian funeral processions they would be doing their best to disturb the harmony which at present exists between them and other portions of the community, and by virtue of which they secure these substantial benefits.[71]

The outcome was most satisfactory: order was secure. 'Although we have been threatened with danger', the *Liverpool Mercury* reported, 'the immediate cause of dread has passed away.'[72] As if for the historical record, the Home Office in February 1868 asked for a list of the names, residences and places of meeting of all known Fenians in Liverpool since the summer of 1865. 'Although there is a large section of this Community who are Irish Roman Catholics and many of them are no doubt sympathisers with the movement, there are no prominent Fenians here', Greig declared emphatically in a prefatory note to

---

[70]   *DP* 19 Sept. 1865.
[71]   *LM* 14 Dec. 1867.
[72]   *LM* 31 Dec. 1867.

his list of some 20 odd haunts. The leading Fenian publicans had either left for America or given up the business. Among those in America were Austin Gibbons; Patrick Mullins, whose Brickfield Street beerhouse had attracted 'a very low class of Fenians, who mustered in great force'; and the 'notorious Fenian' Clinch, formerly bar manager at James Mulloy's pub in Chisenhall Street. Among those still in Liverpool, Miles Lambert had given up his pub, moved into humble lodgings and resumed his trade as a tailor. A number of pubs and beerhouses were still in business but were listed with the remark: 'Fenians cease to frequent there.' Even Rossiter's in Adlington Street, the leading rendezvous ('the place') after Gibbons, Mullins and Lambert had closed, had fallen upon hard times and was now 'almost deserted'. 'In a community like ours there were doubtless many who sympathised with the movement', Greig concluded, 'but its organization was most certainly on its last legs.'[73]

Over the next couple of years, reports from the RIC officers, who remained in Liverpool until 1871, were less confident in tone, suggesting sinister goings on behind the raffles and entertainment at a new slate of Fenian pubs and beerhouses, several of which were run by women, including Mary Reynolds in Park Place opposite St Patrick's Chapel, Mrs Burke in Regent Street and Mrs Wagg of 'Tara's Old Hall', also in Regent Street.[74] Greig, however, was able to reassure the authorities that Fenianism was now essentially social and residual in character. 'There is no doubt a disposition among a circumscribed but low class of persons to keep alive the Fenian movement, and they are doing this by means of Concerts and Raffles', he reported in February 1869: 'There is not the least apprehension on my mind of the movement here ever assuming the same proportions as it did in the years /66 and /67.'[75]

There was a flurry of activity later in the year, however, as 'new Fenianism', to use Comerford's designation, spread through the north-west, following reorganisation of the IRB and the circulation of a new constitution.[76] Liverpool was the hub of a renewed trade in arms shipment, conducted through itinerant figures such as Arthur Forrester from Manchester and Michael Davitt from Haslingden. The 'travelling organizer', Davitt took on the role previously undertaken so adroitly by Rickard Burke, who had shipped specially commissioned consignments of rifles and small arms from Birmingham through Liverpool to Ireland undetected, using the names of respectable drapers and

---

73   LVRO, 352POL2/5, 11 and 13 Feb. 1868.

74   LVRO, 352POL2/5, 23 Apr. 1868 and 5 Feb. 1869.

75   LVRO, 352POL2/5, 5 Feb. 1869.

76   Comerford, *Fenians*, pp.166–67.

labelling the goods as 'American cloth'.[77] 'There seems to be an ardent and earnest desire on the part of Fenian agents to accumulate funds for the purchase of arms', RIC Head Constable Joseph Murphy reported in November, having noted a marked increase in the number of raffles (prizes on offer ranged from 'splendid pictures' of Ireland at Mrs Flynn's in Hook Street, to a goldfinch in a cage at Edward Doran's beerhouse in Athol Street). Much worried by further Fenian infiltration of the 64th LRV, Murphy was nonplussed by Greig's insouciance. 'The police authorities here are in receipt of information to the effect that Fenianism never assumed a more active form, or never boasted of such numerical strength as it does at present in Liverpool', he reported back to Dublin, adding that Greig 'does not deem it judicious at present to report the nature of the information conveyed to him to Colonel Bidwill or his Officers'. Read with historical hindsight, Murphy's detailed reports attest less to a revival of Fenianism than to disputes, suspicions and tensions accompanying its demise in Liverpool.[78] Having reluctantly accepted Davitt's advice not to proceed with an arms raid on Jones's gun shop in Great Howard Street, Forrester became almost paranoid in his suspicion and loathing of informers (prompting Murphy to express concern for the safety of his main informant). Writing under the pseudonym Angus in the *Flag of Ireland*, the Mancunian Forrester expressed his disillusionment with Liverpool Fenianism:

> As to Liverpool, every time I think of that den of distrust, disunion, rottenness and treachery I grow sick. Possibly, in no single town in England are there so many individual Irishmen who combine the three qualities of patriotism, shrewd common sense, and experience so well, as there are in Liverpool. Yet, today, the Irish element in Liverpool is completely worthless. Split up into innumerable cliques, factions and fragments, each vilifying and slandering all the others, disunion reigns supreme, and, as a natural consequence, distrust and demoralisation exists everywhere, and the task of uniting all these antagonistic elements seems almost hopeless. Patience and perseverance may yet make the Irish in Liverpool, what their numbers and the unquestionable patriotism of the majority fit them to be, the greatest Irish power in England; but it will take some time to accomplish that, and in the meantime, owing to the want of union and organisation, swindlers and traitors have it pretty much their own way at present.[79]

---

[77] Denvir, *Irish in Britain*, p.246.

[78] Head Constable Murphy's daily reports, Oct.–Dec. 1869 are in NAD, Fenian Papers R Series, Boxes 9 and 10.

[79] *Flag of Ireland* 13 Nov. 1869 enclosed in Murphy, 15 Nov. 1869.

Fenianism had run its course. The way was clear for a new approach: Home Rule politics.

Within a few days of a dynamite attack on the Town Hall in June 1881, only saved from serious structural damage by the prompt action of police officers in the vicinity, the mayor submitted an exhaustive report attributing the outrage to the policy of 'skirmishing' adopted by Irish-American 'Fenian' extremists. Unrestrained by the codes of military conduct still respected by the homeland IRB, these Irish-American 'terrorists' relied on communication networks provided by Irish seamen on the transatlantic run out of Liverpool. These links apart, however, the bombers were an isolated cell, acting independently of the Liverpool-Irish and their Home Rule politics, although their presence, the mayor rued, accentuated the perpetual concern for the safety of waterfront property:

> my impression is that the number implicated in the conspiracy is small and consists of old Fenians and that O'Donovan Rossa is the leading spirit using the Irish firemen on board the Atlantic steamers as his means of communication and also as his Emissaries.
>
> Our most vulnerable point is our shipping lying in the Docks – the whole of the labour employed in working cargo is Irish and among whom O'Donovan Rossa might find some willing agents. I cannot see that we can do anything to ward off danger in this direction.
>
> Although disappointed that none of our leading Home Rulers have called upon me to express their horror of the crime perpetrated here, I have no reason to suspect that they have any <u>active</u> sympathy with the conspiracy.[80]

Further weight was added to this analysis by the detailed statement to the police by James McGrath, recently returned from America to take charge of Liverpool operations with assistance from a local dock labourer, James McKevitt, originally from Warrenpoint. A former quartermaster on the SS *Italy* on the New York run, McGrath had been in touch with leading American Fenians before emigrating to America. Returning to Liverpool under the guise

---

[80]   HO144/81/A5836 Fenians: Explosion near the Town Hall, Liverpool, 1881–82, 16 June 1881.

of a cattle-dealer (and the alias Robert Barton), he was aware of the lack of support for 'skirmishing' on this side of the Atlantic:

> During my visits to New York I frequently visited the members of the Organization, and some time ago I had an interview with Mr O'Donovan Rossa and others, and it was arranged that persons should be selected to go to England to destroy by explosives, Public Buildings etc, and thus direct attention to the Military and Police, and by that means inspire confidence in Ireland, but the members of the Organization in the Country scout the idea of it, and refuse to contribute to such a cause.

McGrath also admitted his part in the earlier gunpowder attack on the police station in Hatton Garden in May, a bungled and much less serious affair, more characteristic in these respects of the O'Donovan Rossa mould.[81]

In the months before the police station and Town Hall attacks, Liverpool had been on high alert, prompted by rumours of the arrival of bombing gangs in Britain armed not only with gunpowder but also with dynamite. Following the first attack on Salford Barracks in January 1881, extra precautions were put in place around public buildings in Liverpool with particular concern to secure the presumed prize target, the Customs House: 'The Organization are more in favour of damaging Government property than (as they say) property that would have to repaired from the rates.'[82] The local authorities did what they could to strengthen the forces of order: the police force was expanded by four inspectors and 100 constables. Liverpool, the Head Constable explained to the Government Inspector of Constabulary, 'is peculiarly situated as a Seaport, from nearly all the Atlantic traffic passing through it, and involving numerous Detective enquiries from all other parts of the Country as well as from abroad'.[83] The government, however, remained resistant to the demand for the permanent stationing of troops (other than a small detachment of cavalry), much to the annoyance of the local authorities who were compelled to request emergency aid (from Manchester, Preston and Chester) as need arose. The dangerous imprudence of this policy had been underlined by the mayor in 1868 when troops were withdrawn as the Fenian threat receded:

---

[81]　HO144/81/A5836, 13, 16 and 20 June 1881; *Times* 18 May 1881. See also, K.R.M. Short, *The Dynamite War: Irish-American Bombers in Victorian Britain*, Atlantic Highlands, NJ, 1979, p.64.

[82]　HO144/81/A5836, 20 June 1881; HO45/9604/A1370B: Arrangements for further protection of Liverpool Customs House to meet contemplated disturbances 1881.

[83]　LVRO: 352POL2/9, 20 June and 22 Aug. 1881.

it is most desirable that this the second Town in the kingdom should not be left without the protection of Troops, as from the situation of Liverpool it is peculiarly a place which would be liable to suffer from sudden attack, and a vast amount of property might be injured before we could get troops from a distance.[84]

The government insisted that the necessary barracks should be provided at local expense, a policy flatly rejected by successive mayors. A new factor aggravated this on-going dispute in the early 1880s: the safety of the gunpowder hulks moored in the Mersey. Although the hulks (each containing some 100 tons of gunpowder) were the private property of merchants, their location and protection in the Mersey was a security issue which exposed divisions of interest and responsibility not only between government departments – the War Office, the Admiralty and the Home Office – but also between separate riparian authorities. In fear of submarine or some other form of Fenian attack, military reinforcements were despatched in January 1881, including an extra 60 Royal Marines to HMS *Eagle*, while a coastguard cutter was put on station between the hulks, measures welcomed in Liverpool but regarded as inadequate by Toxteth Local Board, more at risk given the upstream anchorage of the explosive hazards. Having been stood down a few months later, these precautions were reinstated hastily in the wake of the Town Hall attack. Much to the annoyance of the Admiralty which had to cover the cost, the cutter remained on permanent (and dangerous) station thereafter.[85]

Through continued vigilance at the docks, the Liverpool authorities captured various consignments of dynamite and 'infernal machines', evidence of a more dangerous and 'professional' form of terrorism sponsored by Alexander Sullivan (and his Chicago 'triangle') who gained control of the Clan-na-Gael in August 1881. Given the high state of surveillance, Liverpool was not itself a main theatre of operations in the ensuing 'dynamite war', but it remained of crucial importance for the shipment of explosives. In March 1883 Denis Deasy, leader of a dynamite gang, was apprehended on disembarking from a Cork steamer, armed with explosives allegedly to blow up St Helens Town Hall. A year later, John Daly, a former New York doctor with a lucrative medical practice, was apprehended at Birkenhead carrying a number of parcels containing brass cylinder grenades filled with dynamite of 73 per cent nitro-glycerine, bombs

---

[84]   HO45/9339/21762: Liverpool precautionary stationing of troops to prevent sectarian violence 1868–81, 22 May 1881.

[85]   HO45/9604/A1370: Explosives. Protection of Mersey Powder Hulks during contemplated disturbances in Liverpool 1881–83.

intended to be thrown from the Strangers Gallery onto the floor of the House of Commons. A major coup for the authorities who categorised Daly as 'the most bloody-minded Fanatic since Guy Fawkes', the circumstances of his arrest were highly controversial, a source of contention for years beyond his eventual release from prison (after a hunger strike) in 1896. Allegations that the bombs were planted by the police were investigated and rejected by a series of Home Secretaries. Suspicions of betrayal by an informer persisted in the underground circles of physical force nationalism in Liverpool, adding to the drink problem of Tom McDermott, son-in-law of the prime suspect, Dan O'Neill. Once a close associate of William McGuiness, the Preston publican and member of the IRB supreme council, McDermott, unable to exculpate himself from suspicion, was gradually reduced by his 'drunken habits' to 'a mere parasite'.[86]

Daly's arrest marked a turning-point. There were alarmist rumours of imminent dynamite attack at times of public gathering and celebration – the opening of the Liverpool Exhibition in 1886 and the royal Jubilee festivities in 1887[87] – but the authorities were confident and relaxed, eschewing undue panic. Soon afterwards, in what was by now a familiar pattern, Daly's 'martyrdom' in prison came to personify Ireland's grievances. The campaign to secure the amelioration of his prison conditions developed in 1889 into the Amnesty Association, seeking not only his release but that of all Irish political prisoners. According to the reports of RIC officers in Liverpool, the Association was 'merely a blind for organising the IRB', but it also afforded the opportunity for political linkages within and beyond divisions in both 'revolutionary' and 'constitutional' nationalism. Among the leading figures were the prominent publican Hugh O'Donnell (Dandy Pat's successor at the Morning Star); Professor Brenard (principal teacher at the International Institute for British and Foreign Students, responsible for drafting resolutions for the gamut of Irish political organisations in Liverpool); Hugh McAleavy, at one and the same time a paid organiser for the IRB and an activist supporter of the Harford brothers; other Parnellites within the INP; and John Geraghty, leading Forester, Bootle INP councillor, the sculptor subsequently chosen to create the memorial to the Manchester Martyrs.[88]

Daly's eventual release in 1896, however, did not help the cause of unity and the prospect of a revived and all-embracing 'new departure'. An unstable

---

86   Short, *Dynamite War*, ch. 4; *Irish Programme* 19 Apr. 1884; *LCH* 4 Sept. 1896 (in LVRO); CBS Précis Box, 3 Jan. 1895, and Box 3, 14 June 1902.

87   LVRO, 352POL2/10, 15 Sept. 1886; *CT* 8 July 1887.

88   CO 904/16, Amnesty Movement. CBS Précis Box 1, 29 Jan. 1897.

and erratic character with dictatorial ambitions, Daly sought to gain command
of the IRB by encouraging those aligned to the latest American import from
the Sullivanite (or anti-Cronin) wing of the Clan-na-Gael, the Irish National
Brotherhood (INB).[89] This 'New Movement', known in the United States as
the Irish National Alliance, was under the control of William Lyman, a teetotal,
non-smoking, wealthy builder, a puritanical and fanatical nationalist devoid of
self-glorification. Forwarded to the Home Office by Major Nicholas Gosselin,
'An Argument in Favour of a full and complete exposure of the Lyman Wing
of the Secret Organisation in the USA' noted that 'instead of stealing the
funds of the Organisation for his own private purposes, as Alexander Sullivan
and others did in former days', Lyman was 'ever ready and willing to use his
private fortune for, and to promote, the cause of Ireland's freedom'. Gosselin,
who cast a cool and critical eye over intelligence reports, expressed genuine
concern about renewed dynamite attacks as Lyman was in command of 'the
strongest and most dangerous men on both sides of the Atlantic'.[90] Although
not to the fore in the spread of the INB in northern England, Liverpool took
the lead in trying to effect reconciliation between the new movement and the
IRB. Professor Brenard announced a new paper, 'The Links of a Nation', to
promote the cause of unity, but the project was abandoned through lack of
funds.[91] Thereafter, as RIC officers stationed in Liverpool reported to Gosselin,
there was a distinct 'want of harmony': 'division prevails', an informant noted
in September 1897, 'owing to petty jealousy and the clashing of extreme and
moderate views'.[92] There was much personal and political animosity between
James Murphy and John Byrne. The main IRB 'suspect' in Liverpool, Murphy,
originally a publican in Scotland Road, moved to the Mitre Hotel, Dale Street,
the venue of the 'inner circle', where visiting 'suspects' were spotted working
behind the bar; he later opened a pub in Boundary Street.[93] An advocate of the
INB, Byrne set up a rival committee at Dan Connolly's pub where plans were
first laid for the centenary commemoration of the 1798 rising.[94] After much
acrimonious rivalry, Murphy and the IRB hijacked the anniversary festivities,
enabling Gosselin to indulge in some cynical reflections on the attritional nature
of internecine dispute. 'As the supreme moment draws nigh', he observed,

[89] CBS Précis Box 1, 14 May 1897; Leon O'Broin, *Revolutionary Underground: The Story of the Irish Republican Brotherhood 1858–1924*, Dublin, ch. 5.
[90] HO317/319: Informers Statements 1896–1914, 15 Oct. 1896.
[91] CBS Précis Box 1, 14 Jan. and 18 June 1896.
[92] CBS Précis Box 1, 24 Aug. 1897.
[93] CBS Précis Box 1, 10 Apr. 1895 and 29 Jan. 1897.
[94] CBS Précis Box 1, 3 Apr. 1897.

'the fervour of the patriots weakens.'[95] Although Liverpool topped the league
in terms of membership of '98 clubs with 880 members (as opposed to 776 in
Glasgow, 600 in Manchester and 95 in Newcastle), the centenary demonstration
was a lacklustre affair with a small attendance despite the appearance of T.P.
O'Connor and some INP councillors.[96] As if to make amends, Liverpool took
a prominent role (with the Harford brothers to the fore) in the memorial for
the Manchester Martyrs, another INB initiative taken over by the IRB. Here
there were hopes of effecting a broad unity among the nationalist community:
there were encouraging signs from across the Atlantic where Lyman had
been expelled and the Clan-na-Gael reunified under Devoy; furthermore the
parliamentary party, torn apart a decade earlier by the Parnell divorce scandal,
was on the verge of reconciliation. Some hardliners, however, refused to have
any truck with the constitutionalists. When John Redmond, leader of the
reunified parliamentary party, set sail on a fund-raising tour of the United States
for a memorial to Parnell, Jackie Nolan intended to follow, heckle and harry him
at every turn. Having stayed a little too long in James Murphy's pub, however,
an inebriated Nolan, somewhat the worse for wear, missed the boat.[97]

A leading 'dynamite emissary', Nolan was kept under close scrutiny by
the RIC officers whenever he visited Liverpool where, Gosselin noted, he
commended the Amnesty Association as 'a good cloak for other work'.[98] The
extent of the surveillance network supervised by Gosselin was thorough and
often over-zealous. Local suspects were accorded numbers: for example, Patrick
Higgins was suspect 237, J.P. O'Connor, number 242.[99] Their every movement
across the Irish Sea was monitored closely, even for holiday visits, as for example
when Hugh Murphy took his wife and three children to stay with his mother in
Buncrana.[100] Commercial travellers frequently came under suspicion: a watch
was kept on Edward Jones, a Liverpool tea merchant who did much business in
the west of Ireland; John Dwyer, a traveller for leather merchants, was spotted
at a secret meeting in Drumconda but detailed investigation by RIC officers
back in Liverpool failed to establish any local IRB involvement on his part.[101]
Owen Grey of Birkenhead, aged veteran of the Chester Castle raid of 1867,

95   CBS Précis Box 2, 13 May 1898.
96   CBS Précis Box 2, 25 May and 1 June 1898.
97   CBS Précis Box 2, 21 Sept. 1898 and 2 Nov. 1899.
98   CBS Précis Box 1, 11 May 1896.
99   Numbers were recorded when reporting deaths of suspects: see CBS Précis Box 1,
20 Feb. 1895 and 18 Dec. 1896.
100 CBS Précis Box 2, 20 July 1898.
101 CBS Précis Box 1, 27 Nov. and 26 Jan. 1895.

was followed to Dublin in 1903 on what proved to be a purely business trip: 'All members of the IRB get boots from him at cost price.'[102] In the other direction, suspects from across the water were followed just as closely even when engaged in family or commercial matters: P.N. Fitzgerald, a prominent Cork suspect, was kept under watch while visiting his daughter, a pupil at the Mount Pleasant Convent; James C. Connolly, a former agent of O'Donovan Rossa, restricted his activities to obtaining perfume samples to display on his stall at the forthcoming Belfast exhibition; and Michael Dunning, an AOH suspect from Londonderry, was judged to be on legitimate business when he accompanied a consignment of sheep to Chester market. Following his election as mayor of Limerick in 1899, John Daly was kept under discreet watch while in Liverpool in connection with business interests in the Limerick Harbour Board and the White Star Line.[103] In assessing the reports, Gosselin kept a sense of proportion and critical detachment, while always recommending extra precautions on royal occasions: in 1897 he ordered RIC officers to pay special attention to inward-bound steamers 'to detect the importation of explosives or the landing of persons likely to commit outrages during the Jubilee festivities'; and extra police were drafted to Aintree in 1903 following unsubstantiated (and improbable) rumours of a plot to attack the king at the races.[104]

Within a few weeks of the shame and embarrassment of missing the boat, Jackie Nolan, sober and chastened, finally set sail from Liverpool for Philadelphia in November 1899, duly watched by the RIC officers. A few months later reports were received from across the Atlantic that Nolan had been arrested following an attempt to blow up lock gates on the Welland Canal in Ontario with the intention of restricting movement of troops and supplies for the South African War.[105] Previously, British military entanglements had been perceived as the most opportune moment for physical force initiatives by Irish nationalists. By the time of the Boer War, however, the 'revolutionary underground' was a spent force in Irish Liverpool, lacking the vigour and dynamism of the new cultural nationalists (studied in chapter 8), Celtic purists who stood forward to condemn the enormities of British imperialism and its vulgar music-hall 'khaki' jingoism. Delegates at the IRB conference in James Murphy's pub in January 1901 bemoaned the current 'inactivity'.[106] The mood persisted: a visit by John T.

---

[102]   CBS Précis Box 3, 25 May 1903.

[103]   CBS Précis Box 2, 18 June 1900, Box 1, 9 Apr. 1895, Box 2, 22 Sept. 1898, and Box 3, 29 Apr. and 1 May 1903.

[104]   CBS Précis Box 1, 15 June 1897; Box 3, 27 Mar. 1903.

[105]   CBS Précis Box 2, 2 Nov. 1899 and 25 Apr. 1900.

[106]   CBS Précis Box 3, 4 Jan. 1901.

Keating, Clan-na-Gael and AOH emissary from Chicago, failed to lift spirits in 1903, the Emmet centenary commemorations notwithstanding; disappointed by the local quiescence, P.T. Daly, secretary of the IRB supreme council, returned straight to Dublin after attending the Manchester Martyrs anniversary meeting in Bootle in 1904.[107]

In the early stages of the Boer War, Sergeant Roche was able to reassure Gosselin about the security of Liverpool: 'there is no material in the Irish population of Liverpool from whom an Irish revolutionary organization could be helped, the better class being too enlightened and the other too degraded and dissolute'.[108] This assessment was too simplistic and dismissive. A residual hardcore of physical force nationalists persisted, ready for reactivation (and wider community sanction if not active support) in more propitious times. Shielded by the 'cover' of cultural organisations, the IRB retained a presence: 'Jacques', a new informer recruited by Sergeant Lynch in 1905, calculated the number of members as 1300 under Daniel McCarthy as head centre and Peter Murphy as secretary.[109] O'Donovan Rossa was accorded a tremendous reception (and a splendid INF guard of honour) when he delivered a lecture in the packed Picton Hall in 1906 on 'Men I have met forty years ago'. Embedded in a culture of commemoration, it was an occasion for nostalgia and reconciliation, in line with the mood across the Atlantic. Speaking at a private supper in McCarthy's house the following evening, Rossa assured those present that 'funds would be forthcoming from America in the near future, as, he alleged, the dispute between the Clan-na-Gael and the followers of the Parliamentary Party was about being settled by arbitration'.[110] Around this time, Head Constable Humphreys of the RIC retired and was not replaced. Once to the fore in Gosselin's purview, Liverpool was barely mentioned in Special Branch reports in subsequent years.

---

[107] CBS Précis Box 3, 9 July and 24 Sept. 1903, and 14 Nov. 1904.

[108] CBS Précis Box 2, 14 Feb. 1900.

[109] CO904/17: Special Branch, 27 Oct. 1905.

[110] CO904/17, 6 Mar. 1906.

7

'Pat-riot-ism': Sectarian Violence and Public Disorder

W HILE the threat of physical force nationalism was sporadic, disturbance and direct action on the streets were endemic in Victorian Liverpool. Contemporary commentators had a ready explanation: the presence of 'riotous' Irish whose propensity to violence was compounded by 'pre-industrial' notions of time and work discipline. Head Constable Dowling described the Irish labourers working on the construction of the dock extensions in the 1840s as 'the most reckless, violent set of people that can be imagined':

> They assist each other, and attack the authorities, whoever they may be; they keep the neighbourhood where they reside, which is the North part of the town of Liverpool, in a constant state of uproar and confusion on Saturday nights, Sunday and Mondays and generally a part of Tuesday.[1]

When a bitter east wind persisted in February 1855, preventing most inbound shipping from reaching port, there were 'old-style' bread riots throughout the impoverished north end, an anachronistic reprise of eighteenth-century collective bargaining by riot with women to the fore: 83 of the 106 people arrested were Irish.[2] The police were to request the aid of the Volunteers when there were fears of similar riots in 1861 and 1867, provoked in the latter instance by the precipitate action of shopkeepers in Scotland Road in boarding up their shops.[3]

Anxiety about riot intensified at times of industrial dispute on the

---

[1]   Quoted in Neal, *Sectarian Violence*, p.143.
[2]   R.M. Jones, 'The Liverpool Bread Riots, 1855', *Bulletin of the North West Labour History Society*, 6, 1979–80, pp.33–42.
[3]   LVRO, 352POL2/1, 15 Jan. 1861; 2/2, 18 Feb. 1862; and 2/4, 21 Jan. 1867.

waterfront, echoing similar concerns at critical moments of political tension. During the 'great strike' on the docks in 1879, troops were called in as fears grew of diversionary rioting in Scotland Road, drawing off the authorities while warehouses belonging to 'those merchants who are lowering the wages of their men' were to be set ablaze. 'The civil authorities and Police all seem in great anxiety today about the public peace of the Borough, the state of mind of so many persons being such that the least thing might lead to a riot', Colonel G.F. de Berry, the officer commanding troops at Liverpool, reported on arrival, adding his concern about the fate of strike-breaking dockers brought in from Glasgow and elsewhere to work the ships, having heard 'suggestive expressions such as "leave them to the Irishmen"'. As tension mounted, the Home Office took legal advice 'as to the question of landing a force of sailors and marines to assist the civil power and as to the legality of the use of arms by a Force so landed', but were informed that such a drastic course of action was legally permissible only in the colonies, not in Britain itself.[4]

In a much-employed trope, commentators frequently equated the riotous Irish north end of Liverpool, riven with faction fights or 'Irish rows', with the 'savagery' of far-flung colonial possessions. *Porcupine* described the 'chronic state of suppressed riot' which prevailed around Fontenoy, Addison and Hodson Streets, disputed border territory between rival Irish factions, as 'a state of savage and untamed life in the very midst of organized civilization'. When the bruised protagonists of a typical faction fight in Key Street in 1864 involving brickbats, bottles and other missiles were brought before the bench, Samuel Holme, the magistrate, commented that 'after hearing such a cause as that, one would be apt to fancy he was living in some of the savage settlements of New Zealand instead of the civilised town of Liverpool'. Despite such notorious incidents as the murderous mugging in Tithebarn Street in 1874, the adjacent city centre was by comparison an 'orderly place'. 'Except from Marybone and Scotland Place (where additional Police have been sent) there has been no well grounded complaint of ruffianism', Head Constable Greig assured the Watch Committee. Public concern about 'corner gangs' such as the infamous 'High Rip' notwithstanding, Greig continued to concentrate his resources on containing Irish faction fights in the north end – 'these require additional Constables in plain clothes, to stop the stone throwing in the afternoon, with more men in uniform at night' – and on the prevention of riot-provoking sectarian processions: 'More than ordinary watchfulness is paid to the mood

---

4   HO144/35/81408: Disturbances. Assistance of Naval and Military Forces to aid civil power during dock strike at Liverpool.

and temper of the persons in low neighbourhoods and especially on peculiar occasions such as March 17th (St. Patrick) and July 12th (Orange), the patrols are strengthened and men held in reserve.'[5]

Sectarian violence became institutionalised in working-class life in Liverpool, Frank Neal maintains, from the first street procession by the Orange Order in 1819.[6] A minority component of the migrant inflow, Ulster Orangemen generally came off worse from any physical encounter in these early years. 'The Catholic labourers from the South of Ireland', Head Constable Whitty observed in 1842, 'share freely in the Catholic hatred of Orangeism, and as they are the more numerous, and not the least reckless body, they are here, in times of disturbance the most difficult to manage.'[7] By this time, however, the balance of power on the streets was beginning to change as the Orange contingent grew in confidence, numbers and muscle, boosted by the tacit sanction of the local Tory establishment. Parliamentary and municipal government reform in the 1830s undermined the time-honoured ways and means by which Tories and freemen trades (such as the shipwrights) had negotiated within a framework of mutual advantage. Briefly ejected from office, the Tories, seeking a wider popular base beyond the diminishing freeman vote, added a sectarian inflexion to their protectionist rhetoric through the demagogic oratory of the Rev. Hugh McNeile, one of Liverpool's 'Irish brigade' of Ulster pastors. Incorporated into the Tory narrative of religious and constitutional freedom, Orangeism became the primary expression of allegiance, the symbol of inclusive national identity, for all Protestants, native and in-migrant alike.[8] By the 1840s, the Catholic clergy were cautioning against St Patrick's Day parades as rampant Orange supporters sought revenge on the streets for earlier humiliation. In a further show of strength, the Orange Order mounted elaborate funeral processions, displaying their colours throughout the city in provocative defiance of the spatial boundaries of sectarian allegiance, leading inevitably to serious rioting.[9]

An escalating pattern of violence and fatality on the streets ensued, fed by an anti-Irish backlash against the cost and character of the Famine influx;

5   LVRO, 352POL2/6, 4 Jan. 1875.
6   Neal, *Sectarian Violence*, p.40 and *passim*.
7   CO 904/9, Whitty's report, enclosed in Rushton, 2 Apr. 1842.
8   Smith, 'Class, skill and sectarianism'.
9   Neal, *Sectarian Violence*, p.62.

indignation at the restoration of the Catholic hierarchy in England; and, on the other side, by mounting accusations of anti-Catholic bias and Orange infiltration of the police, seemingly tragically confirmed when the police attacked a panicking but innocent crowd fleeing from Holy Cross church as the balcony collapsed. After the ferocious riots which followed the procession on 14 July 1851, the largest turn-out staged by Orangemen in England, the *Times* called upon the magistrates to prohibit sectarian parades: 'The Orangemen held themselves justified in walking this time, if one folly can justify another, by the procession which the Hibernian Societies held on St Patrick's Day. But this fruitful source of disturbance must for ever be suppressed.' With matters nearly out of hand in 1852, Head Constable Dowling resigned and the magistrates introduced a ban on processions within the borough boundary. Thereafter, set-piece annual processions were transferred to adjacent towns.[10]

In summer 1872, much to Greig's despair, the Orange Order announced its intention to assemble every Sunday at the George III monument, London Road, and process to Trinity Church wearing orange buttons:

> For 20 years there have been no party processions in this town but the Head Constable has no doubt that if the Orangemen assemble each Sunday and march to Church, more especially with an emblem, however insignificant, it will assuredly lead to the assembling of the opposite party, and from a small beginning this town may be in a state similar to that of Belfast.[11]

The Home Rule struggles of the 1880s were fought out on the streets by rival marching bands 'always accompanied by large crowds of young men and boys and these, on passing buildings belonging to the opposite party, frequently throw stones, hoot etc … The Head Constable has endeavoured to persuade the Bandmasters to desist, but without success.' In the first half of July 1886 alone, there were 91 arrests for stone-throwing and 143 for assault and riotous conduct.[12] By this time, Great Homer Street was the acknowledged boundary between Catholic and Protestant Liverpool with the most partisan Orange district running north of Netherfield Road. Other borders were less clearly defined and hence witnessed frequent sectarian skirmishes. Direct invasions

---

10   Neal, *Sectarian Violence*, ch. 5 and 6; *Times* 15 July 1851. See also D.W. Cahill, *Important Letter from the Rev. D.W. Cahill, D.D., to the Right Worshipful the Mayor, and to the Magistrates of Liverpool. On the disastrous recollections of party strife in England and Ireland on the 12th of July!!!*, Dublin, 1852.

11   LVRO, 352POL2/6, 26 Aug. 1872.

12   LVRO, 352POL2/10, 11 Mar. 1884, 30 Mar., 20 Apr. and 19 July 1886.

into 'enemy' territory, into well-defined enclaves, were comparatively rare and generally ill advised, as was the case with the Salvation Army incursion into the Catholic heartland.[13]

Within the Catholic enclave, the marching culture of open-air processions was an expression of internal pride and possession, a means of celebration not of provocation. The 1890s witnessed a great revival of Catholic processions, led by the 'Famine' parishes commemorating their golden jubilee. Alongside the hallowed and sacred anniversary dates in the nationalist and sectarian calendars of the old country, here was a new commemorative history in the making with its own sites of memory, most notably the memorial cross to the martyr priests of 1847, another commission undertaken by John Geraghty, and blessed with great solemnity in 1898 at St Patrick's. Jubilee processions gave physical form to contribution history, celebrating the growth and development of Catholic Irish Liverpool, even in those north end parishes such as St Augustine's where numbers were on the decline through the clearances of the Insanitary Property Committee.[14] The most impressive festivities were at St Francis Xavier's where the foundation stone had been laid in the blighted 1840s by Richard Sheil, head of the pantheon of 'Notable Liverpool Catholics' honoured in the local heritage pages of the *Liverpool Catholic Herald* – the columns also recorded personal anniversaries, such as the golden wedding of Mr and Mrs Maxwell from Co. Mayo, fluent Irish speaking Famine migrants who had met and married in Liverpool.[15] Encouraged by the success and good order of these jubilee processions, the Catholic Church began to celebrate feast days in the open air, a parallel initiative, as it were, to Lee Jones's efforts to bring colour to the slums through his concerts in alleys and courts. To add to the spectacle, the Italian community brought life-size statues to the processions while makeshift 'altars' were constructed in the courts, specially spruced up for the occasion:

> The court is sometimes a passage between two larger streets and sometimes a blind alley. At the festival the court is washed out and 'dressed up', a table is taken from some kitchen and placed, preferably, at the far end of the court and covered with a cloth. Statues of patron saints and crucifixes are brought from the houses and put upon the table with vases, artificial flowers, and such poor adornments as the very needy can afford. At night

---

13   Murdoch, 'From militancy to social mission'.
14   See reports of jubilees at Our Lady's, Eldon Street, *CT* 24 June; St Patrick's, *CT* 7 Oct.; St Francis Xavier, *CT* 2 Dec. 1898; and St Augustine's, *CT* 15 Sept. 1899.
15   *LCH* 20 Feb. 1909.

candles are lighted upon the tables. Children and young people sometimes say their prayers or sing hymns by these 'altars'.[16]

Self-contained in Catholic slums, this festive culture of display caused no concern to the authorities until George Wise and the Kensits chose to re-direct the demagogic animus of ultra-Protestantism away from ritualism in the upper reaches of the Anglican church (and Tory party) to condemn the rampant Romanism flourishing illegally on the streets of Liverpool. (Indoor events went unchallenged, including 'Lourdes in Liverpool' when the interior of St George's Hall was converted in January 1909 into 'an exact replica of the famous Lourdes, realistic reproductions being shown of the Grotto, the Baths, the Church of the Rosary, the Crypt, the Basilica'.)[17] What made Wise's rhetoric so inflammatory was not simply its unrestrained nature (reinforced by pedantic and punitive interpretation of the 1829 Emancipation Act) but his insistence on outdoor delivery in provocative locations, such as St Domingo Pit, close to Catholic institutions and communities – the Bishop's residence, St Edward's seminary, two convents and three Catholic churches serving a congregation of 12,500 were in the neighbourhood. Catholics endeavoured to exercise restraint in the face of such provocation but they were unable to restrain the retaliatory violence favoured by those described in the local Catholic press as 'pot-house theologians who never bend the knee to a priest, never darken a church door, from year's end to year's end'.[18] 'The fact that a spirit of party antagonism, from which the City has been happily free for many years, has recently revived, cannot be disguised', Head Constable Dunning reported in 1902: 'Religious antipathy, or rather antipathy between those who differ on religious topics, is always more bitter than mere political or social antipathy, and anything which might encourage the open-air discussion of other people's religious convictions may be a misfortune.' Having served in Belfast, Dunning was determined to keep sectarian violence under control, but his attempts to prevent the streets being 'used, or rather abused, as places for the demonstration of adherence to this or abhorrence of that form of religious, political or social belief', proved counter-productive. With the best of intentions, he sought to restrict meetings to an agreed list of sites on 'neutral ground', and then lobbied for amendment of the law to ban unruly processions:

---

16 *Police (Liverpool Inquiry) Act, 1909: Report*, pp.58–59.

17 *LCH* 23 and 30 Jan. 1909.

18 *LCH* 26 Aug. 1904.

whether travelling to or from a meeting or merely parading the streets
they play aggravating tunes and behave offensively, they often choose routes
through recognised danger zones, they attract a rowdy following over whom
the leaders, even if they tried, could exercise little or no restraint; it is these
which keep up the bad feeling and call for some control.[19]

A brilliant self-publicist who courted arrest and imprisonment, Wise refused
to comply with any restrictions, preferring to portray himself as a martyr for
free speech and the victim of police tyranny.

Inflamed by Wise, Orangemen took violent exception to the Catholic
summer processions of 1909 when it was rumoured the Host was to be carried
through the streets in flagrant breach of the 1829 Act. Although the rumour
was ill founded, Orangemen were incensed by the diamond jubilee procession
at Holy Cross in May with priests in cassocks and birettas, idolatrous life-size
statues and road-side altars (as on the site of the Marybone fountain where local
Irish residents believed St Patrick had often preached), enormities seemingly
condoned by Dunning and the police, persecutors of Wise and his Bible Class
parades.[20] There were a number of stand-offs (and minor violent incidents)
before the first major clash of the year at St Joseph's procession the next month,
an ugly confrontation which ignited what John Bohstedt has described in a
scintillating analysis of the riots as a chain reaction of physical violence and
reprisal.[21] Aggravated by the flat-footed response of the police and the culpable
silence of the governing Tory councillors, street violence intensified throughout
the summer and into the autumn. Unprovoked attacks on clergy and religious
institutions (including denominational elementary schools, battle ground of
neighbourhood women who 'fought like vixens'), and head-on clashes at rival
parades were among the more visible aspects of 'a perfect epidemic of terror'.
Violence and intimidation were deployed to effect sectarian cleansing in streets
and workplaces. The *Catholic Herald* drew attention to the dreaded domiciliary
visit 'to ascertain whether Catholics have had the audacity to deny the command

---

[19]   HO144/659/V36777,   Disturbances.   Kensite   disturbances   in   Liverpool;
HO144/704/107039: Disturbances. Anti-Catholic disturbances at Liverpool. Imprisonment
of Pastor George Wise 1903–1909; LVRO, 352POL1/27: Orders of the Watch Committee,
21 Apr. 1903; 1/29, 13 June, 5 Sept. 1904; 352POL2/18, 6 Oct. 1902, 16 Mar. 1904, and
2/19, 29 Aug. 1904.

[20]   HO45/11138, Religious disturbances in Liverpool 1909.

[21]   John Bohstedt, 'More than one working class: Protestant and Catholic riots in
Edwardian Liverpool', in John Belchem, ed., *Popular Politics, Riot and Labour: Essays in
Liverpool History 1790–1940*, Liverpool, 1992, pp.173–216.

of the modern Cromwells that they should "get to Hell or Scotland Road".[22]
'Both sides appear to have their pass-words; but they convict or acquit a man
by signs as well', the *Times* reported:

> The Roman Catholics have driven the Protestants from the Scotland-road
> area; the Protestants have swept Netherfield-road clean of Roman Catholics.
> It is almost incredible in regard to a great English city, but these clearances
> are effected by actual violence ... It seems to be generally admitted that
> for some time at least the Roman Catholics have been less provocative than
> the Protestants.[23]

Following the latest outbreak of violence in Kew Street in September, not
brought under control until 300 police officers arrived on the scene, T.P.
O'Connor put down a question for the Home Secretary asking 'whether as on
previous occasions the outbreak was in no way provoked by any action on the
part of the Catholic population. Whether the system still continues of forcing
out of certain streets in Liverpool by threats and violence some number of the
Catholic inhabitants.'[24]

While most reports acknowledged the Catholics as more sinned against
than sinning, Wise claimed the moral high ground, posing yet again as a
martyr for law and freedom in the face of police tyranny and favouritism
towards Catholics. In mounting a sustained campaign for an inquiry into
police behaviour, Wise for once overplayed his hand. Tory councillors, already
concerned at the mounting cost to rate-payers of police overtime and riot
compensation claims, worried about the expense and outcome of an inquiry.
By insisting on evidence being given on oath, a stipulation that required new
legislation, they contrived to save face, convinced that the government would
not find the necessary parliamentary time. 'When the refusal comes down',
a Liberal councillor alerted the government, 'they will go to their protestant
friends and the people who are clamouring for an enquiry, and say "we cannot
hold an enquiry because this wicked government which is under the thumb of
the Irish and Catholics refuse to pass the necessary bill this session".'[25] Having
secured the support of the Irish MPs through the good offices of T.P. O'Connor,

---

22   *LCH* 3 July and 7 Aug. 1909.
23   *Times* 26 Sept. 1910.
24   HO144/1044/184061: Disturbances: Sectarian Disturbances in Liverpool 1909–11,
6 Sept. 1909.
25   HO144/1044/184061, 3 Nov. 1909.

the government promptly introduced the requisite legislation. Aware that Wise would need time to prepare for the inquiry, the Home Office proposed his early release from prison within a general amnesty for rioters until Shepherd Little, the stipendiary magistrate, demurred: it would be 'almost an insult' to Wise to include him in the same list as the 'shocking ruffians' who remained in prison; 'nor would it do much to appease the Roman Catholics as the Protestants would score heavily both in the number released and in the length of terms remitted'. Wise was released early on his own, leaving the likes of the redoubtable Bridget Conway, who had 32 previous convictions for assaults, disorderly conduct and drunkenness, still in prison for her latest offence in the 1909 riots: she had caused considerable injury to the two police officers who had braved a hostile crowd to arrest her as she toured the streets proclaiming in her cups, '"I'm a fucking Irish girl, I'm no bloody George Wise fucking bastard."'[26]

At the inquiry all charges of preferential treatment of Catholics by the police were swiftly dropped, 'charges absurd on the face of them, and which were demolished as soon as they were put forward in Court', the *Catholic Herald* reported approvingly. Furthermore the Commissioner, A.J. Ashton, readily accepted Austin Harford's proposal to enlarge the scope of the inquiry to consider the causes of the disturbances. Picked out for special mention by Ashton, it was Harford, not Wise, who stole the show:

> I should like to say, as a public man, who has respect for those who differ from me politically and in religion, and who has the respect from these people to myself, that this Inquiry will be perfectly futile unless this campaign against Catholics and their beliefs is stopped in the city of Liverpool.

Lynskey, who acted as solicitor for the Catholics at the inquiry, relished the outcome: Wise had been hoist by his own petard. The report's findings, the *Catholic Herald* proclaimed, 'show that, in the face of great provocation and great temptation, the Catholic body has acted with a dignity, a restraint and a statesmanship that cannot be too highly commended'. With the Tories in control of the council, however, there was no immediate action on the two main proposals of the report: new controls on outdoor meetings and processions, and a Conciliation Board to promote inter-denominational understanding, a recommendation considered unnecessary by preening Catholics.[27]

---

[26]   HO144/1044/184061, Liverpool Stipendiary Magistrate, 6 Nov. 1909.

[27]   *Police (Liverpool Inquiry) Act, 1909: Report. LCH* 16 Apr. 1910.

After the inquiry, the Catholics applied a self-denying ordinance on processions, and the Orange Order reduced its parades from 30 to four a year, but with Wise having resumed his harangues at St Domingo Pit, sectarian violence continued unabated. A Wiseite meeting in Edge Hill in May 1910 was broken up with force and gusto by 300 young men, proudly displaying the badge of the new Catholic Defence League and marching behind a former INP councillor, T. Kelly (brother of fellow councillor P.J. Kelly); a few days later in June, the Catholic Bishop was stoned by a Protestant mob. The first file in the Home Office papers on the 'general strike' in Liverpool in 1911 refers to a particularly violent sectarian attack in April on Protestant workmen travelling from homes in Everton to the night shift at Bibby's Mills – in retaliation for which a Protestant mob secured the eviction of the boot-repairer Mrs Sawey, reputedly the last Catholic resident in Netherfield Road.[28]

As seen by labour historians, the general transport strike of 1911, embracing seamen, dockers, carters, railwaymen, tramwaymen and others, marked a third and decisive step forward in efforts to achieve mass union organisation in Liverpool, following the false dawn of the 1870s and the limitations of the 'new unionism' of the late 1880s.[29] Encouraged by the presence of the syndicalist Tom Mann, Liverpool workers were united in unprecedented class-based industrial militancy, a direct action 'strike wave' which brought the city 'near to revolution'.[30] At the same time, however, the 'excitement' on the streets accorded undue licence to the city's 'rough' elements. Observers agreed the violence of 1911 was provoked not by strikers, whether organised trade unionists or not, but by these denizens of the local culture of 'rowdyism', described interchangeably in official reports as idle, hooligan and Irish, the 'horde of rowdy loafers with which Liverpool is unfortunately infested, who will not work, and avail themselves of disturbances of this kind to loot and rob when occasion offers'. On 'Red Sunday', 13 August 1911, some 80–90,000 assembled in front of St George's Hall to support striking transport workers. According to the official report, violence broke out in a side street behind the Empire Theatre, initiated by 'roughs from the adjoining Irish district'.

---

28   *Times* 26 Sept. 1910; Bohstedt, 'More than one working class', pp.210–11; HO144/1044/184061, 1 May 1911; Waller, *Democracy and Sectarianism*, p.250.

29   See the various studies by Eric Taplin, 'False dawn of new unionism? Labour unrest in Liverpool', in John Belchem, ed., *Popular Politics, Riot and Labour: Essays in Liverpool History 1790–1940*, Liverpool, 1992, pp.135–59; *Liverpool Dockers and Seamen*; and *Dockers' Union*.

30   Eric Taplin, *Near to Revolution: The Liverpool General Transport Strike of 1911*, Liverpool, 1994; H.R. Hikins, 'The Liverpool General Transport Strike, 1911', *THSLC*, 113, 1961, pp.169–95.

This served as sufficient cause for troops and police reinforcements from Birmingham and Leeds, previously concealed, to be sent out to clear the plateau: their ill-disciplined baton charges left hundreds injured, hence the subsequent designation, 'Bloody Sunday'. Austin Harford led the campaign for a general amnesty of those beaten and arrested on 'that terrible Sunday' and then given sentences 'almost appalling in their severity'. Local Liberals wrote to Winston Churchill, the Home Secretary, in support of Harford, reporting that Deacon, the stipendiary magistrate, had 'lost his head and consequently people were sentenced to terms of imprisonment that was simply outrageous'. Patronising officials in Churchill's office, however, curtly dismissed a petition from Messrs Murphy and Sons which, in calling for clemency and the exercise of the royal prerogative, sought to distinguish between irresponsible 'malcontents' and those of 'simple habits and for the most part of innocent conversation and manners [who] were worked upon so that numbers of missiles were thrown at the Police in a spirit of hostility for injuries received by their fellow citizens'. 'This is largely an Irish Petition, and is characterised by Irish vagueness and largeness of heart', the covering memo noted, 'I suggest that it might be treated with Anglo-Saxon phlegm and laid by.'[31]

The 'gung-ho' civic authorities, unrepentant over the events of 13 August, instituted a Committee of Public Safety, requisitioned more troops and welcomed the arrival of a naval gunboat in the Mersey. In defiant response, there was a dramatic strengthening of the 'general' strike and of class solidarity, symbolised by ecumenical attendance at funerals of those killed in later skirmishes with the police. In Dingle Ward, Fred Bower averred, 'they were going to put up another colour – orange on the one side, green on the other, and red down the middle'.[32] However, as public sanction was withdrawn from the authorities and the police, there was an outbreak of lawlessness, a veritable orgy of looting and old-style sectarian violence which rendered Liverpool, in the words of the *Review of Reviews*, 'A Nightmare of Civilisation'.[33] Much concerned by the 'bitter feeling' in Liverpool, the government decided to intervene. T.P. O'Connor and Colonel Kyffin-Taylor, Conservative MP for Kirkdale (and committee member of the

---

[31]   This account of events is based on reports in HO45/10654–10658/212470: Strikes. Liverpool Railway Strike, 1911; and on press reports, including the new Liverpool-published paper, *Transport Worker*, Aug. 1911–Mar. 1912.

[32]   'Red Riot Sunday', *Daily Post and Mercury* 26 Sept. 1911.

[33]   Quoted in Waller, *Democracy and Sectarianism*, p.256. For the continued hold of sectarianism, see A. Shallice, 'Orange and Green and militancy: Sectarianism and working class politics in Liverpool, 1900–1914', *Bulletin of the North West Labour History Society*, 6, 1979–80, pp.15–31.

Protestant Reformation Society) were appointed to a Conciliation Committee, assisted by D.J. Shackleton, the Home Office labour adviser. O'Connor was the driving force, running considerably over budget for expenses, as he brokered deals with employers and trade unionists from rooms in the Adelphi Hotel.[34] It was O'Connor too who encouraged the Committee to extend its remit from industrial to sectarian conciliation by picking up the proposals recommended by the inquiry into the 1909 riots. Chaired by Lord Derby, a 'conciliation conference' amended and strengthened the proposals drafted but not implemented in 1910 to regulate meetings, processions, emblems, music and weapons.[35] Thanks to these new powers, the last stages of the Home Rule crisis before the First World War were uncharacteristically riot-free in Liverpool, although Harford, a member of the conciliation conference, continued to protest at the 'scandalous' partisanship of Liverpool politics: 'Nothing did more to expose the way politics were carried on than the refusal of the dominant Tory Party to punish those responsible for outrages on Catholics.'[36] Here was another area where the INP played a leading role in overturning prejudicial portrayal of the Catholic Irish in Liverpool.

34   For details of O'Connor's not inconsiderable hotel expenses, see HO45/10657–8/212470.

35   Bohstedt, 'More than One Working Class', pp.213–14.

36   *LCH* 10 May 1913

8

Cultural Politics:
National Regeneration and
Ethnic Revival

A NECESSARY MEANS of regaining self-confidence, Irish cultural nationalism acquired accentuated resonance after the collapse of political agitation and outbreaks of 'Pat-riot-ism'. In the aftermath, the first priority was to disabuse host attitudes, to refute the prejudice and ethnic denigration aroused to fever pitch by Irish 'commotion'. However, while confuting the derogatory portrayal of the Irish, nationalist cultural brokers, anxious to ensure against further defamation, exhorted their less fortunate fellow-countrymen along the path of reform, respectability and rehabilitation. Liverpool, they were only too well aware, was renowned for its 'unenviable pre-eminence in the unnecessary superfluity of its moral and material temptations to wrong-doing'.[1] Much more than a rejoinder to ethnic defamation, respectable advocacy of Irish culture offered salvation for exiles of Erin adrift in an alien and corrupting waterfront environment.

Promotion of 'respectable' national values crossed the spectrum, from liberal advocates of integrative assimilation to ethnic purists campaigning for celtic separatism. At the same time, the specious 'anti-political' ethos of cultural activity provided ready cover for a 'revolutionary underground' disillusioned by the depredations, sleaze and compromise of constitutional politics. In trying to unravel some of these ironies and complexities, this chapter follows a chronological path through nationalist cultural endeavour. Most notably, it highlights a significant shift in focus from contestation of host stereotypes to inculcation of 'Irish-Ireland' culture, a project that exposed the gulf between cultural 'purists' and second-generation Liverpool-Irish. Where early nationalist

---

[1]   'Liverpool's Character', *Porcupine* 30 June 1877.

culture brokers sought to rescue their fellow countrymen, confronted by the harsh realities of Liverpool life, from denigration and defamation, the new gaelic cultural nationalists of the Edwardian period displayed no such contextual awareness. Harsh critics of those whose Irishness extended no further than affection for commercially packaged sentimental representations of the 'old sod', the purist extremists disowned the 'low' Liverpool-Irish. There was no place in Irish-Ireland for those contaminated (seemingly irredeemably so by the second generation) with the vulgarities of English popular culture.

Father Nugent, the impresario of 'Irish national entertainment' and self-proclaimed 'people's friend', led the way in the sustained campaign to reclaim Irish virtue and national character. Following the anti-Irish backlash of the late 1840s, the first task was to ensure against undue Irish boisterousness on the streets. Ably supported by the visiting Dr Cahill who delivered a series of sermons on 'the excellent manner in which St Patrick's Day should be celebrated in future', Nugent introduced the indoor soirée in the Concert Hall, Lord Nelson Street, to celebrate the national day in respectable Catholic manner unsullied by 'either party or political purposes'. Within a decade the number of committals for drunkenness on the day following had dropped by over half.[2]

By this time, the National Brotherhood of St Patrick (NBSP) offered 'national regeneration' through a comprehensive range of recreational and cultural projects, the primary purpose of which was to 'draw men from public houses' and render them 'more healthy'. Based in Redmond's Temperance Hotel prior to acquiring its own hall in Devon Street, the NBSP (which rapidly expanded to three branches in Liverpool) sought 'to establish Reading Rooms specially devoted to the cultivation of National literature and to organise lectures on subjects intimately relating to the history and literature of Ireland, or otherwise bearing on her National interest'. As well as an athletics club, the NBSP hosted the Emmet Literary Club where individuals were assigned particular aspects of Irish history and literature to study for weekly discussion, all part of a comprehensive cultural package to 'make the man a better Nationalist, the

2   Denvir, *Irish in Britain*, p.171; Rev. D.W. Cahill, *Letter to his Fellow Countrymen in Liverpool and Birkenhead*, Dublin, 1852. After the introduction of the new pattern of cultural celebration, the number of committals for drunkenness on the day following St Patrick's Day fell from 37 in 1851 to 11 in 1864, 'Father Nugent on the Intemperance of the Irish in Liverpool', *LM* 18 Mar. 1865.

Nationalist a better man'. Confronted by such serious competition, the Catholic Young Men's Societies began to question the integrity of the NBSP, claiming that oath-bound secrecy and links to Fenianism lay concealed beneath the specious veneer of cultural nationalism. Although 'emphatically disclaiming all political agitations', the NBSP had from the start attracted militant nationalists, would-be activists seeking something more than 'a little speechifying' by personages 'truly English in birth and principle' at the annual St Patrick's Day soirées. 'This is all very well for Anglo-Celts', Henry Fildes protested, 'but it does not suit the '48 men', those 'Franco-Hibernians' who now looked to the NBSP 'to extirpate British domination in Ireland'. Amid considerable rancour, a clerically approved short-lived rival society, the Erin-go-Bragh Club, was established at Nugent's Catholic Institute, but it could not match the excitement of the NBSP, reinvigorated by the return from America of George Archdeacon, a Confederate hero of 1848. Archdeacon's assumption of leadership hastened the transition from cultural regeneration to physical force activism for which militants in the NBSP, committed to 'the liberation of our native land from the iron grip of the perfidious Saxon', had wished from the outset.[3]

While exposing Fenianism, the respectable Catholic Young Men's Societies promoted national regeneration through rehabilitation of the Irish from the stigma of stereotype and caricature. There was no place for the 'stage Irishman' on their concert programmes henceforth vetted to ensure 'genuine Irish song and music should be given, or none at all, and the spurious caricature should be rejected'.[4] With characteristic showman's flair, Father Nugent carried the campaign forward with 'a NEW IRISH MIRROR', a novel blend of lecture and performance at the Catholic Institute: 'an Original, Oratorical, Historical, Anecdotal, Illustrative Descantation ... in which the Irish People may be seen in their true colours, and thoroughly vindicated from their slanderers'.[5] The *Emerald*, 'the first Irish Magazine ever brought out in Liverpool', was published in 1864 by a group of young Irishmen of literary tastes educated at Nugent's Catholic Institute, to draw critical attention to

---

3   This account is based on reports in *Irishman* 13 Apr. 1861–3 Oct. 1863, and *United Irishman and Galway American* 25 July 1863–2 Apr. 1864. See also Gerard Moran, 'Nationalists in exile: The National Brotherhood of St Patrick in Lancashire, 1861–5', in R. Swift and S. Gilley, eds, *The Irish in Victorian Britain: The Local Dimension*, Dublin, 1999, pp.212–35.
4   'St Anthony's Young Men's Society', *LFP* 21 Jan. 1860.
5   *LFP* 10 March 1860.

Irish representations, and more especially to Irish misrepresentations, for the vulgar stage representation of them has contributed more than even their own worse conduct has done towards making our countrymen in England objects of contempt, or of a condescending patronage (like the humoring a lunatic or wayward buffoon) which is far harder to bear than down right contempt.[6]

It was dramatic representation, not printed portrayal (the cartoon caricatures much studied by historians), which offended nationalist sensibilities.

Established in tandem with the journal, a troupe of Emerald Minstrels, led by the incipient Fenian John Denvir, shared the regenerative mission of 'elevating the tastes of our people, who had, through sheer good nature, so long tolerated an objectionable class of so-called Irish songs, as well as the still more objectionable "Stage Irishman"'. Through skilful adaptation of Christy-style minstrelsy, Denvir and his fellow cultural nationalists sought to prepare the way for a dramatic identity worthy of their 'race'. The Emerald Minstrels adopted the essential features of the commercial genre: an opening sequence to introduce the entire company (each member of whom 'had some special line as singer, musician, elocutionist, story teller or dancer') presented and performed in obligatory semi-circular manner (which Denvir noted 'gave us much the appearance of a nigger troupe'); an olio or miscellaneous variety section including a stump speech (written by the talented John McArdle, an 'incorrigible punster' with 'an instinctive grasp of stage effect', and performed by Barry Aylmer, a 'great Histrionic Orator' whose mastery of the brogue carried him forward into a successful stage career); and a one-act tableau, suitably transposed from the conventional setting, an idealised paternalist plantation in the Deep South, to a warm and welcoming Irish domestic scene, 'Terence's fireside':

We had a drop scene representing the Lower Lake of Killarney. When it was raised it disclosed the interior of the living room of a comfortable Irish homestead, with the large projecting open chimney, the turf fire on the hearth, and the usual pious and patriotic pictures proper to such an interior – Terence's Fireside.[7]

---

6   *Emerald* 1 June 1864.

7   Denvir, *Life Story*, pp.118–22; R.J. Broadbent, *Annals of the Liverpool Stage*, Liverpool, 1908, p.296; *Porcupine* 14 Sept. 1872.

Much in demand at Catholic, national and charitable events for their 'songs and "blarney"' (including fund-raisers for the reformatory ship *Clarence*),[8] the Emerald Minstrels defined their purpose as 'the cultivation of Irish music, poetry and the drama; Irish literature generally, Irish pastimes and customs; and above all, Irish Nationality'. In this last respect, they disappointed the reviewer from the *Emerald* who accorded the troupe priority in his 'Round of the Liverpool Catholic Amateur Dramatic Societies': 'We would wish this entertainment to be not only Irish, but national; yet that might hinder the good which, in its present state, it will do among the English portion of the audiences by disabusing them of their ridiculous ideas of Irish character.'[9]

In the new self-assertive political mood of the 1880s, cultural nationalism served as inspirational and aspirational force: as with Repeal in the 1840s, Home Rule was more than a political campaign. A founder member of the Liverpool Irish Literary Institute (which quickly subsumed the Irish Musical Society), Denvir immersed himself in Irish idioms, proud to follow 'in the footsteps of Thomas Davis and the zealous and gifted band who in O'Connell's time were known as the Young Irelanders'. Dedicated to 'the cultivation of Irish Art, Music and Literature', the Literary Institute brought a new confidence (and a pre-figurative vision of an autonomous Ireland) to Home Rule activists, 'rendering themselves, as day by day they advanced in culture, more fitted to serve the national cause which they all had at heart'. Attempts to extend this cultural enrichment beyond the activists to boost support and funds for the Home Rule campaign, however, proved disappointing. According to Denvir's *Irish Programme* it was 'nothing but sheer laziness and pure dis-regard that keeps our people from our Lecture halls on Sunday afternoon, and from our special concerts got up to keep alive political associations and to admit of the great Irish working body remitting a trifle to the Executive from time to time'. Without unduly compromising national idioms, Denvir returned to the formula of the Emerald Minstrels, importing elements of the latest popular culture to attract a wider audience. Cheap and cheerful, his 'Penny Irish National Concerts', held in the grandiosely entitled Irish National Hall, a former Methodist chapel in Great Crosshall Street, drew upon

8   *LM* 10 Feb. 1865.
9   *Emerald* 1 July 1864. The troupe appeared in 'appropriate costume' at the St Patrick's Day celebrations of St Peter's Young Men's Society, *LM* 18 Mar. 1865.

the structure and style of the music hall, although with a strict proscription on Saxon vulgarity and the 'stage Irishman'.[10]

By blending national and popular idioms, Denvir sought to prevent the displaced Liverpool-Irish from simply mimicking the Irishness on offer at commercial venues:

> The weak point in so-called Irish concerts and entertainments, even, sometimes, when got up by patriotic Irishmen, is often the element intended to be humorous. To be sure Pat is not now represented in the theatre or concert hall as a tattered semi-savage, only fit to excite the ridicule of the superior creature – the Briton. But he is still depicted by Music Hall singers and their imitators (many of these last being Irishmen who ought to know better) in their generally idiotic productions as a sort of blundering *gomach*, appealing to John Bull in such slavish strains as 'When to old England did Pat prove a traitor?' 'Pat's not so black as he's painted' etc. Now these suit the Music Hall singers well enough, and we cannot blame them so much, as it ministers to the vain glory of their English audiences, but that Irishmen with any claim to self-respect, not to speak of patriotism, should sing or even tolerate the like is a sign that the rust of slavery still hangs about them.[11]

Denvir was particularly concerned to safeguard the ethnic and political integrity of the increasing numbers of second-generation Irish in Liverpool, the young people who flocked to the concerts every Monday night: 'a small percentage, probably, are Irish by birth, but nearly all, we may safely take it, notwithstanding the marked Liverpool accent of most, are of Irish parentage':

> They have been taught, perchance, but little of Irish history at school. How could they at the ordinary board Schools, and how little of Irish history is taught even at schools connected with the Catholic churches since the good Irish Christian Brothers – God bless them – gave up their schools in our large towns? Though it is quite possible that many of those present are more accustomed to the atmosphere of an English Music Hall than of a genial Irish assembly, and though the tongue and even the manner may have become Saxonised, in their hearts the Irish spark is still lit ... So long as the committee resolutely set their faces against pandering to low Music

---

10   *Irish Programme* 19 Jan.–3 May 1884.
11   *Nationalist and Irish Programme* 6 Dec. 1884.

Hall tastes ... so long will it continue to be an influence for good and the
rallying point of Irish Nationality in Liverpool.[12]

An exercise in ethnic activation, Denvir's concerts kept the message simple
and accessible, inflected through the '*Patois*' of the Liverpool-Irish. From the
days of the *Emerald*, Denvir's nationalist project had been conducted in English,
not in gaelic, 'a language which would isolate them, for no useful end, from
the rest of the world'.[13] Having observed the Eisteddfod in Liverpool in 1884,
Denvir confessed to envy at the care with which the Welsh had preserved their
language, music and literature but drew attention to the political cost:

> He consoled himself, however, with the thought that though the Welsh
> had kept their language they had lost their nationality and had quietly
> succumbed to their fate as a conquered people. The Irish on the contrary,
> had never yielded to the enemy. They had carried on the fight so far and
> they were determined to carry it on to the bitter end – till Ireland had
> regained her National Independence.[14]

In rallying support for the 'final' political struggle, Denvir did not demand
re-education in a gaelic past but appealed instead to simple expatriate sentiment,
evoking images and memories of 'home' through readily accessible writings
and songs: *Denvir's Monthly Irish Library* provided what Patrick O'Sullivan has
aptly described as 'a do-it-yourself how-to-be Irish kit, a portable identity, a
way of being Irish outside Ireland'.[15] The reciprocal bond was strengthened by
the prolific works (fact, fiction, prose and poetry blended into 'instructional'
history) of the Sullivan brothers, regular visitors to Liverpool. A.M. Sullivan,
editor of *The Nation*, was a frequent and honoured guest, welcomed by
political and cultural nationalists to expound on 'Ireland's Spirit of Nationhood'

---

12   *Nationalist and Irish Programme* 17 Jan. 1885.

13   *Emerald* 1 July 1864.

14   Denvir's speech to the Liverpool Irish Literary Society reported in *Nationalist and Irish
Programme* 20 Sept. 1884.

15   Patrick O'Sullivan, 'A portable identity'. The series began as *Denvir's Penny Illustrated
Irish Library* in 1873, and, as Denvir quickly noted, was much appreciated by his 'fellow-
countrymen; more particularly those who, like himself, are exiles from their native land.
Here in England, more perhaps than elsewhere, Irish men and women, including the
generations who, though born in this land, still call Ireland mother, require to be protected
from influences calculated to debase the national character', *The (First) Book of Irish Poetry:
Lays of Irish Bards*, Denvir's Penny Illustrated Irish Library, no. 3, Liverpool, 1873, p.49.

(although accompanied on an early occasion by an uninvited Fenian contingent from Dublin who heckled and interrupted his lecture with shouts of 'goulah' and 'informer'). Following his death in 1884, Denvir and others ensured his memory was kept alive:

> The late A.M. Sullivan assured me that in meeting an Irish audience in Liverpool he couldn't imagine he was away from home at all, for the memories of the old land were, he said, kept as green here in Liverpool as if it were a piece cut off from the old sod itself.[16]

His brother T.D. Sullivan, the 'Poet Laureate of the Irish People', maintained the link with Liverpool, 'the Tipperary of England'. Unfortunately he was unable to attend the highlight of Denvir's first concert season, 'A night with T.D. Sullivan', an 'Irish at Home' which came to a fitting climax with Sullivan's 'God Save Ireland', accepted by 'universal consent as Ireland's National Anthem'.[17] Transposed to the commercial stage at the Rotunda by Mr Ludwig and his Celebrated Concert Company, it was a rendition of this anthem (rather than the lustily sung ballads of 1798) which stopped the show, electrifying 'a large audience of mixed nationalities who seemed blended into one for the moment and were aroused to such a pitch of enthusiasm that they spontaneously rose to their feet and chorused it vociferously'.[18] Perhaps the most impressive display of Home Rule nostalgia and unity was the great Irish bazaar held in the City Hall in 1890 (months before Parnell's fall) to raise funds for a new church in St Bridget's parish, a 'poor struggling mission' where Father O'Donovan had devoted twenty years to 'ministering day and night to the people, mostly Irish, among whom his lot has been cast'. Proceedings were opened by political, religious, business and professional dignitaries, including T.P. O'Connor and the ubiquitous Father Nugent. Through 'optical illusions, marionettes and magnetic marvels', the bazaar promised to reproduce old Ireland with 'realistic

---

[16] *Porcupine* 22 Mar. 1862; *DP* 10 Mar. 1864; 'Ireland's Spirit of Nationhood: Mr A.M. Sullivan in Liverpool', *CT* 25 March 1875; *Nationalist and Irish Programme* 25 Oct. and 6 Dec. 1884. For a useful assessment of Sullivan and the sentimental side of Irish nationalism (and a passing reference to the Emerald Minstrels), see D. George Boyce, *Nationalism in Ireland*, 2nd edn, London, 1991, pp.247–54.

[17] *Nationalist and Irish Programme* 6 Dec. 1884. When T.D. Sullivan was elected lord mayor of Dublin, Liverpool branches of the Irish National League sent an address of congratulations to 'the citizens of Dublin for clearing out every trace of West-Britonism from their city', *United Ireland* 9 Jan. 1886.

[18] 'Irish National Music', *CT* 7 Feb. 1890.

fidelity', including ruined abbeys, round towers, Celtic crosses, Irish gateways, a facsimile miniature of Blarney Castle and a 'magnificent view of the far-famed Lakes of Killarney and other scenic beauties of the Emerald Isle'.[19]

Cultural nationalism acquired a more rigorous and exclusive tone in the 1890s, a form of purist reaction to the political disillusionment of the Parnell divorce scandal, internecine division in the parliamentary ranks and Liberal retreat over the delivery of Home Rule. As John Hutchinson and Alan O'Day have shown in their study of the gaelic revival in London, there was a comprehensive rejection of the ways, means and ideology of the Irish parliamentary party and its British model of national development. Cultural nationalists sought either the regeneration of Ireland's ancient gaelic ways to inspire a heroic civilisation of small-scale rural communities or the revitalisation of indigenous mores to build an autonomous nation capable of competing in the modern international economic and political order.[20] As pursued in Liverpool, this latest 'cultural turn' led members of the Gaelic League (GL) to stand defiantly apart from contaminating contact with electoral politics, English popular culture and 'fake' sentimental notions of Irishness. In the process, they distanced themselves from the vast majority of the Liverpool-Irish. Purity, not popularity, was the essential consideration. Freed from Saxon materialism and vulgarity, the pursuit of gaelic ethnic purity would lead through cultural and economic autarky to political separatism, a mission of 'redemption' in which, a pamphlet of 1901 proclaimed, 'we Irish men and women must depend on "ourselves alone with the help of God" – Sinn Fein! Sinn Fein amhain le cabhair De!!!'.[21]

The rejection of politics was complete, extending beyond place-hunting 'professional' politicians, self-seeking 'nationalist' publicans and the 'old gang of sycophants, Whigs and West Britons' to include the militant Harfordites of the INA. Begrudgingly applauded for their patriotic ardour, the latter were enjoined 'to drop the rotten corpse of constitutional politics (with its Donnybrook and Billingsgate orgies), and bear a hand to the work of building a nation from the foundation, by the only way it was ever done, i.e., determined

19   *CT* 31 Jan. and 7 Feb. 1890.
20   J. Hutchinson and A. O'Day, 'The Gaelic revival in London, 1900–22: Limits of ethnic identity', in R. Swift and S. Gilley, eds, *The Irish in Victorian Britain: The Local Dimension*, Dublin, 1999, pp.254–76.
21   *LCH* 4 Oct. 1901.

and persistent educational work on National lines'.[22] 'The making of city and parish councillors', a commentator in the *Liverpool Catholic Herald* rued,

> has been 'the be all and end all' of any Irish organisation that has existed here for many years. Ireland and Irish ideals, the Irish language, Irish music, Irish literature, Irish art, in a word Irish nationalism have been totally and egregiously neglected while our people have been educated – and what an education for the descendants of a saintly and noble race – in English politics and Saxon ways that make for materialism, free thought, and all the unrest of latter days.[23]

As the 'virus of jingoism and khakiism' spread during the Boer War, the new Liverpool Celtic Literary Society (LCLS), an outreach extension of the GL, endeavoured to counter 'the poisonous dregs of the music hall and the immoral ravings of the British journalist and historian': to its promoters' dismay, the weekly programme of Irish songs and music could not reverse 'the Anglicisation which had of late years enveloped so many of their more ignorant countrymen in Liverpool'.[24] The LCLS invited Maud Gonne to speak against Irish enlistment in the English army, but the planned public meeting had to be abandoned when the police, alerted to the prospect of a massive counter-demonstration, denied access to the hall. Gonne, the 'fair fanatic who aspires to be the Irish Joan of Arc', was whisked away to safety deep in the enclave to address small numbers of the faithful in Saltney Street.[25] There was some support for the pro-Boer cause, a stance generally inflected through anti-Semitic denunciation of the 'Jew capitalists who want to seize the rich mines and territory of the Rand'. The Harford brothers were pro-Boer but not as vociferously so as their INP colleague Taggart who was duly expelled from various council committees. The Liverpool Irish Transvaal Committee, which defined its purpose as 'like the Celtic character ... at once noble and idealistic', collected funds for an elaborate flag of green silk adorned by a golden harp and inscriptions: 'God bless the South African Republics'; 'From the Irishmen of Liverpool to the Transvaal Irish Brigade'; and 'Remember Fontenoy'.[26] On the streets, however, huge crowds rapturously cheered the 5th Irish Volunteer

---

22   See Shaun on 'Liverpool Irishmen' in *UI* 6 Oct. 1900.
23   *LCH* 15 Sept. 1899.
24   *LCH* 24 Aug. 1900 and 22 Mar. 1901.
25   *LCH* 14 and 21 Dec. 1900; *Liverpool Review* 15 Dec. 1900.
26   *LCH* 24 Nov. and 15 Dec. 1899, and 9 Feb. 1900.

battalion (King's Own) Liverpool Regiment on their return from the Transvaal, oblivious to the damning criticism tucked away in the cultural nationalist press: 'The crime of these men will be shared by Liverpool Irishmen as long as they do not dis-associate themselves publicly from those who fight England's wicked battles in the name of the Liverpool Irish.' [27] In the jingo mania of 'bacchanalian obfuscation and rowdiness',[28] Catholic buildings were specially decorated for the joyous celebrations on Mafeking night, most spectacularly at St Francis Xavier, desecration bemoaned in the *United Irishman*:

> the tide of Jingoism in our schools, churches, and society rooms is at full flood ... On the occasion of the relief of Mafeking the whole front of the Catholic High School was brilliantly illuminated and adorned with pictures of the Famine Queen and Butcher Baden-Powell, while the reverend directors of the college amused themselves and a gaping crowd by discharging fireworks and singing 'God Save the Queen' ... the Irish in England are being denationalised in spite of our National League, Irish Foresters, and Young Men's Societies and churches, members of Parliament, City Council, and Poor Law Guardians. The work of purifying this Augean stable will be Herculean, but it is none the less necessary.[29]

In pursuit of ethnic purity, the celticists were dismissive of many of their fellow Irish Liverpudlians. There was a familiar ring to their ridicule of those who had come to Liverpool and prospered, satirised either as 'arrant snobs', a term applied with particular force to women who considered it unfashionable to be Irish and took 'special pains to be thought English',[30] or as 'shoneen swells':

> If by some stroke of luck a 'patriot' gets a good billet and resides in a 'classy' neighbourhood he straight away proceeds to hide as far as possible the indications of his nationality. His children, instead of the time-honoured Pat and Bride, are designated Adolphus Edward or Ethel Maud ... Once in a while, when some big M.P., boomed by civic hospitality, visits the town, he condescends to favour Ireland by his attendance at the meeting, but there it all ends.[31]

---

27   *UI* 10 Nov. 1901.
28   *LCH* 8 June 1900.
29   *UI* 23 June 1900.
30   *LCH* 24 Aug. 1900.
31   *LCH* 11 Aug. 1905.

Alongside such time-honoured mockery of middle-class ethnic fade, however, were elements of a harsh new ethno-cultural sociology, denying a place for second-generation migrants brought up in the 'lowest depths' of Irish Liverpool. As seen through the upturned vision of the advocates of Irish-Ireland, prejudicial images and stereotypes of 'Irishness' flowed in reverse direction back across the Irish Sea. The population of the 'whole Emerald Isle', the weekly causerie 'Ireland in Liverpool' expostulated, was 'adjudged, and as a matter of course found "guilty – with no recommendation to mercy" on the standard of a section of the inhabitants of Liverpool'. Where Denvir and the Home Rulers had sought to educate and activate the second generation, advocates of Irish-Ireland appeared to disown them:

> These unfortunate people, who are taken as typical samples of the inhabitants of Ireland, have been born here, they have been nurtured on English customs, on English ways – on English beer and materialism – they have been brought up, without, unfortunately shedding the Irish names of their forefathers, and some of the characteristics that have been 'bred in the bone'. They should no more be considered Irish than the Boers in the Transvaal.[32]

As it turned out, the gaelic essentialists found it difficult to live up to their own 'purist' standards. In the absence of a significant number of resident Irish speakers, the emphasis on language as the essential ethnic signifier proved troublesome and problematic (a similar lack of expertise hindered the efforts of the GAA to implant gaelic sports, as shown in chapter nine). 'Few Irish speakers attend the meetings, because as many of them allege, the Irish we are learning is "Cramp Irish", and not the Irish they speak', the GL reported with regret:

> it is to remedy this that we are so constantly appealing to them to pay us a visit, and we shall not cease to do so till they come, or till we acquire their soft flowing native accent, which we cannot acquire from books. Irish speakers may rest assured, too, that it is the very language they speak, and the way they speak it that we are trying our level best to acquire.[33]

Those who attended Kuno Meyer's classes at the University found his

---

32   *LCH* 22 Sept. 1899.

33   *LCH* 19 May 1899.

'German style' of teaching the Irish language demanding and 'inaccessible'.[34] The *Liverpool Catholic Herald* tried to add a popular dimension by offering to print popular songs translated into gaelic but in the absence of the requisite type-face had to abandon the exercise.[35] The regular flow of gaelic-speaking new priests from Ireland gradually relieved the linguistic teaching burden on old INP stalwarts and fluent Irish speakers such as the Bligh brothers, but it was wisely decided to postpone plans for the recital of the rosary in Irish at special services 'lest the responses should be in such a foreign accent as to be conducive of levity rather than devotion'.[36]

Once it became apparent that 'class work alone, i.e. reading, writing, translating, would soon tire, indeed might repulse, people who had to work hard already for a living', the GL decided 'to include a social movement in its work', offering more relaxing forms of ethnic associational culture.[37] Considerable energies were expended on expanding the range of offerings within the branch premises in Liverpool and Bootle to the point of almost daily provision.

Table 8.1 *Weekly diary of GL activities 1903*

Day	Liverpool	Bootle
Mon	Dancing class (members only)	Fortnightly lectures
Tues	Monthly lecture and ceilidh	Irish history class
Wed	Ladies night	Irish step-dancing
Thurs	Language classes	Language classes
Fri	Singing classes and seanchus	—
Sat	Irish history class	Seanchus
Sun	Language classes	Language classes

Source: LCH 2 Oct. 1903.

Tensions soon developed, however, as social functions rather than linguistic provision proved the main attraction. Dancing classes were restricted strictly to members of the GL and LCLS, 'a very necessary decision, as many of those who are willing to learn Irish dances trouble themselves mighty little about the

---

34   'Gaelic in Strange Places', *Denvir's Monthly Irish Library*, Feb. 1902. See also, Sean O Luing, *Kuno Meyer: A Biography*, Dublin, 1991, pp.4–7.
35   *LCH* 30 June 1899.
36   *LCH* 18 May 1900.
37   *LCH* 22 Sept. 1900.

history or language of Ireland'.[38] The evening timetable for language classes had to be amended to combat the growing habit of members 'dropping in when the classes are almost at an end, but in ample time for the Ceilidh which usually follows'.[39]

Beyond the branch culture, there was an ambitious programme of outreach activities: Austin Harford was recruited to chair the first GL open-air concert in number 6 court, Saltney Street; and there were plans to form 'a minstrel troupe, the object of which is principally to infuse a healthy Irish tone into the social entertainments of the city'.[40] In its relaxed recreational mode, however, the GL was still expected to safeguard ethnic purity: hardline activists would not tolerate any suggestion of caricature Irishness or Saxon immorality, the kind of lapses to which the less rigorous INF was prone at its concerts. Having introduced an annual gaelic St Patrick's Day service at St John's, Kirkdale, Father T. O'Byrne, a 'typical Irish sagart', called upon the GL to ensure that 'the stage Irishman and the vulgarities and inanities of the music hall might be banished from the concert stage as the serpents had been driven out of Ireland'.[41] Whenever cultural derogation was detected at GL offerings, publicity-seeking hardliners, those with 'pretensions to extreme "Irish"-ism', caused 'incidents', as at the Dance and Social Reunion in 1901 when 'an artiste, who figured on the bills of entertainment as a "Refined Irish Humorist" appeared on the platform dressed in true music hall apparel, and sang two songs which were anything but suitable for a concert under the auspices of the Gaelic League'.[42] Other prudish activists toured Irish Catholic concert rooms to protest at cultural obscenities such as the prominence of the lewd 'cakewalk' and the absence of any Irish dancing at the St Patrick's Day entertainment at a north end parish in 1904. Such cultural vigilance, a 'growing danger in the midst of the Catholic social life of Liverpool', provoked 'Unity' to write to the *Liverpool Catholic Herald*, protesting at the 'narrowness' of those members of the GL and LCLS 'who, coming as visitors to entertainments not meant to be specifically Irish, try to arrogate [sic] the right of altering arrangements to suit their own views ... There is a bigotry and intolerance in small matters in some Irishmen which is both un-Catholic and un-Irish.'[43] Undeterred, the Dermod O'Shea branch of the Bootle GL

---

38   *LCH* 28 Mar. 1902.

39   *LCH* 29 Aug. 1902.

40   *LCH* 5 Jan. 1900 and 3 Oct. 1902.

41   *LCH* 20 Feb. 1903 and 26 Feb. 1904.

42   *LCH* 29 Mar. 1901.

43   *LCH* 25 Mar. and 1 Apr. 1904.

subsequently approached the other Irish cultural societies on Merseyside to form a Vigilance Committee 'for the preservation of the Irish name against "stage Irishman" exhibitions and kindred methods of defamation and denationalisation'.[44] It proved a timely proposal given the sensational events at Hope Hall in November 1906, a forerunner of the celebrated riot a few months later at the opening of 'The Playboy of the Western World' at the Abbey Theatre, Dublin.

Guardians of Irish virtue, members of the LCLS and GL stopped the performance by Calder O'Beirne of 'The Boys of Wicklow', staged to raise funds for a new Lady Altar at Sacred Heart Church. An indignant W. Geraghty, vice-president of LCLS, took command of the stage to protest at the production on three grounds: the association of the name of a canonised saint (Patrick) with a pig and a donkey; the 'inordinate display of coarse conviviality, whisky drinking and so on, which was an unjust reflection on Irish life and singularly out of place in a city like Liverpool, where the Catholic clergy were doing so much to suppress intemperance'; and 'imported elements' which 'more fittingly represented Bank Holiday "mafficking" than the decent jollity of Irish life'. Held in the immediate aftermath, in a mood of continued moral indignation, the first meeting of the Vigilance Committee attracted some branches of the UIL as well as the gamut of cultural societies: the GL, GAA, INF and the LCLS, now attached to the Cumann na nGaedheal.[45]

Duly renamed the Federated Irish Societies of Liverpool and District, the Vigilance Committee supervised a fundamental shift in the pattern of Irish associational culture, a development diametrically opposed to the unquestioning inclusiveness of the INP 'machine' and its unceasing efforts to increase the number of 'low Irish' on the electoral register. No longer prepared to compromise ethnic integrity in pursuit of a popular audience, the cultural societies, again with the Bootle GL in the van, abandoned open membership: the new constitution at Bootle required prospective members to take a test, while continued membership was dependent on a satisfactory attendance record.[46] The new exclusivism echoed the recommendations of correspondents to the *Liverpool Catholic Herald*, calling for 'existing Irish Societies to make their conditions of membership more difficult, if they wish for success, and desire to make themselves a greater power than they are'. 'After many years of bitter experience', Brian Colgan observed in his 'Ireland by the Mersey' column, 'it is

44   *LCH* 12 Oct. 1906.
45   *LCH* 30 Nov.–14 Dec. 1907.
46   *LCH* 10 May 1907.

25–27. As these photographs of 1900 illustrate, the 'Good Sisters' of the Convent of the Good Shepherd at Ford, 'an asylum or refuge for penitents', imposed a punitive regime upon its inmates, some 200 or so 'fallen' women. Confined in a communal dormitory at night, their daily routine comprised prayer, sewing and washing. The institution was funded by charitable donation and by laundry work undertaken for the local Catholic community. (Crosby Library)

28–29. The self-proclaimed 'people's friend', James Nugent, one of nine children of a first-generation Irish migrant, brought entrepreneurial skills and showmanship style to charitable and 'rescue' work among the 'low Irish' vulnerable to the depredations of Liverpool street life. By the time of Sir J.J. Shannon's fine portrait (*opposite*) in 1898, he had been elevated to Monsignor, but he remained known in popular affection as Father Nugent. The inscription on his statue in St John's Gardens fittingly chronicles his achievements: 'Apostle of Temperance, Protector of the Orphan Child, Consoler of the Prisoner, Reformer of the Criminal, Saviour of Fallen Womanhood, Friend of All in Poverty and Affliction, an Eye to the Blind, a Foot to the Lame, the Father of the Poor'. (Walker Art Gallery, National Museums Liverpool; Alistair Hodge)

Burrell + Hardman
Liverpool

30. Chambré Hardman's portrait gives some indication of the considerable bulk of
Archbishop 'Dickie' Downey: a mere 5 feet 4 inches in height, he weighed 18 stone. The
pride of the Liverpool-Irish – born in Kilkenny, Downey was brought up and educated in
Liverpool – he was the youngest Roman Catholic archbishop in the world when consecrated
in the pro-cathedral in 1928. (© NTPL/E. Chambré Hardman Collection)

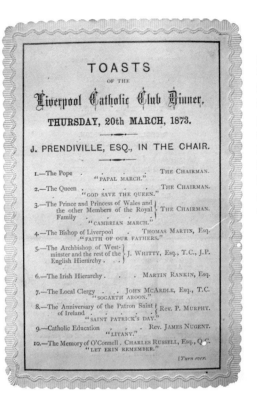

TOASTS
OF THE
Liverpool Catholic Club Dinner.

THURSDAY, 20th MARCH, 1873.

J. PRENDIVILLE, ESQ., IN THE CHAIR.

1.—The Pope . . . . THE CHAIRMAN.
      "PAPAL MARCH."
2.—The Queen . . . . THE CHAIRMAN.
      "GOD SAVE THE QUEEN."
3.—The Prince and Princess of Wales and
      the other Members of the Royal THE CHAIRMAN.
      Family . . . .
      "CAMBRIAN MARCH."
4.—The Bishop of Liverpool . THOMAS MARTIN, Esq.
      "FAITH OF OUR FATHERS."
5.—The Archbishop of West-
      minster and the rest of the J. WHITTY, Esq., T.C., J.P.
      English Hierarchy . .
6.—The Irish Hierarchy . . . MARTIN RANKIN, Esq.
7.—The Local Clergy . . . JOHN McARDLE, Esq., T.C.
      "SOGARTH AROON."
8.—The Anniversary of the Patron Saint Rev. P. MURPHY.
      of Ireland . . . .
      "SAINT PATRICK'S DAY."
9.—Catholic Education . . . Rev. JAMES NUGENT.
      "LITANY."
10.—The Memory of O'Connell . CHARLES RUSSELL, Esq., Q.C.
      "LET ERIN REMEMBER."

[Turn over.

31. An exclusive club of rich Catholic merchants and members of the professions, Irish and otherwise, the Liverpool Catholic Club prided itself on its respectability and conformity to British norms. However, to the ire of otherwise friendly Liberals, the Club persisted in placing the Pope ahead of the monarch in the list of toasts at its annual dinner. (LVRO)

32. An attempt to energise the local Catholic 'urban gentry', the Liverpool Catholic Social Club opened with a suitably lavish banquet in 1881 but for all its good intentions, social and philanthropic, the project was wound up within two years. (LVRO)

Liverpool Catholic Social Club
Limited.
Opening Banquet,

WEDNESDAY, FEBRUARY 16TH 1881.

Charles Russell Esq. Q.C. M.P.

CHAIRMAN.

ROCKLIFF BROS CASTLE ST.

33. Small differences? Despite their association with sectarian violence, street processions were noted for their initial respectable demeanour, a pattern shared by Catholics and Protestants. The iconography of the banners apart, this sodality procession at St Francis Xavier in honour of the visit of Cardinal Bourne in 1913 looks very similar to an Orange Order parade. (LVRO)

34–36. Held in St George's Hall in March 1923, the great bazaar in aid of St Patrick's, Park Place, and its schools was organised by an executive committee led by three members of the city council, Irish Nationalists who were to transfer their allegiance to the (Catholic) Centre Party, including Peter Kavanagh (seated centre) who remains known to this day through the eponymous public house in Egerton Street. In the accompanying souvenir booklet, pride of place was accorded to the female out-door collectors of St Patrick's Children of Mary and to the Council of the Young Men's Society, some of whom appear, however, to be somewhat beyond the first blush of youth. (LVRO)

37. An Ulster Catholic by birth, Terence Bellew McManus, a wealthy forwarding and commissioning agent, was the leader of the Irish Confederates in Liverpool and one of the more heroic participants in the ill-fated Ballingarry rising of 1848. The translation of his remains from exile in California for public burial in Dublin in 1861 was a prototype exercise in stage-managed political/funereal art that brought the Irish Republican Brotherhood to public attention.

38. As commanding officer of the 64th LRV, the Liverpool Irish Rifle Volunteer Corps, during the Fenian years, P.S. Bidwill, a prosperous corn merchant and prominent member of the Catholic Club, endeavoured to proscribe any connection with oath-bound secret societies, bibulous conspiracy and physical-force nationalism. (LVRO)

39–40. A second-generation, upwardly mobile teetotal Irish-Liverpudlian, John Denvir could claim Irish birth, having entered the world in County Antrim when his parents briefly returned to their homeland. A protégé of Father Nugent, he developed into an accomplished political activist and ethnic impresario, moving adroitly between Fenianism, cultural nationalism and electoral politics. At the forefront of the Home Rule campaign in the 1880s, he produced the *Irish Programme* as an organ for the Irish National League and a gamut of supporting cultural, recreational and welfare associations, proudly promoted on the front page. He subsequently moved to London as a national organiser of the Irish cause. (40, photo © British Library)

John Denvir, 1910

LIVERPOOL HOME RULE ASSOCIATION.

ANNUAL BANQUET,

ROYAL HOTEL, DALE STREET.

MONDAY EVENING, 18th MARCH, 1878.

CHAIRMAN, L. CONNOLLY, ESQ. T C. VICE-CHAIRMAN, DR. A. M. BLIGH, T.C.

Bill of Fare.

Soups.

Mock Turtle.   Tomato.

Removes.

Spring Chickens.   Tongues.   Ham.   Boiled Mutton, Caper Sauce.
Boiled Beef.

Roasts.

Saddle Mutton.   Turkeys.   Lamb.

Entremets.

Alexandra Pudding.   Champagne Jellies.   Vanilla Creams.
Rhubarb Tarts.   Custards.   French Pastry.

Dessert.

Grapes.   Oranges.   Apples, &c.

Toasts.

1.—"Queen, Lords, and Commons of Ireland "......The CHAIRMAN.
AIR—"Let Erin remember the days of old."

2.—"The Day we celebrate "............A. M. SULLIVAN, Esq., M.P.
AIR—"St. Patrick's Day."

3.—"The Cause we advocate "......R. O'SHAUGHNESSY, Esq., M.P.
AIR—"The Harp that once."

4.—"The Irish in England "......... MITCHELL HENRY, Esq., M.P.
AIR—"Come back to Erin."

5.—"The Liverpool Home Rulers"........ P. D. GARTON, Esq., T.C.
AIR—"Garryowen."

6.—"The Irish at Home and Abroad ".....................Dr. PARSONS.
AIR—"Home, sweet home."

7.—"The National Press " .... W. MADDEN, Esq.
AIR—"Oh! the Shamrock."

8.—"The Chairman and Vice-Chairman "...........A. CRILLY, Esq.
AIR—"God save Ireland."

41. The social highlight of the political year, the annual St Patrick's Day banquet of the Liverpool Home Rule Association, chaired in 1878 by Laurence Connolly, the first home ruler to be elected to the town council, attracted distinguished guests and MPs from across the water. (LVRO)

TH[E] [COMPANIES] ACTS, 1862 to 1893.

COMPANY LIMITED BY GUARANTEE.

26474

24 MAY 1898

MEMORANDUM OF ASSOCIATION

OF

The Liverpool Irish National Club, Limited,

BY GUARANTEE, AND HAVING A CAPITAL DIVIDED INTO SHARES.

1.—The name of the Company is THE LIVERPOOL IRISH NATIONAL CLUB, LIMITED.

2.—The registered office of the Company shall be situate in England.

3.—The objects for which the Company is established are :—

(a) The facilitating political and social intercourse by providing literature, lectures, meetings, printing and publishing books, or newspapers, renting, letting, or buying property, or any portion or portions of property, and the doing all such other things as are incidental or conducive to the attainments of the above objects.

(b) To carry on all or any of the following businesses, namely, booksellers, bookbinders, stationers, lithographers, and printers.

(c) To purchase, take on lease, or in exchange, hire, or otherwise acquire any real and personal property, and any rights, or privileges which the Company may think necessary or convenient for the purposes of its business.

(d) To sell the undertaking of the Company, or any part thereof for such consideration as the Company may think fit, and in particular for shares, debentures, or securities of any other Company having objects altogether or in any part similar to those of this Company.

(e) To make, accept, indorse, and execute promissory notes, bills of exchange, and other negotiable instruments.

(f) To construct, maintain and alter any buildings, or works, necessary or convenient for the purposes of the Company.

(g) To invest the moneys of the Company not immediately required upon such securities as may from time to time be determined.

(h) To borrow and raise money in such other manner as the Company shall think fit, and in particular by the issue of debentures charged upon all or any of the Company's property (both present and future) including its uncalled capital (if any).

42. Founded amid the excitement of the Home Rule agitation of the 1880s, the Liverpool Irish National Club looked set to establish itself as a profitable commercial venture. According to the file in the Board of Trade Papers, however, the Club had ceased activity by 1892 and was dissolved in 1894. Nationalism flourished in Liverpool but not when promoted on a joint stock basis. (Crown Copyright)

COUNCILLOR JOHN GREGORY TAGGART

MR. GEORGE G. LYNSKEY.
(See page 2).

43–44. In the early 1890s, the *Liverpool Review* ran a series of interviews with Irish Nationalist members of the city council, including the lawyer 'Jubilee Jeremy' Lynskey, the party leader, an autocrat with a penchant for Town Hall receptions and imperial celebration; and J.G. Taggart, employed as a labourer at Tate's refinery when returned for the Vauxhall ward in 1888, the 'first working-man's candidate to enter the City Council'. (LVRO)

DR. COMMINS.

45. A line-drawing of the distinguished polymath Dr Andrew Commins. Born in Co. Carlow, Commins developed a successful career as a barrister in Liverpool, while playing a leading role, as a close associate of both Butt and Parnell, in the development of the Irish Home Rule movement. The first official leader of the Irish Nationalist group on Liverpool council, he also represented a series of Irish parliamentary seats during a lengthy political career. (LVRO)

46. Along with his brother the INP councillor A.M. Bligh, with whom he shared a medical practice in Liverpool, John Bligh acted as host when Parnell visited the town. Born at Castlehackett, John was a fluent speaker of Irish who devoted time and energy to teaching the language to his compatriots, becoming the first president of the Liverpool branch of the Gaelic League. (LVRO)

47. Always dapper in appearance, T.P. O'Connor, MP, was accused by critics of metropolitan high living at the expense of any concern for his poor constituents in the Scotland Division of Liverpool. Regarding his role as representing all the Irish throughout mainland Britain, 'Tay Pay' became a revered figure, holding the seat for over four decades (1885–1929). (LVRO)

48. Jimmy Sexton, a heavy-drinking ex-Fenian well known in Irish Nationalist and Catholic circles on Merseyside, was elected general secretary of the National Union of Dock Labourers in 1893. Cautious and pragmatic in industrial relations thereafter, he also tried his hand at writing plays: his best-known work, 'The Riot Act', portrayed the events of the general transport strike in Liverpool in 1911. (LVRO)

49. Despite his distinguished career in local politics as leader of the Irish Nationalists on the council, Austin Harford was repeatedly denied the post of the city's first citizen. Eventually appointed as Liverpool's first Roman Catholic Lord Mayor in 1943, he died before completing his term of office. (LVRO)

50. The young men of the Liverpool Company, IRA, much involved in simultaneous and diversionary activity during the Anglo-Irish war, photographed on their release from Dartmoor Prison in February 1922 following ratification of the Irish Treaty. John Pinkman, whose memoirs are an important source for this period, appears seated far right.

felt all round that the running of Irish societies on the old spurious, democratic principles, can only bring failure, and that in future record of work done must be the test for membership.' [47]

During this realignment in 1907, the LCLS transformed itself into a local branch of Sinn Fein with a remit restricted to 'education and the support of Irish industries. It would not take any part in municipal or other elections, nor in any form of English politics.' [48] It was soon joined by another branch, the Exiles, based in Great George Street, but after an initial flurry of activity, Sinn Fein appeared to falter in Liverpool. Progress was hindered by a number of factors, including the absence of suitable permanent central premises. Since the centenary commemorations in 1898 there had been plans for a memorial 'Gaelic Hall' to be erected not 'by the millions of an Irish Carnegie, but by the pence of millions of Irishmen' – a suitable successor to the Irish National Hall, venue in the Home Rule excitement of the 1880s of the Liverpool Central Branch of the INLGB, the Liverpool Irish Literary Institute, the Liverpool Irish Musical Society, the Parnell Tontine Society and Denvir's Penny Irish National Concerts. As the years passed, there were repeated attempts to arouse sufficient enthusiasm and resource for a multi-purpose central hall, a gaelic cultural arena for 'the making of Irish Irelanders, the Gaelicising, and saving for Ireland of some small percentage of our huge Irish population', and an economic depot for 'every article of clothing and many other requisites, as well as luxuries, which have been made in Ireland by Irish labour, and not by Jews or starving women'. An essential adjunct of Irish economic autarky, such exclusive dealing represented the best hope of 'combating the bleeding away of our race, and if only 50% of the Liverpool Irish would give preference to the home-made article the emigration figures must be influenced'.[49] In the absence of an all-purpose Irish exchange, the committee of the new Federated Societies undertook to compile a directory of local traders stocking Irish goods, to encourage the formation of an Irish Co-operative Society, and to co-operate with the Catholic School Managers Association in the production of Irish 'readers' for use in schools. Within a few months, however, as the furore over 'The Boys of Wicklow' dissipated, the dynamism dwindled: attendance at committee meetings fell below the levels demanded of ordinary members of the constituent societies.[50] It was not long either before reports of Sinn Fein branch activity

---

47   *LCH* 22 Mar. and 12 Apr. 1907.
48   *LCH* 12 and 26 July 1907.
49   *LCH* 28 Sept.–23 Nov. 1906.
50   *LCH* 1 and 15 Feb. and 19 July 1907.

in Liverpool disappeared from the columns of the *Liverpool Catholic Herald* and from Special Branch reports.

After the sectarian disturbances of 1909–11, cultural essentialism fell further out of favour. Addressing the recently established Irish Society at the University in 1909, T.P. O'Connor struck a familiar conciliatory note: 'An Irish Society meant the culture of Irish nationality, language and literature, and not hostility to other nationalities or a menace to the British Empire'.[51] In 1911, in a move designed to heal sectarian division, the Society was relaunched (with Kuno Meyer as honorary president) as the Irish Society of the City and University of Liverpool, open to 'all classes, creeds, and political opinions'.[52] Although overshadowed by the rapid expansion of the INF, AOH and other agencies of collective mutuality incorporated into National Insurance provision, the cultural societies maintained a tenuous presence. The threat of disturbance by cultural activists promoted the management of the Liverpool Repertory Theatre, having taken police advice, to withdraw a Saturday matinee performance in November 1913 of 'The Playboy of the Western World', thereby incurring the fury of W.B. Yeats.[53] A few months earlier, however, the stage Irishman had reappeared in entertainment mounted under GL auspices at the Lourdes Hall, Rock Ferry in 1913, featuring 'Mr Cornaylious O'Carrollan with his caubeen, dudjeen, tail-coat, red waistcoat, kneebreeches, green stockings and murderous shillalagh [sic]. What was the producer thinking of to allow his ape-like antics, his inane questions and similies, and his idiotic prancing about the stage, as if his brogues were full of hot peas.'[54]

As the final achievement of Home Rule appeared imminent in 1914, the gaelic cultural societies for once co-operated with political nationalists first in joyous celebration on St Patrick's Day (a huge demonstration swollen by the presence of Catholic confraternities whose meetings were postponed to allow their participation), and then as a drilled para-military force of Irish National Volunteers to counteract the Ulster Volunteers and secure the settlement.[55] Drilling occurred in a variety of venues, including GL premises in Liverpool and Bootle.

With the outbreak of the First World War, however, the INP envisaged a redefined role for the Volunteers. Having convened a meeting in the Town Hall of the Irish professional and commercial classes together with representatives

51   *LCH* 20 Mar. 1909.
52   *Liverpool Weekly Mercury* 6 May 1911.
53   *Times* 1 and 3 Dec. 1913.
54   *LCH* 26 Apr. 1913.
55   *LCH* 28 Mar. and 6 June 1914.

Table 8.2 *Irish National Volunteers, 1914*

Place	Date of drilling
Foresters Hall, Bride St, Seaforth	Mon, Wed, Fri
Bootle GL, Derby Road	Every evening
GL, 78 Duke Street	Wed and Fri
Cath. Defence Assoc., Burlington St	Every evening
INF Hall, 4 Jackson St	Mon, Wed, Fri

Source: *Irish Volunteer* 28 Mar. 1914.

from all the local Irish societies, Austin Harford proposed a Liverpool Irish National Volunteer Force for home defence. Enrolment in such a force, he contended, was an obligatory duty given 'the longed-for act of reconciliation between England and Ireland by the granting of Home Rule'.[56] As Home Rule was put in abeyance, pending the conclusion of war, a small number of activists were to define their duty very differently. Nurtured in the Irish-Ireland culture of Edwardian Liverpool, these heirs of the extra-parliamentary tradition were to be in 'the legion of the vanguard' in the Irish 'revolution'.[57]

[56]   *LCH* 29 Aug. 1914.
[57]   John A. Pinkman, *In the Legion of the Vanguard*, Cork, Boulder, CO, 1998, ed. Francis E Maguire. The intense Irishness of Pinkman's Bootle home owed much to participation in local cultural politics and to regular holidays in Ireland.

9

Leisure: Irish Recreation

THIS CHAPTER LOCATES and assesses the cultural mission of the various clubs and associations of Irish Liverpool within the wider framework of commercial provision in a vibrant seaport city. Nationalist societies purportedly gained support in Ireland not so much through political conviction as by filling a social vacuum in recreational provision.[1] For the Irish in Liverpool, the bustling second city of empire, the situation could hardly have been more different. Here, in the fiercely competitive environment of a boisterous 'sailortown' waterfront culture, Irish associations had to compete against a variety of tempting, attractive and lurid commercial offerings.[2] As the study of welfare and collective mutuality has shown, the Irish pub and the Catholic parish offered ready bases for ethno-sectarian 'resource mobilisation'. However, efforts to establish regular forms of Irish associational culture away from either a drinks-based environment or clerical influence and control seldom succeeded for any length of time. The chapter begins with an examination of various failed attempts to offer club and other facilities for the Liverpool-Irish on a joint stock basis, drawing upon previously unused files in the Board of Trade papers. Of itself, Irishness was not enough to underwrite and sustain institutional provision.

At a more informal level, however, ethnicity proved a valuable commercial asset, a form of unique selling-point not just for shopkeepers trading within the enclave but also for artistes and impresarios working the stage circuit around the Irish Sea. By no means a purely politico-cultural project, the re-packaging and re-badging of Irishness was full of commercial opportunities. Rescued from derision, the 'stage Irishman' was to be recast not only on the boards of licensed theatres but also in popular format across an ever-growing entertainment sector: 'authentic' images of Ireland and its people were offered in dioramas,

---

1   R.V. Comerford, 'Patriotism as pastime: The appeal of Fenianism in the mid 1860s', *Irish Historical Studies*, 22, 1981, pp.239–50.
2   Stan Hugill, *Sailortown*, London, 1967.

wax-works and music-hall 'spectacles' with casts of up to 100. While much of this commercial provision operated on a Liverpool–Dublin axis, popular entertainment in Liverpool was enlivened by influences beyond the 'inland' Irish Sea, Liverpool's private celtic empire.[3] The landfall of American popular culture, Liverpool revelled in such imports as blackface minstrelsy, an idiom which spread beyond the commercial stage to become the main attraction in the lecture halls and meeting-rooms of Irish and Catholic associational culture. Through such cross-cultural fusion, the Liverpool-Irish acquired a new ethnic self-confidence.

The chapter concludes with an examination of sport, another significant agent in boosting confidence and pride among the Liverpool-Irish. The flourishing of parish and league-based amateur sport served both to strengthen the self-sufficient structure of Irish Liverpool while facilitating wider civic contact, reinforcing the hyphenated identity of the Liverpool-Irish (and their pluralist approach to the city's two professional soccer clubs). While GAA activists sought to implant gaelic sporting autarky, the Liverpool-Irish preferred to perfect their talents in 'popular' sports and entertainment within their own 'colony', prior to the ethnic Irish delight of beating the British in open competition at their own games.

i. Clubs and Entertainment

For all his success as ethnic entrepreneur and impresario, John Denvir lacked the financial resources to sustain the printing and publication of a weekly Irish nationalist newspaper. Having 'over-taxed' his health and energies at the cost of his 'ordinary business', Denvir closed the *Nationalist and Irish Programme* in February 1885 with an appeal for a limited liability company to take over the operation 'so as to relieve this undue strain and increase its efficiency in many important respects'.[4] Files in the Board of Trade papers point to the failure of such joint-stock proposals. Unable to raise sufficient capital to proceed to business, the Liverpool Irish National Press Company Ltd resolved to allot no shares and voluntarily to 'wind up the whole affair' within a few months of entering its memorandum of association in 1885.[5] The Liverpool Irish

---

3   Scally, *End of Hidden Ireland*, ch. 5. There was much two-way traffic: for example, Liverpool audiences welcomed back Mr Collins, 'the great delineator of Irish character', on his return from Dublin, 'fresh with laurels from the Emerald Isle', *Foot-Lights* 17 May 1865.
4   *Nationalist and Irish Programme* 7 Feb. 1885.
5   BT31/3480/21120, Liverpool National Club Company Ltd.

Publishing and Printing Company, publishers of the *Liverpool Irish Herald* (of which fragments of only one issue have survived) fared slightly better: also established in 1885 it was formally dissolved in 1892 having closed for business some considerable time earlier.[6]

There was a similar record of failure in the various attempts to provide clubs and premises on a joint stock limited liability basis. This was even the case when such efforts enjoyed the support of 'Catholic gentlemen of influence and standing in Liverpool and the county' and were given the blessing of the bishops of Liverpool and Shrewsbury. An elite venture in 'promoting the formation of a new Social Club upon non-political principles', the Liverpool Catholic Social Club opened for business in 1880 in the former premises of the Queen's Hotel in Lime Street, with large dining rooms, a reading room, a billiard room, a smoke-room, several private sitting rooms and 20 bedrooms. Speaking from the chair at the inaugural banquet, Charles Russell MP acknowledged the difficult local demographics as he outlined the proposed membership criteria:

> recollecting that the Catholic population of Liverpool was, in some respects, in a peculiar position, a large proportion not being of what were called in society parlance the upper classes, the club would lay the basis of its membership upon as broad and comprehensive a principle as possible, and that there would be no qualification for membership except personal responsibility and personal high character.

While enjoying the delights of a Catholic library (not of theological works but 'literature of a Catholic kind in history, in biography, in the moral sciences') and a programme of 'soireés musicales' featuring 'negro delineation', gentlemen members were to collect funds to build a school for 'street arabs', an essential first step in helping to mitigate the evils which 'attached' to their less fortunate co-religionists, 'made up in great part of the poor, and being necessarily from their position, most exposed to temptation'. For all the good intentions of its original seven subscribers – two clergymen, two merchants, a stockbroker, an accountant and an MP – the Club failed to energise the Catholic urban gentry. It was wound up within two years.[7]

Drawn from slightly down the social scale, the Newman Club, established

---

[6]   BT31/3546/21656, Liverpool Publishing and Printing Company Ltd. For fragments of the *Liverpool Irish Herald* 31 Oct. 1885, see LVRO, Hf072Mis.

[7]   BT31/2701/14551: Liverpool Catholic Social Club; *DP* 3 July 1880; *CT* 18 Feb. and 2 Dec. 1881, and 3 Feb. 1882.

in 1881 as a social and debating club (renown for its 'At Home' evening in the City Hall, Eberle Street), adopted a limited liability format in 1885 when it moved into new premises in Huskisson Street. The list of shareholders offers important insights into the occupational structure of the growing ranks of lower middle class Catholic Liverpool, headed by book-keepers, accountants, assorted shopkeepers, pawnbrokers, customs officers and small employers on the waterfront. This expanding recruitment pool notwithstanding, the Club was wound up as a limited company in 1887.[8]

Publicans were the single largest occupational category among the shareholders of the most enduring of the clubs founded in the 1880s, the Irish National Club Company. Established in 1883 in premises in Islington previously occupied by the parish-based Xaverian Club, it offered a library, reading room and billiard room 'in which persons of Irish Nationality may assemble for the purposes of amusement, social intercourse and mutual improvement'. Having entered 1885 in 'a most flourishing condition', the Club was 'likely to continue for many years to supply a want a long time felt among the Irishmen of Liverpool', the *Nationalist and Irish Programme* predicted. With the folding of Denvir's paper, however, the Club's activities lost prominent publicity. According to the Board of Trade papers, the Club had ceased activity by 1892 and was dissolved in 1894 with a failed attempt at revival in 1898.[9]

None of the commercial clubs of the 1880s could match the success of Father Nugent's League Hall and Recreation Company Limited. Having developed his entrepreneurial skills in charitable fund-raising, Nugent displayed astute business acumen through commercial provision of entertainment funded by shares cheap enough for purchase by the labourers and poor widows of the north end. From 1874 through to the early 1890s, Nugent offered the 'low Irish' cheap entertainment and a regular 5 per cent dividend on their shares.[10]

Functional rather than ornate, the newly constructed League Hall in St Anne's Street – venue of the Liverpool Catholic Total Abstinence League of the Cross – offered weekly concerts, a fun-packed alternative to the 'rational

---

8   BT31/3529/21523, Newman Club Ltd; *CT* 3 and 24 Nov. 1882, 30 Jan. and 2 Oct. 1885, 29 Jan. 1886, 14 Jan. and 14 Oct. 1887.

9   BT31/3248/19063 and BT31/7997/57483, Liverpool Irish National Club Company Ltd; *Irish Programme* 22 Mar. and 12 Apr. 1884; *Nationalist and Irish Programme* 10 Jan. 1885.

10   BT31/1990/8533: League Hall and Recreation Company Ltd. The success of the League Hall was in marked contrast to William Simpson's Temperance Music Hall in Paradise Street which had to be abandoned after the first season, P.T. Winskill, *History of the Temperance Movement in Liverpool and District*, Liverpool, 1887, p.80.

Table 9.1 *Newman Club: Occupational analysis of register of shareholders as at 30 December 1885*

Book-keepers	17	Wine and spirits broker	2	Oyster dealer	1
Fishmongers	6	Agent	1	Pilot	1
Accountants	4	Baker	1	Poultry salesman	1
Butcher	3	Billiard maker	1	Printer	1
Customs official	3	Boiler maker	1	Sailmaker	1
Master stevedore	3	Chief officer	1	Schoolmaster	1
Pawnbroker	3	Civil engineer	1	Sculptor	1
Commercial traveller	2	Clerk	1	Shop salesman	1
Jeweller	2	Corn merchant	1	Surgeon	1
Journalist	2	Cotton merchant	1	Team owner	1
Master porter	2	Estate agent	1	Tobacco manufacturer	1
Optician	2	Fish inspector	1	Undertaker	1
Provision merchant	2	Fruit merchant	1	Waiter	1
Publican	2	Hotel proprietor	1	Warehouseman	1
Schoolmaster	2	Marine engineer	1	Woollen merchant	1
Solicitor	2	Marine insurance agent	1		
Stationer's assistant	2	Master mariner	1		

Source: BT31/3529/21523.

Table 9.2 *Liverpool Irish National Club: Occupational analysis of register of shareholders as at 24 March 1889*

Licensed victuallers	5	Barrister	1	Hotel-keeper	1
Book-keepers	3	Butcher	1	Manufacturer	1
Collectors	2	Clothier	1	Porter bottler	1
Journalists	2	Coal merchant	1	Provision merchant	1
Printers	2	Cook	1	Wharfinger	1
Schoolmasters	2	Cotton broker	1		
Art dealer	1	Engineer	1		

Source: BT31/3248/19063.

recreation' favoured by Nugent's Protestant counterparts in the struggle against 'Great Grog'.[11] 'I try to catch the taste of the people, and to elevate them', Nugent explained: 'I take care to have a good Irish jig-dancer at least once in a fortnight; negro minstrelsy is also what the people like, and I take care there is

---

[11]   'At Father Nugent's. By a Working-Man', *Porcupine* 29 May 1875.

something of that kind.'[12] Although paid the going rate, the professional artistes (supplemented by such enthusiastic blackface amateurs as the Bootle Amateur Minstrels) were not always of the highest calibre, but the packaged programme of fun and exhortation proved remarkably popular, much to the bewilderment of the refined Liverpool press:

> For about an hour now the audience is amused with a succession of entertainments, in which Irish jigs and negro absurdities predominate ... [then] the rev. chairman comes forward to deliver his weekly address ... the utterances of the rev. father are nothing less than a prolonged scold; and you will wonder what infatuation it is that makes that vast crowd of people go to the League Hall, and pay at the doors, in order to be abused and growled at in such a manner. His address over, the rev. gentleman returns to his place beside the chairman's desk, and Irish jig and negro absurdity hold the audience entranced for about another hour. Now the band plays the national anthem, and the majority of the audience takes its departure ... a large number remain in their places ... Father Nugent is going to administer the pledge. The people kneel down and the reverend father, after another scolding admonition about the gravity of the promise they are about to make, repeats the form of words, the kneeling ones repeat after him, and the proceedings are at an end. In this way the reverend gentleman administers the pledge of total abstinence to a yearly number of about 20,000; and there can be no doubt that some degree of good is accomplished.[13]

To bolster the benefits wrought by the concerts and the pledge, a support and reward framework was introduced with differentiated badges, prizes and entertainment 'reunions' (at which 'darkies' were generally the star turn) for Young Crusaders, League Veterans and the women members in an effort (by no means entirely successful) to curb high levels of lapsing.[14] Then there were the annual highlights such as the St Patrick's Day concert and the summer gala and outing, celebratory occasions with top performers on loan from the professional minstrelsy troupes. Stanley Grey, lead vocalist with Sam Hague's troupe, was a particular favourite for his rendition of 'The harp and the shamrock'. (His

---

[12]   See Nugent's evidence, PP 1877 (171) XI, qq.8194–346.

[13]   'An Evening at the League Hall', *Liverpool Critic* 5 May 1877.

[14]   All such activity was reported extensively in the 'Temperance Record' section of *CT*.

Table 9.3 *League Hall and Recreation Company Ltd: Occupational analysis of register of shareholders as at 31 December 1875*

Labourer	67	Dock porter	2	Estate broker	1	Printer	1
Married woman	28	Engine driver	2	Fish salesman		Railway porter	1
Spinster	16	Esquire	2	(see also		Receiving clerk	1
Workman	16	Foreman	2	Fishmonger)	1	Restaurant	
Dock labourer	9	Fruiterer	2	Fishmonger	1	keeper	1
Widow	7	Furniture dealer	2	Foreman tailor	1	Rigger	1
Hawker	6	Marine store		Forge labourer	1	Saddler	1
Grocer	5	dealer	2	Freight clerk	1	Sawyer	1
Clerk in Holy		Newsvendor	2	French polisher	1	Schoolmaster	1
Orders	4	Provision dealer	2	Fruit salesman		Sempstress	1
Gentleman	4	Shipwright	2	(see also		Servant	1
Tailor	4	Stationer	2	Fruiterer)	1	Ship painter	1
Warehouseman	4	Storekeeper	2	Greengrocer	1	Ship's carpenter	1
Porter	4	Assistant at		Hairdresser	1	Shipkeeper	1
Baker	3	Works	1	Hosier	1	Shopkeeper	1
Carter	3	Billiard table		Housemaid	1	Shore cook	1
Clerk	3	manufacturer	1	Landing clerk	1	Smallware dealer	1
Cooper	3	Boil (sic) maker	1	Letter carrier	1	Smith striker	1
Cotton dealer	3	Boiler Maker	1	Lime merchant	1	Soda water	
Cotton porter	3	Bricklayer	1	Lodging		manufacturer	1
Custom House		Brickmaker	1	housekeeper	1	Solicitor	1
Officer	3	Charwoman	1	Manager Seamen's		Sportsman	1
Gas stoker	3	Chimney-sweep	1	Protective		Stevedore	1
Joiner	3	Club collector	1	Society	1	Student	1
Merchant	3	Coal agent	1	Mariner	1	Sugar boiler	1
Painter	3	Coal merchant	1	Master cooper	1	Surveyor	1
Shoemaker	3	Coalheaver	1	Master tailor	1	Tanner	1
Workwoman	3	Confectioner	1	Miner	1	Tin Plate Maker	1
Artist	2	Corn sampler	1	Optician	1	Traveller	1
Book-keeper	2	Cotton merchant	1	Outfitter	1	Van man	1
Bootmaker	2	Cutter	1	Packer	1	Weight-taker	1
Cab driver	2	Dockyard servant	1	Pawnbroker	1	Woodcarver	1
Cart-owner	2	Dye Sinker	1	Pedlar	1		
Delivery clerk	2	Estate agent	1	Pensioner	1		

NB. A small number of entries either have no occupation or are listed as 'infant' or 'minor'.

Source: BT31/1990/8533.

services were also obtained on the occasion of the Papal Jubilee to lead the singing of 'God bless the Pope'.)[15] The summer outdoor gala always drew large crowds, several thousands strong (it was Nugent's ambition to surpass numbers at the Whitsun celebrations in Catholic Preston): the first such holiday venture, held in the centenary year of the Liberator's birth, began with entertainment by members of the Christy Minstrels accompanied by some Irish fiddlers, followed by athletic sports, and concluded with fireworks, a remarkable *feu d'artifice* displaying the words 'O'Connell 1775'.[16] The annual Easter holiday entertainment, held in the St Anne Street premises, was under the direction of Charles McCarthy, the manager of the Hall, who blacked up for the occasion of 'intense amusement', accompanied by 'a large number of artistes in the role of "darkies"'.[17]

Through the provision of 'Irish jigs and negro absurdities', Nugent trusted to attract the 'low Irish' away from the pubs, temperance being the necessary first step towards recognition of their 'responsibility as citizens of the town, children of the Irish race, and as Catholics'.[18] Given the housing conditions in the north end, he placed little hope in the cultivation of domestic pleasure in 'squalid Liverpool', although he encouraged the women to brighten up the home by distributing free flowers (as well as providing cookery demonstrations). Even here, however, he recognised the need for some fun and entertainment to bring the women in: proceedings at one of his 'Flower Mission' meetings at the League Hall, attended by 4000 women (and graced by the mayor and his wife), opened with a particularly hilarious negro burlesque by the Brothers Vane.[19] Cherishing company and entertainment outside the cramped home, the poor Irish, Nugent rued, were drawn to the pubs:

> If a man finds a public-house at every corner, and that public-house is more comfortable than his own home, the temptation to go in is very strong. This is especially the case with the Irish, who are rather of a cheerful temperament. They go in, perhaps, to get one glass, and that leads to many more.[20]

15 *CT* 23 Mar. and 8 June 1877.
16 *CT* 20 Aug. 1875.
17 *CT* 10 Apr. 1885.
18 *CT* 28 Jan. 1876.
19 *CT* 23 June 1882.
20 *Mortality Sub-Committee.*, pp.195–210.

To rescue and regenerate his fellow countrymen and co-religionists Nugent stepped forward to offer 'innocent recreation':

> One half of the troubles into which the humbler classes fell, sprang from the want of not having opportunities of spending, in a pleasant manner, their time after the labours and anxieties of the day (hear, hear). People who fall into the habits of intemperance, especially the Irish people, fall through company much more than through love of drink ... in the League Hall they were trying to combat nearly all the sources of evil into which the Irish people fall.[21]

Nugent provided entertainment 'second to none in Liverpool', offered at prices (for unreserved places underneath the galleries) which attracted 'the very rag-tag and bobtail of Sawney Pope-street and Scotland-road ... some of them look as if they had taken the pledge not only against the use of intoxicating stimulants, but also of soap and water'.[22] Most of the audience came just for the fun, displaying scant respect for the pledge itself – Nugent 'complained bitterly of persons, especially females, leaving the hall during the performance to go and have the "last glass" before taking the pledge', and duly moved the ceremony earlier in the programme to underline its solemnity.[23] Alongside the stock repertoire of 'laughable Irish and negro sketches' there was a bewildering array of acts: Messrs Wallace and Leathwood's celebrated Austrian Musical Cabinet comprising a large variety of musical instruments of all shapes and sizes from tiny fiddles to musical coffee pots; Professor Atherton's performing dogs; and various depictions of Ireland – beauty spots recreated in minutes by lightning painters or more harrowing images, scenes of distress in the west illustrated by limelight and new 'oxy-hydrogen' technology. Alongside his 'darkie' performances, McCarthy, an accomplished tenor, delighted audiences with his poignant renditions of Irish ballads – in the midst of a limelight 'Trip Round the World', he was called upon to lead the singing of 'The Harp and the Shamrock' when Sackville Street (later O'Connell Street), Dublin, came into (show-stopping) view. Through variety and innovation – 'each week presents some fresh novelty' – Nugent sought to keep pace with commercial Christy minstrelsy.[24]

---

21 *CT* 28 Jan. 1876.
22 *Liverpool Critic* 5 May 1877.
23 *CT* 7 July and 8 Dec. 1882.
24 League Hall reports in *CT* 2 July and 17 Sept. 1875, 2 Apr. 1880, 14 Sept. 1881, 14 July 1882 and 5 June 1885. Local Home Rule politicians were displeased when a lightning artist concluded his performance, presumably on Nugent's instructions, with 'a picture of

An old name, the Emerald Minstrels was revived in the 1880s when McCarthy formed a new troupe as a supporting act for Nugent's extension of activities beyond the north end. The troupe accompanied Nugent on a missionary trip across the Mersey to promote temperance in Birkenhead, and also offered a programme 'mainly composed of Irish songs and music' in the opening season of Nugent's 'People's Free Concerts' in the Rotunda (subsequently Picton) Lecture Hall.[25] An ambitious ecumenical extension of the League Hall project, these Saturday-night concerts (attended by 50,000 in the first six months) sought through 'innocent and rational amusement' to produce 'more kindly and friendly relations between people of different grades in society and different strands of religious and political opinions'. For all the emphasis on the refining influence of concert music, graced by the occasional presence of maestro Rodewald at the conductor's rostrum, Nugent's 'Saturday pops' (to use George Melly's approving designation) were regularly enlivened by the appearance of blackface troupes (with sketches depicting 'Black stupidity'). Crowds had to be turned away and a return visit arranged when the Wandering Darkies appeared in a performance of 'marked originality and absolute freedom from vulgarity'. Blackface disguise facilitated the kind of social interaction which Nugent advocated, bringing together different creeds (as with the Walton Minstrels, 'many of whom were of a different religious persuasion') and, more important, different classes. When the Social Darkies followed their Saturday-evening success at the Rotunda Lecture Hall with a repeat performance at the League Hall on Monday, Nugent stressed the importance of active middle-class social leadership to elevate the Liverpool Irish:

> He thought it was a happy state of public feeling when young men of good position, like those gentlemen, devoted their leisure and their musical abilities to their less fortunate brethren, and such different classes of people were brought together ... If he could band around him some fifty or sixty men of position, education, and influence to join in this movement and work for the interest of their humbler brethren, Catholic men who would sacrifice some of their time in the interests of the people, like those gentlemen who gave that entertainment, they would change altogether the social condition of our people.[26]

a ship in full sail, with the ominous words, "Poor Pat must emigrate"', see 'Father Nugent and Emigration', *DP* 27 July 1880.

[25]   *CT* 17 Apr. 28 Aug. and 25 Oct. 1885.

[26]   *CT* 23 Jan, 1 May and 11 Dec. 1885, 19 March 1886, 28 Jan. 1887, 7 Dec. 1888, 11 Jan., 22 Feb. and 1 Mar. 1889.

Although applauded by civic dignitaries, Protestant philanthropists, shipowners and merchant princes, Nugent's entertainment projects were unable either to break the Liverpudlian mould of institutionalised ethno-sectarianism or, as confidence in Home Rule developed, to offer a sufficiently pure 'ethnic' cultural expression for those of his own faith and fatherland. Having superseded the stage Irishman, blackface minstrelsy spread across classes and creeds: the Kentucky Darkies, a particular favourite in the outreach activities of Liverpool Tories among the Protestant working class, appeared on occasion before Catholic audiences at the League Hall. Some troupes, indeed, reached into parts denied Roman Catholics. The Anglican governors of the National Schools at Seaforth allowed minstrelsy on the premises, but forbade Father Nugent from lecturing on temperance:

> Now, we have no desire to decry the undeniable attractions of the artists in cork-ash and cheap finery, whose lucubrations by aid of 'de ole banjo' and the bones are so justly popular; but we should have thought that the teachings of an experienced and eloquent philanthropist, inculcating sobriety, cleanliness of life and temperance, without reference to doctrine and dogma, would have been at least as useful and acceptable. The school committee, however, can tolerate 'niggers'; but they must draw the line somewhere, and they draw it at Roman Catholics.[27]

While Denvir abandoned minstrelsy to offer the repertoire of 'Young Ireland' for his Penny Irish National Concerts, Nugent persisted with populist idioms and cultural borrowings. Audiences still appreciated the blend, not least the special guest appearance by Billy Richardson, Sam Hague's star stump orator, but there was some consternation when the Negro Nomads provided the entertainment at Nugent's People's Free Concert on St Patrick's Day 1888.[28] Nugent's cultural politics continued to draw upon an array of influences, affiliations and identities, symbolically depicted in the flags and banners which greeted his return to the League Hall after a lengthy recuperative absence on the continent: 'The gallery was backed with the royal standard and the Papal flag while a long scroll in front bore the appropriate motto "*Cead mille failthe,*

---

[27] '"Niggers", but No Popery', *Porcupine* 12 Mar. 1881.
[28] League Hall reports in *CT* 7 and 28 May 1885, 27 July 1887, 13 Apr. and 25 May 1888, and of People's Free Concerts in *CT* 16 and 23 Mar. 1888.

soggarth aroon"; with the stars and stripes, and the green flag with the crownless harp at either side.'[29]

Nugent's relations with Home Rule politicians were ambivalent, dependent on their willingness to recognise sobriety as the precondition for Irish independence. Shortly after his mould-breaking election victory in 1875, Laurence Connolly was the honoured guest at a League Hall concert at which 'the most laughable part of the programme may be considered to be the nigger burlesque by Messrs McCabe and Keeffe'.[30] Nugent made it clear, however, that he would never mix with those 'who discuss national questions in public-houses, and who desecrate the green flag of our race with the excesses of drink'.[31] The point was appreciated by Charles McArdle, who secured Vauxhall for the nationalists after the death of the leading Irish Catholic 'whig' James Whitty in 1876. Attributing his continued tenure of the seat to support provided by the League of the Cross of which he became a Veteran himself, McArdle was a regular speaker at their League Hall reunions, reflecting on how he had 'in his own little way done what he could to elevate the Irish name and character in Liverpool'.[32] At the height of the Home Rule crisis, Nugent was prepared to cancel the weekly concert to allow T.P. O'Connor to use the Hall for election purposes,[33] but he still refrained from unequivocal support of the political project:

> For a long time he had allowed himself to be occupied with only one question, but that was one which he felt to be bound up with the regeneration and prosperity of the Irish people. If he was silent on other questions, it was not that he felt less than others did, but he was convinced that he had one duty and one call ... if he could impress upon their people the necessity of being sober, the necessity of avoiding drink, and of banding themselves in one compact phalanx against their great enemy, he would be doing something to help the Irish people achieve for themselves the greatest religious power and the political power they could exercise.[34]

Throughout the Land War (1879–82), he called upon the Irish in Liverpool to 'boycott' public houses in the name 'not of the Land League, but of the League

---

29 'Father Nugent's Return to Liverpool', *CT* 29 June 1888.
30 *CT* 3 Dec. 1875.
31 *CT* 30 Apr. 1875.
32 'The Liverpool Veterans Grand Reunion', *CT* 3 Feb. 1882.
33 *CT* 2 July 1886.
34 *CT* 19 Mar. 1886.

of the Cross', and warned them especially 'against such public-houses as are decorated with patriotic emblems'.[35] The problem was compounded by changes in the licensed trade as family-run pubs gave way to 'monster establishments' with 'costly fittings' and with Irish managers and barmen. The brewers, Nugent rued, 'knew how to get an Irishman in "to run" the house, who would get people to come there and talk politics, and about the old country, and profess to have sympathy for them, and take the last farthing out of their pockets and leave them paupers'.[36]

ii. The Irish and the Stage

At the bottom end of the market, beneath the licensed theatres and music halls, 'entertainment' was offered in a number of public, beer and refreshment houses, nearly 50 in total in 1866, 'low places' catering for the vast floating, migrant and casual population of the great seaport. Reduced to the crudest stereotype for a multi-national audience, the stage Irishman shared the boards in such dubious premises with other acts luring the unwary into drink and other dangers through device and deception: risqué tableaux vivants in which participants cross-dressed or wore only flesh-coloured cotton tights; and the 'hideous' blacking-up of musicians and dancers such as Mr Nozzle ('a nigger singer with blackened face, striped shirt, tight trousers, and top boots') and Mr Banjo Bones, a favourite who, as Dickens observed, could command a considerable fee.[37] Built around a once-grand theatre, now descended into a disreputable 'gaff', Homer's Gardens, fictional setting ('not far from one of the great thoroughfares leading to the "North-end"') of *The Brandons*, Denvir's serialised story of Irish life in Liverpool, provided lodgings for artistes and street-performers of various nationalities, mainly Irish, Italian and Jewish – Punch and Judy men, acrobats, organ-grinders, musicians, out-of-work artistes

35   *CT* 9 July 1880 and 11 Feb. 1881.

36   *CT* 15 Mar. 1889. Ahead of developments elsewhere, drink in Liverpool had become a 'gigantic business in which large capitalists are embarked', 'Liverpool's Black-Book', *Times* 26 Nov. 1877.

37   See the evidence of Head Constable Greig to 'Report of the Select Committee on Theatrical Licenses and Regulations', PP 1866 (373) XVI, qq.6943–7199; 'The Amusements and Literature of the People: Labour and the Poor, Liverpool, letter xvi', *Morning Chronicle* 2 Sept. 1850; 'The Free Concert Room', in H. Shimmin, *Liverpool Life: Its Pleasures, Practices and Pastimes*, Liverpool, 1857, ch. 4; Charles Dickens, *The Uncommercial Traveller*, final edition, 1869, ch. 5.

and 'burnt-cork niggers now looking somewhat pie-bald after the day's heat'.[38] In cosmopolitan areas such as this, with a floating population of transients, sojourners and settlers, 'sailortown' Liverpool was more akin to Five Points, 'the 19th century New York City neighborhood that invented tap dance, stole elections, and became the world's most notorious slum'.[39] Liverpool, however, seems not to have matched such 'syncretic' fusion between Irish and black culture, although it was always receptive to the latest fashion from across the Atlantic – boys as young as seven took to the cheap concert-room stage to perform clog dances 'à la Juba'.[40] The mainstay of the cheap music halls remained the unreconstructed 'stage Irishman'.

In these 'low places', Greig reported, 'rough acting goes on; Irish characters principally, and comic songs'.[41] Through its 'camera obscura', *Porcupine* offered a glimpse inside one such lowly establishment, housed in premises – 'a cheaply run up, stucco-fronted lecture hall, the work of a Welsh "jerry-builder", turned into a minor concert room' – the evolution of which epitomised Liverpool's distinctive cultural mix:

> Becoming, in rapid succession, a model lodging-house, an "hotel" for poor German emigrants, and a dance-house for foreign sailors. Reverting to something of its original character as a forum for professional atheists – 'fighting permitted after the lecture', and as a meeting-place for the 'Royal Tipperary Friendly Society', the members of which discuss resolutions *vi et armis* over the prostrate body of the chairman. Finally, settling down in life as a hybrid establishment combining the characteristics of a music hall of the rankest, a minor theatre of the cheapest, and a taproom of the dirtiest kind.

Transient or resident, Liverpudlians deserved something better for their dramatic edification, *Porcupine* insisted, than premises such as these and acts as tired and outdated as 'Pat, the funny Irishman'.[42]

On the licensed stage, by contrast, Irishness was a matter of pride and honour, not of ridicule and self-mockery. The efforts of Irish impresarios, performers and playwrights were boosted by the support of compatriot

38   John Denvir, *The Brandons: A Story of Irish Life in England*, London, 1903, previously serialised in *Nationalist and Irish Programme* 30 Aug.–6 Dec. 1884.
39   Tyler Anbinder, *Five Points*, New York, 2001.
40   Shimmin, 'Free concert room'.
41   PP 1866 (373) XVI, q.7015.
42   'Our Camera Obscura: no. vi –A Place of Amusement', *Porcupine* 23 July 1870.

journalists, talented and ambitious professionals for whom Liverpool was an important career staging-post.[43] No opportunity was lost to laud Irish pre-eminence on the boards. Championed as an Irish Catholic, Barry Sullivan, the great Shakespearean tragic actor of the age, rose to fame in Liverpool (where he played eight short seasons at the Amphitheatre and 15 at the Theatre Royal between 1850 and 1870). According to dissentient carping critics, Sullivan had been elevated 'from a very painstaking stock-actor into a "star" of the first magnitude' through the 'persistent writing-up' of Stephen Meany, a leading local journalist (later a prominent Fenian and American politician).[44] Similar patriotic pride was extended to the globe-trotting Irish playwright Dion Boucicault, master of 'sensation' melodrama and commercial opportunism, following his move north from London (and away from bankruptcy) in 1863. Having recouped his fortune by cynical re-packaging of 'The Poor of New York' as 'The Poor of Liverpool' (a stock repertory item for the next ten years or so), Boucicault continued to produce a series of Irish comedy-melodramas (starting with 'The Colleen Bawn' in 1860), which did much to boost Irish self-image, pride and nationalism. In recalling the rising of 1798, 'Arrah-na-Pogue' (1864) pulled in the crowds with dazzling stage effects and popular ballads, one of which, 'The Wearing of the Green', was deemed subversive and, in the aftermath of the Fenian Clerkenwell explosion, temporarily banned from British performances (in later decades, it was to become Frank Harford's party-piece, the highlight of INP cultural gatherings).[45] To the acute embarrassment of the management of the Concert Hall, Lord Nelson Street, a 'Grand Irish Ballad Concert for a Charitable Purpose' held on its premises in February 1869 culminated in an (unannounced) rendition of the still proscribed ballad, the chorus being sung lustily (with 'disloyal feelings') by the audience, some 2000 strong. 'The bulk of those present were men and women of the low population of the north end of the town', Head Constable Greig reported, 'the eye being struck with

---

43   *DP* was founded and edited by M.J. Whitty, 'the father of the penny press', a Catholic from Co. Wexford. A theatre lover who wished to widen its access, he considered it 'a great mistake to associate dissipation with the drama', M.J. Whitty, *A Proposal for Diminishing Crime, Misery and Poverty in Liverpool*, Liverpool, 1865.

44   See the correspondence, 'Is Barry Sullivan a "Great" Actor', in *Porcupine* 26 Oct.–9 Nov. 1872. For Meany, see 'The Career of a Fenian Reporter', *Newspaper Press* 1 Feb. 1867. Despite his punishing schedule of career advancement, Justin McCarthy found time to watch Sullivan perform and to correspond with him, see NLI, Justin McCarthy Papers, MS 3680, diary for 1858, entries for 1, 15 and 21 Oct. and 13 Dec.

45   R. Fawkes, *Dion Boucicault: A Biography*, London, 1979, pp.144–58.

the spectacle of so large an assemblage of the roughest of our population'.[46] Nationalism of this order reached into parts untouched by political Fenianism. When Boucicault subsequently used 'The Shaughraun' (1874), the last of his 'Irish Tryptich', as 'a means of influencing English opinion towards a Fenian amnesty', he lost the support of English liberals who, as *Porcupine* attested, had previously applauded his efforts to present the Irish in more favourable stage light:

> Mr Boucicault has always in his Irish plays proved himself a 'patriot' in one of the highest senses, by rebelling against and revolutionising the Irish drama as it formerly prevailed, when the only type of Celtic character known to the stage was the grossest libel and caricature – a degraded, drunken, dancing, shillelagh-flourishing tatterdemalion, full of coarse Cockneyisms, and revelling in doubtful jokes, ribald songs, and apish antics. In clearing the drama of the 'stage Irishman', and introducing types of national character more lively and entertaining, as well as unexaggerated and harmless in humour, while relieved in their darker phases by the poetry, chivalry, and ingenuousness of the race, the dramatist has been a worthy 'Home-ruler' and done excellent service to the British stage.[47]

Following their success in the licensed theatres, Boucicault's Irish plays transferred to other venues, more accessible to the Liverpool-Irish. Located on the main artery of the migrant enclave, the Rotunda Music Hall in Scotland Road, the 'People's Palace of Entertainment', specialised in catering for Irish tastes (the well-equipped premises also housed American bowling alleys). Here the professional stage Irish – Mr P. Phillips, 'the Gem of the Emerald Isle', was a particular favourite in the 1860s – appeared in nightly variety with an exotic range of other artistes such as Miss Isaacs, the Infant Cantatrice; Mr Sam Bagnall, Shakesperian [sic] comic; Mr Orville Parker, American Comedian and Dancer; and Martin and Conway, 'the Celebrated Ethiopian Deleniators [sic]'.[48] There was the occasional 'Grand Irish Spectacle': one 'enormous attraction' staged in 1870, 'The Cluricaune', featured 'an incidental Colleen Bawn Ballet',

46   LVRO, 352POL2/5, 3 Feb. 1869.
47   'The Shaughraun', *Porcupine* 22 Apr. 1876. As Patrick O'Sullivan notes in his 'Introduction' to *The Irish World Wide*, vol. 3: *The Creative Migrant*, Leicester, 1994, p.9, 'Boucicault's Irish plays quickly achieved "iconic" status for Irish communities throughout the world. Attendance at a performance was a statement of identity, a sacramental celebration of "Irishness".'
48   *Porcupine* 5 Jan. 1867.

the 'Revels of Donnybrook Fair' and a cast of nearly 100.[49] As drama gradually
replaced the 'old concert-hall business', Boucicault's dramatic fare proved no
less enjoyable. 'Arrah-na-Pogue' was the first complete drama performed at the
Rotunda; 'The Shaughraun' was the last before a major fire closed the theatre
and the first to enter the stock repertoire after its re-opening. Performed by
'first-rate' Irish companies, Boucicault's plays stirred 'the quick sympathies
and ready appreciation of the North-end audiences ... Nowhere in Liverpool
are they ever played with such gusto and realism that they acquire on the
Rotunda stage'.[50] At the other end of town, Auguste Creamer, 'the only Irish
Manager in England', took the lease of the Sefton Theatre in Toxteth Park for
his 'Celebrated Irish Comedy-Drama Company' to offer a repertoire including
Boucicault, Edmund Falconer's 'Eileen Oge' (another Rotunda favourite) and
other works of the 'National Drama impersonated by Irish Artistes, true to
nature and the land of their birth'. Where commercial considerations were to
the fore at the Rotunda, this short-lived 'Irish Theatre of Liverpool', advertised
under the banner 'The Wearing of the Green', was a political gesture in less
friendly territory, much appreciated by John Denvir and the Home Rule
militants who applauded Creamer as 'a kind of apostle of Irish nationality
in districts where there is a strong anti-Irish prejudice, and where the Irish
character is misunderstood'.[51] Boucicault's plays were given a new airing in the
League Hall in the 1880s by groups such as the Irish National Dramatic Club and
the Barry Sullivan Dramatic Company, including a shortened version of 'The
Shaughraun' without the 'wake' scene, a bibulous and insanitary Irish cultural
tradition which Nugent refused to sanction.[52]

The Irish plays of Boucicault and Falconer were also adopted with enthusiasm
by Catholic amateur dramatic societies, a flourishing area of activity boosted by
Nugent's encouragement of drama at the Catholic Institute, training ground of
Denvir and his fellow cultural nationalists. The inaugural public production of
'Our Club' (with Denvir in charge of the scenery) was of Cardinal Wiseman's
'Hidden Gem', but Irish material soon came to the fore as new groups were
formed.[53] Politics, faith and drama merged to considerable effect in such
societies as the Saker Amateurs, the main fund-raisers (through performances

---

49   *CT* 12 Feb. 1870
50   *Porcupine* 11 Jan. 1879 and 3 Apr. 1880; Broadbent, *Annals of the Liverpool Stage*,
pp.294–303. The Rotunda re-opened in 1878 with a special performance of Benedict's
'Lily of Killarney' by the Carl Rosa Opera Company.
51   *UI* 23 Sept. and 14 Oct. 1876.
52   *LCH* 13 Apr. 1888.
53   Bennett, *Father Nugent*, p.25; *NP* 8 Feb. 1862. Drama was no less important at the

of 'The Colleen Bawn') for the St Vincent de Paul Society at St Francis Xavier's, and the Boucicault Amateurs (one of whose founders was the future dockers' leader, Jimmy Sexton) who made the round of local parishes and put on special performances at the Rotunda and in the major theatres, 'their appearance for any of our Catholic charities being always attended with good houses'.[54] In the later 1870s they were to pack the Amphitheatre to capacity with a celebratory medley of 'Irish drama', sponsored by the Home Rule Association whose newly elected town councillors were in honoured attendance; and, as severe weather set in, with winter performances of 'The Shaughraun' in aid of the soup kitchens, ragged schools and dispensaries attached to local Catholic parishes.[55] At times of yet more pressing need leading members of the various amateur dramatic societies would combine talents and resources to mount major fund-raising productions. Amid the 'education crisis' of 1870, members of the Catholic aristocracy graced the Royal Amphitheatre to enjoy 'Grand Dramatic Entertainment for the Education of the Poor, By the Amateurs who so successfully rendered the Great Drama of "The Colleen Bawn" in aid of the St Joseph's Catastrophe Fund' (following the death of 15 Catholics, suffocated during the frenzied panic of a false fire alarm).[56] On this occasion, Boucicault's 'Arrah-na-Pogue' was performed (including singing of 'The Wearing of the Green') by special permission of the author who waived his royalty fee and sent a cheque for £5. To help towards the school building programme, the assembled company also staged an entertainment at St Mary's parish, 'The Emerald Isle! Or St Patrick's Night at Home', praised by the *Catholic Times* as 'the best Irish entertainment we have yet seen':

> We have seen Irish entertainment where the performers would insist on the Christy Minstrel arrangement of sitting round in a ring with the comic men at the corners, and an imitation of the nigger 'Johnson' in the middle; but in 'The Emerald Isle' Mr Howard introduces his characters and makes them behave in such a natural manner that a host of sad and pleasant memories flash through the brain, and we fancy ourselves merrymaking at home again, in 'dear old Ireland'.[57]

(rival) Jesuit St Francis Xavier's College where pupils regularly performed Wiseman's play, see *Xaverian* Nov. 1885.

54   *Xaverian* Nov. 1886 and May 1887; Sexton, *Autobiography*, p.55.
55   *CT* 10 Dec. 1875 and 14 Dec. 1877; *UI* 30 Dec. 1876.
56   'Awful Catastrophe in a Catholic Church in Liverpool', *CT* 29 Jan. 1870.
57   *CT* 26 Nov. 1870.

The landfall of American popular culture, Liverpool revelled in such imports as blackface minstrelsy. Whether on the commercial stage, in the outreach activities of nationalist and confessional leaders such as Denvir and Nugent or the recreational efforts of local amateur dramatic societies, minstrelsy in Liverpool was a blend of styles, as transatlantic fashion merged with Irish sentiment. A purveyor of 'wholesome' amusement, Sam Hague, the commercial leader in the field, offered a star quality programme of rollicking fun, 'pathetic' negro minstrelsy and tuneful Irish melody of seemingly universal appeal. In 1880 Hague's 'original slave troupe' (including some 'real niggers') were proud to celebrate a record-breaking 'tenth year of one glorious and uninterrupted season in the St James's Hall, Lime Street', otherwise known as the 'tenth wonder of the town' with its ornate proscenium surmounted by an American eagle. Operating within the well-established professional entertainment circuit across the Irish Sea with a lucrative franchise arrangement for Dublin performances, Hague's shows gave pride of place to the melodious tones of the Irish tenor during the minstrel variety section: the bill always included a selection from the likes of 'Bold Jack Donough', 'Come Back to Erin', 'Let Erin Remember the Days of Old', 'Erin-go-Bragh', 'St Patrick's Day Parade' and (a particular favourite) 'The Harp that once through Tara's Halls'.[58]

In a bewildering process of cultural and commercial fusion and borrowing, 'negro entertainment' spread beyond the professional stage to become the main attraction in the lecture halls and meeting-rooms of Irish and Catholic associational culture. Here the Irish in Liverpool seemed to be following the path of their compatriots across the Atlantic. Irish delight in commercial blackface minstrelsy was an important cultural marker in the multi-faceted process by which they became white, entering the American mainstream to enjoy the 'wages of whiteness'.[59] Shorn of its initial tensions, ambiguities and oppositional force (its racial dialectic of love and theft), blackface minstrelsy became an Americanising ritual, offering socially insecure Irish migrants a sense of superiority over the blacks with whom they were once identified (labelled respectively as 'white negroes' and 'smoked Irish') and from whom they were

---

[58]   *Tenth year of one glorious and uninterrupted season at the St James's Hall, Lime Street, Liverpool. of Hague's Minstrels (the original slave troupe)*, Liverpool, 1880.

[59]   David Roediger, *The Wages of Whiteness: Race and the Making of the American Working Class*, London, 1991, ch. 6; and Noel Ignatiev, *How the Irish Became White*, London, 1995. See also Peter Kolchin, 'Whiteness studies: The new history of race in America', *Journal of American History*, 89, 2002, pp.154–73; and Eric Arnesen, 'Whiteness and the historians' imagination', *International Labor and Working-Class History*, 60, 2001, pp.3–32.

able to distance themselves by parody.[60] But there was a difference. Transposed to Liverpool, blackface minstrelsy enabled the Irish to confirm their whiteness while at the same time asserting their 'ethnic' difference.

As in America, blackface minstrelsy carried the Irish upwards in the cultural market. The antics of blackface 'niggers' provided audiences with the requisite combination of vicarious pleasure, saturnalian release and smug self-satisfaction previously derived from watching the stage Irishman: uninhibited behaviour which was secretly envied but which by its very exuberance served as proof of inferiority.[61] But there was a crucial distinction. Where the stage Irishman was a parody figure with redeemable features (hence the refrain, 'Pat's not so black as he's painted'), the 'nigger' minstrel was beyond civilised reform, purportedly portrayed at his 'semi-barbarian' best in blackface minstrelsy: 'it is only the bright side of his character that is presented to us. We see him in his best dress, in his gayest mood, and indulging in his favourite pastime, not in his indolent sloth, his repulsive filth, and his irreclaimable vice.' [62] With the 'negro' irredeemably below, the Liverpool-Irish acquired a new self-confidence on the stage, as in politics. Irishness was not homogenised into a generic whiteness but accentuated and romanticised in the variety section, the ideal platform for mellifluous rendition of the beauties and delights of the old country, suitably sentimental and nostalgic fare for an expatriate audience 'across the water'. The Liverpool-Irish were able to become white and green simultaneously.

The minstrelsy format remained the mainstay of Irish and Catholic amateur entertainment up until the First World War. The exploits of such troupes as the Negro Nomads, Xaverian Darkies, Cross Darkies, Eldonian Darkies, Vincentian Darkies and the Black Coon Banjo Team in raising funds and caricaturing their Orange opponents ('De sons ob William sing dis song – Doo-dah! doo-dah') were regularly reported in the *Liverpool Catholic Herald*.[63] While minstrelsy continued to flourish within Irish entertainment, any suggestion of engagement with the more modern popular cultural forms emanating from the music hall drew strong censure. A precursor of problems ahead, Dr Cory's 'Irish Diorama',

---

[60]   Eric Lott, *Love and Theft: Blackface Minstrelsy and the American Working Class*, New York, 1995; Robert Toll, *Blacking Up: The Minstrel Show in Nineteenth-Century America*, New York, 1974; and Alexander Saxton, *The Rise and Fall of the White Republic*, London, 1990, ch. 7. See also Robert Nowatzki, 'Paddy jumps Jim Crow: Irish-Americans and blackface minstrelsy', *Éire-Ireland*, 41, 2006, pp.162–84.

[61]   W.H.A. Williams, *'Twas Only an Irishman's Dream: The Image of Ireland and the Irish in American Popular Song Lyrics 1800–1920*, Urbana, IL, 1996, p.85.

[62]   'The "Stars" at the Theatre Royal', *Porcupine* 3 July 1869.

[63]   *LCH* 7 Sept. 1900.

a big hit back in 1870, had relied for its success not only on American minstrelsy (the dancers, a critic noted, performed 'nigger break-downs and indulge, in the course of so-called "Irish jigs", in the old walk-round antics with which patrons of Christy Minstrel performances are so familiar') but also on 'that British institution, the modern "music-hall"' with its 'slap-bang-wont-go-home-till-morning tendency'.[64] By the turn of the century, music-hall was the dominant form of commercial cultural provision: St James's Hall, the former 'Palace of Mirth and Minstrelsy', was duly renamed the Tivoli Palace of Varieties in 1896. Its deleterious influence, the *Liverpool Catholic Herald* rued, extended to the Monday concerts of the Liverpool Irish Fireside Club: 'Ireland possesses a richer store of ballads, songs and lyrics than any other country in the world, notwithstanding which fact we find the officials of an Irish Fireside Club encouraging the bawling of music hall doggerel that is as inane as it is lowering.'[65]

Irishness, however, was not swept away in a tide of British vulgarity and jingoism. While the purists of Irish-Ireland struggled to retrieve their language in cultural isolation, crowds flocked to commercially packaged forms of Irishness which flourished alongside the Saxon music hall. The Rotunda offered regular concerts of 'Irish National Music', including 'The Wearing of the Green' and T.D. Sullivan's 'God Save Ireland' (which had 'acclimatised a well-known American air'), performed to perfection by visiting concert companies such as that of Mr Ludwig:

> With a deep baritone, full of power and flexibility and capable of giving expression to the most passionate as well as the most pathetic feelings – and a combination of passion and pathos is the ground tone of almost all Irish music, certainly all that is associated with the chequered history of that country or its inextinguishable national aspirations – Mr Ludwig is pre-eminently the ablest and most successful representative of the 'Land of Song'.

William Ludwig was a frequent and popular visitor, combining commercial performances with celebrity appearance at associational and amateur gatherings. Having performed a selection of 'rebel songs and street ballads' at a packed concert in the Picton Hall in 1904, he was duly thanked by Father O'Byrne, who presided over the occasion, for 'his work in making his compatriots good Irishmen and good Catholics'. Before leaving town, Ludwig made a star

---

64 'An Irish Entertainment', *CT* 13 Aug. 1870.

65 *LCH* 3 Feb. 1899.

appearance at a special gentlemen's smoking concert of the Old Xaverians Athletic Association chaired by Austin Harford.[66] Beneath Ludwig's nationalist repertoire, sentimental Irish ballads proved enduringly popular, able to withstand the challenge of the music hall (and the censure of GL activists). On melodic return from their first picnic on the Wirral in 1909, the Guild of Holy Angels from St Francis Xavier delighted the accompanying priest by their prowess at musical fusion 'to the extent of changing "I love a lassie" into "Killarney" and the tender old Irish songs'.[67]

In 1898 the Rotunda passed into the hands of Bent's Brewery of which Archibald Salvidge, the Tory 'boss' politician, was a director, but the repertoire remained distinctively Irish.[68] It re-opened after refurbishment in 1899 not with music-hall varieties (as might have been expected) but with Hubert O'Grady's company performing his latest play, 'The Fenian'. Throughout the Home Rule agitation, O'Grady enjoyed great popularity with Liverpool audiences, an appeal attributed to 'the attractive generic conventions of melodrama and especially the plays' relation to Irish history'.[69] The opening night of 'The Eviction' back in September 1880 had caused a considerable stir: 'From beginning to end the audience, especially the gallery and the pit, were in a state of excitement perhaps seldom before experienced in a theatre, and the scene in the Amphitheatre last night had more the appearance of a political demonstration than a dramatic performance.'[70] There were packed houses every night for his next comedy drama, 'Emigration', with its nostalgic portrayal of 'the most conspicuous traits in the Irish peasant's character – his love of home, his innocence and his boundless wit'.[71] In the preface, O'Grady described 'The Fenian' as 'simply a Romantic Irish Love Story', but its political content drew it to the attention of Special Branch. Surveillance was kept on the Irish Sea crossings of Falkner Cox, a second-generation Irish-Liverpudlian, the actor who acquired the rights to 'The Fenian' following O'Grady's untimely death in Liverpool in 1899. His political views, the Dublin police reported, were 'confined to the stage' as 'he does not associate with extremists when in Dublin'.[72]

Based on the dilemmas of virtuous Irish peasants, with a 'dacent boy' and

66 *LCH* 26 Feb. 1904.

67 *Xaverian* Sept. 1909.

68 R.J. Broadbent, *Annals of the Liverpool Stage*, Liverpool, 1908, p.353

69 Stephen Watt, 'The plays of Hubert O'Grady', *Journal of Irish Literature*, 14, 1985, pp.4–13, here p.12.

70 *DP* 14 Sept. 1880.

71 *CT* 8 May 1885.

72 CBS Précis Box 3, 6 Jan. 1902.

a 'fine lump of a girl' as melodramatic heroes tried and tested against a series
of desperate situations, O'Grady's plays, as predictable in their plots as in their
characterisation, offered a winning commercial formula of nostalgia, sentiment
and political message. They were to bring the former upholsterer considerable
riches, as his obituary in the *Liverpool Catholic Herald* attested.[73] At the other end
of the scale, attempts to produce plays in Irish failed to resonate. The Bootle
GL persevered with a production in Irish of 'Caitlin Ni Houlihan' despite
'the depressing effect on the artistes of the small audience, and the want of
enthusiasm amongst those with no knowledge of Irish'.[74] One member of the
branch, Alfons O'Labraidh (A. Lowry), however, scored a minor success with
his one-act comedy, 'A West Briton's Romance', a heavy-handed satire on the
snobbery and refined English vowels of the Clontarf set:

> Now, isn't it a fine state the country is in when such English-aping mongrels
> pull the levers of the machine that rules us. Our own language is the only
> cure for the like of them. By the help of God and the Gaelic League we'll
> have Ireland speaking Irish again. We'll make these *shoneens* and West
> Britons feel that they are foreigners in Ireland.[75]

What attracted audiences in Liverpool was not gaelic purification but
readily accessible representations of the dear old land. Dyson's diorama of 'Old
Ireland' attracted capacity crowds to Hengler's Circus in 1899, to be followed
by a number of similar projects making use of new technology.[76] The Liverpool
agent of the Great Southern and Western Railway of Ireland placed a set of 80
coloured lantern slides showing views of the 'sunny South of Ireland' at the
free disposal of local charities and Irish associations.[77] The first of the free
Corporation lectures in the Jubilee Hall, Burlington Street, organised by Austin
Harford in November 1899 was a lantern show, 'A Scamper Round Ireland',
but the occasion was marred by the music-hall idioms adopted by the Scottish
presenter.[78] To remedy matters, the *Liverpool Catholic Herald* launched its own
series of lantern lectures on the 'Beauties of Ireland', the finest slides ever shown
in Liverpool, interspersed with Irish music and songs, available for societies to

---

[73]   *LCH* 29 Dec. 1899.

[74]   *LCH* 9 Jan. 1909.

[75]   Alfons O'Labraidh, *A West Briton's Romance: A Comedy in One Act*, Dermott O'Shea
Branch Gaelic League, Bootle, 1907.

[76]   *LCH* 15 Sept. 1899.

[77]   *LCH* 20 Oct. 1899.

[78]   *LCH* 24 Nov. 1899.

hire at a 'charge of 10s 6d for each entertainment to cover incidental costs such as the providing of oxygen gas and other effect in connection with the limelight apparatus'. An immediate success, the show was watched by 20,000 people in its first season.[79]

Monitored by the Catholic Stage Guild which attended to the temporal and spiritual welfare of visiting Catholic artistes,[80] theatrical activity in Irish Liverpool ranged from purist pursuit of ethnic essentialism enforced by vigilant censorship to popular forms of commercial innovation enlivened by seaport cosmopolitan fusion. The stage figured prominently in the lives of the leading Edwardian nationalist, ethnic and labour activists. Austin Harford was an accomplished amateur actor. Jimmy Sexton wrote plays: he was forced to rewrite sections of 'The Riot Act', his dramatic portrayal of the events of 1911, having given offence to the women's movement.[81] Jim Larkin brought his 'rank and file' dramatic company across from Dublin for special fund-raising performances in Liverpool after the collapse of the great transport strike: 'Irish songs and dances will be given. The national costume will be worn. From start to finish the plays will be acted by sons and daughters of toil.'[82] Extending beyond the Irish Sea, the various cultural influences at work in pre-war Liverpool can be seen in the fate of Sean Connolly, the first Irish fatality of the Easter Rising of 1916. An accomplished actor, he regularly crossed the Irish Sea to play the Liverpool stage, taking the opportunity to visit Peter Murphy's '98 shop. On one occasion, his performance so impressed an American producer in the audience that he was offered a 'thumping' five-year contract to work in the States. Connolly refused, 'saying that "his country would probably need him before the five years were up and he wanted to be available when the time came"'.[83]

iii. The Irish and Sport

While the stage kept sentimental memories and images of dear old Ireland alive, there was much two-way traffic across the Irish Sea by sports enthusiasts – many of the cross-sea movements of IRB 'suspects' tailed by Special Branch

---

[79] *LCH* 27 Sept. and 17 Oct. 1901.

[80] *LCH* 13 Sept. 1913.

[81] *Liverpool Forward* 13 Mar. 1914.

[82] *Liverpool Forward* 13 Feb. 1914.

[83] 'Captain Sean Connolly', *An-t-Oglach*, summer 1971, pp.9–11; 'On the Run', MS by Nellie Gifford-Donnelly in NLI, 21257, F. Gallagher Papers.

led to horse-racing, boxing and other venues for a flutter on sport.[84] Alongside such perennial pleasures, there was a major expansion (somewhat later than elsewhere) of organised sport in late Victorian Liverpool, a development which brought the Irish into active engagement with the wider community. Its present-day pre-eminence in football notwithstanding, Liverpool was not to the fore in the Victorian origins of organised sport and league competition, hindered by the vagaries of wind, tide and the casual labour market, all of which delayed the introduction of the kind of regular working week with the sporting Saturday half-holiday enjoyed in adjacent industrial areas. Once implanted, however, organised sport was a critical agent in the representation and construction of the inter-locking identities and imagined communities to which the Liverpool-Irish affiliated. The attempt of Irish-Ireland activists to impose a form of gaelic athletic autarky was no match for the vibrant pan-sectarian culture of amateur and professional sport in Edwardian Liverpool.

The inter-parish rivalry which enlivened debating and billiards competition between branches of the Catholic Young Men's Societies acquired a new intensity with the formation of parochial football teams from the late 1880s – St Francis Xavier seem to have been the first in the field with a team formed in 1888.[85] By the early years of the twentieth century, a network of Catholic leagues was in place ranging from young boys in elementary schools (two divisions of eight teams in 1903) through to old boys' teams for top-flight adult players. The *Liverpool Catholic Herald* applauded the 'progressive spirit at present quickening Catholic life' through the development of sports: 'The forming of Catholic football clubs in connection with the parishes or the branches of the Y.M.S. helps to keep football enthusiasts in a Catholic atmosphere.'[86] A new column, 'Sports and Pastimes', provided 'a complete and readable record of all Catholic sports held under the auspices of the Young Men's Society, League of the Cross, United Irish League, and the various school clubs of Liverpool and district'.[87] Above the fiercely held primary identification with the parish, other sporting clubs offered a broader spatial and confessional allegiance, as for example the Liverpool Catholic Cyclists Association, applauded as an important step towards the desideratum, 'a powerful organisation, non-political, but still

---

[84]   See, for example, CBS Précis Box 2, 4 and 13 Mar. 1899, 13 Oct. 1900 and Box 3, 23 Sept. 1901.

[85]   I am grateful to David Kennedy and Peter Kennedy of Glasgow Caledonian University for sending me a draft of their paper, 'An ethnic dimension to football club development in Liverpool: The fate of Liverpool's Irish football clubs'.

[86]   *LCH* 17 July 1909.

[87]   *LCH* 31 Aug. 1906.

able to further Catholic interests whenever opportunity offered'.[88] As with football, of course, cycling was popular across the city's sectarian divide: the George Wise Cycling Club was the largest in Liverpool.

Under the dynamic presidency of its most distinguished alumnus Austin Harford, the pre-eminent amateur sporting club in Catholic Liverpool was the Old Xaverian Athletic Association with three main branches, football, lawn tennis and drama. Its annual dinners in the Exchange Station Hotel were lavish affairs, sometimes graced by the presence of the Archbishop of Westminster, due recognition of its premier status as 'the first Catholic social organisation in Liverpool'.[89] The fame of the club's football team extended far beyond Catholic Liverpool, boosted by tours to Ireland and by its success in open competition in city and county leagues. A crowd of 5000 watched the Old Xaverians defeat the Liverpool Casuals at Goodison Park to win the Lancashire Amateur League in 1903 (a title they were to secure on several subsequent occasions).[90] In the following season, the club participated in the gamut of city, county and national competitions: the Liverpool and District Shield; the Lancashire Amateur League, first and second divisions; the Lancashire Junior Cup; the Lancashire Amateur Cup; and the English Amateur Cup. It was a matter of great pride for the club when two of its players were chosen to play in the Lancashire County team, the only players from Liverpool to be selected.[91]

Having perfected their skills within their own inter-parish leagues, Catholics took considerable delight in vaunting their athletic superiority in open competition and through representative selection, pride which extended down from the Jesuit elite at SFX to the 'low Irish'. Otherwise embarrassed by the disproportionate Catholic numbers in industrial schools, the Catholic press made a special point of drawing attention to the fact that Catholics comprised 12 out of the 22 players selected for the 'North v. South' match, the highlight of the season for the Liverpool and District Industrial Schools Association.[92] Whether on the soccer pitch or in tug-of-war competitions, the sporting prowess of the Catholic Irish of Liverpool gave the lie to alarmist concerns about 'physical deterioration'.[93]

This flourishing of amateur sport notwithstanding, there was no cross-over into an ethno-confessional professional format. Here, Catholic Liverpool stood

---

88   *LCH* 10 Mar. 1905.

89   *Xaverian* Feb. 1909 and June 1910.

90   *LCH* 1 and 22 May, 18 Sept., 16 Oct. 1903 and 22 Jan. 1904.

91   *Xaverian* Feb. and June 1904.

92   *LCH* 24 Apr. 1903.

93   *LCH* 26 July 1907.

apart from the pattern in Scotland and Ulster: Edinburgh Hibernian, Glasgow Celtic, Dundee Hibernian and Belfast Celtic were either forged from amateur parish teams or promoted by senior church figures and nationalist politicians. Liverpool FC were criticised in the socialist press for not allowing a pre-match collection in aid of the striking (and starving) Dublin transport workers, but even after the introduction of a weekly report on Everton, there is nothing in the pre-war Catholic press to suggest any specific sectarian allegiance to either of the two professional clubs, both of which traced their roots back to the St Domingo New Connexion Methodist chapel team. Of the INP councillors, Taggart held shares in Everton, Austin Harford in Liverpool.[94]

Even-handed in its coverage of the two teams, the *Liverpool Catholic Herald* devoted an increasing amount of space to professional league football, a means of ensuring its market share in the competitive popular newspaper business – at the same time, there was an expansion in its sections for women and children. Extensive reports of matches were accompanied by caricatures, or 'Socceratures' as they were called, of leading players. A useful money-spinner, the paper ran its own football pools competition with a £5 prize for the correct forecast of 12 games. Comprehensive in coverage of the top divisions, the paper drew attention to the 'most prominent position of Irish players' throughout the league, but regretted they were not released by their clubs to play for the lacklustre Irish national team.[95]

In Liverpool, as in Ireland itself, the gaelic sports promoted by the Gaelic Athletic Association (GAA) were the most popular aspect of the Irish-Ireland agenda, but they proved no match for the infrastructure of provision, participation and support embedded by amateur and professional forms of British (or 'garrison') sport. Having been rained off by atrocious August bank holiday weather in 1900, the first hurling match in Liverpool was postponed until Easter Monday 1901 at Greenwich Park, Aintree, when the Liverpool Young Irelanders defeated the Manchester Martyrs. Although it attracted surveillance by Special Branch, the match 'excited very little interest, only about 300 spectators being present'.[96] Progress thereafter was halting at best, despite the efforts of gaelic activists to promote 'the grand old pastime of Ireland – a game which was played by our ancestors three thousand years ago, and which has withstood

94   Vickers, 'Civic image', ch. 10; Tony Mason, 'The Blues and the Reds: A history of the Liverpool and Everton Football Clubs', *THSLC*, 134, 1985, pp.107–28; David Kennedy and Michael Collins, 'Community politics in Liverpool and the governance of professional football in the late nineteenth century', *Historical Journal*, 49, 2006, pp.761–88.

95   *LCH* 25 Aug. 1905, 16 Oct. 1909 and 20 Nov. 1909.

96   CBS Précis Box 3, 10 Apr. 1901; *LCH* 12 Apr. 1901.

all the forces of Anglicisation'.[97] There was no problem acquiring hurleys and headgear, specially shipped across from Ireland and available from Flanning's, 72 St James's Place (subsequently the venue of a branch of Sinn Fein).[98] As with language retrieval, the major difficulty was the lack of resident experienced personnel: there was a constant quest for players and referees conversant with the game and its rules. By 1903 the Young Irelanders had been joined by two other Liverpool clubs, Lamh Dearg (inaugurated by members of the GL and the LCLS) and the Exiles of Erin, but they were not always able to field a full complement themselves or to find sufficient other teams within travelling distance for meaningful competition. When the clubs in Ireland started the 1904 season, the three Liverpool clubs, plagued by 'no shows' as opponents failed to turn up, had yet to complete an adequate fixture list for 1903.[99] There was little improvement over the years: the match between Clann na hEirinn, Liverpool, and the Manchester Martyrs in August 1908, for example, started 96 minutes late and was a very one-sided affair, Manchester being two men short.[100] Furthermore, the organisation was poor: the names and addresses of the officials of the Lancashire County Board were unknown to the General Secretary of the GAA.[101]

As practised in Liverpool, in the absence of due punctuality, adequate knowledge of the rules and sufficient players, hurling was not a spectator-friendly sport. Crowds were small unless more popular (and reliable) offerings were also on the programme. Reflecting the new spirit of political union, the Irish Athletic Festival and Gaelic Re-union in Greenwich Park on August bank holiday Monday 1901 was attended by over 9000, keen to catch sight of T.P. O'Connor and to watch the main event, a football match in which the Irish of the south end of Liverpool beat their north end compatriots by two goals to one. The advertised hurling match, however, failed to materialise as the Manchester Martyrs, already unhappy at the UIL sponsorship of the event, refused to take to the field when they saw Union Jacks flying over the grandstand, the competitors' tent and other adjuncts to the ground.[102] The following year, the Irish-Ireland contingent mounted a separate Gaelic festival and *feis* in Birkenhead on August bank holiday Monday, a poorly attended affair, overshadowed by the crowds who flocked to Aintree for the north versus south football match and

---

[97]   *LCH* 16 May 1902.
[98]   *LCH* 12 July 1907.
[99]   *LCH* 22 Jan. 1904.
[100] *LCH* 15 Aug. 1908.
[101] *LCH* 20 Nov. 1910.
[102] CBS Précis Box 3, 12 Aug. 1901; *LCH* 9 Aug. 1901.

the new T.P. O'Connor Challenge Shield awarded to the UIL branch securing the highest points in five events in a traditional British sports programme including egg-and-spoon races, three-legged races, cycle races and tug-of-war. An 'exhibition' hurling match was thrown in for good measure.[103]

Similar problems hindered the attempt to implant gaelic football, compounded by generational and ideological tension between elderly (and vigilant) gaelic activists who founded the clubs and the young bloods who played in the teams. There was outrage at the first ceilidh of the Dermot O'Shea Gaelic Football Club in Bootle when the announcement of a non-Irish dance was welcomed with enthusiasm: 'Coupled with the foreign dancing, there was an amount of horseplay indulged in which, by young Irishmen professing Gaelic League principles, is unpardonable.'[104] Given similar operational difficulties, gaelic football was to prove no more spectator-friendly than hurling. The match between Liverpool and Dublin at the GAA Whitsun sports at Aintree had to be abandoned so that the Dublin team 'might catch the boat'. 'This failure to keep faith with the public attracted to Aintree by the advertising of the match is very bad policy', the *Liverpool Catholic Herald* expostulated, 'and is not calculated to secure support for Irish athletics.'[105]

In one important respect, however, gaelic sports achieved an advance not registered in mainstream British sport: the active participation of women. The first women's hurling match (camoguidheacht) was held at Aintree in August 1906.[106] Within a few years there were three particularly active local clubs (hence the need to send to Dublin for extra camans): the Bootle-based Eileen Nicholl Ladies Hurling Club; the Caitlin ni Houlahan Ladies Hurling Club whose 'social evenings' were 'amongst the most enjoyable Irish-Ireland events of the city'; and another Bootle club, the Sara Curran Ladies Hurling Club, named in honour of Robert Emmet's fiancée.[107] Women's teams from Liverpool, Bootle and Dublin competed in the All-Ireland Hurling Championships held in Aintree in 1913, probably the most successful GAA event on Merseyside.[108] Some months later, however, the *Liverpool Catholic Herald*, champion of the

---

[103] CBS Précis Box 3, 7 Aug. 1902; *LCH* 25 July and 8 Aug. 1902.

[104] *LCH* 27 Jan. and 3 Feb. 1905.

[105] *LCH* 17 May 1913. There is no pre-First World War coverage in *John Mitchels Gaelic Football Club. The Story of the G.A.A. in Liverpool*, n.p., 1984, which notes, p.9: 'Unfortunately there are not sufficient records available to write a "formal" history of the G.A.A. in Liverpool'.

[106] *LCH* 31 Aug. 1906.

[107] *LCH* 8 June, 6 July and 2 Nov. 1912, and 23 May 1914.

[108] *LCH* 9 Aug. 1913.

long-suffering spectators, returned to the familiar critical tenor in its report
of the Whit Monday 1914 Irish sports in Greenwich Park, marred by the late
arrival of members of the south end ladies' hurling team: 'delays of an hour in
starting, long waits between the events, and programmes not completed is not
fair treatment. This sort of thing bids fair to kill what looked like becoming a
successful Gaelic revival.' [109]

One important factor which precluded the emergence of distinctively
different forms of Irish Catholic and/or gaelic recreation in Liverpool was
the Protestant proscription on Sunday entertainment (similar to the disdain
for Sunday funeral 'busters'). A seasoned traveller, Nugent was a life-long
campaigner for the introduction of the continental-style Sunday, having been
impressed by scenes he had witnessed 'at Antwerp, Hague, Dusseldorf, Spa and
other places, showing how the inhabitants enjoyed themselves in their public
gardens, listening to their bands of music, and drinking a beverage dear to
every old Irishwoman, namely tea (laughter and applause)'.[110] Austin Harford
and other INP councillors campaigned vigorously but unsuccessfully for band
concerts in public parks on Sundays. In July 1907, Lynskey applied on behalf
of the GL and GAA for a singing, dancing and music licence to accompany
the proposed Sunday sports and *feis* at Greenwich Park: 'The sports were held
on Sunday because nearly all the attendants and competitors were working
throughout the week, and on Saturday till a late hour, and so it was obligatory
for them to select Sunday.' Led by the Men's Bible Class at the Protestant
Reformers Memorial Church, Netherfield Road, the various local branches
of the PSA, puritanical guardians of the Sunday Observance Act, mounted
a co-ordinated opposition, forcing the organisers to transfer the event to a
Saturday.[111] In Edwardian Liverpool, cultural vigilance and censorship was by
no means restricted to gaelic activists.

---

[109] *LCH* 6 and 13 June 1914.
[110] *CT* 22 Sept. 1876.
[111] LVRO, 352POL1/31, 16 July 1907.

Part Two

———

1914–39

10

The First World War:
Free Citizens of a Free Empire?

T HE SUSPENSION of the Home Rule Bill in September 1914 notwithstanding, the 'Nat-Lab' leaders of the INP were unquestioning in support of the war effort, a stance T.P. O'Connor justified to critical compatriots in America: 'The Irish Party, when they realised that on this occasion England was in the right, did not allow their historical wrongs to prejudice them.'[1] As perceived by Harford and the INP councillors, whole-hearted participation in the war would not only underwrite and guarantee the Home Rule settlement for Ireland; it would also enhance the profile (and improve the lot) of the Liverpool-Irish. Hence their support extended beyond military recruitment to special war-time labour schemes in armaments factories and on the docks, hoping thereby to enhance the future employment prospects of constituents previously doomed to 'blind-alley' occupations and casualism. Throughout the war, politicians and priests vied with each other in patriotic rhetoric, seeking to secure full citizenship rights for Catholics and Irish within the 'free' imperial framework.

A master of the 'sound-bite' ahead of his time, T.P. O'Connor led the way in a famous speech on 'Our Empire' at a recruiting rally at Tournament Hall in September 1914, recalled with glowing approval by dissident Tories in the 1930s:

> Our Empire, founded on freedom, on free institutions, on the respect for nationality. We ask no man to abandon his language. We ask no man to

---

1   *LCH* 10 Aug. 1918.

swerve in his faith. We ask no man to swerve in his individuality. Our flag flies over a wide world and a free Empire.[2]

Written in 1916, his contribution to *Irish Heroes in the War* celebrated the alacrity with which the Irish in Britain had rushed to the ranks:

> the principles for which Irishmen had fought all their lives were revealed to them, as in a flash, as the great spiritual and fundamental issues of the War. They had fought for a small nation; they had fought for the principle of nationality; they had fought for democracy; they had fought for liberty; they had lived in a land where – whatever might be the case in their own country – the freedom of the individual and the representative character of the institutions brought home to them the essential spirit of freedom which lies at the heart of the British Empire ... For the first time in the history of the race, 'God Save the King' was sung – because for the first time these Irishmen were ready to regard themselves as free citizens of a free Empire.[3]

As well as his role as recruiting sergeant, O'Connor encouraged war workers towards new heights of productivity, most notably in his 'Shells! Shells! Shells!' speech delivered at the 'non-political' St Patrick's Day gathering at the Bear's Paw restaurant in 1915: 'I would say to the people of Liverpool that the employer who by his creed, or the workman who by his temper or impatience delays by one hour the armament of our troops, has on his soul the guilt of hundreds if not thousands of human lives.' He was followed by Austin Harford who proudly produced figures which

> proved beyond doubt that to-day a greater number of Irishmen from that city were in the ranks than of any other nationality in proportion to the population ... Recruiting had been so heavy in some streets in Scotland Division that almost every house had a soldier from it fighting at the front.[4]

Among the priests, the most fervently patriotic was the Jesuit Father

---

2   Quoted on the back cover of Barbara Whittingham-Jones, *More about Liverpool Politics: Red Flag, Rome and Shamrock*, Liverpool, 1936.

3   T.P. O'Connor, 'The Irish in Britain', p.31.

4   *LCH* 20 Mar. 1915.

Vaughan who 'spoke of the Empire of Christ and the Empire of Great Britain, observing that not only was there a cry of "Christ and His Church need you" but of "Your King and country need you!" It was his privilege as well as his duty to recruit for both Empires.' Like the labour leaders, Sexton and Milligan, he made a special appeal to the patriotic duty of Liverpool-Irish dock labourers to adjust their work rhythm and workplace culture:

> He would carry forward that cry down to the Merseyside, and shout with all the vehemence of his soul – he would shout out aloud, to his brothers, the dockers – 'Do your duty, and do it now' … He felt sure, if only he could get a grip of hands with each docker along the riverside, and hold him while he poured into his ear the agonising cry for help to crush the foe menacing the existence of our country, that his friend would drop his 'sub' and his 'sup', grip his hook, and brace-up his belt – proud to make any sacrifice to save the flag, which must be kept floating topmast high.[5]

All these efforts were endorsed by the *Liverpool Catholic Herald* which introduced weekly news columns on 'Irish Soldiers at the Front' and 'Catholics at War'. It also accorded special praise to the formation of Dockers' Battalions at the waterfront, with khaki uniforms, guaranteed wages and Irish officers (drawn from officials of the NUDL), 'the harbinger of death to the casual employment evil which has been the bitter curse of the working classes of Liverpool for generations'.[6] However, such enthusiastic participation in the war effort was questioned in some quarters. At parochial recruiting meetings for Harford's Liverpool Irish National Volunteer Force for Home Defence, critics from the floor rejected immediate enrolment, preferring to postpone such commitment until Home Rule was actually implemented.[7] To the anger of the *Liverpool Catholic Herald* there was discord at one of the inaugural meetings for the Dockers' Battalion provoked by 'a large leaven of Socialists, anti-militarists, two-days-a-week men, and anti-Sextonites – for the fact that Mr Sexton is a Catholic, that he does not favour the "down tools" policy except in last resort, and that he has gained many benefits for the men, have made him a goodly proportion of enemies of one kind and another'.[8]

Participation in the war effort was intended to enhance leverage and

---

5   *LCH* 27 Mar. 1915.

6   *LCH* 17 Apr. 1915; Taplin, *Dockers' Union*, ch. 9.

7   *Irish Volunteer* 12 Sept. and 3 Oct. 1914; *LCH* 19 Sept. 1914.

8   *LCH* 24 Apr. 1915.

profile. In championing the interests of the first victims of war, the Belgian refugees, the Liverpool-Irish underlined their patriotism while exposing the prejudicial treatment of Catholics. To the outrage of local Catholics, the refugees, overwhelmingly Flemish Catholics, were consigned by the authorities to 'pauperising' workhouse accommodation. Where the state failed, the Catholic Church proudly stepped forward to arrange an extensive fund-raising and gift-collection service (French books were proscribed) channelled through the *Liverpool Catholic Herald* which also introduced a weekly column in Flemish, 'Oorlog Nieuws voor Belgische Lezers [War News for Belgian Readers]'.[9] Having shamed their Protestant counterparts, the Catholic sense of moral superiority was tarnished when Margaret Robertson, daughter of a wealthy Liverpool-Irish master stevedore, was found guilty at Old Bailey of defrauding £57 18s. while engaged as a voluntary worker in buying second hand clothes on behalf of the War Refugees Committee, to fund her lavish life-style down in London.[10] Given its commitment to welfare, the INP was attentive to the needs of the early casualties of the war on their return to Merseyside. Having intervened to ensure that a wounded soldier who died at Fazakerley was saved the indignity of a pauper burial, Alderman Taggart prevailed upon the council to set apart a separate section at Longmoor Lane cemetery for such deserving cases: 'Thus, thanks to a Catholic Nationalist', the *Liverpool Catholic Herald* reported, 'the city of Liverpool is doing what should be done by the nation, which was apparently content to leave it undone.'[11]

The annual protest over the exclusion of INP councillors from the selection process for the appointment of the lord mayor acquired added intensity during the war, in line with what sociologists label as the military participation ratio. 'It was not a very pleasing reflection for the thousands of Nationalists of the city who had willingly and eagerly placed their lives at the service of the King and country that the old exclusiveness in the selection of a Lord Mayor should continue', Austin Harford protested in 1914.[12] The tone had become far more strident by 1917:

> after the military record of the Irish of Liverpool, it is more than ever necessary to make a protest against the exclusion and isolation of the Irish Nationalists ... Irishmen have made their sacrifices in this war in no small

---

9   *LCH* 24, 31 Oct. and 12 Dec. 1914, and 25 Dec. 1915.
10 *CT* 22 Jan. 1916.
11 *LCH* 10 Oct. 1914.
12 *LCH* 14 Nov. 1914.

measure, and those sacrifices should of themselves put an end once and for all to the hateful policy of the past in dealing with the Irish community – a policy which has been, and still is, a blot upon the municipal and social life of this city.[13]

No less contentious was the nomenclature accorded to the Liverpool-Irish serving in the forces. Sir Lawrence Parsons, the Anglo-Irishman in command of Irish division, refused to accept Irish recruits from Britain. Dismissing the Irish in Liverpool, Glasgow and Cardiff as 'slum birds that we don't want', Parsons sought to counteract Sinn Fein propaganda in Ireland to enlist 'clean, fine, strong, temperate, hurley-playing country fellows'.[14] Nor, despite the efforts of T.P. O'Connor, was there a specifically Irish option in Liverpool at the outset, the Liverpool-Irish simply flooding into existing British units. Thereafter the pride of the Irish in Liverpool rested on the first-line territorials, the Liverpool 8th Irish Battalion, successors to the 'middle-class' Volunteer Force, a heritage extolled by Father Vaughan: 'in Liverpool they were all proud of the 8th Irish Battalion, whose history went back to 1857, and whose members, when war was declared, rallied to the flag and leapt like swords from their scabbards to the King's aid'.[15] Within the Liverpool-Irish enclave, the Liverpool 8th were treated as heroes. St Francis Xavier put its premises at the disposal of the battalion; a rich businessman, Thomas Ryan of Buxton Lime Firms Ltd, 'head of the largest firm of its kind in the world having a capital of £750,000', ensured a regular supply of Irish wolf hounds as mascots.[16] Beyond their own kind, however, the Liverpool 8th were denied the praise, recognition and support they deserved, being treated, the *Liverpool Catholic Herald* repeatedly remonstrated, as 'the Cinderella of the Liverpool Battalions because its members come chiefly from poor homes and have few well-to-do friends'.[17]

In an effort to emulate the laudatory publicity and comforting presents enjoyed by the 'fashionable' 10th, Liverpool Scottish, Harford convened a meeting at the Town Hall in July 1915 to establish the Liverpool Irish Committee Fund (which he subsequently chaired) 'to make arrangements for putting an end to the neglect in the distribution of necessaries and comforts

---

13   *LCH* 17 Nov. 1917.
14   Quoted in Brady, *T.P. O'Connor*, p.221.
15   *CT* 30 Sept. 1916.
16   *LCH* 10 Feb. and 16 June 1917.
17   *LCH* 10 and 17 July 1915.

with which the soldiers of the 8th Liverpool Irish have so far been treated'.[18]
T.P. O'Connor protested vigorously when casualty lists simply referred to the
8th Battalion and finally persuaded the War Office to 'recognise them as the
Liverpool Irish in all future lists'.[19] Having secured official recognition of this
distinctive dual identity, O'Connor was determined it should not be jeopardised
in the subsequent move towards county amalgamation:

> by a system of combining several battalions together, English and Irish, the
> Irish identity of this particular battalion was in danger of being lost. He told
> the War Office, on behalf of the Irish people of Liverpool, that they were
> not going to stand anything of the kind (hear, hear). They insisted that the
> Liverpool Irish Battalion should maintain its Irish character, and they were
> willing to find the Irishmen to keep it up to full strength.[20]

Eventually, the Liverpool-Irish secured due civic recognition at a St Patrick's
Day reception in 1917 for 700 Irish wounded soldiers. Tea and cigarettes were
distributed along with a suitable ethnic gift: 'The Lady Mayoress carried a large
bunch of shamrock tied with vivid green streamers. The daughter and son of
the Lord Mayor and Lady Mayoress, wearing the costume of Irish peasants,
presented bunches of shamrock to all the guests.'[21]

While upholding the honour and valour of the Liverpool-Irish military
contribution, local politicians were keen to consolidate their war-time
civil standing, the necessary foundation for active participation in post-war
reconstruction and the 'people's peace'. Here there were tensions between
politicians and the press. While O'Connor and Harford sought to secure a
post-Home Rule future for a specific 'Irish' party, building upon the 'Nat-Lab'
agenda and the impressive local record in housing reform, the *Liverpool Catholic
Herald* advised the Irish throughout war-time Britain to desert and disband the
UILGB. Come peace, the best future for the Irish in Britain would surely lie
through active participation in mainstream political parties, the course followed
so successfully elsewhere in the diaspora:

> Home Rule being out of the way, we do not want to see the Irish people
> separating themselves from their neighbours, but entering fully and freely

---

18   *LCH* 24 July 1915 and 8 Dec. 1917.
19   *LCH* 31 July 1915.
20   *CT* 30 Sept. 1916.
21   *LCH* 24 Mar. 1917.

into the public life of the country in which they live, taking their part as citizens, and avoiding every course of action that would tend to make the Irish vote a mere pawn in the game of skilful or unscrupulous politicians.[22]

As the war continued (and Home Rule receded), the paper became increasingly critical of 'independent' Irish politics, a worn-out strategy which served Irish Catholics badly in Britain, denying them the kind of advance in war-time civil administration enjoyed by Labour and the Jews who had 'wormed themselves into all kinds of important positions'. Redmond's decision not to join the Coalition cabinet kept the Irish out of the mainstream and away from influence. The Catholic clergy were at fault too: having monopolised control of clubs and associations, they had denied the laity the necessary skills and experience to progress in war-time administration.[23]

Other factors accounted for the failure of the Irish, their patriotic participation notwithstanding, to match the advance attained by other groups during the war. Old labels persisted: the Liverpool-Irish were still stigmatised as riotous and disloyal. Although by no means an exclusively Irish affair, the 'larrikin' element, including Pat O'Mara and fellow Liverpool-Irish 'slummies', were to the fore in the orgy of rioting following the sinking of the *Lusitania* by a German U-boat in May 1915. Shortly before the outbreak of war, the north end had been devastated by the tragic loss at sea of the *Empress of Ireland*: 'almost every member of the crew, from the captain down to the smallest boy, was a native or resident of the city, where there are whole streets, even whole parishes, every house in which contributed its quota to the manning of the great liner'.[24] Even more than the *Empress*, the *Lusitania* was 'the pride of the port of Liverpool': the captain and nearly every man of the crew came from the city, the *Liverpool Catholic Herald* reported under the headline, 'Whole Catholic Parishes Desolated'. The ensuing riots were excused by the *Liverpool Courier* on account of the number of local households affected by the disaster, but recent research has shown that none of those arrested seemed to have lost family members. While bereaved families grieved, more turbulent elements took to the streets, ransacking shops and attacking individuals. What began as a 'crude vendetta' against German-owned premises with women and 'young larrikins' in the van soon extended, the Head Constable reported with alarm,

22 *LCH* 9 Jan. 1915.
23 *LCH* 9 June 1917.
24 'Great Sea Tragedy: The "Catholic Ship" Goes Down', *LCH* 6 June 1914.

to shops 'occupied by anyone with a foreign name, and also to a number of Chinese Laundries and the hooligan classes took the opportunity of looting the damaged premises'.[25] There was furious debate in the press as to the precise starting point of these mindless xenophobic riots: contrary to other reports, the *Liverpool Catholic Herald* insisted the trouble originated not in the Catholic north end but in F.E. Smith's Walton constituency, then spread to Everton and Kirkdale, 'two other strongholds of Toryism and Orangeism'. However, the paper could not dispute the damage done:

> Once again, Liverpool is figuring in the eyes of the nation as a city of riots. Unfortunately, it is a position which Liverpool has become sadly accustomed to occupying, for with the possible exception of Belfast, there is no great centre in the United Kingdom in which these too strenuous ebullitions of public feeling are more frequently witnessed, or more easily provoked.[26]

While swept up in the mood of xenophobia, the Liverpool-Irish were themselves viewed with increasing suspicion, judged not by their own contribution to the war effort but by the motives and behaviour of their transient compatriots passing through the port. There was much critical comment in the press when itinerant harvest workers returned to Ireland in August 1915 to avoid the registration act, only to return shortly afterwards in a 'Celtic invasion' to take work in the docks.[27] Later in the year, there was an outbreak of anti-Irish hysteria as crowds prevented young Irish emigrants (fit and eligible for military service) from boarding the *Saxonia* bound for America. In an exercise in damage limitation, leading figures in the Home Rule movement portrayed the intending emigrants not as disloyal cowards but as marginal figures, peasants from the west of Ireland whose links were with the United States not the United Kingdom.[28] Although some may have been under the misapprehension that conscription had been enacted, the flow of numbers through Liverpool was attributable to two basic factors of migration: prosperity in the United States with a consequent increase in passage money sent back to Ireland; and war-time closure of the Irish

---

25   LVRO, 352MIN/WAT 1/51, 17 May 1915; *Times* 10 and 13 May; *Liverpool Courier* 11 May; and P. O'Mara, *Autobiography*, pp.224–25. For the broader context, see P. Panayi, *Enemy in our Midst*, London, 1991.

26   *LCH* 15 May 1915.

27   *LCH* 2 Oct. 1915.

28   *LCH* 13 Nov. 1915.

ports from which such migrants would normally sail. The Bishop of Limerick spoke up in their defence in a letter to the *Munster News*:

> It is very probable that these poor Connaught peasants know little or nothing of the meaning of war. Their blood is not stirred by memories of Kossovo, and they have no burning desire to die for Servia. They would much prefer to be allowed to till their own potato gardens in peace in Connemara. Small nationalities and the wrongs of Belgium and Rheims Cathedral and all the other cosmopolitan considerations that rouse the enthusiasm of the Irish Party, but do not get enough of recruits in England, are too high-flying for uneducated peasants, and it would seem a cruel wrong to attack them because they cannot rise to the level of the disinterested Imperialism of Mr T.P. O'Connor and the rest of the New Brigade.[29]

Still committed to Home Rule within a post-war imperial framework, the INP repudiated the 1916 Easter Rising in Ireland, contemptuously dismissed by Harford as 'insignificant, unrepresentative and irresponsible'.[30] There was similar condemnation of any suggestion of traitorous consort with the Germans in pursuit of Irish independence. To eschew any hint of disloyalty, the Liverpool-Irish led the way in constant vilification of Kuno Meyer, transmogrified from scholarly doyen of Gaelic Ireland to enemy traitor, 'a German of the worst sort. He was the spoilt pet of Liverpool University, acted as a colleague of Casement in Germany, stirred up sedition in Ireland, and afterwards went to America, where he employed himself in spitting out venom on the hand that fed him.'[31] For all his scholarship, his true attitude to the Irish, as was now revealed by a former colleague, was Teutonic in arrogance and contempt: 'I look at them, he said, "precisely as we (the Germans) regard the Poles, a people only for poetry, rhetoric and sedition"'.[32] Inevitably, there were incidents which tarnished the image of imperial loyalty sedulously fostered by O'Connor, Harford and the INP, particularly after the introduction of conscription in Britain. In 1917, John Hughes, the leading grocer, was sentenced to 12 months' imprisonment having

---

[29]   Enclosed in PRONI, MIC 426.

[30]   *DP* 3 May 1916.

[31]   *LCH* 5 Oct. 1918. Particular offence was taken at Meyer's advocacy of an Irish Brigade recruited from prisoners of war in Germany to fight the British, see O Luing, *Kuno Meyer*, pp.168–75.

[32]   *LCH* 16 Jan. 1915.

been found guilty of bribing the chief military substitution officer in Liverpool with £875 to allow fellow Irish-Liverpudlians to escape military service.[33]

The father of the House of Commons since 1915, O'Connor spent much of the latter part of the war in the United States, raising funds for the *Freeman's Journal*. It was a dispiriting experience as he found himself compelled to 'counteract the poisonous propaganda among the Irish in America directed against the Irish Parliamentary Party and the policy which had been so successfully pursued for the last thirty or forty years'.[34] The attitude of Irish-Americans, he confided in a private letter, was far worse than he had expected:

> I feel as if I hate the whole Irish race – certainly those of them who are in this country. The letters I have read, the articles in the pro-German grafter rags, make my blood boil; and often suggest to me whether I have not wasted my life in fighting for a people of such lunatics and ingrates. Judas Iscariot, paid English agent, these are a few of the terms in letters to me. The Irish politicians have avoided me as if I were a leper.[35]

His eventual return to Britain in 1918 was a considerable relief, although he was perturbed by the consequences, electoral and otherwise, of the 'conscription bomb', the imposition from Westminster of conscription in Ireland. These anxieties were laid aside, however, during the festivities in Liverpool to mark his 70th birthday, 'a sort of perpetual levée', in which he was feted by civic dignitaries and the cheering electorate, now expanded from some 6000 to 30,000 following the Fourth Parliamentary Reform Act.[36]

In the event, there was no place in this extensive measure of electoral reform and redistribution, the foundation for post-war reconstruction, for proportional representation. The proposed scheme for Liverpool drawn up by the Royal Commission had been amended following Harford's trenchant criticism that it would 'endanger the seat of the one member – Mr T.P. O'Connor – who represented the whole of the Nationalists of Great Britain: the Irish Nationalist Party of Liverpool would be wiped out, and sectarian peace would be endangered'.[37] While critical of 'one-ideal fanatics' on the issue, O'Connor's attitude was pragmatic and positive, looking to proportional representation to increase the number of INP seats in Liverpool and beyond.

---

[33]   *LCH* 31 Mar. and 5 May 1917.
[34]   *LCH* 10 Aug. 1918; Brady, *T.P. O'Connor*, pp.240–42.
[35]   NLI, J.F.X. O'Brien Papers, O'Connor 1 Aug. 1917.
[36]   *LCH* 12 Oct. 1918; Brady *T.P. O'Connor*, p.243.
[37]   *LCH* 6 and 13 Apr. 1918.

From Liverpool he wrote to Dillon, the new party leader after Redmond's death earlier in the year, regretting the opportunity lost during his absence in the States:

> It is a curious fact that the abstention of yourself and the other Irish members during the Conscription struggle, by leading as I am told to the defeat of Proportional Representation, deprived us of the certainty of another seat or two here, and perhaps 20 to 23 seats in Great Britain. This is one of the many triumphs of the policy of abstention which the Sinn Feiners are preaching.[38]

O'Connor approached the general election of December 1918 assured of success in his own constituency. 'Harford and the other boys here', he wrote to Dillon, 'have made the seat impregnable.'[39] Thenceforth, indeed, for the remainder of his career, O'Connor was to be returned unopposed for the Scotland Division. But despite the enlarged electorate (and the letters sent by Harford to every Catholic parish in the city to encourage registration), there was be no breakthrough beyond O'Connor's personal fiefdom. As in the past, O'Connor saw his main responsibility as national rather than local, promoting the traditional policy of 'friendship to all the friends of Ireland and independence of all English parties'. However, there was a ready adjustment to the new post-war context in which, as he reported to Dillon, 'Labour is rampant, and I think almost getting to a position of omnipotence':

> It is significant of the hold it has now upon the people that I have had to sacrifice Liberal after Liberal in face of a determined protest on the part of our people in favour of Labour everywhere. Indeed it is, among our people, almost as strong a tide as Sinn Feinism in Ireland.[40]

The list of candidates endorsed by O'Connor for the votes of the Irish in Britain comprised 38 Labour, 12 Liberal and three Independents, one of whom was Austin Harford standing in Liverpool Exchange. As Salvidge the Tory boss was unwilling to allocate Exchange to a Coalition Liberal in this 'coupon' election, the Liberals decided to put a candidate forward, a decision which infuriated the INP, given that the Irish comprised some 40 per cent of the electorate: 'It

---

[38]   TCD, Dillon Papers, O'Connor to Dillon, 7 Dec. 1918.
[39]   TCD, Dillon Papers, O'Connor to Dillon, 7 Oct. 1918.
[40]   TCD, Dillon Papers, O'Connor to Dillon, 7 Dec. 1918.

is a seat that really does belong to us rather than to them, and the Irish here feel that if they allowed their claim to go by this time they would not be able to assert it again.' Nominated by four priests, Harford was brought forward as an Independent, and continued with the candidature after the offending Liberal withdrew. Much to his dismay, O'Connor was thus forced to remain in Liverpool to assist Harford when he should have been supporting sympathetic candidates elsewhere.[41] By simply playing the sectarian card, the Tories (backed by Lloyd George) ensured Harford's defeat.

A personal triumph for O'Connor, the general election of 1918 was nevertheless a disaster which left him without a wider power-base. Although aware of the dramatic shift in Ireland since the 'conscription bomb', his pre-election assessment was wildly optimistic:

> The Irish Constitutional Party is fighting a policy either of a separate Republic through an impossible rebellion or insane policy of abstention from House of Commons where whole fate of British policies has been and can be influenced by Irish representation. If Ireland sent back strong Irish Party it can win Home Rule or destroy Government within one or two years.

As the election approached, there was a slightly more realistic tone in his letters to Dillon whom he hoped would secure 'the necessary 20 or 25 seats to continue the movement'.[42] Sinn Fein, however, swept the board in Ireland, capturing 73 seats while the parliamentary party secured a mere six: a humiliating defeat.

The *Liverpool Catholic Herald* was not dismayed by the outcome. 'The past is gone. So is the Irish Party and its leaders', the paper had already opined in August 1918, noting the rapid advance of Sinn Fein in Ireland: 'We want for Ireland what Ireland wants for herself, and not what we think she should ask or take.' Similarly, and by extension, the UILGB was 'dead as the dodo, slain by just such methods, or want of method, as brought disaster to the Irish Party in Ireland'. The Irish in Britain should transfer allegiance not to Sinn Fein, an insignificant presence in England, but to the Labour Party:

> Inside the Labour ranks the Irish and Catholic electors will be powerful and effective. They can gain influence and weight.

---

41   TCD: Dillon Papers, O'Connor to Dillon, 5 Dec. 1918.
42   TCD, Dillon Papers, O'Connor to Dillon, 21 Nov. and 5 Dec. 1918.

Outside they will be mere pariahs, flies on the wheel, working in the darkness, fighting, not their own battles, but those of others, like the Irish Brigades 'from Dunkirk to Belgrade'.[43]

As the election approached, the paper called for a 'new departure', premised on its previous advice to the Irish in Britain to follow the example of their compatriots elsewhere in the diaspora:

We counsel them to enter fully into the public life of the land in which they live, and not as Irishmen or Catholics, but as citizens pure and simple. They need not be the less ardent Irishman or the worse Catholics because of this ... We advocate then, the ending of the period of isolation and detachment of the Irish in Great Britain. We urge them to drop the policy of being, as it were, a foreign or floating factor in the body politic ... We have been in the public life of the country, but not of it. It is full time we made a change.

The formation of a powerful democratic Labour Party gives us an opportunity.[44]

The move into Labour, however, was to be a lengthy and complex process, rendered all the more complicated by the Irish revolution, the Anglo-Irish War and subsequent civil war. There were other considerations, too, as George Milligan observed as he contemplated the post-war reorganisation of Labour:

With the opening of the gates of the Labour Party to all and sundry the bona-fide workers did not know where they were. They did not want middle-class or higher-class ladies to come to tell them what to do, or theorists like Mr H.G. Wells and Mr Bernard Shaw. The time had come when they ought to start a pure trade union party.[45]

For many in Irish Liverpool, indeed, the Nat-Labism of O'Connor and the INP continued to resonate in the post-war world, suiting their needs better than either Sinn Fein or Labour. Thus, whilst the parent Parliamentary Party collapsed in Ireland, the number of INP councillors in Liverpool increased. Austin Harford was the guest speaker at a national congress in 1916 on 'Home

---

43   *LCH* 24 Aug. 1918.
44   *LCH* 26 Oct. 1918.
45   *LCH* 10 Aug. 1918.

Problems after the War' organised by the National Housing and Town Planning Council, where he drew attention to Liverpool's remarkable record in housing provision for the 'dispossessed', having had 'to grapple with the bed-rock bottom class of the population'.[46] Acknowledged in the national press as the leading progressive force on the council – 'thanks to the Irish', the *Daily Chronicle* observed, 'Liverpool is out and away the leading city of England in all municipal enterprise' [47] – the INP looked confidently forward to a major role in post-war reconstruction.

---

[46]   A. Harford, *The Housing Problem. Memorandum on the Housing of the Dispossessed in Liverpool*, Liverpool, 1916.

[47]   Quoted in *LCH* 2 Feb. 1918.

11

The Liverpool-Irish and the Irish Revolution

THE COMPLEX SUCCESSION of events in Ireland between 1916 and 1923, conveniently condensed by Peter Hart into the single heading of 'revolution' – a rising, an election, a war of independence (with various alternate names), a truce, a treaty, another election and then a civil war – elicited a bewildering array of responses in Irish Liverpool.[1] The various forms of expatriate nationalist activity and expression were all apparent in accentuated form, reinvigorated and fused in a 'revolutionary' compound of competing, occasionally complementary, elements. Having played a relatively minor participatory role in the Easter Rising, the Liverpool-Irish revolutionary underground came to the fore in the Irish wars, drawing upon lengthy experience, stretching back beyond Fenian times, of gun-running, rescue and refuge, simultaneous and diversionary activity. Separatist republican forms of politics, previously overshadowed by repeal and Home Rule formulations, gained new purchase through the Irish Self-Determination League and its first national president, the former Harfordite P.J. Kelly. Co-ordinated and energised by the Council of Irish Societies, there was a resurgence of cultural nationalism with aims and aspirations beyond the ethnic purity and stultifying censorship of the Edwardian years. Thus, there was over-arching cover for underground and other forms of 'revolutionary' activism, including a significant female contribution through the Cumann na mBan. Throughout all this, however, T.P. O'Connor and the INP, seemingly relics of the pre-revolutionary past, consolidated their electoral hold, but with little prospect either of extending their resonance beyond the Liverpool-Irish enclave or of long-term political survival once the 'revolution' in Ireland had run its course.

---

1   Peter Hart, *The I.R.A. at War 1916–1923*, Oxford, 2003, pp.3–29.

As noted already, by no means all the Liverpool Irish were enthusiastic participants in the imperial war effort applauded by O'Connor, Harford and the dockers' leaders. A hard core of nationalists, ably supported by the Cumann na mBan, stuck firm to the Irish Volunteers, shunning any contact with the rival Liverpool Irish National Volunteer Force sponsored by 'so-called Nationalist leaders' such as Harford to 'hoodwink' young Irishmen into joining the British army:

> The seceders are making desperate efforts to form a Union Jack National Volunteer Corps, so far without success. We continue to progress, and though 'our force is few, each man is tried and true' and we have hopes of yet striking a blow – that may not be the least effective blow struck – for Ireland.[2]

Having drifted over to Dublin in twos and threes to evade registration and conscription, some members of the Company took an active part in the Rising, along with the formidable Kerr family from Bootle, Neill and his three sons Tom, Jack and Neill junior, together with a contingent of Volunteers led by Liam McNeive – having read the countermand order, this last group were on their way to Fairyhouse races when they suddenly discovered themselves in the centre of the action.[3]

The role and contribution of the Liverpool-Irish became more important in the aftermath of the Easter Rising. Funding his activities through the '98 shop in Scotland Road (whose stock now included Sinn Fein flags, buttons and badges), Peter Murphy provided 'a safe bridge of escape for any Irish rebel in danger'. Aided by Murphy (and a sympathiser in the seamen's union who provided forged papers to enable him to work as a crew member), Liam Mellows was guided through Liverpool across the Atlantic after the collapse of the Rising in 1916, to be followed by many others subsequently on the run or sprung from prison during the Anglo-Irish War.[4] 'No one who passed through his hands can forget

2   *Irish Volunteer* 7 Nov. 1914.

3   Margery Forester, *Michael Collins – The Lost Leader*, London, 1971, pp.37–38; Thomas Coffey, *Agony at Easter: The 1916 Irish Uprising*, London, 1970, pp.34–35; Pinkman, *Legion*, p.20.

4   UCD, O'Malley Papers, P17b/136, material provided by Paddy Daly.

the lavish hospitality of Peter Murphy and all the "Liverpool Irish", as we called them', Nellie Gifford-Donnelly recollected: 'We recall the twinkle in his eye as he faked up our disguise or fixed a passport bought from some sailor at a handsome figure. I really believe he enjoyed flouting the enemy.'[5] Throughout the revolution, fugitive republicans were either hurried across the Atlantic, concealed or protected by sympathetic seamen, or placed temporarily in safe houses. As acknowledged by Paddy Daly, Neill Kerr's successor as head of the IRB in Liverpool, 'the most essential member of our organisation was the Irish sailor'. No less important were the Irish women who offered safe sanctuary, such as Mrs Dan McCarthy of Aintree, where Cathal Brugha convalesced after being wounded in the Easter Rising, and De Valera stayed on escape from Lincoln Gaol and subsequently en route (disguised as a ship's greaser) to the United States (arrangements supervised by Neill Kerr). Having taken refuge in the premises himself, Daly accorded his host a fitting tribute:

> She was representative of a type, an Irishwoman living in a foreign country and sometimes hostile city, where she went out each day to work for her livelihood. She fed us, put us up and it did not occur to us that perhaps the expense involved was a strain on her financial resources. She thought only of the great satisfaction of helping to strike a blow for that country which she rarely saw.[6]

In May 1919 the Liverpool Irish Volunteers were re-established, at first under the command of Tom Craven, a participant in the 1916 Rising, soon to become 'A Company No 1 Area, Britain, IRA'.[7] The history of this 'Liverpool Battalion', serving in the 'principal military centre outside Ireland', has to be disentangled from myth and misrepresentation of nationalist hagiography, factitious claims exposed in the posthumously published autobiography of John Pinkman, a young apprentice fitter from Bootle, the son of Irish-speaking parents:

> In later years literally scores of men claimed to have belonged to the 'Liverpool Battalion', or, God help us! The 'Liverpool Brigade' of the old IRA, and obtained medals and pensions from the Irish government in recognition of their 'service' in the fight for Irish independence. Some

---

5   Nellie Gifford-Donnelly, 'On the Run' in NLI, Gallagher Papers.
6   UCD, O'Malley Papers, Paddy Daly; Pinkman, *Legion*, pp.108–109.
7   UCD, Richard Mulcahy Papers, P7/A/1, 25 May 1919.

even wrote accounts of their 'exploits' in Liverpool for the gullible Irish newspapers. But there was never a battalion of the Old IRA in Liverpool: there was only one undermanned company – and because I was one of its two mobilisers, I knew every man who belonged to it.[8]

In the early stages, indeed, numbers were insufficient to field two full teams for football matches on Seaforth shore, the preferred method of cover for company meetings. From Dublin, Collins ensured the company was soon knocked into shape by adopting a proper army command structure (instead of its initial committee framework of secretary and treasurer) and by improving its records of arms shipped and funds received – the 'P' section of the Mulcahy papers (the code letter for Liverpool) contains several notes to Collins in the phonetic hand of Neill Kerr, a fitter's labourer on the docks, trying to account for discrepancies between the amount of 'stuff' specified and what was received in Dublin: 'Their must be some thing rong some where.'[9]

In its weekly reports to the Cabinet on Irish revolutionary activity in Britain, the Home Office Directorate of Intelligence accorded less attention to Liverpool than to Glasgow 'where the Irish have a certain amount of industrial power'. Apart from a handful of dockers' delegates, Liverpudlian 'Sinn Feiners' were perceived as an isolated and insignificant force, mainly confined to outlying districts such as Garston, Seaforth and Litherland (where the teenage Pinkman had joined the Roger Casement Sinn Fein Club in 1918 in premises above a bike shop shared with the local INF branch). 'The number of Irishmen passing through the port who keep in touch with the chief members', Special Branch explained in January 1920, 'gives the Sinn Fein movement an appearance of success quite out of proportion to the actual position.'[10] The abortive attempt by P.J. Kelly a few months later to enlist industrial muscle in support of the Irish cause seemingly confirmed the complacent analysis. In support of Irish hunger strikers in Wormwood Scrubs, Kelly sought to bring the docks and city to a standstill through unofficial industrial action involving all 217,000 Irish workers in Liverpool. As it turned out, only 2000 dockers and some 300 coal heavers struck work: a procession of 400 strikers marched north along the dock road for three miles from the Pier Head in a vain effort to persuade all transport workers to abandon work.[11] In reporting this 'severe check to the local Irish

8   Pinkman, *Legion*, p.22.
9   UCD, Mulcahy Papers, P7/A/1, 25 Sept. 1919–15 Apr. 1920.
10   RRO, 15 Jan. and 12 Feb. 1920.
11   *Times* 27 Apr.–1 May 1920; *LCH* 8 May 1920.

extremists', Special Branch noted the deteriorating relationship between the Irish and the labour movement, already strained by persistent rumours of preferential treatment of new arrivals from Ireland in some dockland labour markets ahead of the local unemployed. As a deliberate snub, the Liverpool Trades Council refused to allow Kelly and his supporters to share the platform at the May Day demonstration in Sheil Park, after which the strike quickly petered out. 'The Unions now consider that that the Irish have deliberately attacked them', Special Branch observed:

> The feeling among non-Irish men in the port is raised to fever heat and there has been considerable difficulty in avoiding a clash. Irish placards regarding the strike, in every case where they had not been pulled down, were covered with obscene abuse and remarks about Ireland ... A prominent Labour man, a foreman coal heaver, working in the middle of the worst class of Irish, asked his opinion of the Irish organisation stated: 'It isn't Irish organisations that need worry anybody, it's the Irish roughs that's the trouble here, they want the chance to make a row and pinch something.' [12]

As seen by the authorities, the likelihood of 'serious trouble' in Liverpool extended no further than 'indiscriminate rioting', the kind of 'Pat-riot-ism' prevalent in the past, most recently during the police strike of 1919.

In time-honoured fashion, Liverpool's prominence in the national police strike – and its riotous consequence – were both attributed to Irish factors. 'I fancy the high proportion of men of the Liverpool Police who went on strike was due to the presence of many Irishmen in the force, a class of men who are always apt to be carried away by any wave of enthusiasm', the Commissioner of Metropolitan Police, General Sir Nevil Macready, opined.[13] With half the force on strike, 'hooligan' elements (once again including Pat O'Mara, the 'Liverpool-Irish slummy', a veteran of the *Lusitania* riots) took control of the streets with 'rough-looking' Irish women from the 'volcanic' area of Scotland Road indicating which shops were likely centres of spoil. Central Liverpool was depicted as a war zone: the epicentre of destructive looting, London Road, was described as 'the Ypres of Liverpool'. While most reports (including those from Special Branch) highlighted the 'strong disorderly Irish element', some noted the active participation of foreign sailors in port together with the 'residuum of a cosmopolitan population which contains many elements of

12   RRO, 20 May 1920; Sam Davies, 'P.J. Kelly', pp.169–71.
13   Quoted in Waller, *Democracy and Sectarianism*, pp.284–85.

disorder and violence'.[14] The *Liverpool Catholic Herald* reacted with predictable fury at the continued demonising of the central highway (and synecdoche) of Irish Liverpool: 'By flinging mud enough at Scotland Road some will surely stick to Ireland, and, what is more desirable, the Catholic Church.' Pointing out that 'most of the recovered loot has been taken from Great Homer Street, the main artery of Wiseite Liverpool', the paper endeavoured to set the record straight:

> A sinister fact in connection with the shameful work which went on, is that Catholic and Irish houses were the first attacked. In Scotland Road the business premises of Daly and Co., John Hughes, 'The Gael' Tailoring Establishment, and many others were speedily and completely wrecked. A nice discrimination was shown in the attack on Mr Peter Murphy's '98 Shop' in Scotland Place. One of his windows filled with tobacco and general goods was left untouched. The other one, stocked with Irish literature, music, and statues of Our Lady and other objects of devotion, was smashed to atoms.[15]

Order was restored by a combination of factors: the arrival of troops and gunboats on the Mersey (yet again); the refusal of official trade union leaders to sanction rank and file efforts to extend the strike to the tramways and beyond (the efforts of Milligan and other members of the official Negotiating Committee were concentrated on the vain attempt to secure the reinstatement of the police who had struck and been discharged); and the onset of torrential rain on August bank holiday Monday, a downpour which also washed out the attempt to reintroduce a gaelic sports day.[16] The costs to the rate-payers in compensation claims was considerable, far in excess of the damage caused by the race riots earlier in the year in the south end of the city, reports of which (unlike their counterpart in Cardiff) were free of any specific Irish taint.[17]

---

[14]   *Times* 4–9 and 11 Aug. 1919; RRO, 7 and 14 Aug. 1919; LVRO, 352MIN/WAT/1/56, Minutes of the Watch Committee, 1, 9 and 19 Aug. 1919; O'Mara, *Autobiography*, ch. 30.

[15]   *LCH* 9 Aug. 1919.

[16]   Ron Bean, 'Police unrest, unionization and the 1919 strike in Liverpool', *Journal of Contemporary History*, 15, 1980, pp.633–53; G.W. Reynolds and A. Judge, *The Night the Police Went on Strike*, London, 1968, ch. 11.

[17]   Neil Evans, 'Across the universe: Racial violence and the post-war crisis in imperial Britain, 1919–25', *Immigrants and Minorities*, 13, 1994, pp.59–88; and M. Rowe, 'Sex, "race" and riot in Liverpool', *Immigrants and Minorities*, 19, 2000, pp.53–70; Fitzpatrick, 'Irish

Table 11.1 *Compensation claims for riots in 1919*

Type of riot	No. of claims	Amount claimed	Amount paid	Reduction
Racial, June 1919	54	£2734	£1502	£1232
Police strike, August 1919	583	£163,222	£105,505	£57,717

See 352MIN/WAT 1/58 f.100, 6 July 1920.

As unemployment intensified throughout the period of the Irish troubles, the local authorities feared a recurrence of indiscriminate rioting and looting, a revival of 'the old feud between the roughs and the Police'. When the Walker Art Gallery was occupied by the unemployed in September 1921 (with the young communist Jack Braddock to the fore), the police were criticised by the Recorder of Liverpool for using excessive force in clearing the building. 'This Police Violence idea is the bane of the district', an unnamed but 'well-known' trade union leader confided to the Chief Constable: 'Extremists and others have been working up the subject for months; and the unemployed, fanned by Communists and Irish, are likely to cause serious trouble soon, without anything making them worse.'[18]

The military action undertaken by the Liverpool Company of the IRA was of a quite different order: highly organised, covert and disciplined. From inauspicious beginnings, the Liverpool IRA developed into a sophisticated and enduring organisation, capable of sustaining what Peter Hart has described as 'low-level guerrilla warfare'.[19] There were strict controls over recruitment to prevent infiltration by spies and informers. Where there was doubt or suspicion, prospective candidates were required to apply to James Moran, manager of the INF head office in Liverpool (and chair of the Council of Irish Societies), to join the Foresters' health benefit scheme:

> What the fellow didn't know was that when he handed his completed application form to Mr Moran's secretary, Nan Feeley, she made a copy of the applicant's name, birthplace, parents' names etc., and then sent a copy to IRA Headquarters in Dublin. Michael Collins would then send

in Britain 1871–1921', p.667; John Belchem and Donald M. MacRaild, 'Cosmopolitan Liverpool', in John Belchem, ed., *Liverpool 800: Culture, Character and History*, Liverpool, 2006, pp.311–92, here pp.375–77.

[18]   HO45/11032/423878, Disturbances. Liverpool unemployment riots. Police censured.

[19]   Hart, *I.R.A. at War*, ch. 6.

the information to the IRA intelligence officer in the area from which the applicant hailed and ask for it to be verified. Only when we received from Dublin a satisfactory report on the fellow would we consider accepting him into the company.[20]

Beyond the enrolled 'Company' a wide range of activists and sympathisers provided the necessary facilities, resources and 'cover'. The smuggling of arms and ammunition to Ireland was co-ordinated by Stephen Lanigan, a senior Customs and Excise official and IRB member, the crucial back-room figure who 'was careful to stay away as much as possible from demonstrations, ceilis, and meetings of Volunteers'.[21] A network of seamen ensured the safe passage of the 'stuff', from small-scale operations in coasting craft known as 'pig boats' to regular runs on routes to Newry, Dundalk, Cork and Dublin, notably the SS *Blackrock* of the B and I Line, 'our most frequent source of export'.[22] In the two years before the 1921 truce (after which, however, there was a rapid increase in arms traffic), Peter Hart has calculated that 289 handguns, 53 rifles, 24,141 rounds of ammunition and 1067 pounds of explosives were shipped through Liverpool.[23]

Through the services of the likes of Bernie Kavanagh, a diminutive seaman with a hot temper, a dapper top hat for wearing ashore, and direct contact to Collins, the B and I link served a number of other vital functions. Travelling on the fo'c'sle of the *Blackrock* with Kavanagh to Dublin was 'the recognised method of travel for anyone wishing to avoid the detectives or Auxiliaries at the North Wall'. Sailors on the return run reported to a particular pub close to the Nelson Dock bearing instructions from Collins in an envelope marked 'LP'. 'Generally we had the lounge to ourselves', Daly recollected, 'but if any strangers were present a meeting in the lavatory at the back was effected to convey any particular verbal messages or dispatches from Dublin either to myself or for transfer to New York'. While smuggling whiskey into prohibition America, Irish seamen returned to Liverpool with Thompson sub-machine guns (revered by the gangsters of American popular culture) and other arms for the Irish struggle. The chance discovery by Customs in Liverpool of a consignment of ten sub-machine guns on board the SS *Baltic* in November 1921 was a cause of potential embarrassment to the treaty negotiations. 'This was bound

---

20   Pinkman, *Legion*, pp.21–22.
21   Pinkman, *Legion*, pp.25–26.
22   UCD, O'Malley Papers, Paddy Daly.
23   Hart, *I.R.A. at War*, pp.183–84.

to occur some time', Daly reported to Collins, 'but it may seriously hinder future activities.' Irish seamen on continental European runs out of Liverpool specialised in smuggling German automatic pistols, known as 'Peter-the-Painter' after the Latvian anarchist who escaped from the Sidney Street siege. The most trusted arms smugglers such as Dick O'Neill and Barney Downes on the New York run were also responsible for the safe passage across the Atlantic of fugitive republican leaders, complex operations master-minded by a group of Irish shipping agents in Liverpool, including Kit O'Reilly, Tommy Hoare and Barney Kiernan.[24]

While gun-running was organised through the tried-and-tested networks of the old IRB (Patrick Lively, a baker from Cork, had been the local head centre since 1906),[25] the military operations of the Liverpool IRA were in youthful and less experienced hands. Following Craven's sudden departure for New York, the studious Mike O'Leary – 'Iron Mike' as he subsequently called himself in romanticised recollection – took over the command, but was soon voted out of office (his memoirs claim he resigned) by adolescent members of the Volunteers impatient for military action.[26] One of Neill Kerr's young sons, Tom, was elected the new captain and appointed Pinkman as one of the mobilisers: 'He said I was just the man for the job, because having grown up in Bootle, I knew Bootle, Kirkdale, Litherland and Seaforth like the back of my hand, and unlike most of the other fellows in the company, I spoke with a Liverpool accent.'[27] This local knowledge was deployed to good effect during the 'Liverpool spectacular' of the night of 27–28 November 1920 when squads of armed guerrillas spread along the waterfront attacking 23 warehouses, timber yards and similar buildings, burning 19 of them and causing hundreds of thousands of pounds worth of damage, in the course of which a civilian watchman was shot dead.[28] The authorities were caught napping in complacent conviction that

---

24 UCD, O'Malley Papers, Paddy Daly. UCD, Mulcahy Papers, P7/A/7, Daly to Collins, 1 Dec. 1921.
25 Pinkman, *Legion*, p.19.
26 'The Liverpool Battalion', *An-t-Oglach*, 2, 1967, pp.1–2.
27 Pinkman, *Legion*, p.21.
28 The 'spectacular' accounted for by far the largest sums in NAD, FIN1/1589, Dept of Finance: Claims for compensation in respect of damage to property in England by Irish forces during the War. After extensive investigation by insurance companies and the police, the original claims from Bootle and Liverpool were reduced from £820,000 and £164,000 to £374,000 and £153,000 respectively out of an overall revised national total of £672,000. After protracted negotiation into 'the returns of loss or damage occasioned during the period from 1st January 1919–14th January 1922 and attributable to persons

the IRA was in retreat, following press exposure a few days earlier of papers seized in a raid on Dublin, showing detailed plans and feasibility studies drawn up by Jack Plunkett for Rory O'Connor, the Director of Engineering and 'O/C Britain', for simultaneous attack on various prime targets, notably the Liverpool docks and the Stuart Street power station in Manchester. The *Liverpool Catholic Herald* dismissed the revelations as mere 'fairy tale', the 'scatter brain dreamings of some visionary, intended to shake the nerves of the average Briton and to make circulation'.[29] Undeterred by the revelations, Tom Kerr and the Liverpool Company decided to go ahead, transforming what had originally been intended as a preliminary diversionary activity, setting fire to warehouses and timber yards prior to blowing up the dock gates and pumping stations, into the main operation. The 'scouse' Pinkman served as lookout, relishing his exchange with 'a big, red-faced bobby': '"Eh," I said to him in my best – or worst! – Liverpool accent, "wot the 'ell's goin' on?" "Bleedin' fire!" he muttered. "Those bleedin' Sinn Feiners". "Shinners?" I said. "Bolshies, more like it! ... effin' Russians, I'd say".'[30]

The scale and audacity of the operation could not be gainsaid. 'Outrages on the scale of those perpetrated in Liverpool can be carried out only by a large body of men acting together on a well-prepared plan', the *Times* observed in an interesting analysis of the contextual factors which assisted the arsonists:

> How, then, does it come about so considerable a party could have got across the Irish Sea undetected? The explanation is that but a few have so emigrated. The belief is that men few in numbers but having ideas and the gift of leadership are those who have come to England; that, once here, they may depend upon friends and sympathizers for adequate protection and concealment, and that they are prepared to mobilize not only these to assist them, but also the more desperate characters among the various bodies of malcontents always to be found in a great city – people for whom Sinn Fein may have no great use later on.[31]

Caught out on the night, the police took the opportunity over the next week

---

actuated by Irish political motives', the Irish Free State authorities made a final settlement of £500,000.

29   *LCH* 27 Nov. 1920.

30   Pinkman, *Legion*, pp.33–38; Edward Brady, *Ireland's Secret Service in England*, Dublin, n.d., pp.25–33; LVRO, 352MIN/WAT1/58, 21 Dec. 1920 and newspaper cuttings in Town Clerk's Cuttings 352CLE/CUT1/41.

31   *Times* 30 Nov. 1920.

or so to round up all known Irish activists, many of whom Pinkman noted 'had nothing to do with the Volunteers and had no connection whatsoever with the warehouse and timber yard fires'.[32] 'While in most cases there is a certainty that the arrested men are implicated', Special Branch acknowledged, 'there is not sufficient evidence to convince a Court. As in war, internment appears to be the only solution.'[33] Stephen Lanigan, Mike O'Brien, Liam Geraghty (a Liverpool participant in the 1916 Rising) and several others were duly despatched to the Belfast internment camp under DORA regulations, action commended by the Directorate of Intelligence: 'the last thing these agitators desire is to return permanently to their own Island'.[34] Seven others were committed to trial at assizes: Neill Kerr (57, fitter's labourer); James McCaughey (32, dock labourer); the Brown sisters from Litherland, Sheila (30, schoolteacher) and Kathleen (24, a clerk for John Hughes who also employed Pinkman's sister as a cashier); Henry Coyle (24, a farmer from Ballina, Co. Mayo, a brigade adjutant in the IRA who had nothing to do with the fires but who ran guns from Glasgow to Dublin via Liverpool); Matthew Fowler (27, labourer from across the Mersey in Lower Tranmere); and James McPartlin (19, plasterer). Most were discharged or acquitted, but Kerr and McCaughey (whose 'absolute innocence' was reported by Daly to Collins) were sentenced ('purely on prejudice') to lengthy concurrent sentences for conspiracy to murder and conspiracy to arson. Kerr's sentence on the first charge was subsequently quashed on appeal and his sentence reduced from ten years to two. Fowler was sentenced to two years for conspiracy to arson.[35] Liam Maher, one of those injured on the night of the 'big fires', but not arrested, was reduced to abject poverty thereafter, a pathetic supplicant, along with his unemployed asthmatic father, to the 'Dail Relief bureu [sic]' in 1923.[36]

The arrests, raids, trials and deportations inevitably took their toll on the movement. 'Sinn Feiners in England have been overawed for the moment', Special Branch reported with some satisfaction. Edward Brady recorded a reduction in the military wing on Merseyside from five sections to three with membership down from 150 to 108. 'For the next couple of months after the warehouse and timber yard fires, the Liverpool Company of the volunteers had to lie quiet, very

---

[32] Pinkman, *Legion*, p.38.

[33] RRO, 2 Dec. 1920.

[34] HO317/48, Sinn Fein: activities in the UK, 1920, 2 Dec. 1920.

[35] *LCH* 15 Jan.–19 Feb. 1921; UCD, Mulcahy Papers, P7/A/4, Daly to Collins, 5 Feb. 1921; Pinkman, *Legion*, p.45; T161/138: Law costs: repayment to Corporations of Liverpool and Manchester of costs incurred in prosecution over the Sinn Fein outrages.

[36] NAD, FIN1/1673, Dept of Finance, Compensation case of Thomas Maher.

quiet!', Pinkman recollected.[37] With the leadership decimated, communication from Dublin was at first routed through the elderly John Fitzgerald, a veteran of the IRB, a bachelor who had long since 'decided to dedicate his life to Irish freedom, like a priest dedicating his life to God and the Church'. Collins then arranged for Paddy Daly to be put in charge of arms-running in Liverpool. A young medical student from Dublin, forced to go 'on the run' on account of his IRA activities, Daly secured a job in a cotton warehouse on the Liverpool docks before assuming his responsibilities. 'The older IRB men in Liverpool', Pinkman recollected, 'were wild at the idea of this young pup taking over.'[38] Another young blood from Dublin, Hughie Early, replaced Tom Kerr as the local 'O/C'.[39] Generational tensions were compounded by other jealousies as the more 'public' figures in Irish nationalism in Liverpool stepped forward to offer succour to the families of those imprisoned after the police round up. From his cell, Neill Kerr got word to Daly and thence to Collins that he had no wish for his family and children to be looked after by James Moran and the Council of Irish Societies 'as they are nearly always squabbling with one another (not to any serious extent) and they are in general a crowd of "lime-lighters" whom he always more or less treated with contempt'.[40]

Within a few months, however, the Liverpool IRA had regrouped and undertook a series of daring operations, the first of which displayed, as even the *Times* acknowledged, 'wonderful organization and exceptional executive ability'. Posing as policemen, three groups of IRA men (one of which was under the command of the young Edward Brady) raided emigrants' lodging houses to seize tickets and documents from American-bound Irish 'deserters'. 'This daring and risky incident was given considerable publicity in the press at the time', Brady recorded, 'with the result that it had the effect of cooling the ardour of other intending emigrants'. Pinkman, another participant, noted that the emigrants were not informers and renegades but 'ordinary young Irish men and women whom the Black and Tans had forced to flee their homes and their country'. While noting that the majority were from Galway and Mayo, Daly displayed no sympathy as he reported on the operation to Collins:

> I am afraid that the shipping companies will facilitate the 'victims' to get away as they are issuing duplicates to those who have lost their tickets. It

37   RRO, 16 Dec. 1920; Brady, *Secret Service*, p.33; Pinkman, *Legion*, p.47.
38   UCD, Mulcahy Papers, P7/A/3, 1–12 Dec. 1920; Pinkman, *Legion*, pp.47 and 79.
39   UCD, O'Malley Papers, P17b/110, Hugh Early.
40   UCD, Mulcahy Papers, P7/A/4, Daly to Collins, 28 Feb. 1921.

will show them up anyway. If this affair was published in the Irish press it might make others hesitate. The morale of the local company is very good.[41]

Aided by his close relationship with Collins, Daly brought new dynamism and efficiency both to 'munitions work', his stated area of responsibility, and to the wider 'planning of operations', including ambitious schemes for attacking the oil tanks which supplied the liners using the port. Ahead of another waterfront 'spectacular', he went along with Early's plans for a 'ring of fire around Liverpool'. 'We are having some farm-work tonight', he reported to Collins on 9 March, 'just to keep the local coy [sic] in practice'.[42] Anxious to assert his authority, Early unwisely rejected the list of farms carefully drawn up by Pinkman and others with local knowledge and insisted on attacking targets which led (inevitably and treacherously in Pinkman's view) to arrests and injuries. Between 7.40pm and 8.40pm, some 13 fires were lit in farms across Merseyside, six on the outskirts of the city (in Woolton, Childwall, West Derby and Wavertree) and another seven in Crosby, Aughton and across on the Wirral at Wallasey and Bidston. By no means as extensive as the farm fires stretching from the Tyne to the Tees later in the month, the damage was nevertheless considerable, calculated as at least £15,000, but the night's operation led to the wounding and arrest of Paddy Lowe at Prescot (Rimmer, the farmer who shot him, was later the target of a revenge attack in May), and to the arrest of the hapless Pinkman and four others at Seaforth.[43]

Daly confided to Collins that 'things look very fishy' but Early remained in command for the next couple of months during which there were various other operations, including the smashing of 400 plate glass windows in the leading shops and principal thoroughfares on 1 April (which led to copycat, but not necessarily IRA, incidents in other cities), and, as part of a national campaign of 'new ruthlessness', raids on the homes of relatives of members of the RIC. Details of the home addresses of British ex-officers acting as auxiliary policemen in Ireland were supplied by the Headquarters Intelligence Branch of the IRA for simultaneous attacks in London, St Albans and Liverpool. On 14 May, masked men armed with revolvers broke in to six houses in Liverpool: in an exercise in what Brady described as 'terrorism', inmates were gagged and bound,

41 *Times* 21 Feb. 1921; Brady, *Secret Service*, ch. 4; Pinkman, *Legion*, pp.30–32; UCD, Mulcahy Papers, P7/A/4, Daly to Collins, 21 Feb. 1921.
42 UCD, Mulcahy Papers, P7/A/4, Daly to Collins, 4 and 9 Mar. 1921.
43 Pinkman, *Legion*, ch. 4; Brady, *Secret Service*, pp.38–43; LVRO, 352MIN/WAT1/58, 22 Mar. 1921; RRO, 10 Mar. and 26 May 1921.

and attempts made 'by soaking carpets and clothes with paraffin, to set the houses on fire'.[44] Early was arrested as the next operation began: the disruption of various communication networks with attacks on railway, telegraph and telephone lines. 'Dislocation, paralysis, was the objective', recorded the new commander, the 19-year-old Brady. As with the farm fires, the operation (in which more than 300 wires were cut) spanned Merseyside, was accompanied by a gun-fight at Huyton, and led to a number of arrests. 'We lost five of our best men in the last wire-cutting operation, including the c/o Brady and J. Byrne, second lieutenant', Daly reported to Collins: 'The latter two are a great loss to the company. We are certainly at a greater loss than the enemy. I am trying to re-organise the whole company. The new c/o is Denis Fleming, and about the best man left, and also the most suitable for the position.' [45]

The truce in July brought time for the IRA to regroup, while gun-running along the old IRB networks intensified in preparation for the next round of the struggle (with special efforts to recruit cable operators to improve communications). In September, Rory O'Connor toured English cities at Cathal Brugha's direction 'for the purpose of organising and perfecting plans for an Active offensive to be carried out on the resumption of hostilities'. He discussed a number of proposals at Liverpool, including an attack on the Overhead Electric Railway, but reported in disappointing terms, noting the adverse economic context, the high turnover in personnel, and the lacklustre quality of the new officers in command, 'slow and lacking initiative':

> The Officers are all new, none of them were in the Army six months ago, and I am informed that the rank and file have to the extent of about 50% changed since the successful operations carried out there in last November. This is due to men having to leave the area owing to the unemployment, this is a serious matter from our point of view, as men who are asked to operate in this city will do so with greater confidence if they are familiar with it.[46]

In these circumstances, perhaps the most remarkable feature of the Liverpool IRA was its sheer resilience, its ability to persist and replenish its forces in the

---

[44]   UCD, Mulcahy Papers, P7/A/5, Daly to Collins, 27 Apr. 1921; Brady, *Secret Service*, pp.64–66.

[45]   Brady, *Secret Service*, pp.63, 82–88; UCD, Mulcahy Papers, P7/A/5, Daly to Collins, 7 and 13 June 1921.

[46]   UCD, Mulcahy Papers, P7/A/29: Dept of Engineering. Report on visit to Britain Sept. 1921.

face of worsening economic conditions and an increasingly effective police force: as has been shown, four successive captains of the Liverpool IRA company (O'Leary, Kerr, Early and Brady) were arrested between late November 1920 and June 1921 along with a good number of other activists. Of the 22 names listed in the *Irish Exile* of those deported between January and May 1921, 10 were from Liverpool and Bootle including Phil Coyle and Peter Rowland, lieutenants in the Company.[47]

As with IRB gun-running, IRA activities drew upon wider circles of active support or at least tacit sympathy if not approval within the Liverpool-Irish enclave. Coal merchants carried arms and munitions concealed in coal bags. Other merchants, such as the cattle agent McGrath, offered garage facilities for lorries used for transporting 'supplies', including gelignite appropriated for the cause by Irish workers in mines at St Helens.[48] An elderly couple, Hugh Morris and his wife, let out the backroom at their corner shop on Boundary Street near the Nelson dock as a convenient arms dump.[49] At the other end of the scale, John Hughes was able to provide employment 'cover' for IRA activists within his retail empire.[50] When Daly injured himself in an accident with a .32 revolver, he was treated by a sympathetic doctor in a hospital in St Helens, 'a very convenient place', he reported to Collins, 'for any special case from over the water'.[51]

The Treaty of 6 December 1921 split the republican movement in Liverpool as thoroughly as in Ireland. The aged Nestor of the group, Neill Kerr, stayed loyal to his 'dear Mick' and pledged support for the treaty (as did young Pinkman who on release from Dartmoor joined the Dublin Guards Brigade of the Irish National Army under Collins' command). Daly, however, decided to continue the fight, explaining his reasons in a sorrowful parting letter to Collins:

> It was suggested to me recently that 'stuff' I was sending over might be used to shoot down my fellow-countrymen. If I thought such an idea was entertained on either side I would not have anything to do with it. If I thought that guns I had sent or was sending over were turned on you, believe me, I would rather be riddled a hundred times over than think I had helped in any way to harm you … I am in sympathy with the majority of the IRA, I would wish them to continue now and finish the fight. I want to help

47   'English Justice: Deported without trial or charge', *Irish Exile* July 1921.
48   'The Liverpool Battalion'.
49   UCD, O'Malley Papers, Paddy Daly.
50   Pinkman, *Legion*, p.18.
51   UCD, Mulcahy Papers, P7/A/5, Daly to Collins, 24 Mar. and 8 Apr. 1921.

them to do so. That is my position. To postpone for fifteen or twenty years would be a forlorn consolation. The 'big' businessmen and the politicians will come forward when peace is established and perhaps after some years gain control. Their interest will never demand a renewal of war.[52]

Daly's energies were now channelled to supplying arms to Liam Mellows, the Director of Purchases for '"General" Rory O'Connor's mutinous section of the IRA', including detonators and explosives stolen from mines in St Helens, robberies 'believed to have been carried out by imported IRA Irregulars, assisted by men familiar with the locality'. With the authorities hot on his heels, Daly seems to have left Liverpool to continue his trade. Some of the Liverpool Company, most notably Denis Fleming and his brother Patrick, crossed to Dublin to join Rory O'Connor at the Four Courts. By the summer of 1922, when the Fleming brothers were back in town, the strength of the irregulars under their command in Liverpool was calculated at around 50, meeting at 93 Scotland Road (with Peter Murphy in the chair) and at pubs run by P. Leahy and Jeremiah Murphy in Scotland Place. Dispiriting reports were received from Ireland and morale was lowered further when Denis Fleming was suspended in October on 'a suspicion that he has been making false returns as to prices paid for arms etc, and pocketing some of the money'.[53]

There was one final attempt at revival in the early months of 1923 when Liam Lynch, the Chief of Staff in Dublin, sent out an inquiry to officers commanding the irregulars in England: 'We are considering carrying out active hostilities in England owing to the advanced development of situation here. The activities would mean a general destruction policy. Let me have your views on the possibility – judging by the resources at your disposal.' Much of the ensuing correspondence was intercepted by the authorities, including letters between Fleming, now exonerated, and Patrick Murray, the new 'O/C Britain', mainly concerned with increasing operational difficulties in gun running, particularly to Sligo and Drogheda, and the development of a new safe store for ammunition in a shop in Birkenhead. Having been shown to the press, the correspondence (along with previously intercepted and rather outdated material) served to justify the deportation of 110 Irish men and women en masse to prisons in Dublin on 11 March.[54] 'There is indisputable evidence that the action of the authorities,

---

52   UCD, Mulcahy Papers, P7/A/7, Daly to Collins, 3 Apr. 1922.

53   RRO, 4 May, 15 June, 27 July and 24 Aug. 1922.

54   HO144/3746, Ireland: Irish Republicans in Great Britain illegal deportation and internment in Irish Free State 1923–24.

which led to the wholesale arrests during the week-end, not only removed a potential danger to the Free State, but nipped in the bud a series of outrages in England', the *Times* reported.[55] Figures vary according to the source, but Special Branch reported that of the grand total of 110 deported following nocturnal raids across the country, 19 Irish men and five Irish women were arrested in Liverpool:[56] the list of women prisoners held in Irish 'Concentration Camps' drawn up by Cumann na mBan included Kitty Furlong (subsequently released along with a fellow schoolteacher Mary Finan), Miss MacLively, Miss Spillane and Mrs Leonard (who collected funds for Liverpool members of the IRA in gaol in Ireland).[57] This use of the controversial regulation 14b was challenged successfully in the Court of Appeal and in the Lords, leading to the release of those detained, substantial compensation claims amounting to £64,200, and the hasty passage of a special bill to indemnify the Home Secretary.[58] The legal and financial embarrassment aside, the government was pleased with the outcome: 'the deportations have inflicted a smashing blow upon the irregulars from which they will not recover'. 'The recent deportations entirely disorganized the IRA in this country, and completely upset their plans', Special Branch reported with obvious relief. A few days before he was shot to death by Free State soldiers, Lynch was informed by his deputy in early April that 'the chances of operations in Britain are now negligible, if not altogether impossible'.[59]

Before the deportees were released, arriving in Holyhead on 17 May to shouts of 'Up the Republic' and 'Up De Valera', the usual welfare mechanisms were mobilised among the wider Liverpool-Irish community. 'Owing to the recent deportations many Catholic families here are deprived of their breadwinners, and in consequence are in great distress', the secretary of the Irish Prisoners' Aid Committee explained in a circular letter to parish priests in Liverpool as he sought 'to appeal once more for your kind permission for a collection at your Church'.[60] Sympathetic priests, such as Father Quinlan, delivered special lectures in aid of the 'Dependents Fund', but those who sought to make broader political points were not well received. 'In Liverpool things have been particularly quiet', Special Branch reported in the aftermath of the deportations: 'Harry Harte, a local Labour Sinn Feiner is trying to raise money for the

---

55   *Times* 16 Mar. 1923.
56   RRO, 15 Mar. 1923.
57   *Eire* 21 Apr. 1923.
58   *Times* 7 Mar. 1924; Hart, *I.R.A. at War*, pp.174–75.
59   'The Irish Deportations', typed memorandum in HO144/3746; RRO, 12 Apr. 1923.
60   NLI, MS 10,972 P. Cusack Papers, 16 Apr. 1923.

Defence Fund but is meeting with little success: he is not popular with the local Irish.' A small number of activists, dismissed by Special Branch as 'unimportant men and spitfire women of the school teacher type', stepped forward to 'keep the Republican Flag flying': there were 13 men and nine women at a meeting of the new Thomas Ashe Republican Club in Liverpool in early May 'when it was decided that whatever happened, the Thomas Ashe Club would keep on fighting until Ireland was granted a "Free and Full Republic".' [61] The local authorities intensified their vigilance, seizing 3500 rounds of ammunition, machine-gun parts and correspondence addressed to the 'O/C' Liverpool in a raid on the house of John Finn, a 45-year-old watchman and former Liverpool policeman, a native of Co. Mayo, on 11 May. William Joseph Horan, a 20-year-old Irish-born joiner, and Fleming's replacement as the new local O/C, unwisely entered the house during the raid, was arrested and subsequently sentenced to five years' penal servitude. A few days later, shortly before the formal end of the Irish Civil War, the Fleming brothers were re-arrested on their return from deportation: Patrick was discharged but Denis Fleming was sentenced at the Old Bailey to 12 months' imprisonment.[62]

After the end of the civil war, Special Branch continued its surveillance of 'revolutionary' Irish organisations, but reports from Liverpool were sparse, an occasional source of amusement, no longer of concern. 'The local IRA are quarrelling among themselves, a very usual state of affairs', the first report for 1924 noted, as Peter Murphy tried to reconcile differences over the current O/C (named as Daly or Deely), criticised by the older men but supported by the younger ones. 'There is very little enthusiasm amongst the extreme section of the Liverpool Irish', the report in April noted as energies were transferred into 'constitutional' channels through the ISDL, now renamed as the Irish Freedom League: 'frequent quarrels take place at their meetings, held in 93 Scotland Road, over money matters and positions in the movement. The majority are in favour of giving the Irish Freedom League a chance of success.' [63]

Although it attracted residual members of the Liverpool IRA, the reformulated ISDL under Art O'Brien was by this time a London-based radical rump,

61   RRO, 28 Mar., 3 and 10 May 1923.
62   RRO, 17 May 1923; *Times* 30 June and 1 Dec. 1923.
63   RRO, 3 Jan. and 17 Apr. 1924 in PRO30/69/220: Special Branch Reports 1924.

disparaged and disowned by early promoters of the movement in Liverpool. As viewed by Special Branch, the ISDL was a cunning ploy by De Valera to attract funds and recruits to the republican cause from those who 'fought shy of Sinn Fein', while facilitating a 'secret understanding' with the IRA behind a convenient 'constitutional' cover.[64] Liverpool was the initial stronghold with P.J. Kelly, a Harfordite INP councillor, serving as national chair of the Provisional Central Executive Council, dedicated to two objects announced in its manifesto in June 1919: self-determination to Ireland and the release of Irish political prisoners. Branches spread rapidly in Liverpool despite the opposition of some vested interest groups: when the AOH refused to allow use of its hall to an ISDL branch, the Hibernians were promptly stigmatised as 'the Anglo-Order of Hypocrites or Asquith's Only Hope'. Having severed its links with the INP and its isolationist politics, the *Liverpool Catholic Herald* refused to endorse the new departure since the ISDL, strictly restricted to those of Irish birth or descent, would similarly keep the Irish in Britain out of mainstream politics and thus could not maximise the support necessary to secure self-determination for Ireland: 'To exclude any honest advocate of Irish self-determination from a Self-Determination League, on grounds of racial or national differences, would be a retrograde and an indefensible step.'[65] Such criticism notwithstanding, the ISDL attracted considerable attention and support through a series of demonstrations at Liverpool Stadium (most controversially when Arthur Griffith was the star speaker) which reportedly recaptured the fervour of the 'great repeal meetings of the early 1840s'. In an interview printed in the *Times* on 1 January 1920 Kelly proudly boasted that there were already 15 branches of the ISDL in Liverpool and 12 Sinn Fein branches.[66]

Further progress was hindered by a number of factors, including persistent allegations in the *Liverpool Catholic Herald* of financial improbity and constitutional impropriety, charges which intensified as O'Brien and his London supporters became the dominant force on the Executive. While less open and above board than the UILGB, the ISDL always insisted it was a 'purely constitutional organisation' opposed to any attempt at 'carrying the war into the enemy's country'. There was some overlap, however, with the underground through the likes of Peter Murphy (who briefly served as local treasurer), but the ISDL seems not to have engaged the young men of action. Edward Brady was

---

[64]   There are useful studies of the ISDL in Hutchinson and O'Day, 'Gaelic revival', pp.271–75, and Fitzpatrick, 'Irish in Britain, 1871–1921', pp.685–87.

[65]   *LCH* 7 and 21 June 1919.

[66]   *LCH* 6 Dec. 1919 and RRO, 4 Dec. 1919; *Times* 1 Jan. 1920.

secretary of the Wallasey branch but soon resigned (and had no further contact with the ISDL) to take on duties with the IRA: 'from the purely political and constitutional side of the Sinn Fein movement, I graduated to the *Military* and *Secret* branch'. The banning of public meetings in the Stadium and other major venues which followed in the wake of each IRA 'outrage' by Brady and the Liverpool Company hit the ISDL hard, undermining its most successful medium of fund-raising and propaganda.[67]

Then there were strained relations with the local labour movement. Impassioned in response to Black and Tan outrages in Ireland during the Anglo-Irish War, Kelly was often unguarded in his rhetoric, deviating from the norms of 'Nat-Lab' class politics. 'Notwithstanding the fact that he had sincere friends in the Labour movement, he refused to deal with them on the Irish question', he asserted at a meeting to protest at deportations from Bootle in April 1920: 'it was hypocritical and cowardly for the British Labour party to blame Mr Lloyd George or Mr Winston Churchill – they did not make the guns: the workers were to blame.'[68] As already noted, he incurred the wrath of trade union leaders a few weeks later when he tried to bring the docks to a standstill through unofficial action in support of the Irish hunger strikers in Wormwood Scrubs. Thenceforth, the trade unions were disinclined to respond to calls to prevent the shipment of arms to British forces in Ireland: 'we'll ship all that's wanted to blow hell out of the lot of them', a foreman stevedore averred. 'Councillor P.J. Kelly has not attended any public meeting during the month', Special Branch noted in a following report: 'Many of the local Irish are unemployed as a result of the Dock Strike and he is consequently unpopular with them.'[69] Having offended the official labour leaders, Kelly welcomed local militants of the extra-parliamentary left onto the ISDL platform, such as Rev. Vint Laughland, described by Special Branch as 'a crank who has gathered a following of communists and other extremists'.[70] As the elections approached in 1920, the loyalist press were duly able to depict the contest in terms of 'Union Jack or Red Flag'. The headline in the *Courier* posed the question: 'Constitution or Anarchy? Real Issue for Municipal Electors. Sir A. Salvidge and Labour's "Sinn Fein Bolsheviks"'.[71] Not surprisingly, Labour suffered a major reverse at the polls.

As well as the adverse electoral consequences, Kelly's brand of Irish

---

[67]   *LCH* 19 Mar. and 18 June 1921; Brady, *Secret Service*, pp.10, 17–21.

[68]   *Courier* 12 Apr. 1920.

[69]   RRO, 20 May and 15 July 1920.

[70]   RRO, 7 July 1921.

[71]   *Courier* 20 and 27 Oct. 1920.

republican politics threatened a return to the worst days of sectarian disorder, a matter of grave concern to the local authorities. Speeches at the demonstrations and processions attended by Arthur Griffith at the end of November 1919 prompted Pastor Longbottom and his secretary at the Protestant Reformers Memorial Church to register their protest in ominous terms:

> While recognising the right of all citizens to free speech we trust that steps will be taken to prevent further appeals to violence and rebellion by the Sinn Fein leaders in this City. Further we wish to inform you of our intention in the event of a similar Sinn Fein demonstration to hold a counter Protestant and Patriotic demonstration.[72]

Fears of a Protestant backlash persuaded the authorities to take drastic action a few months later to prevent the controversial figure of Archbishop Mannix, a fervent advocate of Irish self-determination, from landing in Liverpool. With Kelly as president of the ISDL in charge of the extensive arrangements, Mannix's arrival from New York was to be the occasion of a massive demonstration attended by leading Sinn Feiners and other dignitaries from Ireland (where the firebrand Archbishop had already been forbidden to land). 'So far the police have been able to hold the opposing factions in hand', the Chief Constable of Liverpool reported to the Home Office,

> but I am of opinion that should the Archbishop land here, a public welcome by the local Sinn Feiners, who are fairly strong, would result and be considered provocative by the Orangemen. A grave menace to the public peace, which our efforts have hitherto prevented, would then commence, the end of which it would be hard to foretell.

Convinced by other predictions that a 'faction outbreak' would ensue, the government acted decisively: the SS *Baltic* was intercepted, Mannix was transferred to a destroyer and put quietly ashore at distant Penzance. Later in the year, within a week of the Liverpool 'spectacular' which set the warehouses ablaze, Mannix sought to circumvent the continuing ban on his entering Liverpool by accepting an invitation to Bootle. Orange Order lodges across Merseyside announced their intention to mount a massive counter demonstration, prompting the Home Office to issue an order under DORA regulation 9a prohibiting all meetings and demonstrations in the area. 'Police

---

[72]   LVRO, 352MIN/WAT1/57, 6 Jan. 1920.

have kept the Irish and Orangemen apart for some years successfully, but the latter are now "thirsting" to get at the former, after recent events', the Home Office memorandum recorded, noting that the Chief Constable was 'sure there would be bloodshed if the meetings and counter meetings were held'.[73]

As London-based Art O'Brien became the dominant force in the ISDL (he was also the key official of Sinn Fein and the Gaelic League in England), the initiative in Liverpool passed to the Council of Irish Societies. The Council indeed proved more adept than the local ISDL at the necessary accompaniments to propaganda and demonstrations in support of Irish self-determination: fund-raising for the victims of the struggle; and cultural broadening, the reinvigoration of the Irish-Ireland movement after its pre-war decline. The call for funds 'in Aid of the Defence of Ireland' was ceaseless. Over £10,000 was raised in the 12 months to July 1920, after which appeals became more urgent in support of such deserving causes as the striking Irish railwaymen who refused to transport British arms; the White Cross fund; and the Belfast Expelled Workers Fund for the victims of 'Carsonism'. Austin Harford stepped forward to chair the latter fund to the approval of the *Liverpool Catholic Herald* which observed that 'the condition of things in Belfast is well understood in Liverpool, which city happens to be the only one in Great Britain that has anything analogous to the North of Ireland storm centre'.[74] When Harford called for the internees to be released as the treaty discussions began, Peter Murphy ridiculed his sudden and 'miraculous' conversion to Sinn Fein, reminding readers of the *Liverpool Catholic Herald* of Harford's condemnation of the 'treacherous' 1916 Rising.[75] The occasional grand-standing by prominent politicians apart, fund-raising was a constant chore undertaken by hard-working activists, co-operating closely with the Catholic clergy, as in the case of the Council of Irish Societies (Liverpool and District) Prisoners Dependents and Irish Distress Fund whose records were subsequently sent to Ireland as 'an archive of the struggle'. Where O'Brien and his allies in the ISDL were regularly accused of being 'tyrannical, reckless and indefensible spendthrifts', James Moran and Patrick Cusack were the very model of financial probity – significantly, Lanigan had commended Moran, 'a man of business capacity', to Michael Collins as the best person to handle the Liverpool contribution to the Dáil Éireann National Loan.[76] Once the accounts had been duly audited by Patrick Clarke and Father Gerrard, they

---

73   HO144/22281, Activities of Sinn Fein supporter, Dr Mannix, Roman Catholic Archbishop of Melbourne, 1920–21.

74   *LCH* 11 Sept. 1920.

75   *LCH* 15 Oct. 1921.

76   *LCH* 7 Oct. 1922; UCD, Mulcahy Papers, P7/A/1, 6 Sept. 1919.

sent confidential details of the sums raised since July 1920 (some £12,490 by early 1922) to the local priests together with a note of 'our gratitude to the Clergy for the facilities they have afforded us':

> For obvious reasons much of the information supplied is not intended for the general public, but we are anxious that generous and consistent subscribers should have all the information possible concerning the collection and distribution of their subscription and know of no more appropriate method of giving them that information than through their respective Parish Priests.[77]

The resurgence of cultural nationalism began with Father Gerrard's lectures on Irish music, quickly followed by the formation of the Irish Musical Society, an initiative much applauded by the Council of Irish Societies. Arranged by Father Gerrard to support the St Edna's School fund in memory of Patrick Pearse (whose mother was the guest of honour), the Grand National Concert at St George's Hall on 15 March 1920 was hailed as 'a milestone in what is called Irish Liverpool'.[78] Lecturers at the fashionable Irish Fellowship, a Catholic club similar to the American Knights of Columbus, captured the new mood:

> The lighter side, ever inseparable from Irish life, was not forgotten. But those who came to be merely amused ... those almost hopeless Liverpool Irish who even regard the pathos of Irish life as something 'proper awful fooney' and who were present in dozens, had a swift and splendid shock in what followed the humour.[79]

The role of the Council, however, was not to impose censorship but to co-ordinate and encourage a sense of Irish self-determination across the broadest range of cultural, sporting and economic activities, an essential complement to the political struggle:

> This body is composed of representatives of all Irish Societies whose constitution limits membership to persons of Irish birth or descent, and the fundamental rules of which pledge the members to give support to Ireland's claim for national independence, to support Irish manufacture and industry,

---

[77] NLI, Cusack Papers.
[78] *LCH* 7 Jan. and 20 Mar. 1920.
[79] *LCH* 17 Apr. 1920.

and to support, foster, and practise Irish games and pastimes and the study of Irish in art and literature. Under this wide constitution, it approves all Irish events in the City, avoids the clashing of engagements, and throws its whole force in the event that may be on hand.[80]

Immediately after the truce in July 1921, the Council began to redefine its mission to offer leadership to the Irish in Britain. 'The advent of an Irish settlement would make feasible the organisation of Councils, such as existed in Liverpool, in every big centre of Irish people in Great Britain', Moran opined at a congress of Irish societies. Father Gerrard endorsed the proposal, noting that 'although Liverpool had done well, too many Irish were, as yet, untouched: those must be roped in and "Irelandised"'. Henceforth, energies were to be concentrated on the welfare and ethnic awareness of their fellow countrymen in Britain: 'they would, whilst claiming allegiance to the Irish nation, have to discharge the duties of citizenship towards the people amongst whom they lived. The safeguarding of the rights and well-being of the working classes would at all times have the sympathy and support of Irishmen.'[81] Following the treaty, the Council took the lead in organising and preparing athletes to represent (and showcase) Irish Liverpool at the proposed Tailteann Games (or Irish Olympiad) in Dublin. The civil war in Ireland forced the event to be postponed until 1924.[82] In the interim, there was considerable progress in sporting and cultural 'Irelandising' in Liverpool with the opening of a new GAA ground at Dingle Brook Farm, West Derby; new parish leagues for camogie and gaelic football, reported in the weekly 'Catholic Athletic News' column in the *Liverpool Catholic Herald*; and the revival after fifteen years of the GL annual *feiseanna* at Fazakerley.[83] None of this, however, could match the popularity and fierce inter-parochial rivalry of the mainstream sports (including boxing, now 'all the rage') offered by the Catholic Church: the Central Catholic Sports in 1922 involved over 30 parishes, 1400 competitors and 20,000 spectators.[84]

In the ranks of the ISDL, the personal animosity between Kelly and O'Brien served to accentuate internecine dispute over the treaty. Kelly, briefly detained by the Metropolitan Police before the truce, seems to have sensed the prevailing mood on his return north. 'In Liverpool Sinn Fein circles there is a genuine desire for peace' Special Branch reported in the immediate aftermath of the July

80   *LCH* 19 June 1920.

81   *LCH* 3 Sept. 1921; RRO, 8 Sept. 1921.

82   *LCH* 17 June and 22 July 1922.

83   *LCH* 26 May, 23 June and 4 Aug. 1923.

84   *LCH* 21 Apr. 1923 charted the record attendance in 1922.

truce: 'During the week several streets in the Irish district have been decorated and prayers for the peace offered in many of the Catholic Churches. Many Sinn Feiners make no secret of their desire for peace on Dominion Home Rule lines.' Thereafter, political demonstrations about Ireland were not a success: 'the average man is getting tired of this long drawn-out fight in which he really does not count for much except in so far as his subscriptions are concerned'.[85] However, there was a mood of real celebration, boosted by the appearance of the Padraic Pearse Pipe Band, when those who had been deported and arrested arrived back to a heroes' welcome at Lime Street station in December, released under the terms of the treaty.[86] While falling short of the hoped-for republic, the treaty, the *Liverpool Catholic Herald* asserted in an editorial which caught the majority mood in Irish Liverpool, brought matters to a point of acceptable closure: 'AFTER CENTURIES OF STRUGGLE, OF IRELAND'S RIGHT TO HER NATIONAL LIFE, TO HER ECONOMIC, SOCIAL, EDUCATIONAL, RELIGIOUS AND POLITICAL FREEDOM IS NOW A FACT ... WE PROPOSE TO ENTIRELY FINISH THIS CONTROVERSY IN THE PRESENT ISSUE AND TO GET ON WITH OTHER THINGS.'[87] Having accepted the treaty, Kelly rejoined the mainstream of the INP, thereby bringing 'the stormy period of his career to a close'.[88] Other groups which had supported Irish self-determination, such as the INF (always a colourful presence at ISDL demonstrations), underwent similar reluctant adjustment. There was considerable anxiety in INF ranks when the Registrar of Friendly Societies 'intimated that he would not receive registration from them in the Irish Free State'; worse still, to comply with the new dispensation the INF had to appoint a Subsidiary Executive Council for Northern Ireland.[89]

Throughout all this turmoil, T.P. O'Connor persisted in a vain effort to restore and reformulate the UILGB as an independent force in British electoral politics with a two-fold mission: securing Dominion Home Rule status for Ireland (and thus repudiating Sinn Fein republicanism); and promoting the interests of the 'Irishman in Great Britain' in his 'curious middle place between the nationality

85   RRO, 21 July and 1 Dec. 1921.

86   *LCH* 17 Dec. 1921.

87   *LCH* 11 Feb. 1922.

88   Sam Davies, 'P.J. Kelly', p.174.

89   *LCH* 11 Aug. 1923 and 16 Aug. 1924.

to which he belongs and the race among which he lives'[90] (and thus offering an ethnic alternative to class-based Labour). According to the *Liverpool Catholic Herald* such a policy was 'sheer piffle', a hangover from the discredited 'methods of the past':

> the method of keeping up the Irish Ghetto in this country; of deliberately keeping the Irish people out of the public life of the people among whom they live; of 'separate' political, social, racial organisations; of following the policy of the Irish Party in Parliament – a policy right enough in itself and so far as it went, of isolation and abstention from all responsibility for the English method of misgoverning Ireland.
>
> BUT A WHOLLY ERRONEOUS, STUPID AND FATAL POLICY WHEN APPLIED BY THE IRISH PEOPLE IN GREAT BRITAIN TO PUBLIC AFFAIRS HERE.[91]

While not prepared to stand against O'Connor in the Scotland Division, Diamond, the proprietor of the paper, wanted no more truck with the 'bossism' and 'thimble rigging' of 'T.P. and Co.'. Henceforth labelled as 'British Irish', O'Connor and his handful of cronies were now dismissed as 'part and parcel of the anti-national, anti-self-determination forces arrayed against the Irish people'.[92]

To Diamond's amazement, O'Connor persisted with his folly after the treaty was signed in December 1921, oblivious of the fact that 'Irish political organisations outside Ireland have had their roots and justification in Ireland's political enslavement. That is over ... Ireland's Freedom ends the cause and so ends the effort.'[93] Hence when O'Connor sought to revitalise the UILGB ahead of the general election of 1922 on the old Parnellite principle of being 'independent and apart from all existing political parties', he was condemned as being no different from 'the Bourbons who "learnt nothing and forgot nothing"'. 'Just as we have fought in the past against the many attempts that have been made to identify the Catholic cause in this country with the Tory party', the *Liverpool Catholic Herald* thundered, 'so we oppose with equal vehemence any suggestion on the part of Mr O'Connor or anyone else to

---

90   T.P. O'Connor, 'The Irish in Great Britain', p.32.
91   *LCH* 22 Mar. 1919.
92   *LCH* 13 Dec. 1919 and 17 Jan. 1920.
93   *LCH* 24 Dec. 1921.

create "an Irish garrison" in Great Britain or to make a separate Irish political party under a pretence of defending the Catholic Church.' It implored its readers to vote Labour: 'An "Irish National Party" in Great Britain, in local or Imperial affairs, is an anachronism and an absurdity. It should be wiped out.'[94] Although returned unopposed in 1922 – their national agent advised Labour against standing in the Scotland Division – O'Connor cut a forlorn figure, described by the Unionist Sir Leslie Scott as 'that flotsam and jetsam of the Irish Question left here in Liverpool by the passage of the tide, high and dry'.[95] Scott, however, was given a reminder of the strength of this residual feeling when one of O'Connor's associates, Joe Devlin, was brought across from Ulster to stand as an Irish Independent in Exchange Division. Only exceptional organisation and expense, Philip Waller notes, saved Scott's seat.[96]

As the Irish Civil War came to an end in May 1923, O'Connor made one last attempt to reconfigure the old UILGB, drawing upon his Liverpool experience to underline the 'special needs' of the Irish in Britain:

> The Irish had made considerable progress since the days when they came to Great Britain under circumstances of hardship, but it had been achieved only by a struggle. He wanted an organisation if only to visit the sick and comfort the afflicted. In particular he wanted to get hold of some of the poorer children in the Catholic schools when they reached the age of fourteen, take them away from their sordid home surroundings, and train them for the arts and professions for four or five years. Let them have an organisation of that kind in Great Britain for fifteen or twenty years and there would be a new Ireland in Great Britain ... There were still Irish people living in the slums, and it was useless for them to rely on other people, however kindly, for help. The Irish must look after their own. He regarded the new organisation as necessary for the maintenance of racial identity.[97]

In the absence of any response, O'Connor finally abandoned the attempt to resurrect or recreate an Irish organisation in Britain. 'Why WILL ancient actors still lag superfluous on the stage?', the *Liverpool Catholic Herald* asked after T.P.'s

94   *LCH* 14 and 28 Oct. 1922.
95   Quoted in Brady, *T.P. O'Connor*, p.254.
96   Waller, *Democracy and Sectarianism*, p.291.
97   *LCH* 26 May 1923.

unopposed return at the December 1923 general election: 'So far as politics are concerned he still seems to think that he is living in the atmosphere of thirty years ago when he was described, or described himself, as "the Irish Boss in Great Britain".' [98] While remaining an Independent (and therefore accustomed to sit on the Opposition side), O'Connor crossed the floor of the House to join the benches of the Labour Government in 1924 and was made a Privy Councillor a couple of months later.

While O'Connor failed to reactivate the parliamentary party, the record at municipal level was considerably more positive: in defiance of trends elsewhere, the number of INP councillors increased from 14 in 1918 to 23 in 1923, aided in part by the post-war disarray of the local Liberals. The Tories, however, still ruled the roost, appointing one of their own to the vacant chair of the Housing Committee in 1919, a deliberate snub to Harford, the acknowledged expert in the provision of 'homes fit for heroes', who had served with distinction as acting chair during the war while Kyffin-Taylor was away on service. The *Liverpool Catholic Herald* drew the obvious moral, calling for a progressive alliance of INP and Labour: 'Did we but help to return ten Labour men this year, we should acquire a balance of power that would break the bigotry asunder, and there would be a Catholic Lord Mayor of Liverpool next November.' [99] In 1919, at least, the two parties co-operated effectively as Harford issued instructions to Irish electors outside the nationalist wards to vote Labour, a message embellished by O'Connor in the best spirit of post-war reconstruction:

> with the Great War the day has come when as Labour supplied a hundred for every one drawn from other ranks of society, so also for a re-shaping of all the relations between Labour and the other classes of society must be modified ... In this work of national and social reorganisation no class in the community has a deeper interest than the people of our race. This, then, is the appointed time to join in every effort to uplift the working masses, and to give to their progress from lower to higher conditions a much needed acceleration. By the support of the Labour movement, the Irish will best attain that end. Vote Labour! [100]

At this stage there was just one dissentient voice. The veteran Alderman Taggart, once the party's first working-class councillor, placed creed above class,

---

98   *LCH* 8 Dec. 1923.
99   *LCH* 19 Apr. and 25 Oct. 1919.
100   *LCH* 1 Nov. 1919.

eschewing contact with 'socialist atheist' Labour for fears of its consequences on Catholic denominational education. Where Taggart led, Harford and P.J. Kelly were subsequently to follow.

The electoral pact of 1919 proved to be no more than a one-off understanding. Confronted by a Labour challenge in the nationalist wards, the INP entered the elections of 1920 furious at Labour 'ingratitude'. This time, Harford issued strict instructions for Irish electors throughout the city to vote only for INP candidates, drawing attention to the party's proud record in social reform:

> In appealing for the full and active support of the Irish men and women electors of Liverpool, and all progressive forces, we are proud to point to the magnificent services in all departments of the city's government the Irish Party has rendered for generations past. Many sound and beneficial reforms have been obtained by them for the working classes. Our claim to have maintained and upheld a high standard of civic patriotism and public service is justified by our record.[101]

The voters responded in positive manner: the number of INP seats rose from 16 to 21, including Davie Logan's sweet victory over Labour in South Scotland. The turmoil in Ireland notwithstanding, the INP consolidated its position in 1921 and again in 1922 when Labour suffered a net loss of nine seats. By 1923, however, there were indications of serious fracture in the INP and of new political alignments.[102]

In January, Logan defected to Labour, prompting the Irish Club in Stanley Road to call for his resignation from West Derby Board of Guardians and the City Council as he had joined a party that was 'neither Catholic nor Irish'.[103] In March, Jack Hayes, an Irishman and former police striker, won the Edge Hill by-election, Labour's first parliamentary seat in Liverpool, to be presented on his victory with a large shillelagh by the progressive element in the Irish electorate. This group at least, the *Liverpool Catholic Herald* noted approvingly, 'are convinced of the futility of Irish nationalism in England and are aware of the true democrat [sic] reforms which can be made by the Labour Party in power'.[104] As events in Ireland finally seemed settled with the end of the civil war, Harford moved closer to an essentially Catholic (and anti-Labour) platform

---

[101] *LCH* 30 Oct. 1920.

[102] Bernard O'Connell, 'Irish nationalism in Liverpool, 1873–1923', *Eire-Ireland*, 10, 1975, pp.24–37, here pp.35–36.

[103] *LCH* 3 Mar. and 12 May 1923.

[104] *LCH* 10 Mar. 1923.

in the Irish Democratic League, ahead of the renaming of the INP as the Irish Democratic Party (IDP). The municipal elections were more than usually fractious and ill tempered. The liberal press hinted at a secret pact between Harford and the Tories 'to dish Labour who are pressing both the Nationalists and the Conservatives'.[105] Locked in fierce electoral competition Labour and IDP candidates outbid each other in establishing their Catholic credentials. Alderman Robinson, the local Labour Party leader, whose five daughters attended the Notre Dame Convent in Everton Valley, took particular exception to being labelled 'a tin-pot Cromwell' by Harford.[106] Once again the Irish vote held: standing for Labour, Logan was defeated in South Scotland. Harford's authority, however, was clearly on the wane. Without his sanction, and indeed much to his annoyance (given his new understanding with the Tories), William Grogan stood as an independent Irish candidate in Exchange at the general election in December and finished only 229 votes behind Scott on a platform of free trade, labour policies and denominational education. Harford resigned the party leadership to be replaced by P.J. Kelly in February 1924.[107]

Acting on his own initiative, Kelly convened a conference at the Exchange Hotel in July to discuss an electoral truce with Labour, a union of 'progressive forces' to terminate Conservative power. As in his ISDL days, however, Kelly succeeded only in offending Labour. Having opened the conference in non-conciliatory manner with a belligerent speech on 'the conflict up to now, Labour had lost, while we, the Irish Party, had gained', he then laid extravagant claim to eight 'Irish' wards. Not surprisingly, the conference proved abortive. Thereafter, things went badly for the IDP. Logan won the North Scotland by-election for Labour; Grogan defected to Labour; and in the municipal elections, the last at which candidates stood as 'Irish', Kelly himself was defeated by Labour in South Scotland as was the IDP candidate in Sandhills, the two victorious Labour candidates being former members of the INP.[108] As the drift to Labour gathered pace, Kelly and others mounted a rearguard action through the formation of a Catholic party around the motto: 'What we have we hold.'

---

[105] *LCH* 3 Nov. 1923.
[106] *LCH* 27 Oct. 1923.
[107] *LCH* 15 Dec. 1923 and 2 Feb. 1924.
[108] Sam Davies, 'P.J. Kelly', pp.175–77; Waller, *Democracy and Sectarianism*, p.295.

The evolution of an independent Catholic party out of the INP was not surprising. While Ireland underwent revolutionary turmoil and internecine strife, Catholic Liverpool registered significant consolidation and advance. Where previous efforts had concentrated on basic parish and welfare provision, the post-war years saw major expansion of resources and facilities for middle-class Catholic Liverpool. The city now proudly led the way in Catholic 'higher education'. Having outgrown its premises in Hope Street, the Catholic Institute, revitalised by the Christian Brothers on their return to Liverpool, moved in 1919 into St Edward's College whose theological students were transferred to the Upholland seminary.[109] Although originating in Glasgow, the Knights of St Columba, a form of Catholic freemasonry, enjoyed 'wonderful progress' in Liverpool, drawing upon contacts established with the Knights of Columbus at the US wartime military base at Knotty Ash. In the continuing absence of a Catholic Hall, meetings were held in the Homer Cinema where the manager belonged to the Order. Other than an amateur performance of 'The Lily of Killarney', there was nothing specifically Irish in the extensive social and recreational provision to accompany the five-course dinners. By 1925, the Liverpool Province (which included a Council at Liverpool University) numbered over 3000, praised by Archbishop Keating as 'the spear-point for any Catholic movement in Liverpool'.[110] Another import, the Catenians founded in Manchester in 1908, enjoyed similar success in post-war Liverpool, attracting Catholic middle-class professionals and businessmen to a lay association free from clerical supervision and control.[111]

The new sense of self-confidence was most evident in the campaign to build a Cathedral, 'a great House of God in the metropolis of Northern Catholicity'. Having declared the Irish controversy closed in February 1922, the *Liverpool Catholic Herald* immediately transferred all its energies into the Cathedral project, hailed as a fitting memorial to Whiteside, Liverpool's first archbishop who died in 1921. Keating, his successor, had grandiose plans, stretching the fund-raising capacities of the committee chaired (inevitably) by Harford:

---

109 *LCH* 2 Aug., 13 Sept. 1919 and 28 Feb. 1920.
110 *LCH* 22 Mar. 1919, 13 Nov. 1920, 29 Jan., 28 May, 3 Dec. 1921, 22 July 1922 and 5 May 1923.
111 *LCH* 1 May 1920.

there is no place for petty economy. The magnitude of the undertaking must determine the cost; not considerations of cost the magnitude of the undertaking. A Cathedral is not a glorified parish church ... a Cathedral must be situated in the heart of the city, with its doors ever open to all. It must be large enough to accommodate, when required, many thousands of worshippers.

A body of 200,000 Catholics bounded together in all sorts of organisations and having charitable institutions unrivalled in the country, ought to have a great religious centre where its religion could be exhibited in all its splendour.[112]

Progress towards this great desideratum came to a sudden halt in 1925 when the archdiocese suffered a double blow. First, 'a thunderbolt came from Rome, smashing his diocese into two', Keating bemoaned, 'just when he wanted it to be one in order to carry out the great project of the new Cathedral'. Then came a damning report by the Board of Education on the state of Catholic elementary schools in the city, four of which (all in highly crowded areas) were condemned out of hand, while 12 others were deemed in need of substantial structural alterations. Keating reacted with predictable fury: having underlined the disproportionate burden borne by Catholics in providing schools for working-class children in the congested quarters of the city, he refused to be 'swindled out of what they had done'. He would not allow Catholic children to be transferred into non-Catholic provision and demanded that the costs of rebuilding be paid for out of the public purse. Since his arrival in Liverpool, Keating had hoped to steer the INP towards a Catholic programme of opposition to 'divorce, interference in Catholic schools, and the Revolution'. As denominational education came under financial threat, he stood forward to take over the party.[113]

Ahead of the 1925 municipal elections a Catholic Representation Association was formed which Mgr Pinnington, the Vicar General, insisted was 'essentially non-political':

Is it politics to safeguard the Faith of their children? That is all the party is out for. In the time of the old School Board we got our men in, and politics

112 *LCH* 18 Feb., 6 May and 24 June 1922.
113 *LCH* 24 Jan. 1925; Waller, *Democracy and Sectarianism*, p.287.

was never dreamed of. If there is any attempt to renew sectarian trouble it will not come from our side.[114]

Seven candidates, including two priests, were put forward in 'Catholic' wards, on a programme whose 'purpose is defence, not defiance, and its motto may be cited as "What we have we hold"':

> To secure the return of suitable Catholic representatives in proportion to our voting strength on local public bodies.
> To effectively safeguard the Catholic character of Catholic schools, and the interests of Catholic children in so far as they are controlled by the above bodies.
> To strive for the social betterment of Catholic working men and working women.[115]

The results were sensational: one of the priests, Mgr George, secured 80 per cent of the votes cast in North Scotland, and other Catholic candidates triumphed over Labour in South Scotland, Great George and St Anne, losing only in Sandhills. This success was complemented when the Catholics, in defiance of accepted convention, decided to oppose Robinson's re-election as Alderman by running a candidate of their own, none other than P.J. Kelly, not even a city councillor at the time. Kelly's victory was condemned as 'an outrage on the decency of public life' by Luke Hogan, Robinson's temporary successor as Labour leader. A few days later, the Catholics, under Kelly's leadership, adopted the name Centre Party, a designation borrowed from Germany: 'The Centre will include, not only those elected last week as Catholics, but those already sitting members identified with the old Irish Party – on the Council.' The IDP was officially dissolved in December 1925 as the Centre Party announced its policy – 'adopting that of the Catholic Representation Association for the wards the members represent, while being opposed to reactionary Toryism on one side as well as destructive Communism on the other'.[116]

The Centre, however, did not hold. Justifiably outraged, Labour fought back hard with quick and considerable electoral success. Then came a more serious blow when Downey, the new archbishop, called for a change of political direction in 1928, convinced that Catholic interests were better served through

---

114 *Courier* 28 Sept. 1925; *LCH* 10 Oct. 1925.
115 *LCH* 24 and 31 Oct. 1925.
116 *LCH* 14 Nov. and 5 Dec. 1925.

integration into mainstream parties than by an independent presence. With the writing on the wall, Kelly and five colleagues finally crossed the floor to join the Labour Party in 1929 – Harford and a tiny rump remained in the Centre, increasingly dependent on Tory patronage for survival.[117] A few weeks later, T.P. O'Connor died. His Scotland seat, held for over forty years, was assumed by Davie Logan, the first Nationalist councillor who had defected to Labour. A founder member of the Knights of St Columba, Logan pursued a rigid Catholic line on family and other issues. The ensuing tensions in Liverpool Labour have been succinctly summarised by Tony Lane:

> Labour absorbed councillors who had been instruments of the church and it inherited organisations that knew more about clientism, autocracy and priestly patronage than about beliefs in democratic and constitutional procedures which were the hallmarks of the Labour Party and the 'respectable' working class. Although the Labour Party was now formally much larger, it was in practice two parties and the Catholic section, organised as a caucus, was dominant.[118]

---

[117]   Sam Davies, 'P.J. Kelly', pp.180–81.

[118]   *Liverpool: Gateway of Empire*, London, 1987, p.138; republished as *Liverpool: City of the Sea*, Liverpool, 1997. See also A. Shallice, 'Liverpool Labourism and Irish nationalism in the 1920s and 1930s', *Bulletin of the North-West Labour History Society*, 8, 1981–82, pp.19–28.

12

Depression, Decline
and Heritage Recovery

T HE DISTINCTIVE IDENTITY of the Liverpool-Irish was tried and tested in the depressed economic conditions of the inter-war period. Habituated to their 'curious middle place', they conformed neither to the narrow norms of Irishness propounded by the Irish Free State under the 'de Valera dispensation' nor to notions of Britishness which prevailed outside Liverpool in Baldwin's middle England.[1] As economic depression persisted, they were to endure heightened levels of ethnic and sectarian prejudice, a blend of old attitudes and new fears fuelled by alarmist response to the influx of numbers from the Irish Free State. The new arrivals were ready scapegoats for Liverpool's worsening economic plight (apart from those whose specialist skills were essential for regeneration projects, such as digging the Mersey Tunnel).[2] The *Industrial Survey* of 1932 gloomily predicted that 'a vast problem of unemployment will weigh on Merseyside for many years'. Throughout the 1930s the local unemployment rate remained resolutely above 18 per cent, double the national average.[3] Even so, Merseyside was not designated as a depressed area in the legislation of 1934. Still dominated by port-based commerce and transport, Liverpool found itself disabled within inter-war discourse of unemployment and economic policy. Priority was accorded to the problems of the industrial north and other distressed manufacturing areas, while efforts to regain comparative advantage as the world's clearing house were exclusively centred on the City of London.

---

1   Roy Foster, *Modern Ireland 1600–1972*, London, 1988, ch. 22.
2   There were rumours of a substantial Irish influx even before work began on the scheme, see *LCH* 28 Nov. 1925.
3   *Board of Trade: An Industrial Survey of Merseyside*, London, 1932, p.38; S. Davies, P. Gill, L. Grant, M. Nightingale, R. Noon and A. Shallice, *Genuinely Seeking Work: Mass Unemployment on Merseyside in the 1930s*, Birkenhead, 1992.

In the new economic geography, Liverpool was cruelly disadvantaged – to the point at which it eventually ceased to attract Irish migrants.

Throughout the inter-war period, the Liverpool-Irish came under renewed pressure and scrutiny in consequence of an adverse conjuncture of 'second wave' migration, economic depression and political realignments. Categorised in biological and cultural terms by eugenicists, they were to encounter 'racial' prejudice, but even so, they fared considerably better than some other British subjects in 'cosmopolitan' Liverpool. The new arrivals from the Irish Free State, like the long-settled inhabitants of T.P. O'Connor's north end fiefdom, took their place (albeit often lowly) in the 'white' majority, above the discrimination and institutional racism deployed against 'coloured' British subjects of otherwise similar legal status.

The adverse economic climate notwithstanding, the Catholic Church persisted with its prestige project, 'The Cathedral in our Time'. Hailed by Sir John Summerson as 'the supreme attempt to embrace Rome, Byzantium, the Romanesque and the Renaissance in one triumphal and triumphant synthesis',[4] Lutyens's design matched the extravagant ambition of the new Archbishop. The doyen of the 'Kerry gang' of priests in the archdiocese, 'Dickie' Downey (1928–52) was a revered (and typically non-ecumenical) Irish-Liverpudlian, born in Kilkenny but brought up and educated in Liverpool where he attended St Edward's College junior seminary. By dwarfing the tower of the Anglican cathedral (and all but outstripping St Peter's in Rome) the proposed edifice was of immense symbolic importance, attesting to the Catholic contribution to Liverpool. As in the earlier construction of the parochial infrastructure of worship, education and welfare, the burden of finance fell upon hard-pressed ordinary Catholics, now enjoined not only to donate but also to purchase a range of special products such as Cathedral tea and Cathedral cigarettes. Only the crypt was built before funds ran out. It was not until the early 1960s that construction work began on Gibberd's radically different design, to be christened on completion with characteristic scouse wit as 'Paddy's wigwam'.

After the turmoil of the Irish 'revolution', political expressions of Irish nationalism were muted in inter-war Liverpool. Unlike the 'political Hibernomaniacs' of

---

4   Quoted in Joseph Sharples, *Liverpool: Pevsner Architectural Guides*, New Haven, CT, and London, 2004, p.84.

the past, the Irish in Liverpool would no longer continue 'strangers in a strange land'. 'We are aliens no longer', Con O'Leary proclaimed in a specially commissioned article for the *Liverpool Catholic Herald* which drew inspiration from the wider diaspora:

> We accept our citizenship as the Irish in America accept theirs, and we hope in time, as our people make use of the opportunities of education, to play as worthy a part, and incidentally to do as well for ourselves and our children as the Irish in America have done.[5]

Cultural nationalists duly took their place alongside the studious and respectable guardians of Welsh, Scottish and Manx culture in local pan-celtic gatherings at which 'all apparently looked well on England as the land of their adoption and Liverpool as their place of residence, and there was no hanging up of harps or weeping'.[6] Beneath the surface, however, strong feelings still prevailed, prompting the Chief Constable to seek a local ban on a play about 'the Black and Tan times of 1920' considered suitable by the Lord Chamberlain's Office for performance in London and elsewhere in 1929:

> The Chief Constable points out that the large Irish population in Liverpool is somewhat inflammable and says that he thinks it is too soon to permit a play of this character to be performed there ... Liverpool with its large and vocal Irish population is of course the worst possible atmosphere for a play of this character and the Chief Constable appears to have good grounds for his apprehensions.[7]

While seemingly a belated transition from the ghetto politics of Irish nationalism to mainstream British 'class' politics, the shift from the INP to the Labour party prompted a fierce sectarian reaction. There was an angry Protestant response when, in contravention of official party policy that publicly owned land should not be sold into private hands, a majority of Labour councillors voted in favour of the Catholic Church purchasing the old workhouse site on Brownlow Hill in 1930 as the site for the projected cathedral. Labour, it seemed, was

5   *LCH* 19 Jan. 1924.
6   Report of the second annual Celtic Reunion, *LCH* 24 Oct. 1925.
7   HO45/24879: Entertainments. Maintenance of ban on play about Irish troubles because of potential disorder in Liverpool.

under the control of 'Red Flag Shamrock', a Catholic caucus with a confessional mission and machine.[8]

Head Constable Wilson rued the consequences as militant Protestant groups, with Pastor Longbottom to the fore, promptly engaged in 'working up an agitation', bringing an end to a decade of relative quiet on the streets, not least throughout the general strike of 1926. In a reversion to pre-war practice, there were violent sectarian clashes around St Domingo Pit, at times compounded by the presence of unemployed and communist demonstrations.[9] Tension increased in subsequent years, propelled by an issue of perpetual contention, denominational education. Here, too, political realignment served in a no less paradoxical manner to accentuate sectarian division. Previously secularist, the Labour party was converted to the clericalist cause by the Catholic caucus: hence the party called for the maximum grant permitted by the Education Bill of 1936 to enable church schools (many of which still fell below standard) to meet the demands of raising the school leaving age to 15, scheduled to take effect in September 1939. Correctly sensing an opportunity to trounce 'Catholic' Labour at the polls, the Tories underwent their own volte-face: jettisoning their former denominationalism, they insisted that no grant whatsoever be allowed, and duly appropriated the 'no Rome on the rates' rhetoric of the militant Protestants.[10] Alongside these party manoeuvrings, the issue was literally fought out in nightly disorder at St Domingo Pit. 'We were nearer to serious sectarian strife than we have been at any time during the past 25 years', Wilson recorded, as he introduced a ban on all public meetings on the site.[11] Inevitably, there was a more humorous side to Liverpudlian sectarianism, as in the line of rotting kippers strung up across China Street on St Patrick's Day, accompanied by the caption, 'Cured at Lourdes'.[12]

An uneasy compromise over school funding was eventually secured in 1939,

---

[8]   B. Whittingham-Jones, *More about Liverpool Politics*, ch. 2, 'The Ghost of "Tay Pay"'. See also Sam Davies, *Liverpool Labour: Social and Political Influences on the Development of the Labour Party in Liverpool, 1900–1939*, Keele, 1996, pp.69–75 and 178–79.

[9]   HO144/21037: Disturbances: Police arrangements to prevent disorder at public meetings in Liverpool 1931–38. Wilson, 27 June 1938 provided an analysis back to 1909.

[10]   John Davies, 'Irish narratives: Liverpool in the 1930s', *THSLC*, 154, 2005, pp.31–62, here pp.38–39; and '"Rome on the Rates": Archbishop Downey and the Catholic schools question, 1929–1939', *North West Catholic History*, 18, 1991, pp.16–32; Waller, *Democracy and Sectarianism*, pp. 340–42.

[11]   HO144/21037, Wilson, 29 Aug. 1936.

[12]   Boyce, 'From Victorian "Little Ireland" to heritage trail', p.289.

but other financial problems remained, a reminder of the 'disproportionate' social burden borne by Catholics given their commitment to confessional institutions. As 'delinquent' children had to be kept separate from destitute children, the Catholics struggled to provide sufficient places at their own 'approved schools'.[13] There were other divisive issues, not least as women's influence with the Labour party and the promotion of facilities such as birth control clinics diminished in inverse proportion (with the not inconsiderable exception of Bessie Braddock) to the rise of the staunchly anti-feminist Catholic caucus.[14] Instruction in the Catholic line on citizenship with its conservative morality on marriage and the family and a rigid anti-socialist stance was provided by a new agency, formed with the support of the Catenians in 1936, Catholic Social Economic Action, responsible 'for the training of candidates for public service on city or town councils, in trade unions, professional associations, or societies for social betterment'.[15]

The intensified political sectarianism of the 1930s was condemned by 'one nation' Conservatives as retrograde and outdated. In a series of polemical pamphlets Barbara Whittingham-Jones exposed the workings of the Conservative machine under its latest 'boss', Sir Thomas White, operating through the 'tripod' of 'Religious bigotry, Class jealousy and Caucus formation'. Intended to defend the Tory establishment in Church and state against Catholics *and* Nonconformists, constitutional 'No Popery' had been transmogrified into a bigoted militant Protestantism, suspicious of those Anglicans in 'polite society' who failed to display full sectarian fervour. This was all the more to be regretted as the 'motive' for militant Orangeism had disappeared with the establishment of the Irish Free State, yet the Tory caucus, now dominated by Protestant extremists, persisted with the 'phantom' politics of sectarianism. The consequences were dire. The Conservatives were denied key constituencies of support in what was the real political struggle of the times: the mobilisation of an 'Economist' vote to resist the growing force of 'Squandermaniac Socialists'. They lacked leaders of appropriate calibre as leading businessmen, disgusted by the coarse 'shopkeeper' vulgarities and class jealousies of the militant Protestant caucus, declined to offer themselves as candidates. Furthermore, no electoral appeal could be made to the Catholic working class who otherwise would

---

13   MH57/281, Roman Catholic certified schools: correspondence with Liverpool Catholic Children's Protection Society 1938–42.

14   Sam Davies, *Liverpool Labour*, ch. 7.

15   *DP* 18 Nov. 1936.

readily be convinced that they 'will benefit more from Conservative policy – in housing, health, employment, security etc. than from Socialism'.[16]

While repudiating sectarianism, Whittingham-Jones joined her fellow Tories (and those of other political persuasions, including Jack Braddock, the former Communist turned leading Labourite) in ethnic condemnation of the 'second wave' of Irish migrants, drawn to Liverpool from the Irish Free State.[17] Here old prejudices were compounded by new political and economic circumstances in populist denigration of the ungrateful and disloyal Irish. In this emotive discourse, new arrivals from the Free State were held responsible for the persistence of Liverpool's disproportionately high levels of unemployment and of benefit payments in the 1930s, inequitable and seemingly irreversible burdens on rate-payers and the local economy. However, as civil servants and administrators realised, embedded within this rhetoric were a number of contradictions and ironies, factors which were to preclude the introduction of the various proposals – immigration restrictions, repatriation schemes and identity cards – advocated by populist politicians.

First apparent in Scotland, where in 1923 the General Assembly of the Church of Scotland had published a pamphlet, *The Menace of the Irish Race to our Scottish Nationality*, there was a disjuncture between xenophobic public opinion and 'greater British' administrative policy.[18] Following the establishment of the Free State, the 'independent' Irish were judged apart: as R. M. Douglas notes, the 'miscibility' which had applied earlier in the hope of improving the Irish stock by Anglo-Saxon influences gave way to a resurgent racial essentialism in Britain. The Irish in their Free State were configured as a distinct race possessing hereditary and immutable characteristics differentiating them from their nearest neighbour.[19] The most startling example of such 'racial hibernophobia' came from the pen of G.R. Gair of the Scottish Anthropological Society. Seeking to avert 'cancerous decay', he outlined the urgent 'necessity for racial segregation'

---

16   Barbara Whittingham-Jones, *The Pedigree of Liverpool Politics: White, Orange and Green*, Liverpool, 1936; *Down with the Orange Caucus*, Liverpool, 1936; and *More about Liverpool Politics*.

17   For the four 'waves' of Irish migration, see Alan Strachan, 'Post-war Irish migration and settlement in England and Wales', in R. King, ed., *Contemporary Irish Migration*, Dublin, 1991, pp.21–31.

18   HO45/14634, Ireland: Immigration into the UK from the Irish Free State, 1926–28; Enda Delaney, *Demography, State and Society: Irish Migration to Britain, 1921–1971*, Liverpool, 2000, pp.85–97.

19   R.M. Douglas, 'Anglo-Saxons and Attacotti: The racialization of Irishness in Britain between the wars', *Ethnic and Racial Studies*, 25, 2002, pp.40–63.

in a series of essays on 'The Irish Immigration Question' in the *Liverpool Review*. An advocate of scientific racial purity at a time of 'real alien menace', Gair warned that the

> greatest feature of this alien menace lies in the immigration into Britain during the last one hundred years, of Irish of the Mediterranean stock. This is a definite menace, not because these people are undesirable in their own habitat, but because they are in that of a Nordic race ... The unrest and lack of obedience to prescribed ideas in the one, and the great respect for communal institutions in the other are biological as well as purely cultural manifestations.[20]

Although outside the United Kingdom and characterised (at least by eugenicists) as racially apart, the Irish nevertheless remained British subjects. Anathema to de Valera, dominion status placed the Irish within the 'greater Britain' of the 'Old Commonwealth' alongside Canada, Australia and New Zealand, the pride of the British political establishment.[21] A scribbled covering note on the file containing documents relating to the interdepartmental conference in 1927 prompted by Scottish concerns about immigration from the Free State spelt out the constitutional position: 'Irishmen cannot be kept out of U.K. without legislation which would break down the traditional rule of U.K. that any B.S. [British Subject] can come in, whatever may be the practice of the Dominions. Irish should not be referred to as aliens.'[22]

During the Anglo-Irish war, the Dail had condemned migrants as deserters. This hardline stance was perforce relaxed by the Cumann na nGaedheal administration, preoccupied with establishing the legitimacy (and machinery) of the Free State. Rhetoric apart, there was no discernible change of policy when Fianna Fail assumed power in 1932. Indeed, as de Valera's Ireland became characterised by Anglophobia, irredentism, intense Catholicism and the self-sufficient ideal of rural 'frugal comfort', out-migration reached new heights.[23] For Whittingham-Jones and her like, this was to add insult to injury. She sought to impose restrictions on migrants from the Free State to Liverpool 'not because they were Roman Catholics but because they were citizens of a country which had constantly tried to undermine the British Empire and had repeatedly insulted

---

20 G.R. Gair, 'The Irish immigration question, 1–3', *Liverpool Review*, Jan.–Mar. 1934.
21 Randall Hansen, *Citizenship and Immigration in Post-War Britain*, Oxford, 2000, pp.18–19.
22 HO45/14634, 3rd file.
23 Delaney, *Demography*, pp.57–63.

the British Crown'.[24] While repudiating links to Britain, the ungrateful Irish nevertheless relied on unrestricted access to the Liverpool labour market, or rather its generous relief and benefits payments, to compensate for the abysmal poverty and failure of their own economy. 'If we do have an Irish Republic as our neighbour, and it is found possible to return her exiled citizens, what a fine exit of ignorance and dirt and drunkenness and disease', J.B. Priestley mused as he contemplated the Liverpool-Irish 'slummies' of Paddy's Market on his *English Journey*, in a passage blending old attitudes and new prejudices:

> they have settled in the nearest quarter and turned it into a slum, or, finding a slum, have promptly settled down to out-slum it. And this, in spite of the fact that nowadays being an Irish Roman Catholic is more likely to find a man a job than to keep him out of one ... though I suppose there was a time when the city encouraged them to settle in it, probably to supply cheap labour, I imagine Liverpool would be glad to be rid of them now. After the briefest exploration of its Irish slums, I began to think that Hercules himself will have to be brought back and appointed Minister of Health before they will be properly cleaned up, though a seductive call or two from de Valera, across the Irish Sea, might help. But he will never whistle back these bedraggled wild geese. He believes in *Sinn Fein* for Ireland, not England.[25]

When first compelled to investigate the matter in the late 1920s, the government dismissed claims of large-scale immigration and benefit fraud, drawing attention to the high birth rate of those Irish already resident in places such as Liverpool: 'It is in fact the Irish population already established that presents the main problem and the comparatively small migration does not appear to warrant any departure from the traditional policy of allowing the free admission into this country of all British subjects of whatever origin.'[26] Studies by social scientists, however, soon suggested otherwise. Based on figures supplied by shipping companies and the Irish Free State authorities and collated by H. Parker, *A Study of Migration to Merseyside with Special Reference to Irish Immigration*, published in 1931 as a preliminary to Caradog Jones's *Social Survey of Merseyside*, calculated a net inward balance into Liverpool of 4828 in 1927, 4752

---

24   'The Irish in Liverpool', *DP* 26 Apr. 1937.
25   J.B. Priestley, *English Journey*, London, 1934; 1994 edn, pp.244–50.
26   HO45/14635: Ireland: Immigration into the UK from the Irish Free State, 1929–32, printed memo, Jan. 1931.

in 1928, 6015 in 1929 'with the likelihood that 1930 will show greater inward balance'. Indeed, given the nature of the Free State economy, the flow was set to continue undiminished:

> Now that the creation of small holdings in Ireland is practically completed there is no prospect of a further outlet for the population on the land ... The least useful members of the village are thus forced to leave and go elsewhere and seek a livelihood. In the absence of industrial development in Ireland they leave the country. The line of least resistance leads this surplus to cross to Merseyside.[27]

Having seen a pre-publication copy, Carr-Saunders drew up a confidential memorandum in October 1930, warning of the dire consequences as 'the net influx into Great Britain from the Irish Free State has increased and is apparently still increasing during a period in which industrial conditions have worsened'. No longer serving as trans-shipment point following the introduction of quotas by the United States, Liverpool, he noted, carried the greatest burden:

> The problem has not escaped the attention of the co-religionists of the migrants, and the local Catholic societies have sought to deal with the matter. A letter was addressed some time ago to every Irish branch of the Society of St. Vincent de Paul asking that the utmost be done to dissuade Irish from coming to Liverpool owing to the distress prevalent there. Warnings were given in the Irish press and the Irish pulpit, but all to no avail. It seems that the Irish still think that, though America may be even richer, England is also a land of almost limitless wealth. But while America has taken steps to deal with the inflow so caused, we have taken none and therefore we are getting not only the former inflow but also part of that which would have gone to America.

At the very least, Carr-Saunders advised, the government should introduce legislation enabling them 'to deport Irish (or other Dominion) citizens who become chargeable in this country'. A few months later, the Report of the Economic Advisory Council of the Committee on Empire Migration (of which Carr-Saunders was a member) called upon the government to consider entry

---

27   Caradog Jones, *A Study of Migration to Merseyside*.

restrictions, admittedly 'a striking departure from the historic policy of this country'.[28]

Quantitative calculation was accompanied by qualitative assessment as social scientists and economists bemoaned the low skill levels of the new arrivals, adjudged a poor exchange for skilled British workers who were taking advantage of subsidised emigration schemes to the colonies. Caradog Jones's 1931 study concluded by exposing this economic irony:

It appears a little incongruous that the Government and various estimable societies should have spent large sums of money, in emigrating people of a fairly high standard from this district, when no steps have been taken to restrict the entry of labour of inferior quality through the Port of Liverpool.

While claiming to adopt a 'dispassionate approach' to disabuse misconceptions about Irish migration, Caradog Jones's study relied as much on value judgement, articulated through binary oppositions, as on statistical sophistication. In his social surveys, he identified what he termed 'blots' in the otherwise positive impact of migration into Merseyside by contrasting the lowly Irish ('inferior' in skill levels and much else besides to native-born residents) with the resourceful and orderly Welsh, and among 'overseas' migrants, the problem 'negro' (and their abandoned 'half-caste' children) with the industrious and responsible family-oriented Chinese. Jewish migrants were an exemplary class apart, with the most inclusive and highly developed networks to encourage upward and outward mobility from the Brownlow Hill 'ghetto' to the suburbs. Here was damning evidence of Liverpool's new Irish burden: while America skimmed the cream through its quotas, Liverpool had to deal with an influx of unskilled migrants (57 per cent of adult male Irish migrants were unskilled manual labourers as compared with 39 per cent for the whole sampled population), prone to 'particularly high percentages both for overcrowding and poverty'.[29]

The 1931 *Study of Migration* was the point of entry into the debate for a range of interested parties, all of whom claimed to be concerned simply with the economic consequences of the influx from Ireland. Under pressure from local Evangelicals, Bishop David led the way, seeking information from the

---

[28]   HO45/14635, Carr-Saunders, 27 Oct. 1930, and Economic Advisory Council Report, July 1931.
[29]   Caradog Jones, *A Study of Migration*, pp.9–11; and *Social Survey of Merseyside*, vol. 1, Liverpool, 1934, ch. 3, 'The welding together of foreign elements'.

Home Office about reciprocal repatriation agreements with the Dominions, as 'steerage passengers are crossing to us at the rate of 6,000 a year, and many of them are adding to an already heavy burden of maintenance'. 'There is a good deal of trouble pending here', he explained in a subsequent letter, 'and some of us are trying to confine it to broad economic lines, and to exclude as far as possible the old religious animosities.'[30] This was the line adopted by his Anglican colleague, Canon Raven, in discussing 'The Irish Problem' in a series of articles in the *Liverpool Review*. Raven drew attention to three recent critical changes in 'public opinion' in Liverpool: the onset of pessimism about economic recovery ('that Liverpool would never recover was almost an axiom'); the return of strife and disorder ('the religious and racial bitterness for which our city has been unpleasantly notorious is undoubtedly increasing in violence'); and 'the very widespread belief that our social progress is being hampered and our financial stringency increased by the influx of immigrants from the Irish Free State'. In this context, it was vital to ascertain the 'economic' impact of Irish migrants on the labour market, benefit costs and social reform programmes.[31]

This was the beginning of a sustained campaign to stigmatise migrants from the Free State. Extending far beyond diocesan publications, cumulative invective outweighed internal logic. Ready scapegoats for Liverpool's economic decline, new arrivals were condemned as both job-taking 'scabs' and welfare scroungers. In a reprise of old arguments about Ribbonism, Liverpool was depicted as the fulcrum of the 'ganger' system, radiating from Co. Mayo through 'well-organised societies'. 'The influence of Irish foremen and gangers', Raven asserted, 'secures work for newly-arrived Irishmen in preference to resident Englishmen.' Other migrants, often in need of ready cash to pay off debts to gangers who operated as money-lenders, took jobs away by undercutting the wages and conditions of local workers. Such practices were readily condoned by building contractors: '"they work hard and do not worry about Trade Union rules" is the reason given for preferring them to natives'. Alongside these time-old charges relating to the casual and unskilled sectors, the *Liverpolitan*, a leading Conservative periodical, drew attention to new forms of 'economic freemasonry', 'religious cliqueism' and 'nepotism' as the 'Catholic caucus' consolidated its municipal position:

> with the growth of the Irish Catholic community here, it is natural that a
> certain amount of industrial and civic leadership and patronage should have

30   HO45/14635, Bishop David, 10 and 15 July 1931.
31   'The Irish Problem', 'Notes of the Month' and 'Irish Immigration into Merseyside', *Liverpool Review*, May, June and Aug. 1931.

been acquired by the abler and more enterprising members of that body, and it is not surprising to find a strong economic 'freemasonry' existing between employers and workmen, tradesmen and customers, professional men and clients, city councillors and their protégés of the same Catholic faith.

In issue after issue, *Liverpolitan* aired (unsubstantiated) allegations of 'a widespread, lynx-eyed, and ever-active system of favouritism towards Catholics in the various departments of the public service':

> The municipal hospitals, in particular, are said to be happy hunting grounds for Irish medicos and nurses, many of whom fresh from their native land have been given preference over Liverpool-born and Liverpool-trained persons, whose only disability is their Protestantism! ... What it is apparently necessary to emphasise is that Liverpool despite its somewhat cosmopolitan character is still predominantly English and Protestant as to numbers and ratepaying capacity. What is objected to is not a man's nationality or religion but the abuse of English hospitality and tolerance as stepping-stones to usurpation in matters economic. The wealth and the public funds of the city belong in the bulk to English Protestants, and we protest against any back-stair tactics that result in the disinheriting of the main native elements to the advantage of newcomers from over the channel. If one half of what we hear is true a state of scandal has been reached calling for a searching inquiry and the application of appropriate remedies.

Liverpolitan was outraged when, following changes in the administration of the benefit system, disabled ex-servicemen employed as clerks by the local Public Assistance Committee were dismissed while Catholics were retained: 'The public will not believe that ninety-five per cent of those selected on merit for permanent employment are Irish Catholics.'[32]

While favoured in the labour market through under-cutting, gang systems, 'religious cliqueism' and the like, the Irish were also portrayed as consummate welfare scroungers. As in the past, the port of entry bore a disproportionate burden as the place of final recourse, a point underlined in a report drawn up by the right-wing Economic League:

> Many Irish labourers arrive in Lancashire or some other part of the country

---

[32]   *Liverpolitan* Jan. 1936 and May 1937.

to work as navvies or general labourers on some contract job. When the job is finished these labourers usually stay and drift to Liverpool, where many of them have relatives and friends. Their work on a contractor's job has qualified them for unemployed pay. There is little doubt that the dole provides them with a better living than wage labour in Ireland.[33]

An immoveable presence, the new arrivals retarded the city's hard-fought progressive efforts to eradicate slums and casualism. Subsidised by Liverpool rate-payers, Irish migrants settled in the worst slum housing, thence to be placed, quite unjustifiably it was protested, at the front of the queue for new municipal housing.[34] However, it was the extent of benefit fraud which constituted what *Liverpolitan* described as the 'Irish menace':

all hope of a reduction in the number of the city's unemployed or in the P.A.C. rate can be abandoned if no check can be applied. Recently a batch of these immigrants, while pretending to be destitute, had Irish banknotes concealed in the heels of their boots! There ought to have been authority to send them back to Dublin at their own expense.[35]

The point was rammed home by Bishop David in a number of Anglican publications in 1937, drafts of which were apparently sent for checking and approval to Thomas White, the Tory boss.[36] There was no longer any pretence of limiting discussion of 'The Irish in Liverpool' to the economics of migration: the political implications were the crucial consideration.

Our migration treaties with the Dominions are all unilateral. They can send back our nationals who become a charge on public funds, but we cannot do likewise. Consequently, there are a quarter of a million Irish in Liverpool, and they continue to come over every year for the higher dole. Ireland has discovered a way to make England support her surplus population. Their chief effect on Church life is to drive our conservative evangelicals into extremism. The most serious effect is political. They may give control to the local Labour party, which in turn may gain control of

---

33   Quoted in *Liverpool Echo* 19 Jan. 1939.
34   'Influx of Irish', *DP* 19 Jan. 1939.
35   *Liverpolitan* Mar. 1938.
36   John Davies, 'Irish narratives', p.33.

the local government. In this event, Liverpool will be dominated by Roman Catholics.[37]

Henceforth there was no restraint in vehement condemnation of the Irish inflow. R.S. Walshaw, a student of Caradog Jones, tried to dispel misperceptions with a comprehensive statistical study of *Migration to and from Merseyside: Home, Irish, Overseas* (1938). Having conceded that the numbers of Irish migrants were on the increase from 1935, Walshaw found 'no evidence that they come here with the specific purpose of obtaining, when unemployed, assistance from public funds on a more generous scale than is obtainable in the Irish Free State'.[38] The *Liverpolitan* was curtly dismissive of this academic intervention, dismissing Walshaw's statistics as 'just dry bones':

> They tell us nothing of the social, economic and other values involved. The rot has already set in, and if the present rate of movement should be maintained it is not difficult to envisage Liverpool fifty years hence as a city predominantly Irish in race and Roman Catholic in religion ... What has England as a whole to say to a system that permits Southern-Ireland to be the breeding-ground of redundant low-grade elements, free to cross the channel, to debase the British standard of life? [39]

According to Councillor David Rowan, Liverpool's very identity was now at risk: 'in two or three years, if you took a plebiscite, instead of the city being Liverpool, it might be called Dublin ("Shame")'.[40]

Conservative councillor for Princes Park, Rowan was the leading figure in the establishment of the Irish Immigration Investigation Bureau in early 1939, prompted by the latest 'scandal': the preference purportedly accorded to Irish workers at the Speke aircraft factory. Having previously quit their jobs at the factory during the Czechoslovakian crisis to 'shoot back' to Eire to avoid possible conscription, they had now brazenly returned to Speke to be reinstated, so Rowan and others alleged, at the expense of some 160 local workers hastily

37 Having first appeared in a Church monthly, the Bishop's remarks were given a wider airing through his article 'The Irish in Liverpool', *Liverpool Diocesan Review*, Apr. 1937 which drew upon the figures of 'A Lancashire Burden', *Times* 5 Aug. 1936. See also *DP* 24 and 26 Apr. 1937.
38 Robert Stanley Walshaw, *Migration to and from Merseyside: Home, Irish, Overseas*, Liverpool, 1938.
39 'The Irish Influx', *Liverpolitan* June 1938.
40 *DP* 19 Jan. 1939.

discharged from employment. Here was a potent blend of politics and economics, an emotive compound which, as in the past, carried anti-Irish prejudice to fever pitch: job takers and welfare scroungers, the Irish were also demonised as political traitors and cowards. Having denounced the alleged events at Speke at a 'stormy' meeting at Picton Hall which required heavy stewarding, Rowan, supported by other councillors from across the political spectrum (including the chairman of the Public Assistance Committee), called upon the Merseyside MPs to lobby government for the amendment of the immigration laws. To reinforce the campaign, a local 'Anti-Irish Immigration Bureau' was to be established, charged with 'the investigation and exposure of cases where preference is shown for Irish Free State labour to the detriment of Liverpool unemployed, and the protection of the interests of Liverpool workingmen against cheap Irish labour'. In early February, offices were opened in Rigby's Buildings for the new 'non-sectarian', 'non-political' voluntary body, now known by the more diplomatic name of the Irish Immigration Investigation Bureau. Mary Cumella, a former Labour councillor who had lost her seat in Granby in the municipal elections of 1937 fought on the issue of grants to Catholic schools, served as honorary secretary to the all-party committee of councillors and magistrates, from which Alderman Longbottom was deliberately excluded to preserve the non-sectarian façade.[41]

Unfortunately, the published reports of the Irish Immigration Investigation Bureau have been removed nefariously from the Liverpool Record Office. Judging by accounts in the press, the Bureau set about its task in pro-active manner: ahead of the findings of its investigations, it began collecting signatures for a petition for the introduction of laws to restrict immigration and the 'amending of the Act of Settlement between Britain and Eire to ensure that the Government of Eire accepts financial responsibility for its nationals chargeable to local and national public funds'. Rowan was convinced of the operation of widespread benefit fraud as Irish migrants, having benefited from preference in the labour market, 'worked for 30 weeks, qualified for the dole, and then their jobs were taken by their relatives, who did the same thing'. At his instigation, the council ordered the Public Assistance Committee to submit a report on the number of Irish and their dependants who had become chargeable over the last five years together with regular monthly updates of new applicants for relief. When G.W. Molyneux, the Public Assistance Officer, presented the first set of figures, there was a heated exchange between Longbottom, who offered anecdotal evidence that 'a good deal had been going on in the selling of Labour

41   *Liverpool Echo* 16, 19, 20, 28 Jan., 1 and 6 Feb. 1939. *DP* 19 Jan. 1939.

Exchange cards' and Hogan, the Labour leader, who repudiated the entire investigatory exercise:

> All this great scare is simply eyewash. It is based upon something that you have in Liverpool and that you have not got in any other part of the country – a deep venomous hostility to the people, who if trouble breaks out in Europe, you will want to have on your side.

When Molyneux subsequently submitted figures relating to Irish migrants who had 'not resided continuously without relief in Liverpool for a period of five years before their initial application', the number was a mere 67 at a cost of some £3000 per annum, statistics which, as John Davies notes, 'hardly substantiated the popular picture of the number of destitute Irish being supported by the city's ratepayers'. Public support for the Irish Immigration Investigation Bureau was by no means undermined, however, as the political context deteriorated drastically.[42] Appalled by de Valera's insistence on Irish neutrality, Liverpudlians were then outraged when IRA 'terrorists', opposed to the 1938 Anglo-Irish agreement, began a bombing campaign in the city.

The bombing campaign drew inspiration from the 'S-Plan', a republican document drawn up during the civil war proposing a combination of sabotage and symbolic diversionary attacks in Britain to disrupt economic life and create an atmosphere of anxiety. The belated implementation of the plan, however, flew in the face of the essential premise of the strategy: 'In order to exercise maximum effect, the diversion must be carried out at a time when no major war or world crisis is on.'[43] Conducted in the tense international climate of 1939, the campaign backfired, isolating the IRA – and by implication the Irish – as treacherous terrorists and German collaborators. Much inconvenience was caused in the city: the tramway system was disrupted; telephone kiosks and pillar-boxes were wrecked; cinemas were evacuated following tear-gas attacks; explosive devices were dropped through the letter-boxes of commercial premises; and but for the vigilance of a postman, who spotted 47 sticks of gelignite, there would have been a major explosion at a sub-post office in

---

[42]   In the absence of the Bureau's records, this analysis draws upon the press cuttings in LVRO, 352CLE/CUT1/69 and 70, including *Liverpool Echo* 26 and 28 Jan, 1 Feb. and 19 Apr. 1939; *Express* 23 Mar., 19 Apr. and 17 May 1939. See also 'The Influx of Irish into Liverpool. The Investigation Bureau – what it is and what it is doing', *Liverpolitan* May 1939; John Davies, 'Irish narratives', pp.47–55.

[43]   Conor Foley, *Legion of the Rearguard: The I.R.A. and the Modern Irish State*, London, 1992, p.183.

Scotland Road, the main artery of Irish Liverpool.[44] As this last incident suggests, the campaign was for the most part the work of outsiders without local knowledge or contacts. Evidence is sparse, but on the basis of the ready assistance accorded the police in locating suspects and arms dumps, it would seem that these physical force activists no longer enjoyed the kind of community sanction and protection extended to their forbears.

The bombers included the unfortunate Jerry Gildea, a clerk in Guinness's brewery, Dublin, who, as his co-conspirator the adolescent Brendan Behan related, intended to 'go active in England' for the period of his annual summer holidays:

> the inscrutable ways of the Lord being what they are, the first day he was in Liverpool an incendiary primer exploded in his pocket, and he walking up Dale Street, and, with half his face burned off, he was savaged and nearly lynched by the populace, who apparently disapproved of having the kip burned about their ears. The accident happened just in time for the Autumn Assizes, and when the period of his holiday was over, he had been up, tried and weighed off with fifteen stretch under the assumed name of Clarence Rossiter.[45]

Internal standards of vetting and security within the IRA seem to have fallen from earlier days. Vincent Crompton, the main defendant at the October Assizes, sentenced to twenty years' penal servitude on conspiracy and explosion charges, was revealed as 'not even Irish' but a Manchester-born seaman turned adventurer who had served in the United States army, the British army and the International Brigade in Spain. Embarrassed by this exposure in court, Christopher Kenneally, a young co-defendant sentenced to three years in Borstal, sought 'to clear his organisation concerning Crompton. He said that Crompton would not have been allowed to take part in their activities were it known he possessed such a record.'[46] Another teenager, not long off the boat, Brendan Behan was arrested in possession of a suitcase containing 'Pot. Chlor, Sulph Ac, gelignite, detonators, electrical and ignition, and the rest of my Sinn Fein conjuror's outfit': material for bombs intended to be planted on new battleships in Cammell Laird's shipyard in Birkenhead. Awaiting trial, Behan

44   John Davies, 'Irish narratives', pp.55–60; and press cuttings in LVRO, 352CLE/ CUT1/69 and 70.

45   Brendan Behan, *Borstal Boy*, London, 1958, 1990 edn, pp. 36–7.

46   *Times* 28 Oct. 1939.

received some hostile treatment from the Liverpool-Irish, both cell-mates and warders. He shared a cell with Dale who

> told me one day, and I sitting near him, that he was Liverpool-Irish and that his mother was from Westport, County Mayo. He was a bad bastard for all that, and told me in a hurry that he didn't like Irish people, that he was an Englishman himself, and that Irishmen came over to Liverpool to work for scab wages.

To his dismay there was similar Anglicisation among the prison guards: 'Catholic warders were the worst. Irish Catholics, worst of all. They showed their loyalty to the King and Empire by shouting at me and abusing me a bit more than the others.' [47]

Against the background of IRA 'terror', the Irish Immigration Investigation Bureau, supported by the *Liverpolitan*, put forward what were admitted as 'drastic' measures: the restriction of immigration from Eire by the use of identity cards, the holders of which 'should be called upon to comply with the regulations applicable to aliens generally'; and the withdrawal of all Customs Officers of Irish nationality from British ports. Recognising the growing division between new arrivals and the established Irish community, *Liverpolitan* took pains at the same time to commend the loyalty of the latter as war approached: 'Let us rejoice, however, that the loyalty to England of the majority of Liverpool Irishmen is unquestionable, and this is shown by the rapidity with which recruits are coming forward to join the ranks of the re-constituted 8th (Irish) Battalion of the King's Regiment.' [48] The government introduced the Prevention of Violence (Temporary Provisions) Act in July, allowing the deportation of citizens of Eire suspected of IRA activities or connections, but otherwise steadfastly refused to restrict immigration, let alone re-classify the Irish as alien.

Throughout the maze of inter-war negotiations with the Irish Free State, successive British governments sought to gain acceptance of the principle of welfare reciprocity. Ramsay MacDonald described the existing one-way arrangements, so costly for places like Liverpool, as a 'perfect scandal', but the Irish Free State refused to accede to deportation of its subjects from Britain. [49] The

47 Behan, *Borstal Boy*, pp.1, 45–46 and 75.
48 'Between Ourselves', *Liverpolitan* May 1939.
49 PRO30/69/358: Ireland: Immigration to UK, 1929–35, undated memo from Prime Minister to Sir Archibald Sinclair. There are similarities here with Puerto Rican migrants in the United States whose legal status as citizens precluded their being sent back to the

argument extended beyond 'welfare scroungers' to the plight of single expectant Irishwomen, forced in increasing numbers to 'take the boat to England' to escape long-term institutionalisation, exclusion and public shunning in the Free State where unmarried motherhood was considered illegitimate, unsustainable and morally wrong. Of the 992 pregnant single women assisted by the Port and Station Work Society of Liverpool, 940 were Irish. Various repatriation schemes were proposed in an effort to compel the Free State to confront the growing social problem. Here, a hard line was taken by Catholic charities in Liverpool, further evidence of disjuncture between the Liverpool-Irish community and newcomers from the Free State. Previously proud of their ability to rescue Irish women who fell from virtue amid the alien environment of Liverpool, Catholic charities were less accommodating of those who arrived already 'fallen'. In the absence of appropriate action by the Free State authorities, Florence Russell of Liverpool and County Catholic Aid Society called upon Archbishop Byrne of Dublin to try to stem the flow:

> There is, unfortunately, quite a large number of girls who have come from Ireland on the streets of Liverpool and we are obliged often to hear people say that the boast of the purity of Irishwomen is not a true one, and that the fallen Irish girls are turned out of their country to be supported by English charity. We Irish women are ashamed of these girls; they bring disgrace on our religion and our country.[50]

Efforts to repatriate migrants who were a charge on the public purse were forestalled by their continued status as British subjects, a similar set of imperial legal difficulties as applied to 'coloured' seamen and others in 'cosmopolitan' Liverpool. Large numbers of seamen and workers from the colonies were drawn to Liverpool during the First World War, swelling the long-established presence of black and Asian seafaring communities. 'Reports from Liverpool are not reassuring', Special Branch informed the Cabinet, following major race riots in 1919, an ugly aspect of post-war demobilisation and reconstruction: 'Race hatred is still acute in the district, particularly among ex-Service men,

---

country of origin, as was the fate of migrants from Mexico and the British West Indies, upon the expiration of work contracts, see Eric Arnesen, 'Comparing urban crises: Race, migration, and the transformation of the modern American city', *Social History*, 30, 2005, pp.499–507.

[50]   Lindsey Earner-Byrne, 'The boat to England: An analysis of the official reactions to the emigration of single expectant Irishwomen to Britain, 1922–1972', *Irish Economic and Social History*, 30, 2005, pp.52–70

who resent the employment of coloured men in the Liverpool warehouses. They demand that if the men cannot be deported they should be segregated.' [51] Following a hastily convened conference in the Colonial Office, a special repatriation scheme was introduced, offering various inducements to 'British coloureds' (£2 to cover debts and a £5 resettlement grant) to return to the colonies: those with white spouses were to be excluded, however, there being 'no question of providing a passage at government expense for the European wife of a coloured man'.[52] Significant numbers proudly and defiantly asserted the right to remain, although for safety's sake few ventured out of Toxteth, the 'new Harlem of Liverpool', at the other end of the city from the main Irish enclave. Speaking in 1919, on behalf of 'coloured men' who were 'British subjects and are proud to have done what they have done for the Empire', D.T. Aleifasakure Toummanah, Secretary of the Ethiopian Hall, appealed to the British sense of fair play. 'Some of us', he declared, 'have been wounded, and lost limbs and eyes fighting for the Empire to which we have the honour to belong.' His demand was both clear and simple: 'We ask for British justice, to be treated as true and loyal sons of Great Britain.' [53] Unlike their Free State counterparts, however, these 'coloured' British subjects were soon to encounter the full force of British institutional racism.

Tightened legislation against aliens introduced in 1919 and 1920 culminated in the Special Restriction (Coloured Alien Seamen) Order in 1925. Racist in spirit if not in the letter, the Order sought to safeguard union seamen against substitution by underpaid black labour (in particular, Arab seamen from the Yemen) by imposing a special registration certificate on black seamen who could not prove British nationality. The documentary proof required, however, was an impracticable stipulation for thousands of seamen born in Africa, the Caribbean, the Middle East, India and Malaya: their British subject status and right of domicile were snatched away by bureaucratic fiat. Institutional racism was compounded by the notorious extra-legal Elder Dempster agreements of the 1920s and 1930s which allowed the company to engage and discharge 'undocumented' crews in West Africa at discount wages and conditions. In return Elder Dempster undertook to 'control' its labour force while in Liverpool, much to the relief of the overstretched authorities, and to repatriate the men when they had no further need of their services. However, the company

---

51   RRO, 26 June 1919.
52   HO45/11017/377969, Aliens. Repatriation of Coloured Seamen, etc. 1919–20.
53   *Liverpool Post* 11 June 1919, quoted in Laura Tabili, *'We Ask for British Justice': Workers and Racial Difference in Late Imperial Britain*, Ithaca, NY, 1994, p.136.

continued to abandon those considered least satisfactory, a category which included 'troublemakers' and activists as well as the sick and infirm, dumping them in Liverpool rather than returning them to the colonies as promised. The rest of the labour force was 'controlled' through racially segregated company housing in a spartan hostel in Upper Stanhope Street, sparsely furnished with minimal amenities 'in keeping with the normal standard of living of West African seamen'. Over time, Elder Dempster's West African employees developed an array of resistance strategies against their exploitation, acquiring British passports and/or marriage partners (often Irish), entitling them to work (at union rates), relief and social services in Liverpool.[54]

Throughout the inter-war years there were repeated 'moral panics' about the growth of black (and Arab) settlements and the wholesale dumping of 'coloured seamen'. In their most sensational form, these alarms linked 'coloured' men to the 'white slave traffic', including allegations that a number of young Catholic girls 'fresh from Convents' in Liverpool had been 'enticed into brothels controlled by coloured men', prior to being shipped to Malta for 'immoral purposes'. Having checked with the Liverpool police that there was 'no evidence of the existence of any "rings" of coloured "White Slave" traffickers', the Home Office sought to set the record straight about its efforts to restrict immigration:

> We have done what we can to prevent the alien element increasing but there is no power to deal with the British element. It is a penalty of being a mother country with a large mixed Empire. The most that we can do is to discourage coloured seamen from obtaining British passports, so that we can treat them as aliens, when they get here, and prevent them remaining.[55]

By this time, the growth of the black settlement was attracting the attention of academic social scientists based at the University of Liverpool, but their approach differed little from the blend of sex, prejudice and economics favoured by other interested parties, not least Havelock Wilson's seamen's

54 Tabili, *'We Ask for British Justice'*, pp.68–77; Diane Frost, *Work and Community among West African Migrant Workers since the Nineteenth Century*, Liverpool, 1999, pp.80–83. See also the special issue, edited by Frost, on 'Ethnic labour and British imperial trade: A history of ethnic seafarers in the UK', *Immigrants and Minorities*, 13, nos 2 and 3, 1994.
55 HO45/25404, Aliens: Colour problems and white slave traffic in Liverpool and other ports; police reports; correspondence with the Association for the Welfare of Half-Caste Children, memo 3 July 1934.

union in defence of its white members.[56] In his 'Foreword' to M.E. Fletcher's *Report on an Investigation into the Colour Problem in Liverpool and Other Ports* (1930), a frankly racist condemnation of miscegenation in Liverpool, Professor P.M. Roxby, chair of the Liverpool Association for the Welfare of Half-Caste Children, questioned the value of temporary expedients short of the 'total exclusion of negro labour on ships entering the port'. Roxby's Foreword, like Fletcher's text, drew its force from the binary polarities which characterised the social surveys of the 1930s, contrasting the virtue of the Chinese with the vice and 'real social menace' of the 'negro'. The rehabilitation of the Chinese, previously demonised by (among others) INP councillors and Liverpool-Irish trade union leaders, was remarkably rapid, aided perhaps by the post-war relocation of some of the major drug dealers to Hamburg and Rotterdam where they diversified from opium and morphine to heroin and cocaine (a substance yet to find a market in Liverpool) – and by plans (subsequently completed by Luftwaffe bombing) to raze the old Chinatown area around Pitt Street.[57] New explanations were proffered for the 'lure' of the Chinese to English women: 'A Chinaman who marries or keeps a woman does so for the purpose of sexual enjoyment and makes the best of her by letting her lead a life of idleness and luxury, he scrubs the floor and does the washing and loves to lavish luxuries upon her.' Father Primavesi, Roman Catholic priest of St Peter's, Seel Street, was at first horrified by the number of his Irish parishioners marrying Chinese men, but soon changed his mind, explaining to a press reporter on assignment to Chinatown in 1928: 'The Chinese make good husbands, certainly better than the blacks, and the children are intelligent and well cared for.' The journalist found 'many half-caste children, intelligent, well-dressed and having devoted parents',[58] an observation confirmed by Fletcher who added tellingly that 'the colouring and features being far less distinctive than Anglo-Negroids, are not such a handicap'. Fletcher's verdict on inter-racial marriage with negro seamen – described as promiscuous, ridden with sexually transmitted diseases, violent and contemptuous to their women – was damning. Having chosen 'a life which is repugnant', white women 'invariably regret their alliance with a coloured

---

56   Colin Holmes, *John Bull's Island: Immigration and British Society, 1871–1971*, Basingstoke, 1988, p.156.

57   HO144/22498: Dangerous drugs and poisons: reports by Liverpool police on Chinese engaged in drug trafficking, 1923; Gregory B. Lee, 'Paddy's Chinatown, or the harlequin's coat: A short (hi)story of a Liverpool hybridity', in his *Chinas Unlimited: Making the Imaginaries of China and Chineseness*, London, 2003.

58   HO45/25404, report to Harris, 8 Sept. 1925, and cutting from *Daily Mail* 1 Sept. 1928.

man ... It is practically impossible for half-caste children to be absorbed into our industrial life and this leads to grave moral results, particularly in the case of girls.' [59] The propaganda of the Irish Immigration Investigation Bureau notwithstanding, *the* social problem of inter-war 'racialised' Liverpool was not the feckless immigrant from the Free State but the half-caste child.

In resisting the growing clamour from Liverpool for immigration restrictions, successive governments took solace in investigations undertaken by various civil servants, none of whom found evidence to substantiate alarmist claims. A memo drawn up for the Irish Situation Committee by the Ministry of Labour in 1932 noted how the flow had declined since the publication of the *Study of Migration to Merseyside* on account of various effective local measures: tighter operation of the dock labour scheme to hinder 'non-tally holders' from obtaining work; stricter measures by the municipal authorities to restrict employment provided by them to local applicants; and the increased efficiency of Labour Exchanges in filling seasonal agricultural vacancies.[60] Even more reassuring was the report received the following year, noting that 'the Managers of the Merseyside Exchanges agree that there is no evidence to support the suggestion that there is a scheme for enabling Irish labourers to obtain 30 unemployment stamps in order to qualify for Unemployment Benefit'. Now supervised by the Exchanges, the three-year residential clause for Corporation employment was being applied rigorously, while private contractors were also according preference to locals (including the long-established Liverpool-Irish community). Mr Potts, manager of the Leece Street Labour Exchange, reported favourably on his interview with the contractor in charge of construction of the Catholic cathedral:

> I doubt whether he is likely to give employment to newly arrived Irishmen, as I found him sympathetically inclined towards the large number of local unemployed Building Trade workers, more especially as he recognised that very many of them would be making contributions towards the cost of the Cathedral, and should perhaps receive some consideration on that ground.[61]

Amid the furore raised by Bishop David in 1937, civil servants urged careful amendment and limited circulation of the report of the recent interdepartmental

---

[59] M.E. Fletcher, *Report on an Investigation into the Colour Problem in Liverpool and Other Ports*, Liverpool, 1930, pp.11 and 19–23.

[60] LAB8/16, Irish Free State: enquiry on immigration to Great Britain.

[61] LAB2/1346/ET3318/1933, Employment and Training: Overseas: correspondence concerning the influx of Irish labour into Liverpool and Glasgow, 6 June 1933.

committee on Irish migration to prevent misunderstanding and misrepresentation. Its main findings were unequivocal: migrants from the Irish Free State
came for work not for higher levels of unemployment benefit; they undertook
heavy and arduous unskilled labour for which it was 'difficult to find an adequate
supply of equally satisfactory applicants already available in this country'.[62]
In line with this functional analysis, subsequent reports by the Ministry of
Labour highlighted the changing economic geography of migration. Given their
sensitivity to the labour market, the 'second wave' of Irish migrants hastened
through Liverpool to more promising and prosperous areas. Of the 25,469
migrants from Eire who entered insured employment in Britain between 1 April
1937 and 31 March 1938, a mere 13.7 per cent remained in the north west,
while 53 per cent settled in London and the south east, and 16.2 per cent in
the Midlands.[63] The point was underlined by Walshaw in his study of *Migration
to and from Merseyside*: 'differential economic development and a new localisation
of industry have caused many workers to trek southward for work'.[64]

The inter-war period witnessed episodic tension and disjuncture between
the established Liverpool-Irish community and new arrivals from the Free State.
The subsequent diminution in the migrant flow had more profound long-term
consequences. Denied replenishment from Ireland (other than the continued
recruitment into the 1950s of Irish-trained priests), Liverpool was to lose its
primacy among those settling in 'the nearest place that wasn't Ireland'. In itself,
this would not have mattered had the Liverpool-Irish been able to maintain their
self-sustaining, self-sufficient ethno-sectarian enclave. Here, the pace of cultural
and spatial change was already beginning to work against the retention of a
specific Liverpool-Irish identity, undermining the framework of associational
culture. At parish and school level, sport remained fiercely competitive, but
participation in amateur sport failed to keep pace with the spectatorship appeal
of professional sport, notably soccer, conducted in Liverpool (unlike Glasgow
and elsewhere) on non-sectarian lines. The interactive milieu of the music
hall and concert room gave way to the escapist delights of the cinema. Having
struggled to adjust to the legal requirements of the Irish Settlement in the inter-
war years, the network of ethnic and sectarian friendly societies, once the pride
of Irish Liverpool, were to lose their rationale and identity when incorporated
into the post-war welfare state. More serious still was the impact of major slum
clearance schemes. Between the wars, some 140,000 people – 15 per cent of

---

[62] LAB8/16, Report, Apr. 1937.
[63] LAB8/16, typed memo, 'Immigration from Eire'.
[64] Walshaw, *Migration*, p.7.

the total population of Liverpool – were re-housed, many on distant suburban estates without shops, schools, pubs or churches. Even in Holy Cross parish, where Father O'Shea and the other Irish Oblate priests deployed considerable skills in league with Catholic councillors to ensure some re-housing at Fontenoy Gardens within the parish boundary, the population dropped from 4878 in 1933 to 2497 in 1938. Out on the estates there was little improvement over time as the housing committee operated a ban on second-generation houses, forcing the children of the new suburbanites to vacate the neighbourhood on marriage. Without kinship groups or adequate facilities, the new estates lacked the character, culture and welfare networks of the old slums.[65]

As Frank Boyce has observed, this was the beginning of the transition, accelerated by war-time bombing and subsequently the major clearance of the late 1960s to build the second Mersey Tunnel, that was to transform the dockland parishes of the north end 'from Victorian "Little Ireland" to heritage trail'.[66] Heritage has come to serve the Liverpool-Irish well, securing their place in Liverpool's past. In the initial nostalgia boom after the First World War (when the term 'scouse' seems first to have been used), the Irish docker was the great iconic figure resonant of the city's glory days as world seaport, remembered and celebrated for hard graft and hard drinking by George Milligan, first president of the Society of Lovers of Old Liverpool. After the Second World War, the Liverpool-Irish claimed pride of place within a pan-ethnic mood of nostalgia in popular imaginings of 'the Liverpool That Was', a cosmopolitan heritage of Merseypride briefly embraced by Black Liverpool, until as Jacqueline Nassy Brown has noted, its history became as apart as its geography.[67] This spirit is perhaps best personified by Paddy Murphy, or, to give him his correct name, Mr Kanso Yoshida. A second cousin of the Japanese emperor Hirohito, he came to Liverpool before the First World War and became so attached to the place that he stayed, joined the merchant navy, served in both world wars, took British

---

65   McKenna, 'The suburbanization of the working-class', pp.173–89. Application of the 'Rorschach technique' to measure personality configuration among those still resident in one of the older slums in the 1950s pointed to role deprivation, impairment and uncertainty, factors which precluded associational culture, arrested maturation, and left the inhabitants (predominantly Irish) 'unfitted to play complex or more discriminating roles, even when they are offered to them', see Madeline Kerr, *The People of Ship Street*, London, 1958. For uncertainty about the continued viability and vitality of the parish in the modern environment, see Conor K. Ward, 'Some aspects of the social structure of a Roman Catholic parish', *Sociological Review*, new series, 6, 1958, pp.75–93.

66   Boyce, 'From Victorian "Little Ireland" to heritage trail', pp.289–90.

67   Brown, *Dropping Anchor, Setting Sail*, ch. 9.

nationality and – as a true Liverpudlian – was known to all (as his obituary in 1960 recorded) as Paddy Murphy.[68] In this ever more distant and irretrievable past before global trade declined, the empire disintegrated and the old slums were destroyed, the Liverpool-Irish 'slummy' was inscribed as the prototypical 'scouser'.

Where the earlier eponym 'Dicky Sam' related strictly to those born within the 'original parish' of Liverpool, the designation 'scouser', as the *Daily Post* explained in the course of extensive correspondence and investigation during the city's 750th anniversary celebrations in 1957, 'crept into general use in the Scotland Road area of Liverpool after the First World War'. While the origins of 'Dicky Sam' remain obscure and controversial, one interpretation suggesting that it denoted '"Imitation American", a sidelight on the city's pioneer links with the U.S.A.', the term 'scouse', coined along the main artery of Irish-Liverpool, attested unequivocally to Irish influence. Briefly interchangeable with the nomenclature 'wacker' or 'whacker' (probably derived from army slang), 'scouse' soon asserted its dominance (to the dismay of refined Liverpolitans) as the quintessential Liverpudlian badge and signifier. Derived from lobscouse, the sailors' 'traditional concoction of meat, vegetables and ship's biscuit', scouse was Irish stew by any other name, the main ingredient in the Liverpool 'melting-pot'.[69] A popular local dish in the north end, scouse was always eaten with red cabbage pickled in vinegar – the presence of meat depended on economic circumstance, being absent from 'Blind Scouse'. Trade was brisk late on Saturday nights at the 'scouseboat', a steaming cauldron of stew strategically located on the junction of Wellington Street and Scotland Road. 'Scouse Alley' ran underneath Paddy's Market in St Martin's Hall, offering scouse for a 1d a plate and wet nellies, another local speciality, at a halfpenny each.[70] Much more than a dish or an identity label, scouse gave voice to twentieth-century Liverpool, previously subsumed within standard south Lancashire speech. Here too there were other influences – Welsh and catarrh figure highly on the list – but Irish intonation was the dominant constituent of Liverpool's 'accent exceedingly rare'.

In the lucrative market for heritage publications, the unadulterated image of the lowly Irish 'slummy', reckless and feckless, has been adopted as the foundation character in popular history and working-class autobiography, a

---

[68] Fritz Spiegl, *Scouse International: The Liverpool Dialect in Five Languages*, Liverpool, 2000, p.22.

[69] See the volume of newspaper cuttings on 'Dialect and Slang' in LVRO at Hq.427CUT.

[70] Cooke, *Scotland Road*, pp.36 and 52.

symbolic figure of inverse snobbery and pride in the evolution of the real Liverpudlian, the true Scottie Road scouser. As portrayed in wider popular culture, the scally scouser is the latest incarnation of the stage Irishman with an array of dubious tricks, ploys and survival techniques, a source of amusement amid economic adversity.[71] This book suggests other ways in which the Liverpool Irish deserve their place in history.

---

[71]   John Belchem, '"An accent exceedingly rare": Scouse and the inflexion of class', in Belchem, *Merseypride*, pp.55–59.

Bibliography

1. Manuscript Sources

i. National Archives, Kew

Board of Trade Papers
BT31/1990/8533, League Hall and Recreation Company Ltd, 1874.
BT31/2701/14551, Liverpool Catholic Social Club, 1880.
BT31/3248/19063, Liverpool Irish National Club Company Ltd, 1883.
BT31/3480/21120, Liverpool National Club Company Ltd 1883.
BT31/3529/21523, Newman Club Ltd.
BT31/3546/21656, Liverpool Publishing and Printing Company Ltd 1885.
BT31/7997/57483, Liverpool Irish National Club Ltd 1898.

Cabinet Office
CAB24, War Cabinet and Cabinet: Memoranda (includes RRO).
CAB41/33/26, Situation in Liverpool; Dock Strike; Threatened Rail Strike; Irish
    Government Bill, 1911.

Colonial Office
CO 318/352, West Indies, 1919.
CO 904/7–9, Dublin Castle: Ribbonism, vols 1–3, 1798–1867.
CO 904/15, Dublin Castle: Register of Foreign Associations 1890–93.
CO 904/16, Dublin Castle: Register of Home Associations 1890–93.
CO 904/17–18, Dublin Castle: Register of Suspects, I and II.
CO 904/117–20, Dublin Castle: Précis of information received by the Special Branch,
    1905–1917.

Foreign Office Papers
FO 5/483, To Mr Crampton, Chargé d'Affaires, Washington, Jan.–Dec. 1848.
FO 5/484–87, From Mr Crampton, Jan.–Dec. 1848.
FO 5/488, Consuls at Portland, Boston, New York, Jan.–Dec. 1848.
FO 5/502, 1849.
FO 5/516, 1850.

FO 5/533, 1851.
FO 5/549, 1852.
FO 5/568, 1853.

Ministry of Health
MH57/281, Roman Catholic certified schools: correspondence with Liverpool Catholic
   Children's Protection Society 1938–42.

Home Office Papers
HO41/20–23, Disturbances Entry Books, 1848–71.
HO45/184, Ribbonism, 1841.
HO45/674, Prohibition of processions, 1844.
HO45/1080B, Ireland: Potato disease, distress, disturbances and relief, 1845–48.
HO45/1734, Pauper emigrant problem in Liverpool.
HO45/1816, Destitute Irish arriving in Liverpool.
HO45/2369, Irish Disaffection in 1848.
HO45/2410B, Disturbances. Threat of revolution, 1848: Liverpool and Lancashire
   (previously classified as HO45/2410A and recently reclassified as HO45/2410 Part
   2).
HO45/2642, Disturbances. Tour of Lancashire and opening of Gladstone Docks,
   Liverpool by King George V and Queen Mary: anticipated dockers strike; reports on
   labour position in Liverpool.
HO45/2674, Suggested depot for emigrants; Immigration of Irish paupers into England.
HO45/2391, Irish Republican Union in New York.
HO45/6877, Reports of British Consul in New York (1859).
HO45/7268, Liverpool licensing system: complaint of free trade in licenses causing
   increased drunkenness, 1862–67.
HO45/7326, Liverpool Police employed during Birkenhead riots 1862.
HO45/7799, Fenianism.
HO45/9339/21762, Liverpool Precautionary stationing of troops to prevent sectarian
   violence 1868–81.
HO45/9472/A19903, Disturbances. Prohibition of Orange Processions in Liverpool and
   Scotland 1867–73.
HO45/9572/78351C, Catholic Chaplaincy at Liverpool Prison, 1878–89.
HO45/9604/A1370, Explosives. Protection of Mersey Powder Hulks during
   contemplated disturbances in Liverpool 1881–83.
HO45/9604/A1370B, Police: County and Borough: Arrangements for further protection
   of Liverpool Customs House to meet contemplated disturbances 1881.
HO45/10172/B27657, Children: Liverpool City: Street Trading by Children; Byelaws
   1899–1905.
HO45/10654–10658/212470, Strikes. Liverpool Railway Strike, 1911.
HO45/11017/377969, Aliens. Repatriation of Coloured Seamen, etc. 1919–20.
HO45/11032/423878, Disturbances. Liverpool unemployment riots. Police censured.
HO45/11138, Religious disturbances in Liverpool 1909.
HO45/11843, Aliens. Chinese Immigration etc. 1906–25.

HO45/14634, Ireland: Immigration into the UK from the Irish Free State, 1926–28.

HO45/14635, Ireland: Immigration into the UK from the Irish Free State, 1929–32.

HO45/24879, Entertainments. Maintenance of ban on play about Irish troubles because of potential disorder in Liverpool, 1927–29.

HO45/25404, Aliens: Colour problems and white slave traffic in Liverpool and other ports; police reports; correspondence with the Association for the Welfare of Half-Caste Children.

HO100/257, Ireland: Correspondence, Miscellaneous 1837–51.

HO100/263, Ireland: Correspondence, Miscellaneous 1840.

HO144/35/81408, Disturbances. Assistance of Naval and Military Forces to aid civil power during dock strike at Liverpool, 1879.

HO144/81/A5836, Fenians. Explosion near the Town Hall, Liverpool, 1881–82.

HO144/235/A51366, Strikes: Liverpool Dock Strike. Military aid to civil power 1890.

HO144/659/V36777, Disturbances. Kensite disturbances in Liverpool – imprisonment of John Kensit, Jnr., place of trial of John McKeever for murder of John Kensit, senior.

HO144/704/107039, Disturbances. Anti-Catholic disturbances at Liverpool. Imprisonment of Pastor George Wise 1903–1909.

HO144/1044/184061, Disturbances: Sectarian Disturbances in Liverpool 1909–11.

HO144/1050/186261, Police: Liverpool Police inquiry following disturbances 1909–1910.

HO144/3746, Ireland: Irish Republicans in Great Britain illegal deportation and internment in Irish Free State 1923–24.

HO144/21037, Disturbances: Police arrangements to prevent disorder at public meetings in Liverpool 1931–38.

HO144/22281, Activities of Sinn Fein supporter, Dr Mannix, Roman Catholic Archbishop of Melbourne, 1920–21.

HO144/22498, Dangerous drugs and poisons: reports by Liverpool police on Chinese engaged in drug trafficking, 1923.

HO317/37, Irish political societies 1876–1914.

HO317/48, Sinn Fein: activities in the UK, 1920.

HO317/319, Informers' Statements 1896–1914.

Ministry of Labour

LAB2/1346/ET3318/1933, Employment and Training: Overseas: correspondence concerning the influx of Irish labour into Liverpool and Glasgow.

LAB8/16, Irish Free State: enquiry on immigration to Great Britain.

LAB8/105, Irish Immigrations, 1936–39.

Domestic Records of the PRO

PRO30/69/220, Special Branch Reports 1924.

PRO30/69/358, Ireland: Immigration to UK, 1929–35.

Ministry of Transport

MT23/329, Labour trouble at Liverpool, 1914.

Treasury Papers

T1/12465, Colonial Office. Payment of compensation to black British subjects for losses and injuries suffered in race riots in Liverpool.

T161/138, Law costs: repayment to Corporations of Liverpool and Manchester of costs incurred in prosecution over the Sinn Fein outrages 27.11.20.

Treasury Solicitor's Papers

TS25/1290, Roman Catholic Clergy: appointment of clergy in Liverpool gaol without consent of the Town Council, 1862.

ii. Liverpool Record Office

352MIN/SPE1/2, Liverpool Corporation: Special and Sub-Committee Minute Books: Apprehended Riots: Proceedings of Magistrates, March 1848.

352MIN/WAT1, Minutes of the Watch Committee, 81 vols, 1836–1967.

352POL1, Orders of the Watch Committee to the Head Constable, 37 vols, 1836–1915.

352POL2, Reports of the Head Constable to the Watch Committee, 19 vols, 1857–1905.

361CAT1/1, Liverpool Catholic Benefit Society Minute Book, 1850–58.

361CAT2/1, Liverpool Catholic Benefit Society: Annual reports, notices and memoranda, 1810–1914.

361VIN, Society of St Vincent de Paul: Conference of St Mary's, Highfield Street, 1868–77.

364CAT, Records of the Liverpool Catholic Reformatory Association, 39 vols, 1854–1946.

Town Clerks Papers: uncatalogued.

iii. University of Liverpool, Special Collections

D715, Records of Liverpool Sheltering Home for Orphan and Destitute Children.

Rathbone Papers

RPIX 1.167, English caricatures of the Irish.

RPIX 9.21, Scrapbook of newspaper cuttings 1868–80.

RPIX 9.22, Scrapbook of newspaper cuttings 1880–92.

iv. Lancashire Record Office

RCLv, Archdiocese of Liverpool papers, Boxes 28, 40, 56 and 71.

v. Bodleian Library, Oxford

Clarendon Papers, Boxes 12, 16 and 53.

vi. Public Record Office of Northern Ireland

CR5/3, Reformed Presbyterian Church Records: Shaw Street, Liverpool.

D354, Mussenden papers.

D1140, Business letters mainly to William Weir, merchant, Stewartstown, Co. Tyrone from Dublin, Liverpool and Pennsylvania, 1770–1829.

D2166, Papers of R.R. Cherry.

D2723, Correspondence and papers of Samuel Smiley, a sea captain, mainly of Liverpool (1852–4).

D2765, Papers of the Hume Family, Derry, Liverpool and Australia.

D3227, Letters from Patrick O'Doherty to his family at Rock House, Derry Co. Londonderry recording his voyage to America via Liverpool and his initial settlement in New Orleans (1840).

T3539, Emigrant letters relating to the McGinty family, Newtonhamilton, Co. Down and New York, 1847–85.

T1639/6, William Kerr to his father and mother.1855.

vii. Ulster-American Folk Park, Omagh
Irish Emigration Database.

viii. National Library of Ireland, Dublin
MS 812, Briefs for the Counsel in the trial of T.B. McManus.

MS 3679–714, Justin McCarthy Papers: diaries.

MS 5886, Narrative of the Rising of 1848 by R O'Gorman, T B McManus and J Kavanagh.

MS 7675–698, Larcom Papers.

MS 8479, Father Hickey Papers. Letters to Rev. William Hickey, while a curate at St Michael's, West Derby Road, Liverpool.

MS 10,511–16, letters to John M. Kelly, Dublin, 1846–48 from John Brady, Liverpool and Thomas Reilly, Saratoga.

MS 10,972, A file of letters and other papers relating to Pádraig Ciosóg (Patrick Cusack) Hon Treasurer of a Liverpool Gaelic League Branch and member of various Irish nationalist organisations in Liverpool, 1915–22.

MS 13,432, J.F.X. O'Brien Papers: letter from T.P. O'Connor.

MS 13,458, J.F.X. O'Brien Papers: correspondence, T.P. O'Connor.

MS 15,516, Notice of appointment of Patrick O'Brien of Liverpool as Parnell's election agent there and four letters from Parnell to same, 1884–90.

MS 18,431, Copies of two letters from Brown, Shipley and Company, Liverpool to John Shipley in the United States, July 1848.

MS 21,257, Frank Gallagher Papers, typescript account by Nellie Gifford Donnelly of the assistance given to Irishmen after the Easter Rising by Peter Murphy of Liverpool (c. 1940?).

MS 21,557, Photocopies of letters by, and to, members of the family of Cronhelm, and associated families of Crosbie, etc, of Dublin and Liverpool, mainly re family maters but with reference to commercial activity, religious matters, social life, 22 items, 1811–1902.

MS 27,991, Notebook in hand of T.P. O'Connor.

MS 32,483, Letter-book of Richard Henry Sheil, 1850–56.

ix. National Archives, Dublin

Frazer MS 43, Transcript of the books written in short hand found on the person of
  Richard Jones on the 1st October 1839.
23994C, Outrage Papers, Co. Cavan, 1839.
Fenian Papers: F series.
Fenian Papers: R series.
Habeas Corpus Suspension Act: Index.
3/714 Irish National League Box 6.
3/715/1 Police Reports 1882–1921, Box 2.
3/716 Crime Department Special Branch, 1894–1905, Boxes 1–3.
Dept of Finance, FIN1/1589: Claim for compensation in respect of damage to property
  in England by Irish forces during the war.
Dept of Finance, FIN1/1673: Compensation: case of Thomas Maher, ex IRA wounded
  in Liverpool.
Dept of Foreign Affairs, 353/7: Accommodation and furniture of offices abroad:
  Liverpool 1925–42.

x. Trinity College Dublin

MS 6740–44, Dillon Papers: T.P. O'Connor Correspondence 1881–1927.
MS N4/6, Sirr Diaries.

xi. University College Dublin

Richard Mulcahy Papers, P7A/1–7, 24 and 29.
Ernie O'Malley Papers, P17b/110 and 136.
Irish Folklore Commission. Questionnaire: Emigration.

xii. Royal Irish Academy, Dublin

23H41: Correspondence Book of the Irish Confederation, May 1847 – March 1848.
23H44: Minutes of the Council of the Irish Confederation, 19 Jan. 1847 – 6 July 1848.

xiii. All Hallows College, Dublin

Correspondence with the Diocese of Liverpool, 1853–68.

xiv. Dublin Diocesan Archives

Cardinal Cullen Papers.
Archbishop Hamilton Papers.

xv. Diocese of Clogher, Monaghan

Clark Compendium.

2. Newspapers and periodical publications

An-t-Oglach.
Belfast News-Letter.

Bulwark.

Catholic Fireside.

Catholic Institute Magazine.

Catholic Times.

Courier.

Daily Post.

Economist.

Eire.

Emerald.

Foot-Lights.

Homeless: Organ of Father Berry's Homes for Friendless Children.

Irish Exile.

Irishman.

Irish People.

Irish Programme continued as Nationalist and Irish Programme.

Irish Tribune.

Irish Volunteer.

Jones.

Lancashire Free Press and Catholic News.

Liberal Review of Politics, Society, Literature and Art continued as Liverpool Review of Politics.

Liverpolitan.

Liverpool Catholic Herald.

Liverpool Critic.

Liverpool Diocesan Review.

Liverpool Echo.

Liverpool Forward.

Liverpool Irish Herald.

Liverpool Lion.

Liverpool Jewish Magazine.

Liverpool Leader in Politics, Literature, Science and Art.

Liverpool Link.

Liverpool Lion.

Liverpool Mercury.

Liverpool Review.

Liverpool Weekly Post.

Liverpool Weekly Mercury.

Lyceum.

Morning Chronicle.

Nation.

Nationalist.

Northern Press.

Porcupine.

Times.

Transport Worker.

United Ireland.
United Irishman and Galway American.
United Irishman.
Xaverian.

i. Newspaper cuttings, Liverpool Record Office
352CLE/CUT1, Liverpool Corporation: Town Clerk's Newscuttings: Extracts from local and other newspapers, 109 vols, 1867–1967.
352CLE/CUT2, Council Proceedings from newspapers, 15 vols, 1858–1966.

3. Parliamentary papers
PP 1834 (44) XXVIII, First Report from the Commissioners on the Poor Laws.
PP 1835 (476) XVI, Third Report of the Select Committee on Orange Lodges.
PP 1836 (40) XXXIV, Royal Commission on the Condition of the Poorer Classes in Ireland, Appendix G: The State of the Irish Poor in Great Britain.
PP 1839 (486) XII, Report from the Select Committee of the House of Lords appointed to enquire into the state of Ireland in respect of crime.
PP 1866 (373) XVI, Report of the Select Committee on Theatrical Licenses and Regulations.
PP 1867–68 (4072) XXXVII, Report of the Cholera Epidemic of 1866 in England.
PP 1870 (116) LXI, Report from the Committee on the Transit of Animals by Sea and Land.
PP 1870 (259) VIII, Select Committee on Prisons and Prison Ministers Acts.
PP 1872 (514–1) XXVI, RCFBS, 2nd Report.
PP 1873 (842) XXII, RCFBS, 3rd Report.
PP 1874 (916) XXIII, RCFBS, 4th Report.
PP 1877 (418) XI, Third Report from the Select Committee of the House of Lords on Intemperance.
PP 1878–79 (282) XII, Report on the Select Committee on Poor Removal.
PP 1882 (344) XIII, Report from the Select Committee of the House of Lords on the law relating to the protection of young girls.
PP 1888 (389) XII, Report from the Select Committee on Friendly Societies.

4. Unpublished theses
Bailey, Craig, 'The Irish network: A study of ethnic patronage in London, 1760–1840', unpublished PhD thesis, University of London, 2004.
Bryson, Anne, 'Riot and its control in Liverpool, 1815–1860', unpublished MPhil thesis, Open University, 1989.
Farley, I.D., 'J.C. Ryle – Episcopal evangelist. A study in late-Victorian evangelicalism', unpublished PhD thesis, University of Durham, 1988.
Feehan, L., 'Charitable effort, statutory authorities and the poor in Liverpool c. 1850–1914', unpublished PhD thesis, University of Liverpool, 1987.

Grant, Linda, 'Women workers and the sexual division of labour: Liverpool 1890–1939', unpublished PhD thesis, University of Liverpool, 1987.

Jones, Simon, 'Fenianism in the Liverpool Irish Rifle Volunteers', unpublished MA thesis, University of Liverpool, 1997.

Kanya-Forstner, Martha, 'The politics of survival: Irish women in outcast Liverpool 1850–1890', unpublished PhD thesis, University of Liverpool, 1997.

Klapas, J.A., 'Geographical aspects of religious change in Victorian Liverpool, 1837–1901', unpublished MA thesis, University of Liverpool, 1977.

Letford, Lynda, 'Irish and non-Irish women living in their households in nineteenth-century Liverpool: Issues of class, gender and birthplace', unpublished PhD thesis, University of Lancaster, 1996.

McConville, C., 'Emigrant Irish and suburban Catholics: Faith and nation in Melbourne and Sydney', unpublished PhD thesis, University of Melbourne, 1984.

MacGregor, J.A., 'In search of ethnicity: Jewish and Celtic identities in Liverpool and Glasgow 1850–1900', unpublished M.Phil thesis, University of Liverpool, 2003.

O'Connell, B., 'The Irish Nationalist Party in Liverpool, 1873–1922', unpublished MA thesis, University of Liverpool, 1971.

Papworth, J.D., 'The Irish in Liverpool 1835–71: segregation and dispersal', unpublished PhD thesis, University of Liverpool, 1982.

Pooley, Colin G., 'Migration, mobility and residential areas in nineteenth-century Liverpool', unpublished PhD thesis, University of Liverpool, 1978.

Scott, C.L., 'A comparative re-examination of Anglo-Irish relations in nineteenth-century Manchester, Liverpool and Newcastle-upon-Tyne', unpublished PhD thesis, University of Durham, 1998.

Taylor, Iain, 'Black spot on the Mersey: A study of environment and society in eighteenth- and nineteenth-century Liverpool', unpublished PhD thesis, University of Liverpool, 1976.

Vickers, Matthew, 'Civic image and civic patriotism in Liverpool 1880–1914', unpublished DPhil thesis, University of Oxford, 2000.

Watkinson, C.D, 'The Liberal Party on Merseyside in the nineteenth century', unpublished PhD thesis, University of Liverpool, 1967.

5. Contemporary books, pamphlets etc

Adshead, S.D., and P. Abercrombie, eds, *Liverpool Town Planning and Housing Exhibition and Conference, 1914*, Liverpool, 1914.

'Among the Liverpool Irish. By a Missionary Priest', *Lyceum* Feb. 1894, pp.105–108.

Anon., *The Liverpool Irishman, or Annals of the Irish Colony in Liverpool*, n.p., 1909.

Appeal to the Public. Description of the Liverpool Permanent Night Asylum for the Houseless Poor, Liverpool, n.d. [1830?].

Baines, Thomas, *The Agricultural resources of Great Britain, Ireland, and the Colonies, considered in connection with the rise in the price of corn, and the alarming condition of the Irish People*, Liverpool, 1847.

——, *The History of the Commerce and Town of Liverpool, and of the Rise of the Manufacturing Industry in the Adjoining Counties*, London, 1852.

Behan, Brendan, *Borstal Boy*, London, 1958, 1990 edn.

Bell Cox, Rev. James, *Wage-Earning Children: A Paper read at the Southwell Diocesan Conference ... 1899*, Liverpool, 1900.

Board of Trade: An Industrial Survey of Merseyside, London, 1932.

Brabrook, Sir Edward William, *Provident Societies and Industrial Welfare*, London, 1898.

Brady, Edward, *Ireland's Secret Service in England*, Dublin, n.d.

Broadbent, R.J., *Annals of the Liverpool Stage*, Liverpool, 1908.

Buddicom, R.P., *A Sermon Preached at St George's Church, Everton, on Sunday 26th May, 1822, in aid of the fund now raising in Liverpool for the relief of the distressed peasantry of Ireland*, Liverpool, 1822.

Burke, Thomas, *Catholic History of Liverpool*, Liverpool, 1910.

——, 'The street-trading children of Liverpool', *Contemporary Review*, 78, 1900, pp.720–26.

Cahill, Rev. D.W., *Important Letter from the Rev. D.W. Cahill, D.D., to the Right Worshipful the Mayor, and to the Magistrates of Liverpool. On the disastrous recollections of party strife in England and Ireland on the 12th of July!!!*, Dublin, 1852.

——, *Letter to his Fellow Countrymen in Liverpool and Birkenhead*, Dublin, 1852.

Catholic Family Annual and Almanac for the Diocese of Liverpool, 1884, 1888, 1891–92, continued as *Catholic Family Annual and Almanac for the Dioceses of Liverpool and Shrewsbury*, 1903, 1905–1907, 1910 and 1912 (held in LVRO).

Cropper, James, *Present State of Ireland: With a Plan for Improving the Condition of the People*, Liverpool, 1825.

D'Aeth, Frederic G., 'Liverpool', in Mrs Bernard Bosanquet, ed., *Social Conditions in Provincial Towns*, London, 1912, p.38.

Denvir, John, *The Brandons: A Story of Irish Life in England*, London, 1903.

——, *Denvir's Penny Illustrated Irish Library*, Liverpool, 1873 on, continued and re-issued as *Denvir's Monthly Irish Library*.

——, *Denvir's Penny National Irish Almanac for 1889*, Liverpool, n.d.

——, *The Irish in Britain*, London, 1892.

——, *The Life Story of an Old Rebel*, Dublin, 1910.

Derrick, Samuel, *Letters Written from Leverpoole, Chester, Corke, the Lake of Killarney, Dublin, Tunbridge Wells, Bath*, 2 vols, London, 1767.

Dickens, Charles, *The Uncommercial Traveller*, final edition, 1869.

Duffy, Charles Gavan, *My Life in Two Hemispheres*, 2 vols, London, 1898.

Farrie, Hugh, *Toiling Liverpool*, Liverpool, 1886.

Fay, B. Essington, *The Catholic Educational Year-Book, 1914*, Liverpool, 1914.

Finch, John, Jr, *Statistics of Vauxhall Ward, Liverpool*, Liverpool, 1842.

Fletcher, M.E., *Report on an Investigation into the Colour Problem in Liverpool and Other Ports*, Liverpool, 1930.

Forwood, A.B., *The Dwellings of the Industrious Classes in the Diocese of Liverpool and How to Improve Them*, Liverpool, 1883.
Full Report of the Commission of Inquiry into the Subject of the Unemployed in the City of Liverpool, Liverpool, 1894.

Gair, G.R., 'The Irish immigration question, 1–3', *Liverpool Review*, Jan.–Mar. 1934.
Gladstone Miscellaneous Pamphlets, large collection held at Athenaeum, Liverpool.
Grisewood, W., *The Poor of Liverpool and What is to be Done for Them*, Liverpool, 1899.

Harford, Austin, *The Housing Problem. Memorandum on the Housing of the Dispossessed in Liverpool*, Liverpool, 1916.
——, *Speech of Alderman Austin Harford J.P. on his re-election as Deputy-Chairman of the Housing Committee, November 23rd 1917*, Liverpool, 1917.
Harrison, Amy, *Women's Industries in Liverpool: An Enquiry into the Economic Effects of Legislation Regulating the Labour of Women*, London, 1904.
Heinrick, H., *A Survey of the Irish in England, 1872*, ed. Alan O'Day, London, 1990.
History and Album of the Irish Race Convention, Dublin, 1897.
Home Government Association, *Report of the Inaugural Public Meeting of the Home Government Association*, Dublin, 1870.
How the Casual Labourer Lives. Report of the Liverpool Joint Research Committee on the Domestic Condition and Expenditure of the Families of Certain Liverpool Labourers, Liverpool, 1909.
Hume, Abraham, *Condition of Liverpool, Religious and Social*, Liverpool, 1858.

Irish Home Rule League, Dublin, 1875.
Irish Home Rule League. Council for the Year 1876, Dublin, 1876.
Irish National Foresters, *Annual Reports*, 1899–1902, 1907–10 and 1919–22, held in National Library of Ireland.

Jones, David Caradog, *Merseyside: The Relief of the Poor*, Liverpool, 1936.
——, *Social Survey of Merseyside*, 3 vols, Liverpool, 1934.
——, *A Study of Migration to Merseyside, with Special Reference to Irish Immigration*, Liverpool, 1931.
Jones, Rev. John, *The Slain in Liverpool during 1872 by Drink*, Liverpool, 1873.
Jubilee Memorial of Canning Street Presbyterian Church, n.p., n.d.

Leslie, Frank John, *Wasted Lives: The Problem of Child Labour*, Liverpool, 1910.
'Liverpool: Its Moral and Spiritual Condition. By the "Sunday at Home" Special Commissioner', *Sunday at Home*, 1911, pp.813–19.
Liverpool Council of Voluntary Aid, *Report on the Uses of Leisure in Liverpool*, Liverpool, 1923.
Liverpool Dispensaries, *Report of the Committee of the Liverpool Dispensaries, for the Year 1825*, Liverpool, 1826.
Liverpool District Provident Society, *The First Annual Report of the Liverpool District*

Provident Society, for the Year 1830, with the Rules of the Society and a List of Subscribers, Liverpool, 1831.

——, *The Second Annual Report of the Liverpool District Provident Society, for the year 1831*, Liverpool, 1832.

Liverpool Domestic Mission Society, *Report Presented at the Fourteenth Annual General Meeting of the Liverpool Domestic Mission Society, by their Minister to the Poor*, Liverpool, 1851.

Liverpool Society for the Prevention of Cruelty to Children, *First Annual Report, 1884*, Liverpool, 1884

Local Reports on the Sanitary Condition of the Labouring Population of England, London, 1842.

Lowndes, F.W., *The Extension of the Contagious Diseases Acts to Liverpool and Other Seaports Practically Considered*, Liverpool, 1876.

——, *Prostitution and Venereal Diseases in Liverpool*, London, 1886.

Loyal Orange Institution of England: *A Handy Guide to the Various Lodges of the Province of Liverpool, Circuit no. 1*, n.p., 1885.

Lundie, R.H., *The Dark Side of Liverpool*, Liverpool, 1880.

McArdle, John F., *Catechism of Irish History*, Liverpool, 1873.

——, *A Patient in Search of a Doctor*, Liverpool, 1872.

McCarthy, Justin, *Story of an Irishman*, London, 1904.

McGrath, T.F., *History of the Ancient Order of Hibernians*, Cleveland, OH, 1898.

McNeile, Rev. Hugh, *The Famine a Rod of God; its provoking cause – its merciful design. A sermon preached in St Jude's Church, Liverpool on Sunday, February 28, 1847*, Liverpool, 1847.

Martineau, James, *Ireland and her famine: a discourse preached in Paradise Street Chapel, Liverpool ... January 31, 1847*, London, 1847.

Milligan, George, *Life through Labour's Eyes: Essays, Letters and Lyrics from the Worker's Own Point of View*, London and Edinburgh, 1911.

'The mortality of Liverpool and its national danger', *Quarterly Journal of Science*, 3, 1866, pp.311–23.

Mortality Sub-Committee. Report and Evidence, Liverpool, 1866.

O'Connor, T.P., 'The Irish in Great Britain', in F. Lavery, ed., *Irish Heroes in the War*, London, 1917, pp.13–34.

O'Labraidh, Alfons [A. Lowry], *A West Briton's Romance: A Comedy in One Act*, Dermott O'Shea Branch Gaelic League, Bootle, 1907.

O'Mara, P., *The Autobiography of a Liverpool Irish Slummy*, London, 1934.

Owles, J. Allden, *Recollections of Medical Missionary Work*, Glasgow, 1909.

Persecution of the Jews in Russia. Mansion House Relief Fund. Liverpool Commission, Liverpool, 1882.

Picton, J.A., *Sir James A. Picton: A Biography*, London, 1891.

The Picturesque Hand-book to Liverpool; a manual for the resident and visitor, being a new and greatly improved edition of the Stranger's Pocket Guide, Liverpool, 1842.

Police (Liverpool Inquiry) Act, 1909: Report.

Presbyterian Church in Ireland, *Minutes of the General Assembly of the Presbyterian Church in Ireland*, Belfast, 1850.

Presbyterian Historical Society of Ireland, *Minutes of the Annual Meeting of the Eastern Reformed Synod in Ireland at its Meeting in Belfast 1857.*

Priestley, J.B., *English Journey*, London, 1934.

(Proposed) Celtic Chair for Professor Kuno Meyer, Liverpool, 1903.

Rathbone, Eleanor, *Report of an Inquiry into the Condition of Dock Labour at the Liverpool Docks*, Liverpool, 1904.

——, *Report on the Condition of Widows under the Poor Law in Liverpool*, n.p., 1913.

Rathbone, Emily A., ed., *Records of the Rathbone Family*, Edinburgh, 1913.

Report of the Commission Appointed by the City Council to inquire into the Chinese Settlements in Liverpool, Liverpool, 1907.

Report of the Investigation of the Treatment of Roman Catholics in the Liverpool School for the Blind. Reprinted from the 'Liverpool Mail' of February 11, 1841, Liverpool, 1841.

A Report of the Trial of Edward Browne and others for administering and of Laurence Woods for Taking an Unlawful Oath, Dublin, 1822.

A Report of the Trial of Michael Keenan for Administering an Unlawful Oath, Dublin, 1822.

Report on Sunday Funerals by the Executive Committee of the Burial Board for the Parish of Liverpool, Liverpool, 1866.

Salter, Joseph, *The Asiatic in England; Sketches of Sixteen Years' Work among Orientals*, London, 1873.

Samuelson, James, *The Children of our Slums*, Liverpool, 1911.

Saunders, W.H., 'The Making of Liverpool', *Proceedings of the Liverpool Philomathic Society*, 63, 1918, pp.xxxi–xlvi.

Sexton, James, *Sir James Sexton: Agitator. The Life of the Dockers' MP: An Autobiography*, London, 1936.

Shimmin, H., *Liverpool Life: Its Pleasures, Practices and Pastimes*, Liverpool, 1857.

——, *Pen-and-Ink Sketches of Liverpool Town Councillors*, Liverpool, 1866.

Smith, Samuel, *Social Reform*, London, 1884.

Squalid Liverpool: By a Special Commission, Liverpool, 1883.

Substance of a lecture delivered by the Rev. Thos. Butler, D.D., on Sunday evening, April 25, in St Anthony's Church, Scotland Road, containing strictures on certain passages in anti-Catholic discourses preached in this town by the Rev. Hugh M'Neile, Liverpool, 1841.

Tenth year of one glorious and uninterrupted season at the St James's Hall, Lime Street, Liverpool. of Hague's Minstrels (the original slave troupe), Liverpool, 1880.

Treacy, John, *Mr John Treacy's Reply to Mr S.B. Harper*, Liverpool, 1863.

The True and Wonderful History of Dick Liver: shewing how from small beginnings he became a man of substance; and how he was robbed while he was asleep; and relating his ineffectual attempts to get into his own house and recover his property. By Timothy Touchstone, Historiographer, Liverpool, 1824.

United Assurance Society: volume of six pamphlets, 1832–1869 in the British Library.

United Irish League of Great Britain, *Annual Reports*, 1906–1909.

Walshaw, Robert Stanley, *Migration to and from Merseyside: Home, Irish, Overseas*, Liverpool, 1938.

Wasted Lives: The Problem of Child Labour; reprinted with additions from the Liverpool Courier, Liverpool, 1910.

Watch Committee: Report on the Police Establishment 1908, Liverpool, 1909.

Whittingham-Jones, Barbara, *Down with the Orange Caucus*, Liverpool, 1936.

——, *More about Liverpool Politics: Red Flag, Rome and Shamrock*, Liverpool, 1936.

——, *The Pedigree of Liverpool Politics: White, Orange and Green*, Liverpool, 1936.

Whitty, M.J., *A Proposal for Diminishing Crime, Misery and Poverty in Liverpool*, Liverpool, 1865.

Winskill, P.T., *History of the Temperance Movement in Liverpool and District*, Liverpool, 1887.

Wiseman, Cardinal, *The Highways of Peaceful Commerce have been the Highways of Art, an address delivered at Liverpool on Tuesday, August 30, 1853, on occasion of the opening of the Catholic Institute, by His Eminence Cardinal Wiseman*, n.p., 1853.

The Wonderful Monkey of Liverpool who turned barber to shave the Irish gentlemen coming over to reap, Newcastle, n.d.

6. Secondary sources

Akenson, D.H., *Small Differences: Irish Catholics and Irish Protestants 1815–1922*, Montreal and Kingston, 1988.

——, *The Irish Diaspora: A Primer*, Belfast, 1996.

Anbinder, Tyler, *Five Points: The Nineteenth-Century New York City Neighborhood that Invented Tap Dance, Stole Elections, and Became the World's Most Notorious Slum*, New York, 2001.

Appel, J.J., 'From shanties to lace curtains: The Irish image in *Puck*, 1876–1910', *Comparative Studies in Society and History*, 13, 1971, pp.365–75.

Arnesen, Eric, 'Comparing urban crises: Race, migration, and the transformation of the modern American city', *Social History*, 30, 2005, pp.499–507.

——, 'Whiteness and the historians' imagination', *International Labor and Working-Class History*, 60, 2001, pp.3–32.

Aspinwall, Bernard, *Arrival, Assertion and Acclimatisation, or Context and Contrasts: A Preliminary Checklist of Works on the Irish Catholic Experience in the North West of England*, Wigan, 1996.

——, 'The Catholic Irish and wealth in Glasgow', in T.M. Devine, ed., *Irish Immigrants and Scottish Society in the Nineteenth and Twentieth Centuries*, Edinburgh, 1991, pp.91–115.

——, 'The welfare state within the state: the Saint Vincent de Paul Society in Glasgow, 1848–1920', in W.J. Sheils and D. Wood, *Studies in Church History: Voluntary Religion*, Oxford, 1986, pp.445–59.

Ayers, Pat, 'Work, culture and gender: The making of masculinities in post-war Liverpool', *Labour History Review*, 69, 2004, pp.153–68.

Baily, S.L., *Immigrants in the Lands of Promise: Italians in Buenos Aires and New York City, 1870–1914*, Ithaca, NY, 1999.

Barrett, J.R., 'Americanization from the bottom up: Immigration and the remaking of the working class in the United States, 1880–1930', *Journal of American History*, 79, 1992, pp.996–1020.

Barron, R.D., and G.M. Norris, 'Sexual divisions and the dual labour market', in D.L. Barker and S. Allen, *Dependence and Exploitation in Work and Marriage*, New York, 1976.

Bayor, Ronald H., and Timothy J. Meagher, eds, *The New York Irish*, Baltimore, MD, 1997.

Bean, Ron, 'Police unrest, unionization and the 1919 strike in Liverpool', *Journal of Contemporary History*, 15, 1980, pp.633–53.

Belchem, John, '"An accent exceedingly rare": Scouse and the inflexion of class', in Belchem, ed., *Merseypride: Essays in Liverpool Exceptionalism*, Liverpool, 2000, 2nd edn, 2006, pp.55–59.

——, 'A city apart: Liverpool, Merseyside and the North West region', in D. Newton and N. Vall, eds, *An Agenda for Regional History*, forthcoming, 2007.

——, 'Ethnicity and labour history: With special reference to Irish migration', in Lex Heerma van Voss and Marcel van der Linden, eds, *Class and Other Identities: Gender, Religion and Ethnicity in the Writing of European Labour History*, New York and Oxford, 2002., pp.88–101.

——, '"Freedom and Friendship to Ireland": Ribbonism in early nineteenth-century Liverpool', *International Review of Social History*, 39, 1994, pp.33–56.

——, 'The Irish diaspora: The complexities of mass migration', *Przeglad Polonijny*, 31, 2005, pp.87–98.

——, 'Liverpool in the year of revolution: The political and associational culture of the Irish immigrant community in 1848', in Belchem, ed., *Popular Politics, Riot and Labour: Essays in Liverpool History 1790–1940*, Liverpool, 1992, pp.68–97.

——, 'Nationalism, republicanism and exile: Irish emigrants and the revolutions of 1848', *Past and Present*, 146, 1995, pp.103–35.

——, 'Priests, publicans and the Irish poor: Ethnic enterprise and migrant networks in mid-nineteenth century Liverpool', *Immigrants and Minorities*, 23, 2005, pp.207–31.

——, 'Republican spirit and military science: The "Irish Brigade" and Irish-American nationalism in 1848', *Irish Historical Studies*, 29, 1994, pp.44–65.

——, 'Whiteness and the Liverpool-Irish', *Journal of British Studies*, 44, 2005, pp.146–52.

——, ed., *Liverpool 800: Culture, Character and History*, Liverpool, 2006, pp.370–74.

——, ed., *Merseypride: Essays in Liverpool Exceptionalism*, Liverpool, 2000, 2nd edn, 2006.

——, ed., *Popular Politics, Riot and Labour: Essays in Liverpool History 1790–1940*, Liverpool, 1992.

Belchem, John, and Donald M. MacRaild, 'Cosmopolitan Liverpool', in John Belchem, ed., *Liverpool 800: Culture, Character and History*, Liverpool, 2006, pp.311–92.

Belchem, John, and Klaus Tenfelde, eds, *Irish and Polish Migration in Comparative Perspective*, Essen, 2003.

Bennett, Canon, *Father Nugent of Liverpool*, Liverpool, 1949.

——, 'The story of Father Berry's homes', *Cathedral Record*, 19, 1949, pp.149–52.

Bielenberg, Andy, ed., *The Irish Diaspora*, Harlow, 2000.

Bisceglia, Louis R., 'The threat of violence: Irish Confederates and Chartists in Liverpool in 1848', *Irish Sword*, 14, 1981, pp.207–15.

Bohstedt, John, 'More than one working class: Protestant and Catholic riots in Edwardian Liverpool', John Belchem, ed., *Popular Politics, Riot and Labour: Essays in Liverpool History 1790–1940*, Liverpool, 1992, pp.173–216.

Boyce, D. George, *Nationalism in Ireland*, 2nd edn, London, 1991.

——, and Alan O'Day, *The Making of Modern Irish History: Revisionism and the Revisionist Controversy*, London, 1996.

Boyce, Frank, 'From Victorian "Little Ireland" to heritage trail: Catholicism, community and change in Liverpool's docklands', in R. Swift and S. Gilley, eds, *The Irish in Victorian Britain: The Local Dimension*, Dublin, 1999, pp.277–97.

——, 'Irish Catholicism in Liverpool: The 1920s and 1930s', in John Belchem and Patrick Buckland, eds, *The Irish in British Labour History*, Liverpool, 1993, pp.86–101.

Bradley, Joseph, 'Wearing the green: A history of nationalist demonstrations among the diaspora in Scotland', in T.G. Fraser, *The Irish Parading Tradition*, Basingstoke, 2000, pp.111–28.

Brady, L.W., *T.P. O'Connor and the Liverpool Irish*, London, 1983.

Broehl, Wayne G., Jr, *The Molly Maguires*, Cambridge, MA, 1964.

Brogden, M., *On the Mersey Beat: Policing Liverpool between the Wars*, Oxford, 1991.

——, *The Police: Autonomy and Consent*, London, 1982.

Brown, Jacqueline Nassy, *Dropping Anchor, Setting Sail: Geographies of Race in Black Liverpool*, Princeton, NJ, and Oxford, 2005.

Brown, T.N., *Irish-American Nationalism*, Philadelphia and New York, 1966.

Brubaker, Rogers, 'The "diaspora" diaspora', *Ethnic and Racial Studies*, xxviii, 1, 2005, pp.1–19.

Brundage, David, '"Green over Black": Ireland and Irish-Americans in the new histories of American working-class "whiteness"', paper presented to the conference on Racializing Class, Classifying Race, Oxford, 11–13 July 1997.

Burton, Valerie, 'Liverpool's mid-nineteenth century coasting trade', in Valerie Burton, ed., *Liverpool Shipping, Trade and Industry*, Liverpool, 1989, pp.26–66.

Busteed, M.A., 'Little Islands of Erin: Irish settlement and identity in mid-nineteenth-century Manchester', in Donald M. MacRaild, ed., *Great Famine and Beyond*, Dublin, 2000, pp.94–127.

——, 'A Liverpool shipping agent and Irish emigration in the 1850s: Some newly discovered documents', *THSLC*, 129, 1980, pp.145–61.

Champ, Judith F., 'The demographic impact of Irish immigration on Birmingham Catholicism 1800–50', in W.J. Sheils and D. Wood, eds, *Studies in Church History 25: The Church, Ireland and the Irish*, Oxford, 1989, pp.233–42.

Christian, Mark, 'Black struggle for historical recognition in Liverpool', *North West Labour History*, 20, 1995–96, pp.58–66.

Coffey Thomas, *Agony at Easter: The 1916 Irish Uprising*, London, 1970.

Collins, Neil, *Politics and Elections in Nineteenth-Century Liverpool*, Aldershot, 1994.

Comerford, R.V., *The Fenians in Context: Irish Politics and Society 1848–82*, Dublin, 1998.

——, 'Patriotism as pastime: The appeal of Fenianism in the mid 1860s', *Irish Historical Studies*, 22, 1981, pp.239–50.

Connolly, G.P., 'The Catholic Church and the first Manchester and Salford trade unions in the age of the industrial revolution', *Transactions of the Lancashire and Cheshire Antiquarian Society*, 135, 1985, pp.132–33.

——, 'Irish and Catholic: Myth or reality? Another sort of Irish and the renewal of the clerical profession among Catholics in England, 1791–1818', in R. Swift and S. Gilley, eds, *The Irish in the Victorian City*, London, 1985, pp.225–54.

——, 'Little brother at peace: The priest as holy man in the nineteenth-century ghetto', in W.J Sheils, ed., *Studies in Church History* 19: *The Church and Healing*, Oxford, 1982, pp.191–206.

Conzen, K.N., D.A. Gerber, E. Morawska, G.E. Pozzetta and R.J. Vecoli, 'The invention of ethnicity: A perspective from the USA', *Journal of American Ethnic History*, 12, 1992, pp.3–41.

Cooke, Terry, *Scotland Road: 'The Old Neighbourhood'*, Birkenhead, 1987.

Corcoran, Mary P., 'Emigrants, *Eirepreneurs* and opportunists: A social profile of recent Irish immigration in New York City', in Ronald H. Bayor and Timothy J. Meagher, eds, *The New York Irish*, Baltimore, MD, and London, 1997, pp.461–80.

Costello, Ray, *Black Liverpool: The Early History of Britain's Oldest Black Community 1730–1918*, Liverpool, 2001.

Cronin, M., and D. Adair, *The Wearing of the Green: A History of St Patrick's Day*, London, 2002.

Curtis, L. Perry, Jr, *Apes and Angels: The Irishman in Victorian Caricature*, Washington, DC, 1997.

Davies, John, 'Irish narratives: Liverpool in the 1930s', *THSLC*, 154, 2005, pp.31–62.

——, 'Parish charity: The work of the Society of St Vincent de Paul, St Mary's, Highfield Street, Liverpool, 1867–68', *North West Catholic History*, 17, 1990, pp.37–46.

——, '"Rome on the Rates": Archbishop Downey and the Catholic schools question, 1929–1939', *North West Catholic History*, 18, 1991, pp.16–32.

——, 'Sensible economy? Sectarian bigotry? The Liverpool Catholic schools question, 1938–1939', *THSLC*, 155, 2006, pp.85–120.

Davies, Sam, *Liverpool Labour: Social and Political Influences on the Development of the Labour Party in Liverpool, 1900–1939*, Keele, 1996.

——, '"A stormy political career": P.J. Kelly and Irish Nationalist and Labour politics in Liverpool, 1891–1936', *THSLC*, 148, 1999.

Davies, S., P. Gill, L. Grant, M. Nightingale, R. Noon and A. Shallice, *Genuinely Seeking Work: Mass Unemployment on Merseyside in the 1930s*, Birkenhead, 1992.

Davis, Graham, *The Irish in Britain 1815–1914*, Dublin, 1991.

Delaney, Enda, *Demography, State and Society: Irish Migration to Britain, 1921–1971*, Liverpool, 2000.

de Nie, Michael, *The Eternal Paddy: Irish Identity and the British Press, 1798–1882*, Madison, WI, and London, 2004.

Dennis, Richard, *English Industrial Cities of the Nineteenth Century*, Cambridge, 1984.

Diner, Hasia, *Erin's Daughters in America: Irish Immigrant Women in the Nineteenth Century*, Baltimore, MD, 1983.

——, *Hungering for America: Italian, Irish and Jewish Foodways in the Age of Migration*, London, 2001.

Donovan, K., 'Good old Pat: An Irish-American stereotype in decline', *Éire-Ireland*, 15, 1980, pp.6–14.

Douglas, R.M., 'Anglo-Saxons and Attacotti: The racialization of Irishness in Britain between the wars', *Ethnic and Racial Studies*, 25, 2002, pp.40–63.

Doyle, David N., 'The Irish and American labour 1880–1920', *Soathar*, 1, 1975, pp.42–53.

——, 'The Irish in North America, 1776–1845', in W.E. Vaughan, ed., *A New History of Ireland*, vol. 5: *Ireland under the Union*, Oxford, 1989, pp.682–725.

Doyle, P., 'Bishop Goss of Liverpool (1856–1872) and the importance of being English', in S. Mews, ed., *Studies in Church History* 18: *Religion and National Identity*, Oxford, 1982, pp.433–47.

——, 'The Catholic Federation 1906–29', in .J. Sheils and D. Wood, *Studies in Church History: Voluntary Religion*, Oxford, 1986, pp.461–75.

——, *Mitres and Missions in Lancashire: The Roman Catholic Diocese of Liverpool, 1850–2000*, Liverpool, 2005.

Drudy, P.J., ed., *The Irish in America: Emigration, Assimilation and Impact*, Cambridge, 1985.

Du Noyer, Paul, *Liverpool: Wondrous Place. Music from the Cavern to the Coral*, London, 2002.

Durey, Michael, 'The survival of an Irish culture in Britain, 1800–45', *Historical Studies*, 20, 1982, pp.14–35.

Dye, Ryan, 'Catholic protectionism or Irish nationalism? Religion and politics in Liverpool, 1829–1845', *Journal of British Studies*, 40, 2001, pp.357–90.

——, 'The Irish flood: Famine, philanthropy and the emergence of duelling Catholic identities, 1845–1865', *THSLC*, 150, 2001, pp.97–120.

Eagleton, Terry, *Heathcliff and the Great Hunger*, London, 1995.

Earner-Byrne, Lindsey, 'The boat to England: An analysis of the official reactions to the emigration of single expectant Irishwomen to Britain, 1922–1972', *Irish Economic and Social History*, 30, 2005, pp.52–70.

Emmons, D.M., *The Butte Irish: Class and Ethnicity in an American Mining Town, 1875–1925*, Urbana, IL, 1989.

Engman, M., F.W. Carter, A.C. Hepburn and C.G. Pooley, eds, *Ethnic Identity in Urban Europe*, Aldershot, 1992.

Erie, S., *Rainbow's End. Irish Americans and the Dilemma of Urban Political Machines, 1840 to 1985*, Berkeley, CA, 1988.

Evans, Neil, 'Across the universe: Racial violence and the post-war crisis in imperial Britain, 1919–25', *Immigrants and Minorities*, 13, 1994, pp.59–88.

Fawkes, R., *Dion Boucicault: A Biography*, London, 1979.
Fielding, Steven, *Class and Ethnicity: Irish Catholics in England, 1880–1939*, Buckingham, 1993.
Fitzpatrick, David, 'Exporting brotherhood: Orangeism in South Australia', *Immigrants and Minorities*, 23, 2005, pp.277–310.
——, 'How Irish was the diaspora from Ireland?', *British Association for Irish Studies*, 25, 2001, pp.5–9.
——, 'The Irish in Britain, 1871–1921', in W.E. Vaughan, *New History of Ireland*, vol. 6: *Ireland under the Union II, 1870–1921*, Oxford, 2003, pp.653–702.
——, *Oceans of Consolation: Personal Accounts of Irish Migration to Australia*, Cork, 1994.
——, '"A peculiar tramping people": The Irish in Britain, 1801–70', in W.E. Vaughan, *New History of Ireland*, 5. *Ireland under the Union I, 1801–70*, Oxford, 1989, pp.623–60.
Foley, Conor, *Legion of the Rearguard: The I.R.A. and the Modern Irish State*, London, 1992.
Foner, Eric, 'Class, ethnicity and radicalism in the Gilded Age: Land League and Irish America', *Marxist Perspectives*, 1, 1978, pp.6–55.
Forde, Frank, 'The Liverpool Irish Volunteers', *Irish Sword*, 10, 1971–72, pp.106–23.
Forester, Margery, *Michael Collins – The Lost Leader*, London, 1971.
Foster, Roy, 'Marginal men and Micks on the make: The uses of Irish exile c. 1840–1922', in *Paddy and Mr. Punch*, London, 1995, pp.281–305.
——, *Modern Ireland 1600–1972*, London, 1988.
——, *W.B. Yeats: A Life*. 1: *The Apprentice Mage, 1865–1914*, Oxford, 1998.
Frost, Diane, *Work and Community among West African Migrant Workers since the Nineteenth Century*, Liverpool, 1999.
——, ed., 'Ethnic labour and British imperial trade: A history of ethnic seafarers in the UK', special issue, *Immigrants and Minorities*, 13, nos 2 and 3, 1994.
Funchion, Michael F., ed., *Irish-American Voluntary Organizations*, Westport, CT, 1983.

Gabaccia, Donna R, 'Do we still need immigration history?', *Polish American Studies*, 15, 1998, pp.45–68.
——, *From the Other Side: Women, Gender and Immigrant Life in the U.S. 1820–1990*, Bloomington, IN, 1994.
——, *We Are What We Eat: Ethnic Food and the Making of Americans*, London, 1998.
Gallagher, T., 'The Catholic Irish in Scotland: In search of identity', in T.M. Devine, ed., *Irish Immigrants and Scottish Society in the Nineteenth and Twentieth Centuries*, Edinburgh, 1991, pp.19–43.
Gallman, J. Matthew, *Receiving Erin's Children: Philadelphia, Liverpool and the Irish Famine Migration, 1845–1855*, Chapel Hill, NC, and London, 2000.
Gerber, D.A., 'The immigrant letter between positivism and populism: The uses of immigrant personal correspondence in twentieth-century American scholarship', *Journal of American Ethnic History*, 16, 1997, pp.3–34.

Gifford, Lord, Wally Brown and Ruth Bundey, *Loosen the Shackles. First Report of the Liverpool 8 Inquiry into Race Relations in Liverpool*, London, 1989.

Gilbert, Bentley B., *The Evolution of National Insurance*, London, 1966.

Gilley, Sheridan, 'The Roman Catholic Church and the nineteenth-century Irish diaspora', *Journal of Ecclesiastical History*, 35, 1984, pp.188–207.

Gilroy, Paul, *The Black Atlantic: Modernity and Double Consciousness*, London, 1993.

Ginsberg, L., 'Industrial Life Assurance', in W.A. Robson, ed., *Social Security*, London, 1948, pp.261–88.

Gosden, P.H.J.H., *Self-Help: Voluntary Associations in the Nineteenth Century*, London, 1973.

Gray, Peter, ed., *Victoria's Ireland? Irishness and Britishness, 1837–1901*, Dublin, 2004.

Green, Nancy L., 'The comparative method and poststructural structuralism: New perspectives for migration studies', in J. Lucassen and L. Lucassen, eds, *Migration, Migration History, History: Old Paradigms and New Perspectives*, Berne, 1997, pp.57–72.

——, 'Time and the study of assimilation', *Rethinking History*, 10, 2006, pp.239–58.

Gwynn, Denis, *Young Ireland and 1848*, Cork, 1949.

Hall, Catherine, '"From Greenland's Icy Mountains ... to Afric's Golden Sand": Ethnicity, race and nation in mid-nineteenth-century England', *Gender and History*, 5, 1993, pp.212–30.

——, Keith McClelland and Jane Rendall, *Defining the Victorian Nation: Class, Race, Gender and the Reform Act of 1867*, Cambridge, 2000.

Hansen, Randall, *Citizenship and Immigration in Post-War Britain*, Oxford, 2000.

Harris, Ruth-Ann, *The Nearest Place That Wasn't Ireland*, Ames, IO, 1994.

Hart, Peter, *The I.R.A. at War 1916–1923*, Oxford, 2003.

Heery, P., *The History of St Francis Xavier's College, Liverpool, 1842–2001*, Liverpool, 2002.

Hepburn, A.C., *A Past Apart: Studies in the History of Catholic Belfast 1850–1950*, Belfast, 1996.

Herbert, Michael, *The Wearing of the Green: A Political History of the Irish in Manchester*, London, 2001.

Hickman, Mary, *Religion, Class and Identity: The State, the Catholic Church and the Education of the Irish in Britain*, Aldershot, 1995.

Hikins, H.R., 'The Liverpool General Transport Strike, 1911', *THSLC*, 113, 1961, pp.169–95.

Hollett, D., *Merseyside and the Nineteenth-Century Emigrant Trade to Australia*, Birkenhead, 1988.

Holmes, Colin, *John Bull's Island: Immigration and British Society, 1871–1971*, Basingstoke, 1988.

Hopkins, Eric, *Working-Class Self-Help in Nineteenth-Century England*, London, 1995.

Hornby-Smith, M.P., and A. Dale, 'The assimilation of Irish immigrants in England', *British Journal of Sociology*, 39, 1988, pp.519–44.

Hugill, Stan, *Sailortown*, London, 1967.

Hutchinson, J., and A.D. Smith, *Ethnicity*, Oxford, 1996.

Hutchinson, J., and Alan O'Day, 'The Gaelic revival in London, 1900–22: Limits of ethnic identity', in R. Swift and S. Gilley, eds, *The Irish in Victorian Britain: The Local Dimension*, Dublin, 1999, pp.254–76.

Ignatiev, Noel, *How the Irish Became White*, London, 1995.

Jackson, Dan, '"Friends of the Union": Liverpool, Ulster and Home Rule, 1910–1914', *THSLC*, 152, 2003, pp.101–32.

Jensen, Richard, '"No Irish Need Apply": A myth of victimization', *Journal of Social History*, 36, 2002, pp.405–29.

John Mitchels Gaelic Football Club. The Story of the G.A.A. in Liverpool, n.p., 1984.

Johnson, Paul, *Saving and Spending: The Working-Class Economy in Britain 1870–1939*, Oxford, 1985.

Jones, Gareth Stedman, *Outcast London: A Study in the Relationship between Classes in Victorian Society*, Harmondsworth, 1976.

Jones, R.M., 'The Liverpool Bread Riots, 1855', *Bulletin of the North West Labour History Society*, 6, 1979–80, pp.33–42.

Kanya-Forstner, Martha, 'Defining womanhood: Irish women and the Catholic Church in Victorian Liverpool', in Donald M. MacRaild, ed., *Great Famine and Beyond*, Dublin, 2000, p.168–88.

Kazal, R.A., 'Revisiting assimilation: The rise, fall and reappraisal of a concept in American ethnic history', *American Historical Review*, 100, 1995, pp.437–71.

Kearns, G., and P. Laxton, 'Ethnic groups as public health hazards: the Famine Irish in Liverpool and lazaretto politics', in E. Rodriguez-Ocana, ed., *The Politics of the Healthy Life: An International Perspective*, Sheffield, 2002, pp.13–40.

Kelly, Michael, *Liverpool: The Irish Connection*, Liverpool, 2003.

Kennedy, David, and Michael Collins, 'Community politics in Liverpool and the governance of professional football in the late nineteenth century', *Historical Journal*, 49, 2006, pp.761–88.

Kennedy, David, and Peter Kennedy, 'An ethnic dimension to football club development in Liverpool: The fate of Liverpool's Irish football clubs', article not yet published.

Kennedy, John, *St Francis Xavier's Liverpool, 1848–1998*, Liverpool, n.d.

Kenny, Kevin, *The American Irish: A History*, Harlow, 2000.

——, 'Diaspora and comparison: The global Irish as a case study', *Journal of American History*, 90, 2003, pp.134–62.

——, *Making Sense of the Molly Maguires*, New York and Oxford, 1998.

——, 'The Molly Maguires and the Catholic Church', *Labor History*, 36, 1995, pp.345–76.

Kerr, Madeline, *The People of Ship Street*, London, 1958.

Knobel, Dale T., *Paddy and the Republic. Ethnicity and Nationality in Antebellum America*, Middletown, CT, 1986.

Kolchin, Peter, 'Whiteness studies: The new history of race in America', *Journal of American History*, 89, 2002, pp.154–73.

Koseki, Takashi, 'John Donnellan Balfe and 1848: A note on a Confederate Informer', *Saothar*, 23, 1998, pp.25–32.

Lane, Tony, *Liverpool: Gateway of Empire*, London, 1987; republished as *Liverpool: City of the Sea*, Liverpool, 1997.

Lawton, R. 'The population of Liverpool in the mid nineteenth century', *THSLC*, 107, 1955, pp.89–120.

Lawton, R., and C.G. Pooley, 'The social geography of Merseyside in the nineteenth century', final report to the SSRC, July 1976, Dept of Geography, University of Liverpool.

Lee, Gregory B., 'Paddy's Chinatown, or the harlequin's coat: A short (hi)story of a Liverpool hybridity', in his *Chinas Unlimited: Making the Imaginaries of China and Chineseness*, London, 2003.

——, *Troubadours, Trumpeters, Troubled Makers: Lyricism, Nationalism and Hybridity in China and its Others*, London, 1996.

Lee, W.R., 'The socio-economic and demographic characteristics of port cities: a typology for comparative analysis?', *Urban History*, 25, 1998, pp.147–72.

Lees, Lynn Hollen, *Exiles of Erin: Irish Migrants in Victorian London*, Manchester, 1979.

Letford, L., and C. Pooley, 'Geographies of migration and religion: Irish women in mid-nineteenth-century Liverpool', in P O'Sullivan, ed., *The Irish World Wide*, vol. 4: *Irish Women and Irish Migration*, London, 1995, pp.89–112.

Lott, Eric, *Love and Theft: Blackface Minstrelsy and the American Working Class*, New York, 1995.

Lowe, W.J., *The Irish in Mid-Victorian Lancashire: The Shaping of a Working-Class Community*, New York, 1989.

——, 'Lancashire Fenianism', *THSLC*, 126, 1977, pp.156–85.

——, 'The Lancashire Irish and the Catholic Church, 1846–71: The social dimension', *Irish Historical Studies*, 20, 1976, pp.129–55.

Lucassen, Leo, *The Immigrant Threat: The Integration of Old and New Migrants in Western Europe since 1850*, Chicago, 2005.

Lunn, Ken, 'The seamen's union and "foreign" workers on British and colonial shipping', *Bulletin of the Society for the Study of Labour History*, 53, 1988, pp.5–13.

McAllister, T.G., *Terence Bellew McManus 1811(?)–1861*, Maynooth, 1972.

McCartney, Helen, *Citizen Soldiers: The Liverpool Territorials in the First World War*, Cambridge, 2005.

McCleod, John, *Beginning Postcolonialism*, Manchester, 2000.

McDiarmid, Lucy, *The Irish Art of Controversy*, Ithaca, NY, and London, 2005.

McFarland, Elaine, 'A reality and yet impalpable: The Fenian panic in mid-Victorian Scotland', *Scottish Historical Review*, 77, 1998, pp.199–223.

McKenna, Madeline, 'The suburbanization of the working-class population of Liverpool between the wars', *Social History*, 16, 1991, pp.173–89.

McLeod, Hugh, 'Building the "Catholic ghetto": Catholic organizations 1870–1914', in

W.J. Sheils and D. Wood, *Studies in Church History: Voluntary Religion*, Oxford, 1986, pp.411–44.

——, 'Popular Catholicism in Irish New York, c. 1900', in W.J. Sheils and D. Wood, eds, *Studies in Church History 25: The Church, Ireland and the Irish*, Oxford, 1989, pp.353–73.

McManus, Kevin, *Céilís, Jigs and Ballads: Irish Music in Liverpool*, Liverpool, 1994.

MacRaild, Donald M., *Culture, Conflict and Migration: The Irish in Victorian Cumbria*, Liverpool, 1998.

——, *Faith, Fraternity and Fighting: The Orange Order and Irish Migrants in Northern England, c. 1850–1920*, Liverpool, 2005.

——, 'Irish immigration and the "Condition of England" question: The roots of an historiographical tradition', *Immigrants and Minorities*, 14, 1995, pp.67–85.

——, *Irish Migrants in Modern Britain, 1750–1922*, Basingstoke, 1999.

Mac Suibhne, Peadar, *Paul Cullen and His Contemporaries*, 5 vols, Nass, 1967–77.

Mason, Tony, 'The Blues and the Reds: A history of the Liverpool and Everton Football Clubs', *THSLC*, 134, 1985, pp.107–28.

Meagher, T.J., *Inventing Irish America: Generation, Class and Ethnic Identity in a New England City, 1880–1928*, Notre Dame, IN, 2001.

——, ed., *From Paddy to Studs: Irish-American Communities in the Turn of the Century Era*, New York, 1986.

Miller, Kerby A., *Emigrants and Exiles: Ireland and the Irish Exodus to North America*, New York, 1985.

Milne, Graeme, *Trade and Traders in Mid-Victorian Liverpool: Mercantile Business and the Making of a World Port*, Liverpool, 2000.

Mitchell, M.J., *The Irish in the West of Scotland 1797–1848*, Edinburgh, 1998.

Moch, Leslie Page, *Moving Europeans: Migration in Western Europe since 1650*, Bloomington, IN, 1992.

Montgomery, David, 'The Irish and the American labor movement', in D.N. Doyle and O.D. Edwards, eds, *America and Ireland, 1776–1976*, Westport, CT, 1980, pp.205–18.

Moran, Gerard, 'Nationalists in exile: The National Brotherhood of St Patrick in Lancashire, 1861–5', in R. Swift and S. Gilley, eds, *The Irish in Victorian Britain: The Local Dimension*, Dublin, 1999, pp.212–35.

Morawska, Ewa, 'The sociology and historiography of immigration', in V. Yans-McLaughlin, ed., *Immigration Reconsidered*, New York, 1960, pp.187–238.

Munro, Alasdair, and Duncan Sim, *The Merseyside Scots: A Study of an Expatriate Community*, Birkenhead, 2001.

Murdoch, Norman H., 'From militancy to social mission: The Salvation Army and street disturbances in Liverpool, 1879–1887', in John Belchem, ed., *Popular Politics, Riot and Labour: Essays in Liverpool History*, Liverpool, 1992, pp.160–72.

Murphy, J., *The Religious Problem in English Education: The Crucial Experiment*, Liverpool, 1959.

Neal, Frank, 'The Birkenhead Garibaldi riots of 1862', *THSLC*, 131, 1982, pp.87–111.

———, *Black '47: Britain and the Famine Irish*, Basingstoke, 1998.

———, 'A criminal profile of the Liverpool Irish', *THSLC*, 140, 1991, pp.161–99.

———, 'English-Irish conflict in the north west of England: Economics, racism, anti-Catholicism or simple xenophobia?', *North West Labour History*, 16, 1991–92, pp.14–25.

———, 'Lancashire, the Famine Irish and the Poor Laws: a study in crisis management', *Irish Economic and Social History*, XXII, 1995, pp.26–48.

———, 'Liverpool, the Irish steamship companies and the Famine Irish', *Immigrants and Minorities*, 5, 1986, pp.28–61.

———, *Sectarian Violence: The Liverpool Experience 1819–1914*, Manchester, 1988.

Newsinger, John, *Fenianism in Mid-Victorian Britain*, London, 1994.

Nowatski, Robert, 'Paddy jumps Jim Crow: Irish-Americans and blackface minstrelsy', *Éire-Ireland*, 41, 2006, pp.162–84.

O'Broin, Leon, *Revolutionary Underground: The Story of the Irish Republican Brotherhood 1858–1924*, Dublin, 1976.

O'Connell, Bernard, 'Irish nationalism in Liverpool, 1873–1923', *Éire-Ireland*, 10, 1975, pp.24–37.

O'Connor, T.H., *The Boston Irish: A Political History*, Boston, MA, 1995.

O'Day, Alan, 'Irish diaspora politics in perspective: The United Irish Leagues of Great Britain and America, 1900–1914', in Donald M. MacRaild, ed., *Great Famine and Beyond*, Dublin, 2000, pp.214–39.

———, 'The political organization of the Irish in Britain, 1867–90', in R. Swift and S. Gilley, eds, *The Irish in Britain 1815–1939*, London, 1989, pp.183–211.

———, 'Varieties of anti-Irish behaviour in Britain, 1846–1922', in P. Panayi, ed., *Racial Violence in Britain in the Nineteenth and Twentieth Centuries*, London, 1996, pp.26–43.

———, ed., *A Survey of the Irish in England, 1872*, London, 1990.

O'Farrell, Patrick, *The Irish in Australia*, Kensington, NSW, 1986.

O'Leary, Paul, *Immigration and Integration: The Irish in Wales 1798–1922*, Cardiff, 2000.

———, ed., *Irish Migrants in Modern Wales*, Liverpool, 2004.

O Luing, Sean, *Kuno Meyer: A Biography*, Dublin, 1991.

O'Sullivan, Patrick, 'A portable identity', unpublished conference paper.

———, ed., *The Irish World Wide: History, Heritage, Identity*, 6 vols, Leicester and London, 1992–97.

O Tuathaigh, M.A.G., 'The Irish in nineteenth-century Britain: Problems of integration', *Transactions of the Royal Historical Society*, 5th series, 31, 1981, pp.149–73.

Panayi, P., *Enemy in our Midst*, London, 1991.

Paz, D.G., 'Anti-Catholicism, anti-Irish stereotyping, and anti-Celtic racism in mid-Victorian working-class periodicals', *Albion*, 18, 1986, pp.601–16.

'Perspectives on the Irish diaspora', in *Irish Economic and Social History*, 33, 2006, pp.35–58, with contributions by Enda Delaney, Kevin Kenny and Donald M. MacRaild.

Pinkman, John A, *In the Legion of the Vanguard*, Cork, Boulder, CO, 1998, ed. Francis E Maguire.

Pooley, Colin G., 'The Irish in Liverpool *circa* 1850–1940', in M. Engman, F.W. Carter, A.C. Hepburn and C.G. Pooley, eds, *Ethnic Identity in Urban Europe*, Aldershot, 1992, pp.71–97.

——, 'The residential segregation of migrant communities in mid-Victorian Liverpool', *Transactions of the Institute of British Geographers*, II, 1977, pp.364–82.

——, 'Segregation or integration? The residential experience of the Irish in mid-Victorian Britain', in R. Swift and S. Gilley, eds, *The Irish in Britain 1815–1939*, London, 1989, pp.60–83.

Poovey, Mary, 'Curing the "social body": James Kay and the Irish in Manchester', *Gender and History*, 5, 1993, pp.196–211.

Pope, D.J., 'Liverpool's Catholic mercantile and maritime business community in the second half of the eighteenth century: Parts 1 and 2', *Recusant History*, 27, 2004, pp.244–79 and 383–414.

Quinlivan, P., and P. Rose, *The Fenians in England 1865–1872*, London, 1982.

Read, G., 'The flood-gate of the Old World: A study in ethnic attitudes', *Journal of American Ethnic History*, 13, 1993, pp.31–47.

Rex, John, 'Ethnic mobilisation in multi-cultural societies', in J. Rex and B. Drury, eds, *Ethnic Mobilisation in Multi-cultural Europe*, Aldershot, 1994, pp.3–12.

Reynolds, G.W., and A. Judge, *The Night the Police Went on Strike*, London, 1968.

Richards, Eric, *Britannia's Children: Emigration from England, Scotland, Wales and Ireland since 1600*, London, 2004.

Roediger, David, *The Wages of Whiteness: Race and the Making of the American Working Class*, London, 1991.

Rossi, J.P., 'Home rule and the Liverpool by-election of 1880', *Irish Historical Studies*, 19, 1974–75, pp.156–68.

Routledge, Chris, *Cains: The Story of Liverpool in a Pint*, forthcoming, 2008.

Rowe, M., 'Sex, "race" and riot in Liverpool', *Immigrants and Minorities*, 19, 2000, pp.53–70.

Ryan, Mark, *Fenian Memories*, Dublin, 1946.

Samuel, R., 'The Roman Catholic Church and the Irish poor', in R. Swift and S. Gilley, *Irish in Victorian City*, London, 1985, pp.267–300.

Sanchez, George J., *Becoming Mexican American: Ethnicity, Culture and Identity in Chicano Los Angeles, 1900–1945*, New York, 1995.

Sanders, J.M., and V. Nee, 'Limits of ethnic solidarity in the enclave economy', *American Sociological Review*, 52, 1987, pp.745–67.

Saville, John, *1848: The British State and the Chartist Movement*, Cambridge, 1987.

Saxton, Alexander, *The Rise and Fall of the White Republic*, London, 1990.

Scally, Robert, *The End of Hidden Ireland: Rebellion, Famine and Emigration*, New York, 1995.

Shallice, A., 'Liverpool Labourism and Irish nationalism in the 1920s and 1930s', *Bulletin of the North-West Labour History Society*, 8, 1981–82, pp.19–28.

——, 'Orange and Green and militancy: Sectarianism and working class politics in Liverpool, 1900–1914', *Bulletin of the North West Labour History Society*, 6, 1979–80, pp.15–31.

Sharples, Joseph, *Liverpool: Pevsner Architectural Guides*, New Haven, CT, and London, 2004.

Sherwood, Marika, *Pastor Daniels Ekarte and the African Churches Mission*, London, 1994.

Short, K.R.M., *The Dynamite War: Irish-American Bombers in Victorian Britain*, Atlantic Highlands, NJ, 1979.

Sinclair, Robert C., *Across the Irish Sea. Belfast–Liverpool Shipping since 1819*, London 1990.

Sloan, W., 'Religious affiliation and the immigrant experience: Catholic Irish and Protestant Highlanders in Glasgow, 1830–50', in T.M. Devine, ed., *Irish Immigrants and Scottish Society in the Nineteenth and Twentieth Centuries*, Edinburgh, 1991, pp.67–90.

Smith, Joan, 'Labour tradition in Glasgow and Liverpool', *History Workshop Journal*, 17, 1984, pp.32–56.

Smith, Joan, 'Class, skill and sectarianism in Glasgow and Liverpool, 1880–1914', in R.J. Morris, ed., *Class, Power and Social Structure in British Nineteenth-Century Towns*, Leicester, 1986, pp.158–215.

Smith, Philip, '"I've got a theory about Scousers": Jimmy McGovern and Linda la Plante', in Michael Murphy and Deryn Rees-Jones, eds, *Writing Liverpool: Essays and Interviews*, Liverpool, forthcoming.

Spiegl, Fritz, *Scouse International: The Liverpool Dialect in Five Languages*, Liverpool, 2000.

Strachan, Alan, 'Post-war Irish migration and settlement in England and Wales', in R. King, ed, *Contemporary Irish Migration*, Dublin, 1991, pp.21–31.

Tabili, Laura, *'We Ask for British Justice': Workers and Racial Difference in Late Imperial Britain*, Ithaca, NY, 1994.

Taplin, Eric, *The Dockers' Union: A Study of the National Union of Dock Labourers*, Leicester, 1986.

——, 'False dawn of new unionism? Labour unrest in Liverpool', in John Belchem, ed., *Popular Politics, Riot and Labour: Essays in Liverpool History 1790–1940*, Liverpool, 1992, pp.135–59.

——, 'Irish leaders and the Liverpool dockers: Richard McGhee and Edward McHugh', *Bulletin of the North West Labour History Society*, 9, 1983–84, pp.36–44.

——, *Liverpool Dockers and Seamen 1870–1890*, Hull, 1974.

——, *Near to Revolution: The Liverpool General Transport Strike of 1911*, Liverpool, 1994.

Toll, Robert, *Blacking Up: The Minstrel Show in Nineteenth-Century America*, New York, 1974.

Treble, J.H., 'The attitude of the Roman Catholic Church towards trade unionism in the north of England, 1833–42', *Northern History*, 5, 1990, pp.93–113.

Van der Linden, Marcel, ed., *Social Security Mutualism: The Comparative History of Mutual Benefit Societies*, Berne, 1996.

Walker, W.M., 'Irish immigrants in Scotland: Their priests, politics and parochial life', *Historical Journal*, 15, 1972, pp.649–67.

Waller, P.J., *Democracy and Sectarianism: A Political and Social History of Liverpool 1868–1939*, Liverpool, 1981.

Walton, J.K., M. Blinkhorn, C. Pooley, D. Tidswell and M.J. Winstanley, 'Crime, migration and social change in north-west England and the Basque country, c. 1870–1930', *British Journal of Criminology*, 39, 1999, pp.108–109.

Walton, J.K., and A. Wilcox, eds, *Low Life and Moral Improvement in Mid-Victorian England: Liverpool through the Journalism of Hugh Shimmin*, Leicester, 1991.

Ward, Conor K., 'Some aspects of the social structure of a Roman Catholic parish', *Sociological Review*, new series, 6, 1958, pp.75–93.

Watt, Stephen, 'The plays of Hubert O'Grady', *Journal of Irish Literature*, 14, 1985, pp.4–13.

Williams, W.H.A., *'Twas Only an Irishman's Dream: The Image of Ireland and the Irish in American Popular Song Lyrics 1800–1920*, Urbana, IL, 1996.

Williamson, Jeffrey G., 'The impact of the Irish on British labour markets during the industrial revolution', *Journal of Economic History*, 46, 1986, pp.693–721.

Wilson, Carlton E., 'Racism and private assistance: The support of West Indian and African missions in Liverpool, England, during the interwar years', *African Studies Review*, 35, 1992, pp.55–76.

Index

Index entries followed by the letter 't' indicate references within tables.